36.00

DATE DUE			
MAR 10 1995			
APR 5 1995			
APR 2 6 1995			

Critical Essays on

ROBERT BLY

CRITICAL ESSAYS
ON
AMERICAN LITERATURE

James Nagel, General Editor
University of Georgia, Athens

◆

Critical Essays on

ROBERT BLY

◆

edited by

WILLIAM V. DAVIS

G. K. Hall & Co. / New York
Maxwell Macmillan Canada / Toronto
Maxwell Macmillan International / New York   Oxford   Singapore   Sydney

G. K. Hall & Co.
Macmillan Publishing Company
866 Third Avenue
New York, New York 10022

Maxwell Macmillan Canada, Inc.
1200 Eglinton Avenue East
Suite 200
Don Mills, Ontario M3C 3N1

Library of Congress Cataloging-in-Publication Data

Critical essays on Robert Bly / William V. Davis [editor].
    p.   cm. — (Critical essays on American literature)
    Includes bibliographical references and index.
    ISBN 0-8161-7316-8
    1. Bly, Robert—Criticism and interpretation.   I. Davis, William
Virgil, 1940–   . II. Series.
PS3552.L9Z62   1992
811'.54—dc20
                                                                92-28712
                                                                    CIP

The paper used in this publication meets the minimum requirements of
American National Standard for Information Sciences—Permanence of Paper
for Printed Library Materials. ANSI Z3948-1984.∞™

10   9   8   7   6   5   4   3   2   1

Printed in the United States of America

Contents

◆

General Editor's Note	xi
Publisher's Note	xiii
Introduction	1
WILLIAM V. DAVIS	

PRELIMINARIES

North of Jamaica	21
LOUIS SIMPSON	
Thinking About Robert Bly	23
WILLIAM MATTHEWS	
Young Bly	27
DONALD HALL	
Inward to the World: The Poetry of Robert Bly	30
WILLIAM HEYEN	

REVIEWS

Four Voices in Recent American Poetry	35
RALPH J. MILLS, JR.	
Poetry Chronicle [Review of *Silence in the Snowy Fields*]	40
RICHARD HOWARD	
Two Languages	42
HARRIET ZINNES	
A Sadness for America	44
PAUL ZWEIG	
Jeremiads at Half-Mast	46
ROBERT MAZZOCCO	

Brief Reviews [Review of *The Teeth Mother Naked at Last*]   51
  MICHAEL HEFFERNAN

Bly: Man, Voice and Poem   53
  ANTHONY PICCIONE

Where They All Are Sleeping   57
  JOYCE CAROL OATES

Books [Review of *The Morning Glory*]   60
  STANLEY PLUMLY

This Book Is Made of Turkey Soup and Star Music   62
  PHILIP DACEY

[Review of *This Tree Will Be Here for a Thousand Years*]   65
  ANONYMOUS

[Review of *The Man in the Black Coat Turns*]   66
  CHARLES MOLESWORTH

Sepia Photographs and Jazz Solos   68
  FRED CHAPPELL

Robert Bly and the Trouble with American Poetry   70
  ROGER MITCHELL

The Poetry of Robert Bly   75
  ROBERT RICHMAN

Minnesota Transcendentalist   89
  JOYCE PESEROFF

Robert Bly [Review of *Selected Poems*]   92
  ASKOLD MELNYCZUK

Robert Bly's *Iron John* and the New "Lawrentian" Man   96
  STEPHEN KUUSISTO

ESSAYS

Back to the Snowy Fields   107
  WAYNE DODD

The Live World   114
  PAUL A. LACEY

Robert Bly Alive in Darkness   135
  ANTHONY LIBBY

Robert Bly's *Sleepers Joining Hands*: Shadow and Self   148
  MICHAEL ATKINSON

Tiny Poems   165
  HOWARD NELSON

"The Body with the Lamp Lit Inside": Robert Bly's
New Poems   176
   RALPH J. MILLS, JR.

Domesticating the Sublime: Bly's Latest Poems   185
   CHARLES MOLESWORTH

From Silence to Subversion: Robert Bly's Political
Surrealism   194
   WALTER KALAIDJIAN

A Sensible Emptiness: Robert Bly and the Poetics of
Immanence   212
   LAWRENCE KRAMER

Nature, Human Nature, and *Gott-Natur*: Robert Bly
in the Seventies   224
   RICHARD P. SUGG

The Man in the Black Coat Turns and *Loving a Woman
in Two Worlds*   240
   WILLIAM V. DAVIS

Captain Bly   257
   TED SOLOTAROFF

OVERVIEWS AND CONCLUSIONS

Which Way to the Future?   267
   ROBERT REHDER

The Startling Journeys of Robert Bly   283
   PETER STITT

Redefining the American Poet   292
   RICHARD P. SUGG

Index   294

For My Brothers

General Editor's Note

♦

This series seeks to anthologize the most important criticism on a wide variety of topics and writers in American literature. Our readers will find in various volumes not only a generous selection of reprinted articles and reviews but original essays, bibliographies, manuscript sections, and other materials brought to public attention for the first time. This volume, *Critical Essays on Robert Bly*, is the most comprehensive collection of essays ever published on one of the most important contemporary writers in the United States. It contains both a sizable gathering of early reviews and a broad selection of more modern scholarship, as well. Among the authors of reprinted articles and reviews are Louis Simpson, Joyce Carol Oates, Ted Solotaroff, and Lawrence Kramer. In addition to a substantial introduction by William V. Davis, there are also three original essays commissioned specifically for publication in this volume, a charming reminiscence by Donald Hall of meeting Bly for the first time at Harvard, an assessment by Robert Rehder of Bly's place in contemporary verse, and an exploration of the journeys in Bly's poetry by Peter Stitt. We are confident that this book will make a permanent and significant contribution to the study of American literature, and we are delighted to have it as part of the *Critical Essays on American Literature* series.

JAMES NAGEL
University of Georgia, Athens

Publisher's Note

◆

Producing a volume that contains both newly commissioned and reprinted material presents the publisher with the challenge of balancing the desire to achieve stylistic consistency with the need to preserve the integrity of works first published elsewhere. In the Critical Essays series, essays commissioned especially for a particular volume are edited to be consistent with G. K. Hall's house style; reprinted essays appear in the style in which they were first published, with only typographical errors corrected. Consequently, shifts in style from one essay to another are the result of our efforts to be faithful to each text as it was originally published.

Introduction

♦

WILLIAM V. DAVIS

Just as Robert Bly's formal career as a poet was about to begin, Donald Hall noticed in his work, and in that of his contemporary Louis Simpson, something that was "genuinely new." He called it "a kind of imagination new to American poetry." This new movement, Hall thought, was "subjective but not autobiographical." It involved a colloquial vocabulary; a "special quality" of diction that resembled Georg Trakl and Pablo Neruda (poets Bly translated); an imagination "irrational," but without any "straining after apocalypse"; the use of simple language; and "inward" images of "profound subjectivity."[1] Cleanth Brooks quickly contradicted Hall, arguing that Bly and Simpson were doing nothing new.[2] And so, even before Robert Bly had published his first book, the critical response to his work had already begun.

For almost thirty years now this response has continued to be as wide-ranging, as controversial, and, often, as personal as Bly's poetry and his own criticism has been. And although this book is focused as much as possible exclusively on Bly's poetry, it is inevitable, even immediately and conspicuously so, that Bly's achievements as critic and translator, as well as his activities as social and political activist, are inseparable from his poetry, and they have often been linked in the critical responses to his poetry—as, indeed, Bly himself has regularly linked all of these endeavors together.

The situation is further complicated by the fact that, although Bly has been, and continues to be, a very visible public figure (perhaps no other American poet is more immediately recognized both inside and outside the literary community), he has always been, and he remains, an extremely private person. Furthermore, in the absence of substantial, definitive biographical materials on him, there is little reliable evidence linking his life and work. What is available comes primarily from Bly himself, and he is notorious for contradicting himself and, in various ways, carefully covering his tracks.[3]

Obviously, Bly's poetic career is far from over, just as the final critical estimate of his work remains incomplete. This book, then, is an attempt to document the most important stages in the criticism of his career up to the moment.

1

REVIEWS

Silence in the Snowy Fields received more than forty reviews. This kind of attention would be astonishing for any book of poetry; for a first book it is almost unheard-of. The range of response was not nearly as wide nor as diverse, however, as some of Bly's later books would elicit, usually with fewer reviews. The word most frequently used to describe the poems in *Silence* was "simplicity." Various readers found the simplicity "deceptive," "naive," "fresh," "achieved." The poems themselves were called "subtle," "evocative," but "abstract," "vacuous and sentimental," "boring," and "intensely subjective." Two of the most substantial reviews set the tone for the critical response to follow. Louis Simpson called *Silence* "one of the few original and stimulating books of poetry published in recent years."[4] Ralph J. Mills, Jr., in a review essay, linked Bly's earliest criticism (published primarily in his journal *The Fifties* and *The Sixties*) with the practices of his poems in *Silence* and found in *Silence* "a poetry of concentrated understatement" and a "pointed moral sense."[5]

The poems in *The Light Around the Body*, Bly's most controversial book to date, were appreciably different thematically, if not stylistically, from the poems of *Silence*. It was to be expected, then, since Bly had taken readers rather by surprise, that *Light* was greeted with a wider variety of conflicting critical responses. Reviewers were particularly, inevitably, drawn to the overt political poems that attacked the Vietnam War and, especially and specifically, attacked the American involvement in the war.

The critical concentration on these poems led to an interesting and somewhat curious division of responses in terms of the American as opposed to the British reviewers (approximately one-fourth of the numerous reviews of *Light* appeared in British periodicals). American reviewers either found a "curious externality" in the book, which they variously described as "weak poetically" at the same time that it was "dangerously alluring," or they saw it as "monotonous in the cumulative effect," with the political poems "predictable, even pious"; or as "an honorable failure"; or "one of the most significant American volumes to be published in years," by "one of the few poets in America from whom greatness can be expected."[6] British reviewers, on the other hand, saw the book in more general terms. They spoke of Bly's "generalized despair" even though at least one of them felt that he might be considered "a currently fashionable American White Hope."[7] Among all reviewers, Kenneth Rexroth was perhaps most perceptive in seeing *Light* as the culmination of Bly's struggle (which had been going on now for a number of years—long before even *Silence* was published) "to return American poetry to the mainstream of international literature."[8]

Bly's next major book, *Sleepers Joining Hands*, like both *Silence* and *Light*, was widely reviewed. In some ways a book that attempted to synthesize the first two, but also to go beyond them, *Sleepers* was treated both retrospectively and prophetically, sometimes both ways simultaneously. Some reviews saw *Sleepers* as an attempt to synthesize the inner and outer reality of *Silence* and *Light*.[9] Others saw it as pretentious or preachy,[10] even shamefully dishonest.[11] A number of reviewers separated out the central prose essay from the poems surrounding it,[12] or they isolated the powerful long antiwar poem, "The Teeth Mother Naked at Last," for special attention,[13] or they focused on both the prose piece and "Teeth Mother."[14] Perhaps the most comprehensive review was by Joyce Carol Oates, who found the book, "a remarkable collection of poems"; indeed, "one of the most powerful books of any kind I have read recently." Oates stressed the "internal development" and the "dramatic tension" of the book and found it, poetry and prose, "unique at the present time."[15]

Bly continued his habit of making each new book unique with his next major collection, *The Morning Glory*, a book of prose poems. Although *Morning Glory* got fewer reviews than the books already mentioned, there was greater agreement about it than about most of Bly's earlier collections. Critics saw this book as suggesting return, renewal, and rebirth; the ecstatic, the visionary, and the apocalyptic. Bly was described as having found "new poetic powers."[16] William V. Davis saw the book as Bly's attempt to move away from the "abstraction" of the cultural situation, following Vietnam, and, through the genre of the prose poem, of trying to find "a way of maintaining the possibility of poetry in an age about to abandon it."[17] Stanley Plumly found it "remarkably free" of the preoccupations of *Light* and *Sleepers* and called Bly "our Thoreau," a "visionary of detail, of the small unattended moment."[18] And James F. Mersmann saw *Morning Glory* as the culmination and climax of Bly's career to date, "a poetry that ecstatically rediscovers a world of profound correspondences, that realizes . . . that all things are intricately connected . . . in a common ground and center."[19]

This Body Is Made of Camphor and Gopherwood was greeted by clearly mixed reviews, the reviewers sometimes taking both positive and negative positions simultaneously. The reviews ranged from charges that the book was "overweight and pretentious," filled with the sort of "soothing aphorism" found in "stationery stores," to suggestions that the poems had a strong hallucinatory quality that evoked beautiful images in their own "stillness."[20] In a flamboyant review essay, Philip Dacey suggested that *This Body* was "emphatically a book of deep religious longing," which had both "a prophetic quality" and "a grandiose purpose bordering on battiness." He concluded that Bly wanted "nothing less than to be a saint." Thus, to wish him success would "be out of place . . . because to journey toward such a goal is already itself an exemplary arrival."[21] No matter what positions they took, most reviewers would have agreed with Charles Molesworth when he argued that *This Body* signaled "a decisive change in Bly's poetry." They might not, however, have gone as far as Molesworth did when he described the poems as "nodes of psychic energy" and, thus, overtly poems of "religious vision" that attempted to "domesticate the sublime."[22]

Bly's next book, *This Tree Will Be Here for a Thousand Years*, like *This Body*, received mixed notices. A number of reviewers used Bly's preface, "The Two Presences," as a springboard for their comments.[23] Arguing that Bly's notion of the "two presences" was "Swedenborgian nonsense," or that the poems themselves were "hermetic" and "elitist subjectivism," and even then only seldomly "successful," a number of the critics nonetheless found the book fresh and intriguing, and themselves "caught" by it.[24] Eliot Weinberger wrote the most caustically critical review of *This Tree*. He began by attacking Bly himself: "Robert Bly is a windbag, a sentimentalist, a slob in the language." Still, since poetry today is "a useless pleasantry" and "largely ignored," the considerable success of Bly, a "cozily irrelevant poet," is "less disheartening" than it might have been at some other time.[25]

But perhaps the variety of reaction to this book can best be seen by two differing interpretations of several lines from it:

> Sometimes when you put your hand into a hollow tree
> you touch the dark places between the stars.[26]

Weinberger said that this "remark" "might be charming if uttered by a 6-year-old" (Weinberger, 504). Hayden Carruth, on the other hand, said, "Not many of Bly's readers have done that, I imagine, but I . . . *have* done it. I'm damned if he isn't right" (Carruth, 79).

The ambivalence that had greeted Bly's last several books continued, at least in part, in the early responses to *The Man in the Black Coat Turns*. Perhaps part of the negative response was the result of the fact that Bly had become increasingly visible as a popular figure, both as a poet and as a proselytizer for poetry as well as for various social and political causes. Whatever the reason, some of the reviewers saw the book as evoking "conditioned responses," or filled with poems which seemed to have been written to fulfill the requirements of Bly's theories; therefore, they thought that, although the poems meant "little," they had "the facade of Bly's earlier, better" work. Other reviewers saw the book as an impressive part of the "modern mainstream," filled with powerful poems; indeed, Bly's "richest, most complex book."[27]

Four reviews in particular deserve specific notice. Marjorie Perloff saw Bly's poetry (here turned more definitively toward the autobiographical) as a sentimental falling off from his earlier, stronger, poetry of images.[28] For Donald Wesling Bly was a "preacher or wisdom-writer," and thus, apparently, "incapable of masterpieces." Even so, *Black Coat* contained some of the "very best" poems he had written.[29] Charles Molesworth, taking account of each of the three sections of the book individually, found the poems "challenging," poems that extended the "variety of Bly's structures," and showed that "he is genuinely a poet of growth."[30] Michael S. Reynolds saw *Black Coat* as "meditative" and "death-ridden," and the title "character" as either "the poet turning toward new vistas" or "death who turns to wait for the poet." For Reynolds, although this book "looks back to some of Bly's most effective work" and also "reaffirms his visionary stance," it finally remains an important transitional book: "What comes next will be crucial for Bly."[31]

Loving a Woman in Two Worlds, Bly's most recent individual book of poems, received the fewest number of reviews of any of his major books.[32] One reason for this paucity of reviews no doubt had to do with the fact that Bly's *Selected Poems* quickly followed *Loving*. Another reason was that reviewers didn't quite know what to do with *Loving*, a book of love poems. Although Bly had changed his themes, his forms, and his directions from book to book, he had never before made such drastic changes, both thematically and stylistically, simultaneously. The surprise, chagrin, disappointment, and confusion reviewers found in this book is reflected in the reviews, perhaps most conspicuously in the negative reviews.

The most outspoken negative review was brief and anonymous. After suggesting that the "two worlds" of Bly's title described "human thought and the dark, elusive world of animal mystery," and thus echoed his "familiar themes," the reviewer found that the poems nonetheless "fall flat or appear contrived," and often "amount to little more than cliches, both verbal and emotional. I mean, this book stinks, folks. No kidding."[33] Other essentially negative reviews were somewhat more generous, but frequently even these notices found the book "embarrassing" in its inability to describe emotional states effectively, and many reviewers believed that *Loving* could "only detract from Bly's already somewhat problematic reputation."[34] The positive reviews saw the poems as "beautiful, strange, tender and powerful," "*great* poems," even if "a bit preachy." They were poems that made "grief mystical" and "sadness liberating," and the book was resonant "with meaning: Beautiful."[35] Thus, the majority of critics agreed with Fred Chappell that *Loving*, finally, even if it "holds no surprises," has "broken no promises," and therefore remains an important addition "to a body of work that has impressively persuaded a generation of poets and readers."[36]

Reviews of selected or collected books of poetry are obviously quite different from reviews of individual books. Even so, the reviews of Bly's *Selected Poems* were appreciably different from the reviews of the typical "selected" poems. Perhaps this was not surprising—given the course of Bly's career and the atypical nature of this book itself.

The book was unique in several ways. First, Bly took his title seriously. Considering the number of poems he had published in his career, this rather thin "selection" from his previous work might be thought of as extremely modest. Second, his book contained a large number of heavily revised or, indeed, totally rewritten, poems. Third, it contained early, "new," poems—some never before published, others never before collected. Fourth, Bly rearranged the order of the poems from the previously published individual books for the sake of a new thematic unity in the *Selected*—even moving poems originally published in one book to a section largely devoted to another. Finally, Bly added short explanatory prose prefaces to each of the nine sections of the book, and appended two additional critical essays as "afterthoughts." In short, Bly's *Selected Poems* was as unconventional as, in some ways, each of his earlier individual books had been. And, clearly, Bly intended it to be "a kind of reader's guide to his own work."[37] As Joyce Peseroff said, "This is not just an anthology of Mr. Bly's best work; its 11 new essays and its particular method of organization require a fresh look at the poet's achievement."[38]

Peter Stitt has suggested that a sense of "place" is often the typical organizational principle for books of poetry, especially for a "selected" volume. However, Bly's *Selected* was "quite different from most such volumes" in that it "reaches the most indefinite locus of all—an area of the mind that is analogous to the deepest level of nature" (Stitt, 1022, 1024). Other reviewers echoed this position, even though, they thought, it seemed somewhat surprising in Bly—given all the specific details, in terms of place, in his poems from the beginning. Roger Mitchell, for instance, discovered a "disinterest in history" in Bly ("history destroys timelessness and the eternal"), and an almost ethereal state of mind in the poems, in which "Minnesota is almost incidental."[39]

And, thus, in attempting to treat the "idiosyncratic affair" of Bly's *Selected Poems,* "either a tombstone or a capstone" to his career,[40] various reviewers saw it variously. The responses, like the responses to so much of Bly's poetic career, ran the gamut from one extreme to another. On the one hand *Selected* was seen as "a disappointing book . . . because we had been lulled into thinking over the years . . . that more had been accomplished"; on the other hand, it was seen as a fitting climax and "stepping stone" in which the poems "included here from his last two books" (*Black Coat* and *Loving*) were seen as "his finest yet."[41] Perhaps inevitably, most reviewers finally settled for a central position and saw the book as "a mellow ending to a good journey, one that is not over yet" (Peseroff, 2).

CRITICISM

The criticism of Bly's poetry can be divided into categories associated with the various "genres," movements, or "currents" Bly has been placed in or into which, by virtue of his practice in the various stages of his career, he has placed himself. Among these the most obvious are considerations of his work in terms of the thought of Jacob Boehme and "deep image" poetry; criticism with an overt political focus, focused on his overtly political poems; myth criticism (with special emphasis on a Jungian approach, following Bly's practice); specific attention to the prose poems in terms of Bly's extensive use of this genre; and, finally, male-female "consciousness" criticism. These concentrations or emphases within the body of the criticism devoted to Bly's poetry, although they overlap considerably and frequently, follow a roughly chronological sequence associated with the chronological development of the poetry, and they include most of the major criticism in terms of individual articles and essays, as well as the several full-length studies Bly's poetry has received. These critical movements will be considered, then, in the order that most naturally follows the order of the poetry.

The "deep image" focus associated with the thought of Jacob Boehme relates primarily to Bly's early poetry. "Deep image," the term most frequently applied to Bly's early poems, has never been clearly or fully defined. The term itself was coined by Jerome Rothenberg,[42] and it remains the term most commonly used to refer to these poems—although other critics have used different, if related, terms for the same poems (poetry of the "subjective image," the poetry of the "deep mind," the "poetics of immanence," "incorporative consciousness," "deep image surrealism," etc.).[43] Several things can, however, be agreed on: Bly's "deep image" poetry was indebted to Boehme; Bly's theories about it were "generative,"[44] both for Bly himself and for others. Furthermore, Bly's practice of the "genre" of the "deep image" was especially important in and to his early career, and to the careers of many other poets at about this same time.

Most of the important criticism of Bly's early work (although it by no means can be limited exclusively to his early work) can be associated with theories and practices of "deep image" poetics. Charles Altieri and Dennis Haskell have provided perhaps the most elaborate critical framework for considering the "deep image" poetry.

Altieri saw Bly as a representative of one of the several "self-consciously postmodern positions" of *"radical presence"* that resulted from the dissatisfactions with the "epistemological and cultural implications of the New Critical aesthetic," and made for one of the "varieties of immanentist experience" among the poetics of the 1960s. Through his own intuition, and his use of "deep images," Bly was able to adopt "his theological model," in "secular terms," and thereby provide "the reader with a new level of awareness."[45]

Haskell, in an excellent long article on the "deep image" movement, was wider-ranging in his analysis and more definitive in terms of the sources of the movement and in terms of his examples. He defined the "content of a deep image poem" as something "created by the association aroused by individual images and by the manner in which these clusters of association come to be related to one another." He saw Bly as "the most active spokesman for the deep image movement," which he called "a mode of seeing or of vision as much as a poetic technique." Bly, according to Haskell, has "drawn heavily from Boehme" and, not surprisingly, his poems "gain something of a moral stance" even though the "final value of deep image poetry [Bly's or anyone else's] is difficult to judge." Nonetheless, together with "confessional verse," deep image poetry remains "one of the two most important strands to emerge in American poetry since the War."[46]

Among critics who have focused specifically on Bly's early "deep image" poetry, Ralph J. Mills, Jr. (in an essay mainly devoted to James Wright) picked up a reference to "inwardness" in a book review Bly published in the same year that *Silence* appeared,[47] and argued that Bly and Wright rely "to a considerable degree on sources below the level of consciousness or of rational thought." Their poems have a "fluid, dreamlike construction," and an "intense subjectivity," and they typically include an epiphanic "moment of extreme perception," which is "capable of stirring subtle and profound responses in the reader." Such work, Mills argued, has "advanced our imaginative frontiers."[48]

Several other critics considered Bly's "deep image" poetry: Ingegard Friberg found these poems "reminiscent of Emerson's ideas of poetic creativity"; Richard Howard and William V. Davis detailed the Boehmean associations; Charles Molesworth, although he argued that the "positive aspects of Bly's poetics revolve around his concentration on the image," also cautioned that, gone awry, such poetry ran the risk of producing an "endless series of sensory fragments"; finally, Walter Kalaidjian, in one of the few negative analyses of Bly's use of the "deep image," argued that this "essentially conservative aesthetic" had drained the "discursive power" from the poetry of *Silence.*[49]

Although it was evident earlier, the relationship between poetry and politics first became explicit with Bly and for his critics with the publication of *Light* in 1967, and in the events surrounding the National Book Award and Bly's turning the money for the award over to the draft resistance.[50] In one form or another, poetry and politics have continued to be a persistent issue both for Bly and for his critics since the mid-1960s, although, properly seen, this dichotomy in his work and the emphasis on it go back to his poetic beginnings and beyond—since some of the "political" poems in *Light* were written before *Silence.*[51]

Bly's "political" poetry (as opposed, often, to his political actions and his essays) is largely protest poetry, and cause oriented—even though his "causes" are not always overtly political ones. Therefore, although Bly would, perhaps grudgingly, admit that "poetry makes nothing happen," like Auden, he found himself caught by and caught up in the social and political climate of his times, and, his imagination and social conscience fueled by the war in Vietnam, he took his stand in poems and actions, essays and speeches. If, ultimately, even his most blatant political poems made more powerful poetic statements than they did political ones, not all of his critics, then or now, agreed either with what he said or with the way in which he said it.

In his essay "Leaping Up into Political Poetry," Bly dealt with the position taken by some critics "that poetry on political subjects should not be attempted" because "political events are beyond the reach of . . . literary sensitivity." For Bly, however, a "true political poem" is not simply an "opinion" but "a political act" that "comes out of the deepest privacy" and "moves to deepen awareness."[52] Bly's theoretical position, typically unsystematic, linked with the practice of his poetry itself, confused critics—who argued, in part justifiably, that the confusion was his.

If most critics agreed that Bly was one of the finest antiwar poets and that in *Light* and, especially, in his long antiwar poem, "The Teeth Mother Naked at Last," he had "reached a stage far in advance of most of the antiwar poets" and actually written "political analysis,"[53] there, nevertheless, remained considerable differences among them in terms of any final estimate both of the poems and of the politics. While Charles Altieri contended that Robert Duncan was "the only contemporary poet successfully to include the sufferings of the war in Vietnam within his myth," Cary Nelson, among others, argued that such a "claim seems difficult to sustain in the light of Bly's 'The Teeth Mother Naked at Last,'" even if, as Walter Kalaidjian stated, "[f]or many critics 'Teeth Mother' is a controversial work whose high moral tone verges on the very propaganda it indicts."[54] Other critics found in Bly's political poetry: "a deep voice choking on its own anger and going shrill"; instances in which "political struggle is . . . reduced to psychic melodrama"; "psychoreligious . . . atonement" that was "the only solution" to the war in Vietnam; or work "which insists that public events have spiritual meaning."[55]

Several critics attempted to include Bly's political poetry in a broader theoretical discussion. Cary Nelson argued that, in America, poetry and history "are especially dependent on one another" because American poetry "continually addresses the world at large" as "a dream of the people we might become," and, even though "it continually flowers out of its failure," it "is singularly addressed to . . . the future." In Bly's case, his "phenomenological method" with its "increasingly surrealistic edge . . . includes a destructive element he may not fully understand."[56]

James F. Mersmann introduced his important study of poets and poetry during the period of the Vietnam War by pointing out that the poetry that grew out of the Vietnam War (in contrast to the poetry inspired by the two world wars) was unique in several respects: it was written by civilians, not soldiers, who simultaneously felt "the necessity to speak" and "a certain helplessness and futility" with respect to their words. Turning to Bly, "one of the most annoying and most exciting poets of his time," Mersmann detailed how the "'I' of the private vision" of *Silence* became "the 'we' of the public vision" of *Light* (and, indeed, anticipated the myth-oriented poems of *Sleepers*), as these political poems merged the "inward/outward, spiritual/material dichotomy in Jacob Boehme's writings" with the "*animal/animus* dichotomy" of Jung. These "divisions," subtly, and often covertly, became "the most important unifying theme" of Bly's protest poetry.[57]

Thus, whatever else is true, most of Bly's critics agreed that his political poems were "the most specific, the most detailed and the most controversial poetic anti-war statement of the period"; were, indeed, some "of the most stunning political poems in American literature."[58]

In his essay "Developing the Underneath" Bly described Jung's theory of the four "intelligences" and argued that poets (and critics) needed to develop their "inferior" functions, the "underneath."[59] In his essay "I Came Out of the Mother Naked" (which served as the central section of *Sleepers*), Bly summarized the sources behind his poems with "psychological" themes.[60] These two essays, and especially "I Came Out of the Mother Naked," have provided the essential theoretical background for most of the critical commentary focused on the mythic, psychological, and religious approaches to Bly's poetry.[61]

Since this commentary is widely scattered throughout the body of the criticism and since it is frequently unsystematically argued, with comments blurring into one another and overlapping indiscriminately, the easiest way to indicate the scope and the significance of this criticism is simply to summarize the most important contributions chronologically.

Anthony Libby described Bly's theory of "the Great Mother" and showed how it developed from his earlier poetry (in *Silence* and *Light*) and how, finally, though Bly's "vision of the death which feeds life is neither exactly traditional nor really transcendental," his myth and mystically oriented poetry became "prophetic."[62] Michael Atkinson, in a detailed consideration of *Sleepers*, focused on the relationship between Bly's poems and his central thematic essay and discussed the "implicit and continuous parallelism" of Jungian psychological elements in the book and especially in the long title poem.[63] Julian Gitzen described the "various states of mind" detailed in Bly's poetry in general and argued that *Sleepers* added "an additional dimension to Bly's spiritual quest."[64] William V. Davis described the "poetic, religious, psychological struggle" Bly undertook in *Sleepers* and, through a kind of "psychic archaeology," attempted to uncover and describe Bly's exploration of "the substrata of the psyche" and his use of mythic sources and "new brain" theory.[65] David Seal described Bly's debt to Jung, simultaneous with his "unconscious" resistance of Jung, as well as the "anomalies in the Jungian model" in "Sleepers Joining Hands," the title poem of *Sleepers*.[66] Howard Nelson dealt with Bly as a "poet of the inward life," an "inheritor of Whitman," whose "concerns and attitudes are fundamentally religious" (Howard Nelson, 76, 74, passim). Richard P. Sugg, heavily committed to a Jungian approach to Bly in general, traced in close detail Bly's commitment to Jung's "psychospiritual goals of personality development" in "I Came Out of the Mother Naked" and in *Sleepers*, and found in the poem "Sleepers Joining Hands" "a veritable theodicy for the twentieth century" (Sugg, 82, 102, passim). Finally, in an analysis and argument that is perhaps more important to the male/female consciousness criticism to be considered below, Walter Kalaidjian contended that Bly's "'feminine' argument" in his essay "I Came Out of the Mother Naked" and his psychological/mythological-oriented poetry in general "is flawed" because Bly failed "to reflect critically on the sources of his depth psychology" (Kalaidjian, 140–41, passim). And, although Kalaidjian's argument represents a minority position, it may well suggest the direction that future criticism of this phase of Bly's work will take.

The next stage of Bly's career and of the criticism devoted to it focused on the prose poetry. For criticism, the obvious question was: "What does a poet try to accomplish by the paradoxical act of writing poetry in prose?" Stephen Fredman answered this question by arguing that "the American poet," proceeding "from an initial position of alienation," attempted "to create, through attentive receptivity, a space of permission in which the world is allowed to appear as it is." Furthermore, he argued that prose poetry was "central to our time" in that it worked to create "a moment in which poetry, philosophy, and criticism begin to coalesce," because, by its very nature, prose poetry is "unafraid of ideas . . . playful, moving, revelatory, temporally grounded, and critically serious."[67]

Michael Benedikt identified five special properties of the prose poem: attention to the "particular logic" of the unconscious; the use of colloquial and "everyday" speech; a "visionary thrust"; humor; and "a kind of enlightened doubtfulness or hopeful skepticism."[68] All of these properties specifically apply to Bly; they have been conspicuous, quintessential elements in all of his poetry, and are certainly key "properties" in the prose poems. Likewise, they have assumed crucial importance in the criticism devoted to the prose poems.

In his study of the history and practice of prose poetry, Jonathan Monroe considered Bly's work as a rejection of the "subversive historical function" of the prose poem for a "more mystical and religious" approach that focused on "everyday" concrete objects and events and "depoliticized" the "polemical, form-smashing genre for the sake of ecstatic religious content and a focus on domestic concerns and the inner life."[69] And Charles Molesworth provided a succinct summary of Bly's slow "unobtrusive" mastery of the form of the prose poem. "Bly's seeing has seldom been more precise" than in these "self-effacing . . . celebrations of an exacerbated private sensibility" that moves from "one tack-sharp observation to another," through "similes and metaphors proposed but not pursued," which "clear their own ground as they go" (Molesworth, 119–24).

Bly has written extensively on the genre of prose poetry and has written a large number of prose poems.[70] Likewise, a number of important critical studies have been devoted to his theory and practice of prose poetry. In two individual articles Ralph J. Mills, Jr., considered Bly's prose poems in detail. In the first of these, Mills pointed out that Bly's use of the genre of the prose poem goes back to *Silence* and that his "substantial accomplishment" in this genre complements his work in lined poems.[71] In the second piece, Mills traced the unique "organic" development of Bly's prose poems in terms of his theory and found that these poems "stand as a fine coherent achievement."[72] Victoria Frenkel Harris considered Bly's prose poems in terms of "female consciousness," "reliance on intuition," and "psychic integration." In poems like "Walking Where the Plows Have Been Turning," she argued, Bly "constructs a mythology of human experience."[73]

In several separate essays, William V. Davis considered the history of the

prose poem and the literary and theoretical backgrounds behind Bly's extensive use of this form seemingly so ideally suited to him both personally and
poetically. Just as Bly believed that prose poems tend to appear in a culture
when it is getting dangerously close to abstractions, so Bly's prose poems
became dominant in his career following *Sleepers,* his most "abstract" book. In
the prose poems, then, Bly attempted to heal the abstractions he found in his
own work, and, since these poems were close to the poems in *Silence* both in
terms of theme and imagery, he went back, through them, to his poetic
beginnings for a thematic sense of renewal—at the same time that, through
this new genre, he provided himself with a new beginning.[74]

The poems in *Loving,* Bly's most recent individual collection, took critics
by surprise, confused them, perhaps even a bit embarrassed them. Certainly,
most critics were not prepared for overt love poems. For these reasons, and
because there has been less time for critical responses to these poems, what
criticism has appeared (by comparison with the considerable critical attention
devoted to the poems in each of the earlier periods of Bly's career) is slight,
sketchy, unsystematic, and largely unsympathetic.

Although there have been a few dissenting opinions, the major thrust of
this criticism has suggested that the "male-female consciousness" that these
recent poems explore resulted in some of the weakest poems Bly has written.[75]
Of course, given the short time critics have had to consider these poems, such
early opinions may constitute only a kind of interim report, and, like any full
and final estimate of Bly's complete poetic output, still be far from definitive
or final.

The reading, thinking, and writing behind Bly's most recent poems have
already been partially traced to Jung and others, as attested to by the earlier
criticism. One of the most important influences on Bly, however, and especially so in the second half of his career, was Erich Neumann, a disciple of Jung.
Jung said, "The creative process has a feminine quality, and the creative work
arises from unconscious depths . . . from the realm of the Mothers."[76] And
Neumann pointed out that "matriarchal consciousness is not confined to
women," but exists in men as part of their "anima-consciousness. Furthermore,
this is particularly true of creative people" because "the creative is by its
inherent nature related to matriarchal consciousness."[77]

The earliest important background essay in the critical canon to focus
specifically on these new poems was Anthony Libby's analysis of the poetic
theory and the schema of psychological trappings that Bly based some of his
earliest and many of his later poems on. Libby pointed out the Jungian
dichotomy important to Bly's notion of "sexual consciousness": masculine
consciousness involved "logic, efficiency, the advancement of material civilization, repression, and control of the natural world"; feminine consciousness,
"intuition, creativity, mystic acceptance of the world." And, because "only
women are biologically creative," men feel the "aesthetic urge to create"

outside of their own bodies. Libby indicated that, as early as 1970, Bly had seen "the mother coming up" through the psyche, "returning."[78]

In several essays, Victoria Frenkel Harris dealt both generally and specifically with these issues as she focused on the feminine in Bly's work. First, she considered the significance of intuition to poetry in general and of the "incorporative consciousness" in one of Bly's early poems; then she dealt more specifically with the concept of "female consciousness" in another poem. Finally, in a more recent essay, Harris extended and broadened her argument in terms of questions of sexuality in Bly's work. By "valorizing intuition" via Jung, she argued, "Bly's well-intentioned brand of feminism conceals remnants of the patriarchy he denounces." In *Loving*, then, when "an actual woman appears," she often "retains the position typifying patriarchal portraits of women." Therefore, while *Loving* "delivers an actualized female . . . the woman . . . is trivialized" and "never speaks herself."[79]

Finally, Walter Kalaidjian has considered "Bly's later attempts to elide history through a feminist poetics based in depth psychology" and found that Bly's "feminist verse is contaminated by patriarchal representations that oppress even as they seek to celebrate feminine experience." Therefore, because Bly failed "to reflect critically on the sources of his depth psychology," his poems continue to "escalate" the "psycho-sexual conflict" (Kalaidjian, 135–41) that has been evident, even conspicuous, in his poetry since the beginning of his career.

Notes

1. Donald Hall, ed., Introduction to *Contemporary American Poetry* (Baltimore: Penquin, 1962), 24–25. In his essay, "On Current Poetry in America," Bly talked of "the new style or the new imagination" that he found in Jiménez, Machado, and Lorca and found lacking in British and American poetry. (See *The Sixties* 4 [Fall 1960]: 28–29.)

2. Cleanth Brooks, "Poetry Since 'The Waste Land,'" *Southern Review*, N.S. 1, no. 3 (1963): 498–99. Hall's "Introduction" and Brook's criticism of it sparked an ongoing critical reaction. Ronald Moran and George Lensing, in an important early essay, described the "emotive imagination" of Bly's work and argued that his poems and those of James Wright, Louis Simpson, and William Stafford represented a "new departure" in contemporary American poetry. (See Ronald Moran and George Lensing, "The Emotive Imagination: A New Departure in American Poetry," *Southern Review* N.S. 3 [January 1967]: 51–67. A revised version of this essay became the first chapter of Lensing and Moran's book, *Four Poets of the Emotive Imagination: Robert Bly, James Wright, Louis Simpson, and William Stafford* [Baton Rouge: Louisiana State University Press, 1976].) A further reaction to the Hall, Brooks, and Moran-Lensing pieces was G. A. M. Janssens's "The Present State of American Poetry: Robert Bly and James Wright," *English Studies* 51 (April 1970):112–37.

3. The most useful sources for biographical information on Bly are: Deborah Baker, "Making a Farm: A Literary Biography of Robert Bly," *Poetry East* 4/5 (Spring/Summer 1981): 145–89 (reprinted in Richard Jones and Kate Daniels, eds., *Of Solitude and Silence: Writings on Robert Bly* [Boston: Beacon Press, 1981], 33–77), hereafter cited as Jones and Daniels; Howard Nelson's "Chronology" in *Robert Bly: An Introduction to the Poetry* (New York: Columbia

University Press, 1984), xxvii–xxxvii, hereafter cited as Howard Nelson; Robert Bly, "Being a Lutheran Boy-god in Minnesota," in Chester G. Anderson, ed., *Growing Up in Minnesota: Ten Writers Remember Their Childhood* (Minneapolis: University of Minnesota Press, 1976), 205–19.

4. Louis Simpson, "Poetry Chronicle," *Hudson Review* 16 (Spring 1963): 139.

5. Ralph J. Mills, Jr., "Four Voices in Recent American Poetry," *Christian Scholar* 46 (Winter 1963): 341, 344.

6. See Michael Goldman, "Joyful in the Dark," *New York Times Book Review*, 18 February 1968, 10, 12; Robert Mazzocco, "Jeremiads at Half-Mast," *New York Review of Books*, 10 June 1968, 22–25; Herbert Leibowitz, "Questions of Reality," *Hudson Review* 21 (Autumn 1968): [553]–57; Harriet Zinnes, "Two Languages," *Prairie Schooner* 42 (Summer 1968): 176–78; Louis Simpson, "New Books of Poems," *Harper's Magazine*, August 1968, 74–75.

7. See Alan Brownjohn, "Pre-Beat," *New Statesman*, 2 August 1968, 146; and Julian Symons, "New Poetry," *Punch*, 24 July 1968, 136

8. Kenneth Rexroth, "The Poet as Responsible," *Northwest Review* 9 (Fall/Winter 1967–1968): 116–18.

9. See, for instance, Alan Helms, "Two Poets," *Partisan Review* 44, no. 2 (1977): [284]–88; Anthony Piccione, "Bly: Man, Voice and Poem," *Ann Arbor Review*, 15–16 (August 1973): 86–90; and Donald Hall, "Notes on Robert Bly and *Sleepers Joining Hands*" *Ohio Review* 15 (Fall 1973): 89–93.

10. See *Choice* 11 (1974): 434; Seamus Cooney, "The Book Review," *Library Journal*, 1 October 1977, 3163.

11. Paul Ramsey, "American Poetry in 1973," *Sewanee Review* 82 (Spring 1974): 401–402.

12. See, for example, Chad Walsh, "Wry Apocalypse, Revolutionary Petunias," *Washington Post Book World*, 1 April 1973, 13.

13. See Lewis Hyde, "Let Other Poets Whisper . . . You Can Hear Bly," *Minneapolis Tribune*, 25 February 1973, 10D–11D. Hyde called "Teeth Mother" "the best poem written during the last decade."

14. Ray Lindquist, *New* 22/23 (Fall/Winter 1973–1974): 88–89.

15. Joyce Carol Oates, "Where They All Are Sleeping," *Modern Poetry Studies* 4 (Winter 1973): 341–44.

16. Anonymous review, *Booklist*, 15 April 1976, 1162.

17. William V. Davis, "Defining the Age," *Moons and Lion Tailes* 2, no. 3 (1977): 85–89.

18. Stanley Plumly, "Books," *American Poetry Review* 4 (November/December 1975): 44–45.

19. James F. Mersmann, "Robert Bly: Rediscovering the World," *Aura* 6 (Spring 1977): 40.

20. See James Finn Cotter, "Poetry Reading," *Hudson Review* 31 (Spring 1978): 214–15; anonymous reviewer, *Kirkus Reviews*, 1 October 1977, 1087; Hugh Kenner, "Three Poets," *New York Times Book Review*, 1 January 1978, 10; Francine Ringold, *World Literature Today* 52 (Summer 1978): 471.

21. Philip Dacey, "This Book Is Made of Turkey Soup and Star Music," *Parnassus: Poetry in Review* 7 (Fall/Winter 1978): 34–45.

22. Charles Molesworth, "Domesticating the Sublime: Bly's Latest Poems, *Ohio Review* 19 (Fall 1978): [56]–66.

23. In his preface Bly said that the poems in *This Tree* "make one book" with the poems in *Silence*. This preface has been much discussed—especially so since *Silence* was so favorably received. For comments on the relationship of the preface to the book, see Peter Stitt. "The World at Hand," *Georgia Review* 34 (Fall 1980): 663–66; and William V. Davis, *Understanding Robert Bly* (Columbia: University of South Carolina Press, 1988), 32–39; hereafter cited as Davis.

24. See Hayden Carruth, "Poets on the Fringe," *Harper's Magazine*, January 1980, 79; hereafter cited as Carruth; Joseph Garrison, "Book Review," *Library Journal*, August 1979, 1569; James R. Saucerman, *Western American Literature* 16 (Summer 1981): 162–64.

25. Eliot Weinberger, "Gloves on a Mouse," *The Nation*, 17 November 1979, 503–504; hereafter cited as Weinberger.

26. Robert Bly, *This Tree Will Be Here for a Thousand Years* (New York: Harper & Row, 1979), 41.

27. See *Booklist*, 1 January 1982, 582; Brown Miller, "Searching for Poetry: Real vs. Fake," *San Francisco Review of Books*, 8 July 1983, 22; Paul Stuewe, *Quill & Quire* 48 (January 1982): 39; Peter Stitt, "Dark Volumes," *New York Times Book Review*, 14 February 1982, 37. Miller, referring to Stitt, said, "Unfortunately, Bly's reputation is so formidable it can cause a reviewer in *The New York Times Book Review* to call this collection Bly's 'richest most complex book,' an absurd statement from my viewpoint."

28. Majorie Perloff, "Soft Touch," *Parnassus: Poetry in Review* 10 (Spring/Summer 1982): 221–30.

29. Donald Wesling, "The Wisdom-Writer," *The Nation*, 31 October 1981, 447–48.

30. Charles Molesworth, *Western American Literature* 17 (November 1982): 282–84.

31. Michael S. Reynolds, [Review of "The Man in the Black Coat Turns,"] in Frank N. Magill, ed., *Magill's Literary Annual 1983* (Englewood Cliffs, N.J.: Salem Press, 1983), 439–42.

32. Andy Brumer said that *Loving* was "not a book meant for reviewers." (See "Loving as the Bridge," *Poetry Flash* 152 [November 1985]: 6; hereafter cited as Brumer.)

33. Anonymous, "Notes on Current Books," *Virginia Quarterly Review* 62 (Winter 1986): 27.

34. Paul Stuewe, *Quill & Quire* 51 (1985): 29.

35. Brumer, 1, 6; Alex Raksin, *Los Angeles Times Book Review*, 22 February 1987, 10; Sam Hamill, "Lyric, Miserable Lyric (Or: Whose Dog Are You?)," *American Poetry Review* 16 (September/October 1987): 31.

36. Fred Chappell, "Sepia Photographs and Jazz Solos," *New York Times Book Review*, 13 October 1985, 15.

37. Peter Stitt, "Coherence Through Place in Contemporary American Poetry," *Georgia Review* 40 (Winter 1986): 1024; hereafter cited as Stitt.

38. Joyce Peseroff, "Minnesota Transcendentalist," *New York Times Book Review*, 25 May 1986, 2; hereafter cited as Peseroff.

39. Roger Mitchell, "Robert Bly and the Trouble with American Poetry," *Ohio Review* 42 (1988): 89, 86; hereafter cited as Mitchell.

40. Askold Melnyczuk, "Robert Bly," *Partisan Review* 55, no. 1, (1988): 167, 170; hereafter cited as Melnyczuk.

41. See Mitchell, 91; Melnyczuk, 170.

42. See Robert Kelly, "Notes on the Poetry of Deep Image," *Trobar: a magazine of new poetry* 2 (1961): 14. Cf. Jack Myers and Michael Simms, *Longman Dictionary and Handbook of Poetry* (White Plains, N. Y.: Longman, 1985), 77. After acknowledging that the term " deep image" had never been "specifically defined," Myers and Simms suggest that "in general" it "refers to an IMAGE that connects the physical world with the spiritual world." By way of "contemporary associations" they quote Bly's essay on Francis Ponge, "Two Stages of an Artist's Life," *Georgia Review* 34 (Spring 1980): 105–109.

43. See Stephen Stepanchev, *American Poetry Since 1945: A Critical Survey* (New York: Harper Colophon, 1967), 15–16; Donald Hall, "American Expressionist Poetry," *Serif* 1 (December 1964): 18–19; Lawrence Kramer, "A Sensible Emptiness: Robert Bly and the Poetics of Immanence," *Contemporary Literature* 24 (Winter 1983): 449–62; Victoria Frenkel Harris, "Criticism and the Incorporative Consciousness," *Centennial Review* 25 (Fall 1981): 417–34; Walter Kalaidjian, *Languages of Liberation: The Social Text in Contemporary American Poetry* (New York: Columbia University Press, 1989), 18, 42; hereafter cited as Kalaidjian. For a brief summary of Bly's specific relationship to "deep image" poetry, see Davis, 23–25.

44. See James E. B. Breslin, *From Modern to Contemporary: American Poetry, 1945–1965* (Chicago: University of Chicago Press, 1984), 181.

45. Charles Altieri, *Enlarging the Temple: New Directions in American Poetry during the 1960s* (Lewisburg: Bucknell University Press, 1979), 78, 85–86; hereafter cited as Altieri. In a later article, "From Experience to Discourse: American Poetry and Poetics in the Seventies," *Contemporary Literature* 21 (Spring 1980): 191–224, Altieri took a much more negative view of the practice of the "deep image" by Bly and others during the 1960s, arguing that these early "deep image" poems were primarily representative examples of the social and cultural pressures of the 1960s on American poetry.

46. Dennis Haskell, "The Modern American Poetry of Deep Image," *Southern Review* (Australia) 12 (1979): 140, 141, 143, 155, 161, 163.

47. Robert Bly, "Prose vs. Poetry," *Choice: A Magazine of Poetry and Photography* 2 (1962): 65–80.

48. Ralph J. Mills, Jr., *Contemporary American Poetry* (New York: Random House, 1965), 211–12, 217. Bly himself has often mentioned in passing his use of "deep images." For his most definitive comments, see "A Wrong Turning in American Poetry," *Choice: A Magazine of Poetry and Photography*, 3 (1963): 33–47; "Recognizing the Image as a Form of Intelligence," *Field*, no. 24 (Spring 1981): 17–27. Both of these essays were reprinted ("Recognizing" as revised by Bly in 1989) in his *American Poetry: Wildness and Domesticity* (New York: Harper & Row, 1990), 7–35, 273–81, respectively.

49. See Ingegerd Friberg, *Moving Inward: A Study of Robert Bly's Poetry* (Göteborg, Sweden: Acta Universitatis Gothaburgensis, 1977), 208–209; Charles Molesworth, *The Fierce Embrace: A Study of Contemporary American Poetry* (Columbia: University of Missouri Press, 1979), 115, 145, hereafter cited as Molesworth; Richard Howard, *Alone With America: Essays on the Art of Poetry in the United States Since 1950* (New York: Atheneum, 1969), [38]–48; William V. Davis, "'Hair in a Baboon's Ear': The Politics of Robert Bly's Early Poetry," *Carleton Miscellany* 18 (Winter 1979/1980): 74–84; William V. Davis, "'Still the Place Where Creation Does Some Work on Itself': Robert Bly's Most Recent Work," in Joyce Peseroff, ed., *Robert Bly: When Sleepers Awake* (Ann Arbor: University of Michigan Press, 1984), 237–46; Davis, passim; Kalaidjian, 127.

50. For a description of these events see *The Nation,* 25 March 1968, 413–14. For the text of Bly's speech, see *Commonweal,* 22 March 1968, 17.

51. One critically important fact, often lost sight of, is that Bly's canon is almost seamless. He subtly prepares his transitions in advance and constantly synthesizes, blending in, overlapping, or eliding his theoretical buttresses as he goes along in precisely the same ways that he glides from one thematic movement to another in the poems, and book by book. Thus, Bly's career and his canon are, for all their seeming variety and in spite of the apparently sudden shiftings, every much a single fabric. The only clear clue he has given to this "seamlessness" is the rather constant similarity of form throughout his career. (Indeed, it may be for this reason that Bly has always been so reticent to talk about form in poetry.)

52. Robert Bly, "Leaping Up into Political Poetry," *London Magazine* 7 (Spring 1967): 82–87 (reprinted in Bly, *American Poetry,* 243–54). See also, Bly, ed. *Forty Poems Touching on Recent American History* (Boston: Beacon, 1970), 7–17; and Bly and David Ray, *A Poetry Reading Against the Vietnam War* (Madison, Minn.: The Sixties Press, 1966). Cf. Richard P. Sugg: "His extensive experience with politics and poetry had prepared Bly uniquely to write the best poetry of the Vietnam period; but it had also encouraged the overdevelopment of a public persona in an individual who had been devoted to solitude and inwardness all his life" (*Robert Bly* [Boston: Twayne, 1986], 41); hereafter cited as Sugg.

53. Todd Gitlin, "The Return of Political Poetry," *Commonweal,* 23 July 1971, 377. Bly's "The Teeth Mother Naked at Last," originally published by City Lights Books in 1970, was revised by Bly for inclusion in *Sleepers* (1973) and that revision further revised for the *Selected Poems* (1986). Of course, most of the critical commentary refers to the first or second versions, although Davis (73–78) based his analysis on "Bly's final version" in *Selected.*

54. Altieri, 168; Cary Nelson, *Our Last First Poets: Vision and History in Contemporary American Poetry* (Urbana: University of Illinois Press, 1981), 143, hereafter cited as Cary Nelson;

Kalaidjian, 133. In some cases critics make a clear distinction between the poems in *Light* and "Teeth Mother." See, for instance, Paul A. Lacey, *The Inner War: Forms and Themes in Recent American Poetry* (Philadelphia: Fortress Press, 1972), 32–56.

55. See Alan Williamson, "Language Against Itself: The Middle Generation of Contemporary Poets," in Robert B. Shaw, ed., *American Poetry Since 1960: Some Critical Perspectives* (Chester Springs, Pa.: Dufour Editions, 1974), 65; Paul Breslin, "How to Read the New Contemporary Poem," *American Scholar* 47 (Summer 1978): 369; Sugg, 61; Howard Nelson, 64.

56. See Cary Nelson, 23, 25.

57. James F. Mersmann, *Out of the Vietnam Vortex: A Study of Poets and Poetry Against the War* (Lawrence: University Press of Kansas, 1974), 25, 113, 121, 136.

58. Davis, 50; Dana Gioia, "The Successful Career of Robert Bly," *Hudson Review* 40 (Summer 1987): 220.

59. See Robert Bly, "Developing the Underneath," *American Poetry Review* 2 (November/December 1973): 44–45.

60. See Robert Bly, "I Came Out of the Mother Naked," in *Sleepers Joining Hands* (New York: Harper & Row, 1973), 29–50.

61. Cf. Robert Bly, "The Dead World and the Live World," *The Sixties* 8 (Spring 1966): 2–7 (reprinted in Bly, *American Poetry*, 233–39). Valuable information on these areas in Bly's work can also be found, in scattered comments, throughout many of the numerous interviews he has given over the years. See especially the interviews included in Bly's *Talking All Morning* (Ann Arbor: University of Michigan Press, 1980), 3–46; 207–212; 213–23; 224–34. Cf. also Shepherd Bliss, "Balancing Feminine and Masculine: The Mother Conference in Maine," *East West Journal* 8 (February 1978): 36–39.

62. Anthony Libby, "Robert Bly Alive in Darkness," *Iowa Review* 3 (Summer 1972): 78–89. However, Libby cautioned, "To see Bly's poetry as dependent on anyone's theory, on Jung's, Neumann's, or even Bly's own, is not only to deny his belief in the irrational psychic sources of poetry but also to dilute the unique force of his poems." Cf. Libby, "Fire and Light, Four Poets to the End and Beyond," *Iowa Review* 4 (Spring 1973): 111–26; and Libby, *Mythologies of Nothing: Mystical Death in American Poetry 1940–70* (Urbana: University of Illinois Press, 1984), 153–84.

63. Michael Atkinson, "Robert Bly's *Sleepers Joining Hands:* Shadow and Self," *Iowa Review* 7 (Fall 1976): 135–53.

64. Julian Gitzen, "Floating on Solitude: The Poetry of Robert Bly," *Modern Poetry Studies* 7 (Winter 1976): 231–41.

65. William V. Davis, "'At the Edges of the Light': A Reading of Robert Bly's *Sleepers Joining Hands,*" *Poetry East* 4/5 (Spring/ Summer 1981): 265–82 (reprinted in Jones and Daniels, 250–67). See also Davis, 68–99.

66. David Seal, "Waking to 'Sleepers Joining Hands,'" *Poetry East* 4/5 (Spring/Summer 1981): 234–63 (reprinted in Jones and Daniels, 219–48).

67. Stephen Fredman, *Poet's Prose: The Crisis in American Verse* (Cambridge: Cambridge University Press, 1983), 2, 6, 10. Fredman, however, argued that Bly, as well as W. S. Merwin, Russell Edson, and David Ignatow, have more in common with the tradition of the European prose poem than the "more innovative" and "extra-generic qualities" typical of American prose poetry as practiced by William Carlos Williams, Robert Creeley, and John Ashbery, among others. Cf. Jonathan Holden's interesting analysis of the "prose lyric" in terms of his specific reference to Bly in *The Rhetoric of the Contemporary Lyric* (Bloomington: Indiana University Press, 1980), 57–68.

68. Michael Benedikt, *The Prose Poem: An International Anthology* (New York: Dell, 1976), 48–49.

69. Jonathan Monroe, *A Poverty of Objects: The Prose Poem and the Politics of Genre* (Ithaca: Cornell University Press, 1987), 275–303.

70. Bly's most important essays on the genre of the prose poem are: "What the Prose Poem

Carries With It," *American Poetry Review* 6 (May/June 1977): 44–45; "Two Stages of an Artist's Life," *Georgia Review* 34 (Spring 1980): 105–109; and "The Mind Playing," in Stephen Berg, ed., *Singular Voices: American Poetry Today* (New York: Avon, 1985), 17–19. See also Bly's early essay "Poetry in an Age of Expansion," *The Nation*, 22 April 1961, 350–54. Cf. Rochelle Ratner's interview with Bly, "On Writing Prose Poems," *Soho Weekly News*, 11 December 1975 (reprinted in Bly, *Talking*, 115–19).

71. See Ralph J. Mills, Jr. "'The Body With the Lamp Lit Inside': Robert Bly's New Poems," *Northeast* 3 (Winter 1976–1977): 37–47.

72. See Ralph J. Mills, Jr., "'Of Energy Compacted and Whirling': Robert Bly's Recent Prose Poems," *New Mexico Humanities Review* 4 (Summer 1981): 29–49.

73. Victoria Frenkel Harris, "'Walking Where the Plows Have Been Turning': Robert Bly and Female Consciousness," *Poetry East* 4/5 (Spring/Summer 1981): 123–38 (reprinted in Jones and Daniels, 153–68, and in Peseroff, 208–222).

74. See William V. Davis, "'Camphor and Gopherwood': Robert Bly's Recent Poems in Prose," *Modern Poetry Studies* 11 (1982): 88–102; "'In a Low Voice to Someone He is Sure is Listening': Robert Bly's Recent Poems in Prose," *Midwest Quarterly* 25 (Winter 1984): 148–56; Davis, 100–132.

75. Even Bly himself seemed to shy away almost apologetically from the poems he included in his *Selected Poems* from *Loving*. In the brief prefatory note to these poems, he wrote, "The poems are still close to me, and I won't say much about them. . . . Love poems . . . ask for every bit of musicianship we have, because they can so easily go out of tune." (See *Selected Poems* (New York: Harper & Row, 1986), 172.) *Iron John: A Book About Men* (Reading, Mass.: Addison-Wesley, 1990), Bly's most recent book, even though it is focused on "men," is also quite relevant to his thinking about "male-female consciousness." Cf. also Bly, "Symposium: What's New in American and Canadian Poetry," *New* 15 (April/May 1971): 17–20, and Bly's interviews with Bill Siemering, "The Mother: An Interview with Robert Bly," *Dacotah Territory* 12 (Winter/Spring 1975/1976): 30–34; Keith Thompson, "What Men Really Want," *New Age Journal*, 7 May 1982, 30–37, 50–51; and Jeff Wagenheim, "The Secret Life of Men," *New Age Journal*, October 1990, 106–113.

76. C. G. Jung, *The Spirit in Man, Art and Literature* (*Collected Works*, vol. 15), trans. R. F. C. Hull (Princeton: Princeton University Press, 1971), 103.

77. Erich Neumann, "On the Moon and Matriarchal Consciousness," trans. Hildegard Nagel, in *Fathers and Mothers: Five Papers on the Archetypal Background of Family Psychology* (Zürich: Spring Publications, 1973), 43, 58. See also Neumann's *The Great Mother: An Analysis of the Archetype,* trans. Ralph Manheim (New York: Bollinger Foundation, 1963), and *Art and the Creative Unconscious,* trans. Ralph Manheim (Princeton: Princeton University Press, 1969).

78. Libby, "Robert Bly Alive," 85. Indeed, Bly has indicated that "In 1973 . . . I began the poems that eventually became *Loving a Woman in Two Worlds*" (*Selected,* 172). But it might be possible to go even further back than that, to "A Man Writes to a Part of Himself" (*Silence,* 36) in which a "husband" thought of his "wife, starving, without care" and wondered, "Which of us two then is the worse off? / And how did this separation come about?"

79. See Victoria Frenkel Harris, "Incorporative Consciousness," 417–34; "'Walking Where the Plows,'" 123–38; "Relationship and Change: Text and Context of James Wright's 'Blue Teal's Mother' and Robert Bly's 'With Pale Women in Maryland,'" *American Poetry* 3 (1985): 43–56; "Scribe, Inscription, Inscribed: Sexuality in the Poetry of Robert Bly and Adrienne Rich," in Marleen S. Barr and Richard Feldstein, eds., *Discontented Discourses: Feminism / Textual Intervention / Psychoanalysis* (Urbana: University of Illinois Press, 1989), 117–37.

PRELIMINARIES

◆

North of Jamaica

Louis Simpson

Robert Bly grew up on a farm in Minnesota and went to St. Olaf's College—the only other person I knew of who had gone to St. Olaf's was the Great Gatsby—then to Harvard, and had spent a few years thinking for himself. When I met him in New York his outer garment—the blue or grey business suit that even poets were wearing in the fifties—disguised a seething mind. He bought a Viking helmet with horns and contemplated wearing it to poetry-readings.

Bly was dissatisfied with nearly everything that had been taking place recently in American poetry and was looking for new ideas. He had been reading modern Spanish poets in particular. His own writing up to this point was typical of the 1940–1950 younger poets; he had been as able as anyone to write rhymed stanzas in literary language, but now he was growing irritated with this and searching for new ways of poetry in the writings of

> Pablo Neruda . . . Garcia Lorca and Cesar Vallejo; in the Swedish tradition, Ekelöf, in the French Char and Michaux, in the German Trakl and Benn—all of them writing in what we have called, for want of a better word, the new imagination, and making contributions to that imagination as enormous as Eliot's or Pound's and with a totally different impact, and on totally different roads.

Bly wanted poems that would not explain everything in the plodding, rationalistic way of the poetry of the forties. The new poems would be based not on English tradition, nor upon the—in Bly's opinion—exclusive, snobbish, psychically crippling ideas of critics such as T. S. Eliot and Allen Tate. Away with abstract language! Down with literary writing! Bly wanted writings in images, and the images must be new.

His description of the new images, however, was vague. He thought that the Imagists had been merely making pictures, and the images of the French Surrealists came out of trivial associations, they lacked depth. The new image would be "deep." Bly found the Spanish Surrealists more to his taste.

> An imagination, a content, a style exists that has a magnificence of suggestion and association. I think it is mistaken to think that if we work in this style our

works will resemble Eliot's or Pound's. Two things make me think different. First, some profundity of association has entered the mind since then. Freud's ocean has deepened, and Jung's work on images has been done. To Pound an image meant "Petals on a wet black bough." To us an image is "death on the deep roads of the guitar" or "the grave of snow" or "the cradle-clothes of the sea."

What would be the difference between Bly's use of surrealistic images and the old kinds? It was easy to see what he was against, but not so easy to see what he would make that would be new. That would depend on the quality of the life of the poet himself. If this surrealism were new, it would be so because it was written by men who were not French or Spanish, but American. So, at the same time that Bly's new magazine *The Fifties* spoke of neglected avant-garde traditions in Europe, South America and China, it was furiously American, printing poems that spoke of American earth, farm landscapes and highways. It was a curious, and at times awkward, combination of eclectic theorizing and local colour.

In his own poems Bly seemed to be trying to reconcile the irreconcilable.

> the gold animals, the lions, and the zebras, and the pheasants,
> Are waiting at the head of the stairs with robbers' eyes.

He asked for a poetry that would include "the dark figures of politics, the world of street cars, and the ocean world"—by the ocean he meant "this profound life," a life of the spirit. It is easier to call for spiritual life than to represent it in poems, and yet he was beginning, in certain poems about Minnesota, to give the sensation of his ideas.

Thinking About Robert Bly

WILLIAM MATTHEWS

For some people *The Light Around the Body* legitimized an incipient Bly backlash. Earlier, they compared Bly (to his disadvantage) to the poets associated with *The Sixties* and his influence. Now they remember with nostalgia the unique force of *Silence in the Snowy Fields*—its remarkable power to evoke emotions almost wholly absent from the American poetry of recent years.

For all his talk of solitude Bly has come to dominate American poetry.

*   *   *

Bly's incendiary criticism and crusade for the poetry he admires have annoyed many and threatened not a few. When *The Light Around the Body*, which includes some bad poems, came out, open season was declared on Bly. One young poet who heard I was going to do a piece on Bly said, "Good, it's time somebody got him." He assumed I wouldn't write for any other reason. It is very difficult to think straight about Robert Bly. I'm writing these notes to help me try.

It is nearly impossible to overemphasize the importance of Bly's criticism. John Haines was the first to say in public that there has been nothing so interesting or influential since Ezra Pound began sending reviews to *Poetry*. Poets who are also critics write not only about other poems but always, in an elaborate code, about their own—both those they have written and those they aspire to write. We can learn a lot about *The Light Around the Body* from Bly's criticism.

*   *   *

The poems in *The Light Around the Body* are based in a virile mysticism, a secular faith drawn partly from the writings of Jacob Boehme and partly from Rilke's *Letters to a Young Poet*. Like Rilke, Bly relies on the value of solitude as a condition the poet cannot escape; indeed, he cannot prize it too fiercely. From Boehme he draws the idea that there is an inner and an outer world. As Boehme wrote, "Since then we are generated out of both worlds, we speak in two

Reprinted from *Tennessee Poetry Journal* 2, no. 2 (Winter 1969): 49–57. Reprinted by permission of the author.

languages, and we must be understood also by two languages." A glow around the body would show that the two worlds have met there.

Some poems in the book stay in the outer world while the poet seethes inside his skin—these are the poems overloaded with prose ideas. Others want to go infinitely inward, like the vanishing perspective of a High Renaissance painting.

*   *   *

Bly's belief in the value of solitude enforces his faith in the language of the inner world considered apart from the language of the outer world. We get Robert Bly, solitary saint.

Yet this man is housed in the same body with Robert Bly, fiery preacher, who reminds me of D. H. Lawrence.

Like Lawrence, Bly is interested in the spirit of nature, the dark gods, and in a meaningful secularization of religious energies.

*   *   *

The Light Around the Body . . . is Bly's attempt to save himself from the horror of the Asian War without, as no moral man could contemplate, ignoring it.

*   *   *

The war has brought on in Bly another similarity to Lawrence, a tendency to preach. Some consider this an unbearable breach of decorum, like burping at table; I do not. I am tired of the ironists who sit around protecting themselves with cynicism while men like Bly, Dr. Spock, and Rev. Coffin go out on a limb. I'm glad that poets have begun to write about politics and the tone of national life, which they cannot honestly fail to notice. Furthermore, preaching gives expression to a side of Bly's personality which he has suppressed in his poetry. He obviously enjoys his roles of editor and critic; he enjoys literary correspondence; he enjoys his antiwar activity though he detests that it is appropriate. There are moving poems in *Silence in the Snowy Fields* about drinking with friends, being near friends, driving to town late at night to mail a letter. These themes don't appear in the new book. Friends are no longer people whom one loves no matter what; there are instead those who have made the right moral decisions: "the small colonies of the saved." This is an unhappy by-product of preaching.

Or maybe I should put it this way: Bly has written of the attribute of some Oriental poets, "good will toward the self." *Silence in the Snowy Fields* is filled with it. The Asian War and the stifling of the inner life in America disrupt this hard-won peace. In *The Light Around the Body* there is a more muscular, rhetorical, ambitious style. Its ambition is to hold the saint and the preacher together. Many people talk the book's style as if it were an excess in manner, like wearing spats to bed. It's clear though that Bly's style has changed for a reason: to cope with and discover new content. There are crucial issues at stake: reading the book, we watch a man trying to deal with them.

Of course there are failed poems in the book. I have named some I didn't like and tried to say why. The title image is richly suggestive. Some poems leap into the outer world in a mixture of fury and compassion; but they bog down in prose ideas and outer-world debate. Others dive inward in despair and an attempt to stay whole. But it is at the meeting point of the two worlds where the whole man wants to be. Never mind that he cannot stay there, that he is always shooting by like a skier who hasn't learned to stop yet. Still, he is always aiming for that balance, though he knows it will not hold. The best poems in *The Light Around the Body* contain the apparent paradox of seeking a balance that will not hold. It is a risky enterprise.

*　　*　　*

I'm not sure Bly needs a remedy. One thing nobody noticed about *Silence in the Snowy Fields* is its moral seriousness. Most people have talked about the book as if its great achievement were the development of a personal formula—a spare syntax bearing rich imagery—for presenting emotions. Clearly, though, the book is concerned with placing man in the universe, seeking a basis for moral judgment, and with the conflict between any person's need for human contact and the poet's special need for solitude and inwardness. And at no time does he pretend he has solved these problems. The book instead moves toward a consistent attitude toward them: one not so firm it will construct a falsely fixed model, but one coherent enough to give a man integrity. I cannot think what problems might be more important to a poet.

The problem, I take it, is that a man must be morally serious; he must want to be honest. Traditionally, moral understanding is grounded in metaphysics; a metaphysical system guarantees that a moral understanding drawn from it is not capricious. But systems are false: as D'Annunzio had it, "Anatomy presupposes a corpse." This is not a new but an enduring problem. So one tries to base an honest life on an understanding of experience that will not fix, systematize, or otherwise falsify experience. Poetry is a very subtle tool—art is subtler than the intellect—for this impossible job.

To put it too simply, Robert Creeley is always talking to and James Wright about himself. Everyone knows they are serious. Because Bly comes at it more obliquely, some readers miss the point and talk about his style.

Of course earnestness alone will not make a reader share that worthy intention. It is important to notice what poems don't mean as much to us as others. Some poems in *The Light Around the Body* flatly fail for me. Because the book attacks crucial problems, problems I recognize because they haunt my own life, I find the book exciting and painful to read. It is not a "lesser" book than the first one. The good poems are wonderful. Only Bly could have written them.

*   *   *

Bly could become too much embroiled in the outer world. He could become like André Breton—self-consciously a leader of a literary movement, a literary figure in radical politics, a man who diffused a great talent (if you doubt that, read *Nadja*) in too public a life.

In reaction to that possibility he could become a mystical believer in a solitude that excises the legitimate pleasures of human contact and seeks, finally, one to uphold itself.

Too, he could write too much criticism, lessening energies and instincts that would otherwise drive his poems.

My guess, though—even the failures in *The Light Around the Body* confirm it—is that he will continue to take risks, to over-reach. He will continue to face important questions in his poems. I imagine his new poems are already moving toward new dilemmas. Bly has tremendous imaginative power. A serious application of it should produce wonderful poems, as it has many times. Because he has been personally overpublicized and because his literary personality is strong and dominating, we need not fail to notice his bad poems, his achievement and power, the new air his poems and essays allow us to breathe, and the pleasure we take in the difficulty of thinking about Robert Bly.

Young Bly

Donald Hall

He didn't seem young at the time. In February of 1948, my freshman year at Harvard, I first met Robert Bly—in the sanctum of the *Harvard Advocate* on Bow Street. He was Bob for twenty years, and he will remain Bob as I recollect him here. The magazine occupied several rooms on the second floor above the Gold Coast Valeteria, near Adams House and adjacent to the more prosperous *Harvard Lampoon*. I read a notice advertising this term's competition for the *Advocate* and I decided to compete, to try to join a literary board that included Kenneth Koch and Robert Bly. I'm not sure when John Ashbery became an editor.

Not that I knew whom I was joining. I was merely terrified, an infant among the grown-ups. Most of the *Advocate*'s editors (as of 1948) were veterans of the war that ended two and a half years earlier. I came to college straight from boarding school and sat next to people two years older, who had fought in France or Saipan: the ordinary difference of age seemed as if multiplied by seven. In 1991, Robert Bly and I are the same age, but in February 1948 Bob seemed as old and as bronze as John Harvard in the Yard. His naval career had taken place in technical schools studying radar, and then in a hospital where he had rheumatic fever—but I didn't know that.

Although it's unlikely, I think I remember our first meeting: he wore a three-piece brown tweed suit and brown shoes with a narrow maroon tie, striped with green, showing above his vest; he was skinny, incredibly skinny. I assumed from excess of intelligence and scholarship; he wore intelligent horn-rimmed glasses; he spoke rarely, opening his mouth narrowly, with compunction and reticence: He never, ever smiled.

Probably I thought he was thirty, some extravagant figure of years. We talked poetry right away, about Robert Lowell I believe; Lowell really *was* thirty. We both admired him, and we spoke of an *Advocate* dialogue about *Lord Weary's Castle*. The literary ambience was different in those days, and people argued passionately about Lowell's enjambments; friendships dissolved in disagreement over Lowell's eccentric caesurae. Bob and I saw eye to eye—with the result that we found each other intelligent. Mind you, if we had acknowledged our judgment, we would not have used the word "intelligent." At

This essay was written specifically for this volume and is published here for the first time.

Harvard in 1948, people spoke a special language, and "rather bright" was high commendation. For "rather bright" read "extremely intelligent" throughout; for "not very bright" read "incredibly stupid" throughout.

At some point soon, Bob Bly and I dropped our guards and became best friends—which we have remained over decades of affection and argument. When I knew him at first, his poems occupied the closet and he was known as a critic: I suspect that poetry was too important, too much heart-work to be taken public at cutthroat Harvard. But it was not long before we were showing each other our poems, revising each other, reading other people's work, and arguing about what we read. I remember vividly the excitement of his young energy, his enthusiasm, and the generosity of his attentions to my work. Maybe twice a week we met to talk, to argue, to rewrite each other. We took no courses together, until two years later when we were both in Archibald MacLeish's first creative writing class, but we handed to each other what we learned elsewhere. John Kelleher was Bob's tutor, and as a result I felt as if I had a half-tutorial with John Kelleher.

At the *Advocate* the editors stayed up half the night arguing over whether a given poem was good enough for our magazine. Doubtless our solemnity derived from self-importance—but the seriousness of our arguments helped us grow up. Not that we were serious on all occasions. We had marvelous parties, especially when poets came to town to read in the Morris Gray series. Remember that until a decade later poetry readings were rare in the United States. We distributed gallons of martinis at parties for Eliot, Thomas, and the Sitwells.

It was Bob who discovered Adrienne Rich at a Radcliffe jolly-up, telling me that he had met a girl from Baltimore who knew *all* about modern poetry. He introduced me, and we double-dated at Jim Cronin's, Bob with another girl. One time when he was a senior, Bob and I drove to Bennington for a blind double-date—he had a vast green Buick—and on the way home Bob screeched to a stop beside a field of alfalfa. He handed me the keys, so that he might remain with the alfalfa; he thumbed back to Harvard while I drove his car.

In the first summer of our friendship we hitchhiked down south together; or we started to. We spent one night in the woods sleeping on springs in a lean-to we happened upon. Shortly after we settled in, a troop of Boy Scouts arrived, properly outfitted with sleeping bags and cooking equipment. When we exposed our supplies—two cans of Vienna sausage, as I remember—the scoutmaster's mouth dropped open: "Is *that* your *gear?*" The next day Bob stopped a car, claiming that we had been chased by a bear, and we conned ourselves a ride. That night we rented a four-dollar room in a small Tennessee town, to get a little sleep, and the next day we argued over who would thumb rides standing in the sun while the other napped in the shade of a stone wall. I headed back north by myself. I thought: I'll never see *him* again!

We overlapped three years, writing and arguing and double-dating together. When we won Harvard's Garrison Prize for Poetry in his senior year, he beat me out. We waited together at Warren House for the winner's name to be posted. When it was, Robert remembers, I immediately claimed: "I'm not jealous." I won it the next year, only because the prize was still reserved for men; Adrienne Rich was Yale Younger Poet as I won the Garrison. A year ahead of me, Bob graduated and went to New York, which made Harvard lonely in my senior year.

He was extraordinary, even then, for his unceasing curiosity—and his volatility. Both of us kept moving, rocketing among enthusiasms, but he was quicker. He wrote lyrics influenced by Lowell, blank verse monologues less influenced by Lowell, plays, Shakespearean sonnets. . . . When I was at Oxford in the winter of 1951–1952, he sent me a handful of sonnets, which I started to go over—revising, making notes—until I received a letter from New York. I think of that letter as foreshadowing the Robert Bly who emerged so strongly in the 1960s: Don't bother with those sonnets, he wrote me; they're too old-fashioned. . . .

Inward to the World: The Poetry of Robert Bly

William Heyen

For several years I disliked what Robert Bly had done in *Silence in the Snowy Fields* (1962). Indeed, I was surprised that the book had even made it into print. His risks, I felt, were all bad ones. And his dust jacket remarks to the effect that "any poetry in the poems . . . is in the white spaces between the stanzas" offended me. I didn't expect these poems. The ones I had happened to read, in magazines and in the first selection of *New Poets of England and America,* were noisier, more ambitious, I thought that his collection was a mistake, a group of journal jottings.

Where was his "heightened speech"? How, if to suggest something is to create it and to state something is to destroy it, could he write lines such as "I have awakened at Missoula, Montana, utterly happy" ("In a Train") and "There is a privacy I love in this snowy night" ("Driving to Town Late to Mail a Letter")? Didn't he know such bare statements were against the rules?

*   *   *

. . . How, in the Age of Eliot, could he write poems that defied serious inquiry and involved explication? What did these poems *mean*? I couldn't surround them, couldn't grip them, couldn't imagine discussing them. What could one say about them?

Silence in the Snowy Fields was like a cluster of gnats. No matter what else I did, I couldn't remain neutral about Bly's poems. It will be impossible for me to discuss my change of mind rationally, but I've come to believe that my reservations about Bly were only nigglings, that measuring the accomplishment of his work against petty objections is something like dismissing *Moby-Dick* because Melville loses track of his point of view. Bly is free from the inhibitions of critical dictates many of us have regarded as truths. He manages, in fact, to write poems that are themselves suspensions of the critical faculty. The poems had to become what they are. They are quiet, unassuming. They are uninsistent, unrhetorical; they depend, often, on one another for total effect. They do not lead to the kind of intellectual pleasure (an antipoetic pleasure) one gets from having traced down all the allusions in *The Waste Land* or from having used the unabridged dictionary to come to terms with "The Comedian as the Letter C."

Reprinted from *The Far Point* 3 (Fall/Winter 1969): 42–50. Reprinted by permission of *The Far Point*.

In the full senses of the words these are—may I attach labels to poems that defeat labels?—"symbolic" and "mystical" poems.

*　　　*　　　*

Bly's poems do not wear thin. Our inner lives speak in them, speak out from the silence and solitude of the American Midwest. And there is a profound correspondence between "the man inside the body" ("Silence") and the oceans of air and water and land through which he moves. A car is a "solitude covered with iron" ("Driving Toward the Lac Qui Parle River") and so is the man moving inside his struts of flesh and bone. For years I felt that Bly's poetry pointed at a mysterious and dissatisfying nothingness that was a nonsubject. But he has one subject that speaks out from the spaces between lines, stanzas, and poems and unites them: The Self.

*　　　*　　　*

REVIEWS

◆

Four Voices in Recent American Poetry

RALPH J. MILLS, JR.

A volume of poems by Robert Bly has long been awaited, and *Silence in the Snowy Fields* proves that the waiting has not gone unrewarded. Mr. Bly, both as an editor of his journal *The Sixties* (formerly *The Fifties*) and as a practicing poet, has made a great effort to lead contemporary American verse away from its current tendencies and preoccupations: he wishes to introduce fresh influences into it. If I understand correctly what I have seen of his editorial and critical views, he aims at a purification of poetry, a cleansing of all the elements which get into poems and do not, as he thinks, belong there. The elements to be rid of are intellectual, ideological, social, and cultural. Like Denise Levertov and Robert Creeley, he keeps his work close to his individual experience and remote from the world of ideas. Mr. Bly writes rather brief poems as a rule, informal, and with a marked emphasis on the contemplative observer-narrator, who is the poet himself and not some imagined speaker. His approach is made plain in the first of his poems, "Three Kinds of Pleasure":

I

Sometimes, riding in a car, in Wisconsin
Or Illinois, you notice those dark telephone poles
One by one lift themselves out of the fence line
And slowly leap on the gray sky—
And past them, the snowy fields.

II

The darkness drifts down like snow on the picked
*   cornfields*
In Wisconsin: and on these black trees
Scattered, one by one,
Through the winter fields—
We see stiff weeds and brownish stubble,
And white snow left now in the wheeltracks of
*   the combine.*

Reprinted from *The Christian Scholar* 46, no. 4 (Winter 1963): 340–45, by permission.

III

It is a pleasure, also, to be driving
Toward Chicago, near dark,
And see the lights in the barns.
The bare trees more dignified than ever,
Like a fierce man on his deathbed,
And the ditches along the road half full of a
　　private snow.

The movement of these poems is always slow, with a scrupulous attention to accuracy of detail. Yet the purpose of such accuracy seems to me less that of a devotion to realistic principles than a desire to create what the poet conceives as the full image—an image which is brimming with unspoken feelings that are awakened in the reader through its mediation. It is, then, a poetry of concentrated understatement. The imagery, purged of intellectual or ideological reference, bears the weight of the experience presented, while the experience itself emerges from the poet's own circumstance. Thus the substance of a poem mirrors the poet's mind in contemplation, his inwardness if you will, or is a perception of and meditation of nature enlarged by simile and association. The latter is easily comprehended once we know that Mr. Bly lives on a farm in Minnesota, and that his poetic experience originates in this somewhat isolated rural life. "The fundamental world of poetry is the inward world," he says in some notes about his work. "We approach it through solitude." We become conscious of that condition of solitude behind each of the poems; and not only solitude, but a certain kind of silence which surrounds the poetry and undoubtedly derives from the author's attitude toward the world he watches with such careful regard. "There is no beginning to silence and no end: it seems to have its origins in the time when everything was still pure Being," writes the Swiss philosopher Max Picard. "It is like uncreated, everlasting Being."[1] That description would fit Robert Bly's poetic landscape, which is not characterized by a complete lack of sound but is permeated by a profound silence from which particular sounds come forth with a clarity and resonance that invests them with singular value. "After Working" is a fine illustration of this relationship between silence and sound in what the poet perceives:

I

After many strange thoughts,
Thoughts of distant harbors, and new life,
I came in and found the moonlight lying in the room.

II

Outside it covers the trees like pure sound,
The sound of tower bells, or of water moving under
　　the ice,

The sound of the deaf hearing through the bones of
their heads.

III

We know the road; as the moonlight
Lifts everything, so in a night like this
The road goes on ahead, it is all clear.

The environment in which Mr. Bly lives and which fills his poetry is one selected for artistic as well as personal reasons, or so it must appear. Though the Minnesota farmland was apparently the place where he grew up, he obviously made a definite choice, a meaningful one with regard to his work, in returning there. Certainly something very positive may be said for freedom from and independence of literary circles, of the cumbersome load of college teaching and lecturing which comprises the daily routine for so many poets these days. But beyond that one can detect a connection between Mr. Bly's intentions as a poet and his geographical location. In "After Working"—and this might be said of the majority of poems in his book—we see him using those surroundings, his experience of a particular locale, as the means of realizing a poetry of suggestive images, a poetry which sustains its kinship with the things of earth, nature and the seasons, but firmly rejects any framework of ideas. Mr. Bly has insisted that we should read our Spanish, German and Italian contemporaries to learn this view of poetic art and to witness it in practice; and he has felt strongly enough about this matter to publish many translations—of Montale, Trakl, Jiménez, Vallejo, Neruda, Rilke, and others—in his journal and through his press, and so support his contentions. Of course, a writer like Pablo Neruda has been notoriously mixed up in political affairs for a good number of years. I have no notion of Mr. Bly's political opinions, nor do I think he is much concerned with Neruda's. What he discovers in that Chilean poet can best be exemplified through a short passage from Neruda's essay "Toward an Impure Poetry" (which is, I imagine, in essential agreement with Robert Penn Warren's more complicated defense of poetic impurity):

> It is well, at certain hours of the day and night, to look closely at the world of objects at rest. Wheels that have crossed long, dusty distances with their mineral and vegetable burdens, sacks from the coalbins, barrels and baskets, handles and hafts for the carpenter's tool chest. From them flow the contacts of man with the earth, like a text for all harassed lyricists. The used surfaces of things, the wear that the hands give to things, the air, tragic at times, pathetic at others, of such things—all lend a curious attractiveness to the reality of the world that should not be underprized.[2]

This paragraph by Neruda reads, in its own fashion, like a comment on Mr. Bly's poetic aims, on the quality of his observation and reflection. And one cannot doubt that what Mr. Bly is doing consists in just this attentiveness to the residual life in things and to the accumulated human history which the imagination searches out there. But another important element ought to be mentioned in these poems, and that is the mind of the poet himself. We are usually aware of the presence of this mind as the contemplative consciousness through which the world appears and, in addition, as the agent of association and analogy whereby words and images are made to carry emotional weight.

Mr. Bly also offers us poems that initiate with his feelings, his personal moods and moral outlook, and move outward to interpret the world and things in it through them. He remarks that the poetry he writes is about the present rather than the past, and thus it becomes involved with both nature and the unconscious, which exist in the present. We have already spoken briefly of the place nature occupies in his work. The unconscious is disclosed in the poet's reliance on dream and the fluid associations of the mind, especially in the sort of poem which begins with his private feelings. The kind of order we see in one of these poems reflects the motions of the poet's mind in a state of dream and meditation mixed. The poem "Unrest" will serve to introduce this side of Mr. Bly's art and also his pointed moral sense:

> A strange unrest hovers over the nation:
> This is the last dance, the wild tossing of Morgan's seas,
> The division of spoils. A lassitude
> Enters into the diamonds of the body.
> In high school the explosion begins, the child is partly killed,
> When the fight is over, and the land and the sea ruined,
> Two shapes inside us rise, and move away.
>
> But the baboon whistles on the shores of death—
> Climbing and falling, tossing nuts and stones,
> He gambols by the tree
> Whose branches hold the expanses of cold,
> The planets whirling and the black sun,
> The cries of insects, and the tiny slaves
> In the prisons of bark:
> Charlemagne, we are approaching your islands!
>
> We are returning now to the snowy trees,
> And the depth of the darkness buried in snow, through
>   which you rode all night
> With stiff hands; now the darkness is falling
> In which we sleep and awake—a darkness in which
> Thieves shudder, and the insane have a hunger for snow,
> In which bankers dream of being buried by black stones,
> And businessmen fall on their knees in the dungeons of sleep.

The entire poem retains the particular characteristics of the author's thought, the shifting streams of memory and intuition, but these images command, as we continue reading, an increasing objectiveness so that the final effect is one of apocalyptic vision or prophecy. Such a poem, however, does not owe allegiance to any specific system of ideas or institutionalized belief; its criticism of values is implied through imagery, not by abstract or logical formulation. Robert Bly, like Anne Sexton, Dilys Laing, and Robert Hayden, looks to his individual perceptions as the basis for moral attitudes and judgments of worth. Poets of the generation of Pound and Yeats could still think of a comprehensive body of thought which their writing might support. But our world has changed so rapidly in forty years that the poet today, hemmed in on all sides by so many hostile developments, finds it inconceivable to entertain the larger assertions of his predecessors. Yet the reduced sphere of the poet has not lessened his intensity, in fact it may have magnified that because poetry has been brought so close to the flesh and bone and spirit of its makers. Within the circle which is the poet's own existence and the home of his imagination the art of poetry arrives at the honesty of vision that is its essence and includes craft as well.

Notes

1. Max Picard: *The World of Silence*, translated by Stanley Godman, Chicago, Henry Regnery, 1961, p. 1.
2. From *Selected Poems of Pablo Neruda*, edited and translated by Ben Belitt, New York, Grove Press, 1961, p. 39.

Poetry Chronicle
[Review of *Silence in the Snowy Fields*]

RICHARD HOWARD

Transforming images of his bleak or blatant midwest landscape, his empty towns and choking farms, into the sense of a buried life in the body, a kind of somatic fantasia on themes of revelation, Robert Bly's success in *Silence in the Snowy Fields* has been to confer upon even the simplest words a weight and consequence as of new things. It is not a difficult or even a structured poetry he writes; Bly is often content with only just enough; like his invoked master Stevens, he often speaks "below the tension of the lyre":

> I am full of love, and love this torpid land.
> Someday I will go back, and inhabit again
> The sleepy ground where Harding was born.

But he manages to invest his seasons and spectacles, however dull or even dreary, with so much felt life that the simplest monosyllables speak to him, and to us; after dismissing the dove and even the swallow as messengers for *his* ark, Bly chooses:

> The crow, the crow, the spider-colored crow,
> The crow shall find new mud to walk upon.

There is more, though, than the historyless scenery of Minnesota or Wisconsin, the box-elder and the telephone poles; there is a more momentous subject here, urged first by the volume's epigraph from Boehme, "We are all asleep in the outward man." In his best poems, Bly turns the "snowy fields" into correspondences; take a typical Bly scene and act, *Hunting Pheasants in a Cornfield*, in twenty-one lines he presents the field with a single, leafless willow in it, then wonders, "Why do I love to watch / the sun moving on the chill skin of the branches?" The answer is the last stanza:

> The mind has shed leaves alone for years.
> It stands apart with small creatures near its roots.

Reprinted from *Poetry* 102 (June 1963): 184–86. Copyrighted by The Modern Poetry Association (1963) and reprinted by permission of the editor of *Poetry*.

> I am happy in this ancient place,
> A spot easily caught sight of above the corn,
> If I were a young animal ready to turn home at dusk.

Here the landscape that had seemed so "merely" natural becomes an inner event. The outward man is wakened, nature is shown, as by that other poet of correspondences, to be a temple with "living pillars," and we celebrate a metamorphosis, site becoming self and spirit. This strategy of country pieties serves Bly well enough; yet he can move beyond them; in *Waking from Sleep* the ordinance of his imagery is anything but provincial: introducing the figure of mariners in the first beautiful line, "Inside the veins there are navies setting forth," the body is released from sleep, midway through the poem: "Shouts rise from the harbor of the blood, / Mist and masts rising," until at the end;

> Now we sing, and do tiny dances on the kitchen floor.
> Our whole body is like a harbor at dawn;
> We know that our master has left us for the day.

It would be easy to peck at Bly's poems for their sagging prosody, their reliance on a set of declarative aspects that precludes drama or humor; yet their successes are so readily their own and so hard to miss that I feel churlish being anything but grateful for this "afternoon snowfall" from the last poem:

> The barn is full of corn, and moving toward us now,
> Like a hulk blown toward us in a storm at sea;
> All the sailors on deck have been blind for many years.

This is a poetry I should like to show a foreign visitor from some abrupt, overcolonized coast—our own, for instance—to suggest what the West is like. Not since the early Glenway Wescott has anyone found moral emblems so adequate to its possibilities.

Two Languages

Harriet Zinnes

The Light Around the Body is one of the most significant American volumes to be published in years. Maybe literary America is waking up. Maybe it has learned that "inwardness" is not necessarily looking at one's navel, listening to "the way they ring the bells in Bedlam" à la Sexton or tortuously describing the abnormalities of one's aunt or father. The seemingly uncontrollable malignant forces around us do indeed lead us to look inward, but it is at the least sentimental and at the most destructive of the creative self to allow that inward eye complete authority.

Robert Bly uses as an epigraph to his second volume a quotation from the mystic Jacob Boehme. The quotation is actually a kind of paradigm for the poetic necessity to join the inward with the outer eye. Boehme wrote: "For according to the outward man, we are in this world, and according to the inward man, we are in the inward world. . . . Since then we are generated out of both worlds, we speak in two languages, and we must be understood also by two languages." As a contemporary poet, Robert Bly uses these two languages. His images, layer upon layer, come swiftly (and controllably) as he probes deeply into our preconscious selves to avoid being suffocated by those "accountants [who] hover over the earth like helicopters." Bly's vision, like Boehme's, comes from his discarding "those things that have felt this despair for so long"—the corrupt layers of things. It does not come from the serpentine coils of the confessional self. In Bly's poetry, a reader can never forget that there is an "I" who despairs. "Once more," he writes, "the heavy body mourns," or he says, "That is why these poems are so sad." Again, he writes: "There is a bitter fatigue, adult and sad." But this despair is not located in the vacuum of self-pity, of maudlin sentimentality, or of the necessarily slick morbidity that comes from looking at the suffering self with too much analytical cool. The despair in this volume is a despair that is more general. It is general *all over America*. It comes, Bly implies throughout the volume, from the recognition of a sickness in our Great Society that is engaged in an immoral war.

*　　　*　　　*

Reprinted from *Prairie Schooner* 42, no. 2 (Summer 1968): 176–78. Reprinted by permission of University of Nebraska Press. Copyright © 1968 University of Nebraska Press.

The poetry that Robert Bly is writing now—as well as such poets as James Wright, Louis Simpson, and W. S. Merwin, for example—is poetry that has finally joined Whitman to a European tradition. It is a poetry which describes in the words of an article in Bly's own magazine *The Sixties* "new experiences and inner sensations for which there is no precedent in English poetry." Poets such as Bly find more in common not only with Rilke, Lorca, and Neruda, but with other European and Latin-American poets such as Georg Trakl; or Jiménez and Antonio Machado of Spain; and Enrique Gonzalez Martinez of Chile, Cesar Vallejo of Peru. In the works of these poets (many of whom Bly and others have translated in his magazine) the new American poets find the source for the truly "modern" poem, an intense, personal poem in which the subconscious and the unconscious are expressed. Furthermore, this intense personal poem is joined unashamedly with political content. It is this junction which makes the new poems of Bly so thoroughly part of a "modern" tradition—a tradition which excludes the Eliotic narrowness and embraces the cosmic or the mystic by means of controlled release of the self through groups of images derived from, as Ralph J. Mills, Jr., writes in his *Contemporary American Poetry*, "subliminal regions of the mind and joined by associations of an emotional, symbolic, and lyrical kind."

*   *   *

There are many poems in the book with obvious and open political content. Such poems as "Those Being Eaten by America" ("the world will soon break up into small colonies of the saved"), "Smothered by the World," or such poems with specific references to recent and dubious episodes in American history as "Sleet Storm on the Merritt Parkway," "The Great Society," and the whole third section of the book with its poems on the Vietnam war—such poems are not mere propaganda poems, poems like those written freely in the 30's. They are not merely doctrinal. Although they are social protest poetry, they are not simplistic and doctrinaire. They are deeply poetic. They fulfill the needs of art, not those of politics. These poems, it must be remembered, are being written after the symbolists, the post-symbolists, written at a time in all the arts when the chief subject matter is art itself. The aesthetic emphasis is apparent here too, but it is an emphasis not on a sterile impersonality; not on a narrow formalism, on a fetishist autonomy of the work of art; not on disengagement, but on a reality stemming from a concerned, emotional self, inward and released, and from an outward self, yearning for a "glimpse of what we cannot see,/Our enemies, the soldiers and the poor." This is poetry justifiably calling upon Boehme; it is poetry with a vision, a poetry of two languages:

> We did not come to remain whole.
> We came to lose our leaves like the trees.

A Sadness for America

PAUL ZWEIG

Robert Bly's imagination is like a light moving around a central wick. The title of his book describes it well: the light around the body; a darting, flickering illumination, extending the private energies of the body into a circle of images. His poems do not assume the form of an argument, or an ongoing parable. They return to the inward spring of the body and move away again, line by line, until slowly the shape of the poem has emerged.

* * *

It is this ability to move between the inward and the outward emotion that makes Robert Bly one of the finest political poets in America.

* * *

The sadness in *The Light Around the Body* is a sadness for America. The book quietly, but firmly, translates the inward mystery and melancholy of which Boehme speaks, into an expansive public language.

To be sure, not all the poems in Bly's volume sustain this clear language. There is a tendency in some poems to evoke a cast of "accountants," "bankers," "executives," "dentists," who float heavily across the scene, without ever really emerging. They are negative characters, and often boring.

There is another fault which tends to limit the impact of some poems. At times the spiritual moment of which Bly writes has been so entirely transposed into fantasy, that one misses the enveloping shape of the human. The poem "Suddenly Turning Away" is about a crisis of love between people. It begins:

> *Someone comes near, the jaw*
> *Tightens, bullheads bite*
> *The snow, moments of intimacy waved*
> *   away,*
> *Half-evolved antennas of the sea snail*
> *Sink to the ground.*

Reprinted from *The Nation*, 25 March 1968, 418–20. Reprinted by permission of *The Nation* magazine/The Nation Company, Inc., © 1968.

Missing here is the simple gesture, the familiar situation which must encircle and anchor the fantasy. By taking us so far inward, Bly has paradoxically left us outside. He has kept the secret of suddenly turning away.

These faults mark a danger in Bly's imagination. But they are only minor blemishes in a book as richly and as variously sustained as is *The Light Around the Body.*

Jeremiads at Half-Mast

Robert Mazzocco

The Light Around the Body is a meditation on politics, fatigue, failure, war, where we are now. In its theme and sensibility, its eerie passivity and suppressed anguish, it is, I suppose, a jeremiad at half-mast.

> The President dreams of invading Cuba.
> Bushes are growing over the outdoor grills,
> Vines over the yachts and the leather seats.

All of the poems in Robert Bly's second collection spread themselves in the same sad, gray, moonlit language, the emotions deceptively bedded deep below the surface, a sort of postcontemplative, postsurrealist style, the mind drained of its data, possibility wrung dry. Yet, too, the poems seem ennobled by the small rightness of tone, images, indictment, and modest urgency of the poet's response.

Like Thoreau and Tolstoy, Robert Bly is a Puritan at heart. I think he would renounce art for truth, the imagination for "reality," and both, should he be forced to do so, for morality—perhaps an unappealing middle-western morality, thin-lipped, reedy, self-righteous. In Bly's America, an America very much of the moment, everything's a cheat, or everything's *ersatz*, or everything becomes so, even, at times, Nature. The silence in the snowy fields (the title of the poet's first collection) becomes here the official silence of injustice, or the babble of the insane.

> Bishops rush about crying, There is no war,
> And bombs fall,
> Leaving a dust on the beech trees . . .

The good Germans drink cokes and watch the hockey match, dressed in different suits, different roles, but aimless, apprehensive. The swinging society swims into sight like some barren planet tufted with tokens of USA today: "Tiny loaves of bread with ears lie on the President's table." The President is the great devourer, the smyler with the knyfe beneath the cloke, everyone's monster. . . .

Reprinted from *New York Review of Books*, 10 June 1968, by permission of the *New York Review of Books* and the author.

Bly is a strange poet, austere yet tender. A sense of distaste or personal disquiet haunts much of his work: the poet himself, in his wayward, intensely musing way, drawn close to disintegration. But he is also strong-willed, carefully armored, defensively settled in his beliefs and sense of place or of history. He is tremendously subjective, but his subjectivity has always been pitted against objectivity. In *Silence in the Snowy Fields* the contrast was between his self-enclosure and his everyday existence, his Minnesota farm, horses, hunting. In *The Light Around the Body* the dramaturgy is that of the poet's interior journey through Vietnam, imperialism abroad, materialism at home. The new poems are political, but not agitprop.

Very likely all of these poems should really be read as one poem, or as a set of variations on a single complaint. "Merchants have multiplied more than the stars of heaven," a sardonic echo of Kant's "the moral law within and the starry heavens above," is the first line of the first poem. Luxury, indolence, boredom, the TV set, the Chase National Bank, Johnson's cabinet, people existing in an affectless calculating well-fed indifference—these thematic properties appear again and again, giving an air of noxious confinement. "Accountants hover over the earth like helicopters / Dropping bits of paper engraved with Hegel's name"—system-building estrangement, decision-making machinery all about man, beyond man.

Throughout, the tendency is to present a fantasylike landscape of drift and disjunction, or scenes from our day in a more or less newsreel setting:

> The saint is born among tin cans in the orchard;
> . . . .
> Black beetles, bright as Cadillacs, toil down
> The long dusty road into the mountains of South Dakota.

Narrow-eyed pitiless montages. The indifferent voice of the news media tripping over the wires, the bulletins, antiseptic, caressing: "We have violet rays that light up the jungles at night, showing / The friendly populations . . ." Figures from the past (Jackson, Theodore Roosevelt, Kennedy) are introduced, democratic institutions seen as another form of deceit or detachment, the American dream disappearing in conquest, avarice, recriminations:

> Last night we argued about the Marines invading Guatemala in 1947,
> The United Fruit Company had one water spigot for 200 families,
> And the ideals of America, our freedom to criticize,
> The slave systems of Rome and Greece, and no one agreed.

The focus is the Vietnam War, though many of the poems dealing with it are among the least successful in the collection. Here the psychological and political footholds grow deeper and duller, a drudging back and forth, the tone hardening. Often Bly's imaginative resources get lost in the purity of his appeal, the sensitivity seeming secondary to the Jacobian effects. The particulars themselves become abstractions, like the titles: "Asian Peace Offers Rejected without Publication." Beyond that, an amorphous lament, suggesting the smash up of the great society in slow motion, with the poet as the dying commentator, recording the split in man and his two worlds, identity and environment, the inner and the outer, and in another part of the morass, history thrashing about fatalistically, intent on a wrong turning, a cornered beast. . . .

Let me present a typical poem:

> There is another darkness,
> A darkness in the fences of the body,
> And in moles running, and telephone wires,
> And the frail ankles of horses;
> Darkness of dying grass, and yellow willow leaves;
> There is the death of broken buttonholes,
> Of brutality in high places,
> Of lying reporters,
> There is a bitter fatigue, adult and sad.

The poem is called "Listening to President Kennedy Lie about the Cuban Invasion." But it seems to me it could just as well have been called "Watching Television" or "Turning Away from Lies" or "The Hermit" or practically any of the other titles in Robert Bly's collection. Like most of Bly's work, the poem is distinctive and arresting, with its own sort of spiraling queerness ("the fences of the body," "the death of broken buttonholes"), but many of its lines could be transplanted quite easily into neighboring poems, and lines from neighboring poems transplanted right back into the empty spaces, with few readers the wiser.

Bly has arranged his volume in five sections, with each of the sections repeating some theme, some nuance from every other section. Demarcations are made only to evaporate or overlap. So the most damaging remark to be leveled against The Light Around the Body, even while granting its necessarily oppressive or "alienated" atmosphere, is that there's still something monotonous in the cumulative effect, and something a little arbitrary in its aesthetic strategy. After a while, too, the political content, I'm afraid, seems predictable, even pious. Some of the poems, for instance, suggest hapless mutations, an "ironic" cross between The Other America and Thinking About the Unthinkable, or copy from the National Guardian and the National Review inexplicably entangled—an all-too-easy, and currently all-too-familiar, juxtaposition of the Left and Right, the angelic and satanic, the pop apocalyptic. "Tonight they throw the firebombs, tomorrow / They read the Declaration of Independence." "Rusk's assistant eat hurriedly / Talking of Teilhard de Chardin." The anger in the first statement, and the satire in the second, come across as purely perfunctory, or as wasted gestures.

Not doubt, it is easy enough to assent to Bly's political commitments. Certainly they are warranted by the times. But time is fickle. Auden on the Spanish Civil War, some of Brecht, some of Neruda, Aragon's *Front Rouge*— you can't really say there have been many lasting marriages between politics and poetry, not in our culture, probably not in any culture.

Actually, the one instance that I know of where the individual imagination and what Marxists call a revolutionary consciousness do *naturally* engage each other, is in the work of Cesar Vallejo, the comparatively unheralded Peruvian poet and Loyalist fighter who died in Paris in the late thirties and whose grave and beautiful poems have, not surprisingly, influenced Bly. Also, I believe, through Bly's example, others such as James Wright ("Eisenhower's Visit to Franco, 1959") and W. S. Merwin ("The Asians Dying"). What Bly seems to share with, or has taken from, Vallejo, aside from technical models (the Peruvian's singular metaphors, dry lyricism, the movement from the colloquial to the obscure and vice versa), is a feeling of loss or isolation so pervasive, or so famished by, or for, experience, that surrender to it is all: a new sort of stoicism, a new humility arises.

Paradoxically, too, there's the creation of an underlying communion with man and nature and the pressure of the times—especially in Vallejo, who knew poverty and imprisonment. No thunderous statements are made. Instead, the poetry presents an accretion of small illuminations, sunken images, memories, contacts, a dream world, but without the flamboyance and libidinal extremity of dreams—with the impenetrability of dreams, but more earthy, lifelike, Vallejo, undoubtedly, is an important figure, piercingly human, full of blindingly right moments or accents which once heard, even if the reader's understanding of Spanish is rudimentary, he does not forget:

> Cesar Vallejo ha muerto, le pagaban
> todos sin que el les haga nada . . .

Bly is more ascetic, thinner in texture and ideas, a little edgy and evangelical. Bly is always seeking to atone:

> Therefore we will have
> To go far away
> To atone
> For the sufferings of the stringy-chested
> And the small rice-fed ones, quivering
> In the helicopter like wild animals,
> Shot in the chest, taken back to be questioned.

In the concluding poems the poet retreats to a private demesne, robbed of growth and purpose, becoming an analogue of contemporary disrelation and affluence: melancholic interior mutterings, new fallen snow, a funeral, waters rising, wind "rising, swelling, / Swirling over everything alive," a ship sinking. Later, the dying bull "bleeding on the mountain" till the "mountains alter and become the sea." "The Executive's Death," the opening poem of the collection, is a mosaic of decay; the final poem, "When the Dumb Speak," a muted celebration of innocence. As prefaces to four of the sections there are quotations from Jacob Boehme, pretty much the Boehme of *Life Against Death,* the chapter entitled "The Resurrection of the Body."

The remarkable quality in Robert Bly's work is the detail: it is clear cut, disturbingly imagistic, at times cunningly evocative, with rarely a word produced by sloth or insensitivity, as in "Opening an Oyster." Still, unlike Vallejo, unfortunately, little on the whole really quickens, really develops, little's revelatory. More than anything, there's always that sense of movement across vast stretches of waste, or a sense of sequences and impressions enacted in double focus: the sociopolitical notations of condemnations, and a series of mystical redemptive rendezvous, *pro remedio animae* à la Boehme. With Bly, the politics of concern, however heartfelt, tend to sound somewhat hortatory, nagging, secondhand. With Vallejo, both the political temper and the particular psychology are indelibly inscribed: instinct, indictment, vision are one, sans any intimation of posture at all. . . .

Brief Reviews
[Review of *The Teeth Mother Naked at Last*]

MICHAEL HEFFERNAN

Robert Bly's *The Teeth Mother Naked at Last* is a thoroughly uncompromising long poem about the Vietnam war. Bly presents the Supersabre jet as one of his principal motifs, calling it a "knot of neurotic energy," a "death-bee" whose long needle stabs into the earth in a gesture which is at once personal and corporate, the act of an individual airman as well as the final horrifying expression of American economic dominion: "This is Hamilton's triumph. This is the advantage of a centralized bank."

Bly's argument is difficult to reason through, here or elsewhere in this frequently unbearable poem, precisely because of the massive irrationalities which the war itself compels the mind to contend with. Bly's tactic is a perfectly consistent attempt to fit his poem to its occasion. All war, he suggests, is a lie, and this war especially is a brutalizing derogation of human flesh and intelligence, a complex of tremendous compulsions as powerful as those which created America:

> The ministers lie, the professors lie, the television lies,
>   the priests lie. . . .
> These lies mean that the country wants to die.
> Lie after lie starts out into the prairie grass,
> like enormous trains of Conestoga wagons. . . .

Bly may venture an explanation of the war, but it is deliberately irrational and irksome, as if to suggest that the prosperous complacencies of American domestic life and the barbarities of American wars are both paradoxical elements in a grisly harmony:

> It's because the aluminum window-shade business is
>   doing so well in the United States that we roll
>   fire over entire villages
> It's because the milk trains coming into New Jersey
>   hit the right switches every day that the best
>   Vietnamese men are cut in two by American bullets

Reprinted from *Midwest Quarterly* 12 (Spring 1971): 355–56, by permission of the editor.

> that follow each other like freight cars
> This is what it's like to send firebombs down in 110°
>   heat from air-conditioned cockpits, . . .
> It's because tax-payers move to the suburbs that we
>   transfer populations.
> The Marines use cigarette lighters to light the
>   thatched roofs of huts
> because so many Americans own their own homes.

This is a nightmare of a poem proposing the logic of the nightmare as a resolution. It is a total experience, drenching the mind with its images and its plain assertions, urging by its desperate brutalities a return to human things.

Bly: Man, Voice and Poem

ANTHONY PICCIONE

Several middle-ground critics found *Silence In the Snowy Fields* (1962) too joyful, too meditative. When *The Light Around the Body* (1967) uncovered too much public reality too quickly, they longed for [Bly's] return to mid-western silence. For most, *Sleepers Joining Hands* is a book to rejoice in. Bly resides confidently and warmly in both worlds, having found the balance, and the voice to lead us there.

Still, how does one enter a Bly poem? The basic enigma of "deep image" poetry is that it is not so much a technique as it is a state of being: "deep image" is a mode of thinking, an arrival at inner vision achieved through the poet's sustained awareness and experience of the perceptual, unconscious state. The poem exists as the process of its expression; its potential experience for the reader lies in his attunement to the conditions through which the unconscious is engaged and communicated. Specifically, the poem's *content* is a particular aspect and/or idea of the outer world seen from within, from the spiritual. Its process recreates the frameworks and correspondences which lead to new and wider associational awareness, and thus to the ecstatic state. Typically, negative response to this type of poetry is often steeped in a blatant distrust of the unconscious, the inner being that is still incompatible to the traditional contemporary scene, although the expression of spiritual vision has been evolving in art from its genesis.

We have the feeling that Bly's calm warmth for humanity is his real psychic self speaking, not the poetic voice which we associate with technique. Thus, to speak of style or technique or theme is to obscure the central essence of this astounding poetry. The title and the book itself are the assertion, once and for all, that this poetry is an arrival at the universal threshold, the "unconscious speaking to the unconscious," as we've so often put it. Well, that notion no longer seems strange.

From the very beginning, in "Six Winter Privacy Poems," Bly takes great risks to align the reader with the book. Immediately, inner man and outer world are one, and compressed perception is not technique, it is simply an expression of the "new" world perceived:

Reprinted from *Ann Arbor Review* 17 (1973): 86–90, by permission of the author.

> About four, a few flakes.
> I empty the teapot out in the snow, feeling
> shoots of joy in the new cold.

In part 4 ("Sitting Alone"), Bly begins the journey to the interior, and it is at this point that the readers either leap up or lie there, like filings mixed with straw. The point is, of course, that critical cynicism is not a concern here, because Bly is speaking with and *through* poetry not just to "readers" but to all those who are attuned to their own inner beings. Thus this totally new unself-consciousness reaching out from a calm assertion of something stupendous:

> Sitting in this darkness singing,
> I can't tell if this joy
> is from the body, or the soul, or a third place.

The last section of this poem becomes the very center of the book: each poem is the expression of a psyche deeply in touch with two worlds. This is not the poet; this voice, this man, is Bly:

> When I woke, new snow had fallen.
> I am alone, yet someone else is with me,
> drinking coffee, looking out at the snow.

Thereafter, man and voice and poem are one. The separate poems become isolated, time units of deep consciousness, all leading to the phenomenon of psychic/spiritual sleepers awakening. It is all a state of constant arrival:

> O yes, I love you, book of my confessions,
>
> . . .
> So much is still inside me, . . .
> These lines themselves are sunk to the waist in
> the dusk. . . .

And the search is real because it is always thus: he is "only half risen," in the state of becoming. He stands "at the edges of the light, howling to come in" until finally

> There is a consciousness hovering under the mind's feet, ... It is a willow
> that knows of water under the earth, I am a father who dips as he passes over
> underground rivers, who can feel his children through all distance and time!

Bly's long anti-war poem, "The Teeth Mother Naked At Last" (issued separately in an earlier version in 1970) and "Hair" serve as reminders, in real terms, that for us words like "surreal" need redefining. We want to say to "Teeth" that the horror and distortion and the grotesque are recognizable techniques, when in fact, for anyone who has read the poem, the so-called "surreal" is the real world of American foreign policy seen clearly for the first time, from the inner being stripped of its many daily personae. Thus we linger at a new level of horror: the *real*.

This is a strangely alive book: it seems to "talk." In the middle of the book is an exciting prose essay, "I Came Out of the Mother Naked," in which Bly traces the Great Mother cycles and in so doing illuminates much of his thinking on psychic lives and energies in America. Significant to Bly is the notion of brain differentiation: that man possesses three brains (the reptile, the mammal or paleo-cortex, and the neo-cortex), not one. Crucial to this discussion is the assumption that we are constantly leaping from one brain to another, although, for most of us, the neo-cortex is the rational conceptual control. Thus, for instance, to speak of the dichotomy between the mammal brain (feminine, benign, creative) and the neo-cortex (masculine, aggressive) is to speak of "national psychic" energy and, therefore, to describe the spiritual/psychic origins of our outward societal actions.

Continuing after the interlude, the book deepens its province. Four separate pieces form the long poem, "Sleepers Joining Hands." The first, "The Shadow Goes Away," is a masterful blend of social and psychic energy, and both meet in the "new" non-poetic voice.

*   *   *

The poem continues as a type of time travel, back through the brain[s] to the Sioux who have been ravaged, the Puritan Ministers, shadows, other lives, the Old Testament, back up to Vietnam, American technology, our own psychic deaths, historical fact seen as dream vision, nonetheless very real.

"The Night Journey In the Cooking Pot" becomes at once autobiographical *and* mysterious, as the consciousness within it soars, flounders and soars to discovery of inner being. It too begins as dream vision: "I float on solitude as on water . . . there is a road. . . ." But soon sleeping and waking are one great awareness.

*   *   *

The next poem in sequence travels deeper along this "road." Sensing his arrival at self, and also the passing of the body, he states:

> There is another being living inside me.
> He is looking out of my eyes.
> I hear him
> in the wind through the bare trees.

Appropriately, the poem does not end, exactly; we are left in a state of anticipation, of "continuous" culmination. In this remarkably simple way, the image process (of inward turning) is also directly part of its content.

*   *   *

The final poem is a garland, unashamedly open and warm: "An Extra Joyful Chorus For Those Who Have Read This Far." It is a last meeting place of voices and ideas, images and visions, and its *process* approximates the acts of traveling through the "separate" brains. After a series of "I am" lines ending in the joyful "I am no one at all," Bly transcends his conceptual consciousness, and the poem, as well as the book, begins the act of completion in the reader, after the final word has sounded:

> The panther rejoices in the gathering dark.
> Hands rush toward each other through miles of
>   space.
> All the sleepers in the world join hands.

Where They All Are Sleeping

Joyce Carol Oates

This is a remarkable collection of poems, in fact one of the most powerful books of any kind I have read recently. It is beautifully unified—the "sleepers of the world" do indeed join hands in Robert Bly's imagination—and it possesses the kind of internal development, the accumulation of dramatic tension, one usually associates with a single work, whether of poetry or prose. The book is divided into three sections, the first consisting of a number of brief meditative poems, some longer works ("Hair," for one) that move rapidly and dizzyingly through surrealistic, mock-casual observations, and the small masterpiece, "The Teeth Mother Naked at Last," which will probably be remembered as the finest poem to have grown out of the antiwar movement of the Sixties. Like other poems of Bly's, it is both intellectual and relentlessly emotional; it seems to strike at us from all sides at once, so that the reader does not read the poem so much as experience it. It is nine pages long and yet so concise, so intricately imagined, that to isolate a few lines for consideration is somehow to violate the pace of the poem. Yet:

> Helicopters flutter overhead.   The death-
> bee is coming.   Super Sabres
> like knots of neurotic energy sweep
> around and return.
> This is Hamilton's triumph.
> This is the advantage of a centralized bank.
> B-52s come from Guam.   All the teachers
> die in flames. The hopes of Tolstoy fall asleep in the ant heap.
> Do not ask for mercy.

In Bly's vision it is pointless to ask even for sanity: for the nation, perhaps the entire Western world, is infatuated with the prospect of its own death. The lies of our leaders are our own; "the longing we all feel to die." When the Teeth Mother (or the Terrible Mother) draws us back into the Unconscious, into a ceasing of the ego's efforts at consciousness, how can sanity itself resist!

*   *   *

Reprinted from *Modern Poetry Studies* 4 (Winter 1973): 341–44, by permission.

Part II is a prose piece, "I Came Out of the Mother Naked," in which Bly discusses the Great Mother cultures of the world, not content to communicate only through what he calls the "dream-voice" of the poems. Following his frequent practice in *The Seventies*, he pursues a single philosophical line of thought, touching upon psychology (mainly Carl Jung's analytical psychology) and anthropology (Johann Bachofen, known for his *Mother Right* of 1861, the first book to argue for the primacy of the matriarchy), and including work by other poets (John Keats's "La Belle Dame Sans Merci" and Rainer Maria Rilke's "We Must Die Because We Have Known Them"). The essay is fascinating, since it puts into urgent and very timely images the more generalized, diffuse arguments of Erich Neumann, and ties in the tragedy of America's involvement in Indochina with Jung's warning about the catastrophe that awaits the world unless civilized man is willing to face the maniacal depths of his own psyche. But the rationalist West, especially the United States, is simply too shallowly optimistic to imagine that a return to the Unconscious might involve more than a cheerful relaxation of the rigors of patriarchal ideals: hence the exaggerated interest in the past decade in drug-experimentation, in dropping out of society. The awakening of deeper layers of the psyche is, Bly feels, an inevitable phenomenon, which must be understood so that its dangerous aspects can be avoided. Otherwise there may be world catastrophe.

> The increasing strength of poetry, defense of earth, and mother consciousness, implies that after hundreds of years of being motionless, the Great Mother is moving again in the psyche. Every day her face becomes clearer. We are becoming more sensitive, more open to her influence. She is returning, or we are returning to her; everyone who looks down into his own psyche sees her. . . . The pendulum is just now turning away from the high point of father consciousness and starting to sweep down. The pendulum rushes down, the Mothers rush toward us, we can all feel the motion downward, the speed increasing.

Unlike some angry prophets who hope for the apocalypse, perhaps only to punish the world which has disappointed them, Bly emerges as reasonable, logical, and extremely persuasive: he does not downgrade father-consciousness, but argues that the traditional distrust and despising of the feminine soul has been the cause of some of our great disasters. But the "feminine" soul, the anima, is both good and evil, both benevolent and deadly; it is necessary that one consciously integrate both aspects of personality and, on a larger scale, that society recognize both as equally valuable.

Part III, "Sleepers Joining Hands," is a long work, consisting of four separate but related poems. The poet meditates upon the evolution of his own consciousness, the progression of his soul which is complete, pure, fulfilled perfectly in love—and yet often hidden from him, so that his own life, and the larger world in which he lives, is a mystery to him.

*   *   *

Robert Bly's work—poetry and prose—seems to me unique at the present time. It is always directed toward a moral position, yet it is curiously dramatic, mysterious, even suspenseful; it is extremely "intellectual," yet Bly's fastidious concern for language never allows it to seem argumentative or didactic. Its shorter, more vivid thought-poems are reminiscent of Zen poetry, yet who besides Bly could imagine these lines!—

> I sit down and fold my legs. . . .
> The half dark in the room is delicious.
> How marvelous to be a thought entirely surrounded by brains!
> ("Shack Poem")

Books [Review of *The Morning Glory*]

STANLEY PLUMLY

The Morning Glory is a collection of prose poems written over the better part of the last ten years and in several settings, primarily California and Robert Bly's native Minnesota. Considering Bly's "political" passions of this period, it is a book remarkably free of the preoccupations of his most famous work—that is, the War poetry of *The Light Around the Body* and the Mother Culture pronouncements in *Sleepers Joining Hands*. If these prose poems suggest anything about this poet's career, they should remind us that, in spite of the intervening years since his first book, he is essentially still a poet of solitude and snow. Moral outrage aside, Bly is our Thoreau. "Whoever wants to see the invisible has to penetrate more deeply into the visible," he states in his introductory note. He is a visionary of detail, of the small, unattended moment. Again and again, these prose pieces locate him in a landscape of bird's nests, turtles, starfish, salamanders, and the "dry grass beneath." The chief advantages of the prose-poem form are the space and time available, the circumvention of immediate pressures. There is potentially more room for Bly's big body to move around in, sit down in, think. Perhaps too often, though, Bly keeps the space too small, the time too short and ends up muscling his way through. It is a fault common enough in all his poetry—the will doing the work of the imagination. "Looking at a Dead Wren in My Hands" concocts an unlikely combination, even for a leaper: "Your tail feathers open like a picket fence, and your bill is brown, with the sorrow of an old Jew whose daughter has married an athlete." Whatever the relative merits of such a perception, the integrity of a well-established and serious tone has been violated. In longer pieces, such as "Sitting on Some Rocks in Shaw Cove, California," the similes are more inlaid than integrated—we are offered five comparisons in the first six sentences—so that the effect is obfuscation rather than insight. Bly is a poet of epiphany, even unto the Christian sense. To penetrate, to reveal, to restore, the image, however rendered, must be employed with care and timing, because it is, after all, a small door. Ironically, Robert Bly is one of the masters of simile and metaphor. And there are more examples of this fact than not throughout the collection. The Point Reyes poems, already published as a pamphlet, occupy, appropri-

Reprinted from *American Poetry Review* 4, no. 6 (November/December 1975): 44–45, by permission of the author.

ately, the center of the book. They define the size of the emotional and empathetic concerns. But the third, and last, section, especially the final four or five poems, is what *The Morning Glory* is about. "August Rain," "Grass from Two Years," and "Christmas Service at Midnight at St. Michaels" amount to revelations—the building of complete spiritual constructs. Bly by himself, in Minnesota, in the rain, "watching the soaked chairs . . . the sky low, everything silent, as when parents are angry"; by himself, in a place of low branches and dry grass, "a heavy, nervous man who feels more joy than anyone alive"; by himself, at Christmas, six months after his brother's death, the snow outside laboring "its old Manichean labors to keep the father and his animals in melancholy." At the close of this last poem, Bly has Father Richter hold up the two halves of the dry wafer, the broken body, which like so many acts, is permanent.

This Book Is Made of
Turkey Soup and Star Music

PHILIP DACEY

*   *   *

Bly's *This Body Is Made of Camphor and Gopherwood*, a collection of prose poems, is emphatically a book of deep religious longing. The focus throughout on the body is the function not of materialism or hedonism but of a Romantic trust that the body, with its instincts and its close relationship to the earth, provides the surest counsel to spiritual pilgrims.

*   *   *

Bly's new book . . . has both a prophetic quality that distinguishes it from most contemporary work and a grandiose purpose bordering on battiness. Nevertheless, as a descendant of all those who opposed the dualistic heresy of Manichaeism, which proclaimed the evil of the body, of, indeed, all matter, Bly struggles with his own Lutheran heritage, as well as with American puritanism more generally. In response to a question about his ties to Asian thought, Bly once said, "Don't forget I'm not a Sufi; I'm a Norwegian Lutheran."

*   *   *

. . . He is a poet of despair and of longing for deliverance from it. The deliverance will come, he cannot help believing, from "lumps of dirt," out of which, naturally, a body can be made, and from the female water, which for Bly is virtually synonymous with unconscious, instinctual life, an amniotic home. The dirt and water combined suggest mud, which, in a Bly poem, is a nearly talismanic substance. From the first, in *Silence in the Snowy Fields* (1962), Bly loved mud: the "spider-colored" crow of "Where We Must Look for Help," the crow released from the ark, would find "new mud to walk upon." The mud is both a sign of devastation and a promise of renewal. In "Galloping Horses," the hooves "push into the mud." The effect is that of masculine brutalization of yielding feminine form. Finally, then, "upward" is the key word in the quotation from "A Dream of What Is Missing": saving grace not from on high,

Reprinted by permission of Poetry in Review Foundation: *Parnassus: Poetry in Review* 7, no. 1 (Fall/Winter 1978): 34–45.

from a transcendent absolute, but from Bly's version of the "foul rag-and-bone-shop of the heart."

In a recent, rare autobiographical essay,* Bly confesses that as a child he was a boy-god. What he means by that term is crucial to an understanding of his work generally and this new book in particular.

> [Boy-gods] are boys, and yet they feel somehow eternal, out of the stream of life, they float above it. . . . If someone were suffering, or in a rage, I would feel myself pull away, into some safe area, where I did not "descend" to those emotions. . . . The mood of Lutheran Sunday School only speeded up that tendency. It taught us that the body—that is, woman—was evil, and that purity lay in the eternal, in what was "up". . . . "I will leave you" is the everlasting cry of the boy-god. He wants to be tied down to no one, especially not to a woman.

*   *   *

Bly's boy-god is close kin to the "fallen man" of Jacob Boehme, the "Teutonic Theosopher," who has supplied Bly with numerous epigraphs, certain attitudes (for example, Boehme's claim, made almost four hundred years ago, that "in a quarter of an hour [spent meditating] I understood more than if I had been many years at a university," bears an uncanny resemblance to Bly's baiting of his college audiences), and, more importantly, an entire moral framework in which to situate himself. But Bly has given to Boehme's ideas a torque owing much to modern depth psychology. For one thing, whereas "light" was Boehme's term of highest commendation, Bly's is "dark," and, for another, Bly's fallen man has fallen not into sexuality but from it and must, to be saved, fall into it again.

*   *   *

So much for some of the ideas, values, biases, and plain cant that populate Bly's poems. What of his means? (Technique is, of course, a dirty word to Bly.) Leaping has been for a long time Bly's favorite *modus operandi*. In brief, leaping is a movement "from one world to another," a shuttling between the unconscious and the conscious. He calls that movement "an ancient freedom," seeks to embody it in all his work, and goes so far as to say that the "farther a poem gets from its initial worldly circumstance without breaking the thread, the more content it has." Bly flatly opposes the "old banal American realism." What this means in practice is that "Going Out to Check the Ewes" can have almost nothing to do with ewes, even though Bly contends that the prose poem serves to foster close observation of the physical world. It also means that Bly feels free to end a poem like so:

> We talk all morning of the confusion of others, and in daylight the car slides off the road, I give advice in public as if I were adult, that night in a dream I see a

policeman holding a gun to the head of a frightened girl, who is blindfolded, we console each other, and opening a *National Geographic* see an old woman lying with her mouth open.

("Falling into Holes in Our Sentences")

The context does not readily clarify that paragraph, as virtually none of its elements occur previously in the poem. The line between leaping and incoherence is one Bly constantly needs to re-draw. His aesthetic problem may be rooted in Jung's idea that the contents of the unconscious undergo important changes when they enter into consciousness. If it follows from that idea that the unconscious and its way cannot be conscripted into consciousness, then Bly's wish to wed his poems to the unconscious as intimately as he does is basically wrong-headed, a grand but misguided, ultimately anti-literary and self-defeating venture.

*　　　*　　　*

. . . Bly wants nothing less than to be a saint, albeit a saint of The New Age as described by Solzhenitsyn, the time when "our physical nature will not be cursed as in the Middle Ages, but, even more importantly, our spiritual being will not be trampled upon as in the Modern Era." To wish Bly success would probably be out of place, not least of all because to journey toward such a goal is already itself an exemplary arrival.

Note

*"Being a Lutheran Boy-God in Minnesota," *Growing Up in Minnesota*, ed. Chester Anderson (University of Minnesota Press, 1976).

[Review of
This Tree Will Be Here for a Thousand Years]

ANONYMOUS

Disillusioned by experience, Bly has returned in this impressive gathering of 44 new poems to the transcendental contemplation of nature that animated his first collection. "Silence in the Snowy Fields." What he now finds in that middle-American landscape is bleaker, more melancholy, no longer self-contained. In a short preface, Bly professes that his avowedly mystical new poems attempt to enter into "the consciousness . . . in creatures and plants." Poems such as "Amazed by an Accumulation of Snow" or "Pulling a Rowboat Up Among Lake Reeds" possess a rare simplicity and clarity of vision that restore the reader to the real world. Still, the book's predominant tone is a sense of abandonment. Images of cows awaiting dusk, of a Christ who will never return suggest a Godot never to appear. If there is more artifice in these new poems, there is also a more piercing and compassionate vision of the human predicament.

Reprinted from the 2 July 1979 issue of *Publishers Weekly*, published by R. R. Bowker Company, a Xerox Company. Copyright © 1979 by Xerox Corporation.

[Review of *The Man in the Black Coat Turns*]

CHARLES MOLESWORTH

Robert Bly's new book of poems has three untitled sections, each with a loose stylistic unity. The first section includes poems that will be familiar to readers of *The Light Around the Body* (1967) and Bly's eight other previous volumes. Thematically the section deals with blocked energies and institutional failure ("the Empire / dying in its provincial cities"), but there are also hope and "days that pass in / undivided tenderness." An elegy for Pablo Neruda is included as well, perhaps Bly's most touching, scrupulous poem. Throughout, Bly tries to release the numinous qualities of everyday things, and to bring into everyday consciousness the Jungian perspectives of oneiric space and time.

The second section is comprised of six prose poems, and the longest and best of these is "Finding an Ant Mansion." Here Bly's spiritual allegorizing is starkest and most forceful, as he literally domesticates a natural object, a "wood-chunk," and in the process focusses his associative search for a "complete soul home." After a careful, almost microscopic description, ecstatically heightened, he has the "mansion" harbor "the souls of the dead," particularly those of his relatives and neighbors. While turning the wood into a memorial of human labor and destiny, he is also freed to see it as subject to natural forces, "still open to the rains and snows." In many ways the poem epitomizes Bly's work in the genre of the prose poem, where he has successfully joined the vigor of natural history to the ecstasies of desire and memory. The prose poems are to my mind Bly's best work, because his ear is resistant to fixed measures and he works more comfortably with a prose rhythm that relies on an alternation of intensity and relaxation of stress and watchfulness. Many poets turn slack in the prose poem, becoming indulgent in their use of imagery and too precious in their cadences. But Bly, having absorbed such French models as Ponge, finds in this genre just the right mixture of play and contemplative energy. In a sense we can see Bly at work in his prose poems; he has less need to hide the secret springs of his thought and feeling, and so puts us closer to the heart of his enterprise.

The third section of this book contains a dozen poems, all demanding and different from what have come to be Bly's distinctive lyric forms. These will take some getting used to even for Bly's partisan readers, but they show us he

Reprinted from *Western American Literature* 17, no. 3 (Fall 1982): 282–84, by permission of the editors.

is genuinely a poet of growth. His whole project and ethic are founded on the principle of growth, on breaking through convention and repression to reinvigorate the joys of transformation and discovery. He has lived up to his own demands in this regard.

But a few of the poems in this section are for me unsuccessful, most clearly "A Sacrifice in the Orchard" and "What the Fox Agreed to Do." These rely on images too exclusively, or make too great a demand on their own centering thrusts by excessive "leaping." Imagistic density and associative leaping are central elements of structure in Bly's work, of course, but if used too drastically or too purely, they harm the overall effect. This is only another application of the aesthetic truism that any stylistic feature cannot in itself sustain a well-made artifact.

The best poems of the third section, however, are challenging because they extend the variety of Bly's structures. Here the best examples are "Four Ways of Knowledge," "Crazy Carlson's Meadow," and "Words Rising." These poems are distinctive, but they share some features, specifically a concern with plotting the mind's curves and submersions on its way to self-awareness. Still far from being a discursive poet, Bly has turned from the sheer enactment of imagistic condensation and expansion (which sometimes made his poems too willful, too driven, despite his claims of spontaneity), to a subtle examination of the intersections of waking and archaic consciousness. These examinations require differing structures, so the pace of the poem's unfolding varies more frequently. There is more abstract language than Bly formerly allowed ("Noble loneliness held him."), and more reliance on setting a scene. Certain themes persist and are carried over from the first two sections, especially the need to confront and accept the father, but there is a feeling of improvisation, of true searching, despite a more formalized sense of structure. "Well, if I know how to live, / why am I frightened?" Bly asks in one poem. In another he answers, speaking of the habit of ignorance and the need to "learn by falling": "This time we live it, / and only awaken years later." To put it simply, Bly is showing us how he's learned that there is more than one approach to the deep, more than one sounding of the cave, and so there must be many different lines and many different songs.

Sepia Photographs and Jazz Solos

Fred Chappell

A poet who fashions an extreme individual style, as Robert Bly surely has done, may find he has forged his own manacles to a limited means of expression. Whatever his subject or emotions, his poems may melt together in a monochrome haze. The ostensible subject of "Loving a Woman in Two Worlds" is romantic love, but many of the poems—even those containing the phrase "man and woman"—are hard to distinguish from Mr. Bly's other poems of landscape and mystic reverie. The verses become creatures of a habit not necessarily their own. The problem is aggravated by the kind of idiom Mr. Bly has fabricated. So many lines weighted with reverent pauses, stolid with monosyllables, muffled by end stops, can make poems not suggestive but stonily incommunicative. There is too much easy Orientalism, as in "The Turtle."

*   *   *

In "The Roots" and "The Hawk," he is still playing Tarzan; and he still takes flying leaps—"I float in the current, calm and mad as a sleepy cork."

On the other side is the plain fact that his new volume is an addition, weak or strong, to a body of work that has impressively persuaded a generation of poets and readers. Mr. Bly is an undiscountable element of contemporary poetic taste. His wistful shamanizing and stringently elemental diction can still have power. The silly line just quoted is followed by a lovely warm stanza.

*   *   *

Among the fine new poems here are "What Frightened Us," "The Two Rivers," "The Artist at Fifty," "Shame," "The Good Silence," and "In the Month of May." These poems and some others can be admired, I think, even by readers who do not suffer an automatic thrill upon seeing nouns like "mist," "earth," "river," "horse," "star" and "wind" in print. It is an asset of an extreme style that even its most customary mannerisms may result in a good poem.

*   *   *

"Loving a Woman in Two Worlds" holds no surprises, yet the poet has broken no promises. We read here a book written unmistakably by Robert Bly. It must be nearly impossible to write with the kind of mother earth inevitability that Mr. Bly desires and to be surprising at the same time. But a sentence that is only smooth cliché, "The love of woman is the knowing of grief," is not helped by a companion sentence that is merely calculated naïveté, "The loving man / simmers his porcupine stew."

A reader who would like a book of love poems to have some immediate drama, some clash of impulse, some agony of doubt, as well as sexual and romantic jubilation, must go to another poet. What he will find in Mr. Bly's love poetry is mostly a kindly gratitude, a distanced salute—not the sweet and savage rose but a wanly scented pressed wildflower.

The extreme individual style is the one that turns quaint before our eyes. By the time we come to the last line a whole poem has taken on the sepia tone of an aging photograph; it recedes into time past—where most of even the freshest poems end up sooner or later—as if it were constructed in order to do just that. It leaves with us a small, moist animal murmur.

Robert Bly and the
Trouble with American Poetry

ROGER MITCHELL

Robert Bly's poems make me want to rush out and take another look at the world. Or rush out and say something to it. The emphasis is on "rush." Though much of the writing and the thought that lies behind it have been accumulated the way we pick up dropped pencils and smooth stones on our way from here to there, finally it is a convulsive motion we are witness to. "I am driving; it is dusk; Minnesota," to take a well-known example.

It is not always a place Bly rushes to, like the Lac Qui Parle River. Often it is a state of mind.

> There is a restless gloom in my mind.
> I walk grieving. The leaves are down.

Gloom, grief, and the end of vegetation. A swift plunge in an icy river. As it turns out, it is always a state of mind that Bly rushes into or out of. Minnesota is almost incidental. Bly may have given us the small, mostly failed, farm country of the upper Midwest, but that is not what he set out to do.

"If the poem veers too far toward actual events, the eternal feeling is lost in the static of our inadequacies." Though said about love poems in one of the short sub-introductions which have come to be standard in a Bly book, it applies to all of his work. What is astonishing about the silence in the snowy fields is not that we see rural Minnesota there but that we "see" the eternal. It may have the look and feel of Minnesota, but what matters is that the eternal or something like it has come down out of the sky to sit at our table. Minnesota clings to these poems only as a faint scent.

> When our privacy starts over again,
> How beautiful the things are we did not notice before!
> A few sweetclover plants that blossom yellow
> Along the road to Bellingham. . . .

Reprinted from *Ohio Review* 42 (1988): 86–92. Reprinted by permission of *The Ohio Review*.

Along the road to anywhere, really. "Privacy" or "inwardness" were Bly's early words for what we lacked. He was right, I think, but "inwardness" was just another word for "the eternal." It suited a psychological age better than that sodden word, eternity.

But what does a great longing for inwardness do to a poetry over a period of time? Robert Bly's poems, which now cover thirty-five to forty years, begin to tell us.

When the rationalists of the eighteenth century set about relieving us of our superstitions, it was inevitable that a day would arrive when we would want something like those superstitions back, when they would seem mythic and profound. The eighteenth-century mind eventually recoiled from itself, but it did so in an eighteenth-century way. Fairy tales were cataloged, folk tales and nursery rhymes indexed, crumbling castles scrupulously painted. Scholarship and her twin, the Gothic, were born. Conservators of the old ways—the gothic, the primitive, the rural—shot up everywhere. Frazier's *The Golden Bough* is one culmination of this urge.

Bly has become our principal tie to the residually primitive and mythic. If Thoreau—whose work he has just excerpted for the Sierra Club—took us back to the natural world, Bly has made the effort to take us back to that state of consciousness which the Enlightenment tried to do away with. It is a state which abhors sophistication. Sophistication is the enemy of wonder. It is imposed adulthood. False adulthood, at that: a decorum, a holding of the emotions still, a surmounting of the feeling self, a silencing of the voices. Rise up, says Bly,

> The strong leaves of the box elder tree,
> Plunging in the wind, call us to disappear
> Into the wilds of the universe,
> Where we shall sit at the foot of a plant,
> And live forever, like the dust.

Or,

> How strange to think of giving up all ambition!
> Suddenly I see with such clear eyes
> The white flake of snow
> That has just fallen on the horse's mane!

Borrowing, as he is always happy to do, this time from the ancient Chinese.

Bly's search for the eternal often takes him back into the unsophisticated literatures of the past. Shadows of Norse and German mythology, folk and fairy tale, and Biblical narrative show up everywhere in his work. He says that the poems of *Silence in the Snowy Fields* and *This Tree Will Be Here For a Thousand Years* owe a debt to Arthur Waley's Chinese translations and to Frank O'Connor's translations of ancient Celtic poems. What distracts from the childlike

wonder are what he calls "the thousand things," material culture, the bourgeois life. The back roads and failed farms of rural Minnesota make a conve-
nient, even a symbolic, place in which to turn one's back on the constant pour
of the "things" which, as Emerson warned us, sit in the saddle and "ride
mankind."

History is another distraction. Like the poets of the T'ang dynasty (who,
incidentally, suffered a particularly violent and corrupt history), Bly would
prefer "A few friendships, a few dawns, a few glimpses of grass,/ A few oars
weathered by the snow and the heat," if he were not also forced now and then
to face the nature of our national life. Bly could not ignore the Viet Nam War.
No one could. No mountain was high or remote enough to distance ourselves
from a thing which, as taxpayers, we could not prevent ourselves from aiding.
Instead, Bly did the thing many of us value him most for doing, descended into
the marketplace and howled.

> These are the men who skinned Little Crow!
> We are all their sons, skulking
> In back rooms, selling nails with trembling hands!

Bly's surrealism, if that's what it is, is a perfect mirror for the monstrousness of
the corrupt state. Many of the images in these poems, especially in their
juxtaposition and their child-like exaggeration, remind us of the rage at
human corruption in the paintings of Hieronymous Bosch. "Wings appear
over the trees, wings with eight hundred rivets," for instance. Here is the
menace our technology is to nature, even when it assumes one of the forms of
nature.

> Here the citizens we know during the day,
> The ministers, the department heads,
> Appear changed: the stockholders of large steel companies
> In small wooden shoes; here are the generals dressed as gamboling lambs.
>
> Tonight they burn the rice supplies; tomorrow
> They lecture on Thoreau . . .

At the same time, these poems have the effort of removing history and the real
world from a discussion of our national failings. They make impressive curses,
but they weaken our understanding by implying that our problems are moral,
when they seem to be social and political, and that they can be dealt with in
some useful way by the kind of moral outrage exhibited.

Bly's disinterest in history is not hard to explain. For one thing, history is
another invention of the Enlightenment, another way of focusing on, by
ordering, the world's experience, another creation of human reason. History
destroys timelessness and the eternal. History ties everything to a place and a

clock. History, if you will, is the religion of materialism. As R. G. Colling-wood points out, history forces one to live in the present. History is not an alternative or an antidote to the present. It is the past brought into and made pertinent to the present. The snowy fields of rural Minnesota may have been, as Bly obviously thought they were, a place to encounter the world anew. But it is impossible not to conclude that they were also, especially in the 1950s and 60s, a place to get away from the life created by monopoly capitalism. The suburbs, the "giant finned cars," as Lowell called them, the movies, pop music, the overly assured poetry of the time, much of it based on the travel made possible by our new affluence, all were ways of participating in the culture of capitalism.

Bly wanted none of that. He first tried isolating himself in New York City. "I lived for several years in various parts of New York City, longing for 'the depths.'" The later removal to Minnesota was a political gesture made in the belief that he could will himself out of the culture, that like Thoreau or Bartleby, he could "prefer not to." The Viet Nam War shattered that illusion, making it impossible to concentrate on what mattered to him, the private, the inward. And yet, his poems of the time do not concern concurrent wars, or the warlike nature of societies down through history, or the warlike nature of humankind itself. They concern just that war that Americans could not turn away from since it was on their televisions every night. Insofar as they analyze the dilemma—and the few allusions to our oppression of the Indians show that Bly sought explanations in history—these poems rely almost entirely on the straightforward antimaterialist idealism familiar to us in Transcendentalism. The lecturer may be lecturing on Thoreau, but he's making money doing it and at a time when the world is on fire. When the war's over, will it be all right to go back to Minnesota or to Thoreau? Bly's poetry since *The Light Around the Body* and *The Teeth Mother Naked at Last* indicates that it was. For Bly the war was wrong, not the natural consequence of our way of life. I suggest that a great longing for inwardness can prevent a poetry from seeing and understanding "actual events."

*   *   *

Bly's moral idealism transformed Americans into monsters, things out-side society and outside history. It worked as long as he was talking in generalities—"the ministers, the department heads," etc.—but when it came to a real person, Dean Rusk, it fell flat. It not only fell flat, it was false. Dean Rusk was a man and, what was worse, he did not seem to be a particularly bad man. Bly's moral idealism, in fact, blinded him to a wonderful opportunity. Here was an intelligent, decent man—Robert McNamara was another—who followed the logic of their class to the point that they turned themselves and us into little more than mass murderers. "I gave them my son, and they gave me back a killer," one agonized mother told a reporter at the time of the My Lai massacre. To turn us all into sellers of nails makes a nice imaginative leap back to Christ's crucifixion, but it obscures and falsifies what went on. Were we crucifying a Christ? Was our opponent in the conflict, however oppressed, free of imperialist ambition? And so on.

Bly's criticisms of the world are often just, but a poetry that avoids so much of our material lives runs the risk of not seeing the world very well. I wish Bly would invest less in myth, archetype, and childlike wonder. I would like to hear him connect his idealism to the world we really live in, which would require that he see that world differently and, I believe, more deeply than he does.

Eliot once spoke of avoiding personality in poetry. He was the chief architect of the house of objectivity and formalism, and most poets in the middle of this century, including Bly, lived in that house. It had dumbwaiters in the walls and windows that slid smoothly up and down in waxed grooves. Bly helped dismantle this structure, for which we are all in his debt. He helped bring the feeling self back to poetry. Now he is the prophet of inwardness, spontaneity, solitariness, the leap. "Prophet" is too strong a word, but he does need to explain. He has things to teach. I no longer learn as much as I once did from him, but I admire him as a teacher and for his willingness to teach. Gertrude Stein once called Pound " a village explainer," and Robert Bly belongs to that—if I may call it such—noble tradition. He comes down into the marketplace where we are shopping for a little enlightenment and hawks his wares. As did Whitman. We love them both for caring enough about us to address us directly, for wanting to change our lives.

At the same time, it must be said that the *Selected Poems* is a disappointing book. Not because it does not have good—even a few great—poems in it, but because we had been lulled into thinking over the years, partly by his urgency, partly by his provocative essays, that more had been accomplished. American poetry was enlarged by Robert Bly, but that was twenty and twenty-five years ago. He helped free American poetry of its "genial, joshing tone" and its specious externality. But has it not been replaced by a free-floating internality or something like it? That Bly has not yet found a way beyond his accomplishments is, I believe, less the failing of Robert Bly than it is the failing of American poetry to free itself of an inherent idealism and to truly engage itself, not just with "actual events," but more importantly, with an effort to comprehend those events. Think of the obstacles, though—a poetry which institutionally commits itself to showing and not telling, a poetry which goes in fear of abstractions, a poetry still so sunk in Romantic esthetics that it has no working relationship with knowledge. And think of the failures—Pound throwing his best insights away by blaming the Jews for the disintegration of western culture, Olson by an idealist disregard for the lives people really lead.

I would like to say that Robert Bly is now poised to write the great work his work has always promised. I think of Milton before *Paradise Lost*, Blake before the prophetic books. But it will take a new engagement with reality. I hope he undertakes it.

The Poetry of Robert Bly

ROBERT RICHMAN

With the publication this year of Robert Bly's *Selected Poems*[1]—a volume preceded by a number of books celebrating this writer's work[2]—the time has surely come to take a closer critical look at one of the most "radical" poetic careers of our time. Robert Bly himself has always insisted that, of the many poetic movements spawned during the Sixties, none was more radical than his. To establish the priority of his own literary outlook, Bly has spent much time belittling that of his rivals in this period—the confessional and New York School poets, on the one hand, and, on the other, the formalist poets who survived the Sixties. In Bly's view, "both cooked and raw poetry in a certain sense in the United States is head poetry." To deal with the objects of the external world, as both the confessionals and the New York School poets do, is, in his view, to be in thrall to the "logic" of that world. True free-associational surrealism, which is what Bly has long advocated for poetry, is achieved by turning inward, "into" the body and away from the "head" and the world. It is therefore hardly surprising that the only criterion of quality for this poetry of "weird" and "deep images" is said to be its resistance to analysis. Bly's best poetry, according to William Heyen in *Robert Bly: When Sleepers Awake*, has always "defied serious inquiry and involved [that is, complex] explication." "The prized conditions," according to Donald Wesling, another admirer of his work, "are Not Understanding and Not Saying."

A look at the recent publications devoted to Bly's writing suggests, however, that far from defying serious inquiry and explication, Bly's poetry is as full of explicable matter as *The Waste Land.* And the question of form in Bly's poetry has also been recently opened for review. Bly himself has lately abandoned the harsh antiformal polemics that used to be his stock-in-trade. In the new *Selected Poems* he has chosen to include a few previously unpublished poems from the late Forties and early Fifties written in iambic pentameter. In addition, Bly's comments, interspersed throughout the book, show the poet far more willing to make concessions to the value of form in general and to acknowledge its presence in poems we had been previously asked to perceive very differently. This is not to say Bly has abandoned every vestige of his radical outlook. Indeed, one of the more amusing things about the *Selected Poems*—as

Reprinted from *The New Criterion* 5, no. 4 (December 1986): 37–46 by permission of the author.

well as many of Bly's prose writings of the Eighties—is the rhetorical hole he digs himself into by trying to maintain his old radical principles while flaunting an admiration for form: "It is not iambic," he says about one group of poems in the *Selected Poems*, "but free verse with distinct memories of form." For a writer whose unequivocal rantings against form and meaning were long a familiar feature of the literary scene—most of them on the order of, "I refuse to say anything at all about prosody. What an ugly word it is!" and "It's so horrible in high school when they say, 'What's the interpretation of this poem?'"—even this small shift in outlook acquires a certain significance. Clearly a concerted effort is being made by Bly and his many supporters to present a more tempered picture of his aesthetic position for posterity. But does this revisionist view of Bly's poetry really account for what he has written and what he has claimed for it?

Robert Bly was born sixty years ago in the rural farming community of Madison, Minnesota. He belongs to the impressive generation of American poets that emerged in the years immediately following the war. Bly's fellow students at Harvard—he was there from 1947 to 1950—included Richard Wilbur, Donald Hall, Adrienne Rich, Kenneth Koch, and John Ashbery. Like many of his classmates, Bly was under the sway of the formalist impulse then governing American poetry. According to the chronology in Howard Nelson's *Robert Bly: An Introduction to the Poetry*, Bly had "virtually memorized" Robert Lowell's *Lord Weary's Castle*, which had been published the year before Bly entered Harvard. But unlike most of his contemporaries, he chose to withhold from publication the book of formalist poems, entitled *The Lute of Three Loudnesses,* which he had assembled after graduation. The work from this book that is now included in the *Selected Poems* reveals an immature but by no means inconsiderable talent:

> Spring has come; I look up and see
> The agile companies of April sit
> As quaint and graceful as medieval guilds.
> Grouse feathers float away on the still lake.
> Summer and reeds; summer and partridge
>   chicks.
> Then bees: eaters of honey till their death.
> The honey gatherers, coming and going, drive
> Their endless honey circles to the hive.
>
> The sedge root in the river lifts and frees,
> And blackbirds join in flocks, their duties
>   through.
> And now the last autumnal freedom comes,
> And Zumbrota acorns drop, sun-pushed as
>   plums,

> To half-wild hogs in Carolina trees,
> And disappointed bees, with half-gold feet,
> Sail home. For me this season is most sweet,
> And winter will be stamping of the feet.

Bly's dissatisfaction with the poems of *The Lute of Three Loudnesses*—"I heard a whisper of Milton," writes Bly in the *Selected Poems*, and "something in it didn't fit me"—led to a period of self-imposed isolation in New York City and Cambridge from 1951 to 1954. These years of reading and reflection have taken on a considerable importance in the Bly mythology, almost as important as the suppressed first book of poems. According to Bly and his commentators, this period was crucial in the transformation of the writer from a craftsman in rhyme and meter (what Bly would later call "antique work") to a surrealist free-verse poet. For this period of loneliness, as Bly describes it in the *Selected Poems*, "made clear to me [the] . . . interior starvation" which had given birth to the formal poetry Bly had been so unhappy with.

In 1954 Bly enrolled in the writing program at the University of Iowa, and the following year he married Carolyn McLean. In 1956, Bly travelled to Norway on a Fulbright grant to translate Norwegian poetry. Bly is of Norwegian descent but knew no Norwegian at the time. It was in the Oslo Public Library that he encountered the work of the South American poets Pablo Neruda and Cesar Vallejo, the Spanish poet Juan Jiménez, and the German poet Georg Trakl. Overwhelmed by what he perceived to be the imaginative freshness of the work of these "surrealist"poets—far more authentic, Bly believed, than the French surrealists—Bly promptly started a literary magazine when he returned to the United States. Its express purpose was to provide a forum for translations of the work of these writers. But *The Fifties*, as the magazine was called (it would eventually become *The Sixties, The Seventies*, and *The Eighties*), was also used as a vehicle for attacks on the poetry establishment. The editorial in the inaugural issue, published in 1958, read, in part: "The editors of this magazine think that most of the poetry published in America is too old-fashioned." Bly sent copies to all the contributors to *The New Poets of England and America,* the anthology of formalist poetry edited by Donald Hall, Robert Pack, and Louis Simpson which had appeared that same year. By the time the second installment of *The Fifties* appeared in 1959—featuring the first surrealist-inspired work of James Wright, a young poet who, like Bly, had abandoned the formalist path—Bly's commitment to his new aesthetic was solidly established.

In 1958 and 1959 Bly interrupted work on the surrealist "country poems" that would appear in his first published book, *Silence in the Snowy Fields* (1962), in order to finish a book of political poems. It was called *Poems for the Ascension of J. P. Morgan*, and failed to find a publisher. (A few of these poems would turn up in *Silence in the Snowy Fields* and *The Light Around the Body*, Bly's second published book, which appeared in 1967). Bly remained undeterred in his sense of poetic mission. American poetry was then going through a tremendous upheaval: Allen Ginsberg's *Howl* had appeared in 1956 and Robert Lowell's *Life Studies* in 1959—and Bly was anxious to be a part of the new movement. In 1961 he brought out *Twenty Poems of Georg Trakl*, translated by himself and James Wright. By this time Bly had forged more alliances with poets, among them Donald Hall and Louis Simpson, two of the editors of *The New Poetry of England and America* who were experiencing crises of confidence in their own formalist verse. Bly also met Galway Kinnell and David Ignatow around this time, two more poets sympathetic to his cause.

    Silence in the Snowy Fields was the first major contribution to Bly's burgeoning surrealist movement. The first poem in the volume, entitled "Three Kinds of Pleasures," provided the movement with a kind of brief poetic agenda:

I

> Sometimes, riding in a car, in Wisconsin
> Or Illinois, you notice those dark telephone
>   poles
> One by one lift themselves out of the fence
>   line
> And slowly leap on the gray sky—
> And past them the snowy fields.

II

> The darkness drifts down like snow on the
>   picked cornfields
> In Wisconsin, and on these black trees
> Scattered, one by one
> Through the winter fields—
> We see stiff weeds and brownish stubble,
> And white snow left now only in the
>   wheeltracks of the combine.

III

> It is a pleasure, also, to be driving
> Toward Chicago, near dark,
> And see the lights in the barns.
> The bare trees more dignified than ever,
> Like a fierce man on his deathbed,
> And the ditches along the road half full of
>   a private snow.

Bly's pleasures are indeed threefold: the surreal, as tentatively evidenced in the image of the leaping telephone poles in the first stanza; the freedom to assert one's emotional state rather than conjure it through an elaborate network of poetic devices, as in "It is a pleasure, also, to be driving . . ."; and the freedom to construct a poem out of a series of plain, if finely drawn, random observations. Most of the other poems in the book are made up of sequences of description—also occasionally interspersed with "surreal" images—that are far more random than this. As Bly remarked, "when the poems of *Silence in the Snowy Fields* came, I set them down with very little rewriting, maybe one or two lines only . . . they arrived as complete as they came." They were, he said on another occasion, finished "in the thirty or forty seconds that it took to write the poem." The final stanza of "Driving Toward the Lac Qui Parle River" seems to confirm Bly's remarks:

> Nearly to Milan, suddenly a small bridge,
> And water kneeling in the moonlight.
> In small towns the houses are built right on
>   the ground;
> The lamplight falls on all fours on the grass.
> When I reach the river, the full moon covers it.
> A few people are talking, low, in a boat.

By attempting to "penetrate down into an evolutionary part of the mind," as Bly felt Neruda, Trakl, and Vallejo had done, the poet challenged the orthodoxies not only of the formalist poetry of the late Forties and early Fifties but of the modernist poets as well. In the poetry of Eliot, for example, seemingly disparate images and allusions are united by an underlying intellectual structure. Bly's bursts of private subjectivity, on the other hand, seek to do without such structural links. If the imagery happens to cohere, as Bly insisted, the poem had to be disposed of. According to the poet, the most "genuine line" in a poem is the "weirdest line . . . the one that apparently doesn't make any sense. . . ." "To Pound an image meant 'petals on a wet, black bough,'" said Bly. "To us an image is 'death on the deep roads of the guitar.'"

Silence in the Snowy Fields also repudiated Eliot's notion of the objective correlative. In Bly's view, the emotion that the correlative objectifies is destroyed by the very process of its objectification. Bly's "deep" poetic images, emerging from "within," purportedly contained purer emotions whose psychic energy was still intact: "If I reached my hands down, near the earth,/I could take handfuls of darkness!" or "The sun lies happily on my knees." Bly's other way of challenging the objective correlative (for which he is perhaps more famous) is to make simple statements of his feelings. Two well-known examples of this in *Silence in the Snowy Fields* are "I have awakened at Missoula, Montana, utterly happy" (the last line of "In a Train") and "Oh, on an early morning I think I shall live forever!" (the first line of "Poem in Three Parts").

It is easy to understand why Bly's aesthetic—or anti-aesthetic—became so popular in the Sixties and Seventies. It found sympathetic readers among the growing number of people who resented the complexity of modernist—and postwar—poetry. Eliot made no bones about the fact that the poet must be learned and his work difficult. It was those who felt themselves to be disenfranchised from Eliot's exclusive club that Bly claimed as his own. Being a poet could not be simpler, he told them, because each one of us

> has our own psychic rhythms. . . . Anybody at his peak moment, who wants to sit down and write a poem, can write it. . . .

All one needed was a little "inner animal imagery," or, failing that, the ability to state that one was happy, sad, or indifferent in a given town at a given time of day. The idea spread like wildfire.

It is not surprising that many perceived Bly's poetry to be a long-awaited resurgence of Romanticism. But the nineteenth-century English Romantic poets' suffusion of their being into the external world is vastly different from Bly's solipsistic engorging of the world. As Robert Langbaum points out in *The Poetry of Experience* (1957), the Romantic poets did not so much seek to overwhelm the world with their subjective being as confirm their inner experiences in the crucible of the world. "There remains," Langbaum tells us, "the hardheaded critical awareness [on the part of the poets] that the self is something other than the object" of the poet's attention. The Romantics never sought, as Langbaum says, "to put the head to sleep." Putting the head to sleep is a perfectly apt description of the poetic program of Robert Bly.

Silence in the Snowy Fields was not entirely devoid of poetic virtue, however. There is something to be said for the freshness of Bly's language, and for the poet's attempt to bring a wide-eyed wonder to the Minnesota countryside. But the solipsism of this poetry—perfectly embodied in Bly's barren, unpopulated landscapes—all but obscures the musicality of the language.

As appealing as the solipsistic poetry of *Silence in the Snowy Fields* was, it lacked the single element crucial in the Sixties for a truly popular—and critical—success: politics. This element was firmly entrenched in Bly's next book, *The Light Around the Body*, which was published in 1967 and received the National Book Award for poetry in 1968. The conflation of surrealism and politics—a practice Bly also borrowed from his South American models—is evident in "War and Silence"—

> The bombers spread out, temperature steady.
> A Negro's ear sleeping in an automobile tire.
> Pieces of timber float by, saying nothing.

*　　　*　　　*

Bishops rush about crying, "There is no war,"
And bombs fall,
Leaving a dust on the beech trees.

* * *

One leg walks down the road and leaves
The other behind; the eyes part
And fly off in opposite directions.

* * *

Filaments of death grow out.
The sheriff cuts off his black legs
And nails them to a tree.

—as well as in "Driving Through Minnesota During the Hanoi Bombings":

The sergeant said,
"I felt sorry for him
And blew his head off with a shotgun."
These instants become crystals,
Particles
The grass cannot dissolve. Our own gaiety
Will end up
In Asia, and you will look down in your cup
And see
Black Starfighters.
Our own cities were the ones we wanted
to bomb!

In "The Teeth Mother Naked at Last"—first published by City Lights Books
in 1970 and included three years later in *Sleepers Joining Hands*—surrealistic
imagery is for the most part disposed of. Replacing it is a sustained, hate-filled
invective against everything in American life that Bly loathed:

Helicopters flutter overhead. The death-
bee is coming. Super Sabres
like knots of neurotic energy sweep
around and return.
This is Hamilton's triumph.
This is the triumph of a centralized bank.

* * *

The ministers lie, the professors lie, the
television reporters lie, the priests lie.
What are these lies? It means that the country
wants to die.

* * *

This is what it's like for a rich country to
make war.
This is what it's like to bomb huts (afterwards
described as "structures").

> This is what it's like to kill marginal farmers
> (afterwards described as "Communists").
>
> *   *   *
>
> It's because the average hospital bed now costs
> two hundred dollars a day
> that we bomb the hospitals in the north. . . .

Any poet not mentioning the war in 1970 ran the risk, of course, of being implicated in the "genocide." All the same, this appeared to be an egregious about-face for Bly. Unlike the confessional poets, for whom politics was a logical next step, Bly had presented himself as the poet of interior life. He had claimed, again and again, that society and culture threatened the purity of the poet's psychic rhythms. He had vociferously campaigned against what he called the "journalistic mind" in poetry, and had criticized poetry in which the words, as he said, had "their energy corrupted" by evil external forces. If *Silence in the Snowy Fields* demanded a poetry truly free of the rhetoric of the world, then *The Light Around the Body* seemed to be an outright betrayal of the earlier book. It was a book swamped by the rhetoric of the world.

Bly had an explanation, of course. The political poems of *The Light Around the Body*, he reasoned, were attempts to show "that the political poem comes out of the deepest privacy." "Neruda, Vallejo, Antonio Machado, Aleixandre, and Lorca," says Bly in the preface to the section of poems from *The Light Around the Body* in the *Selected Poems*, taught him that it was "just and natural to write of important national griefs in one's poetry as well as of private griefs." As long as these "national griefs" emerged from one's body, insisted Bly, they were not simply political rhetoric but the authentic subjective eruptions of a deeply grieved person. And who was to say whether these poems emerged from one's inner soul or were the product of the fallen world? Why, the poet himself! What we were offered was, in short, the same old solipsism. And as before, anyone who dared to question whether political imagery could be of the requisite psychic depth was automatically accused of using the superannuated critical tools of a dying culture. In the Sixties and Seventies, few wanted to be guilty of this crime.

Even if we take *The Light Around the Body* and "Teeth Mother" in their own terms—as attempts to expiate the alleged sins (greed, commercialism, aggression) of America—they still miss their target. Bly's high moral fervor is undone by some gross miscalculations. Most obvious of these is Bly's repeated stereotyping of people. "No one in business can be a Christian," says Bly in one poem. Accountants, executives, advertising men, and Indians are all similarly typecast (the last in a poem entitled "Hatred of Men with Black Hair"). This alarming attitude crops up in Bly's other works and statements from this time as well. In an interview from 1966 Bly declared that "the typical football player . . . mistreats women, because he has always mistreated the woman that is inside him." What this stereotyping now looks like is the inevitable point of view of someone who has dwelled too long in the unpopulated landscapes of his own subjectivity.

Bly's political poetry corresponded to some real-life activism during these years. In 1966 he organized the first anti-war poetry readings at Reed College and the University of Washington. The same year he co-founded American Writers Against the Vietnam War. In 1967 he took part in a Pentagon demonstration, and was arrested for blocking the entrance to an induction center. And in 1968, at the ceremony for the National Book Awards, Bly in his acceptance speech urged the young people in the audience to defy the draft. At the same ceremony he donated his award money to the "resistance." Ten years later Bly was still castigating his fellow poets—John Berryman was his bête noire—for "refusing to get up on one of those [anti-war] stages." Much of the other work Bly produced during the late Sixties and early Seventies—*Twenty Poems of Pablo Neruda* (1969), translated by Bly and Wright, *The Morning Glory* (1969), a chap-book of prose poems, *Twenty Poems of Tomas Tranströmer* (1970), and *Neruda and Vallejo: Selected Poems* (1971)—was obscured by the running political commentary. In 1971 Bly predicted "a very swift disintegration of all the structures of society" replaced by a world of isolated, self-sufficient communes. Clearly, Bly's primary interest was in taking his solipsism to the streets.

"The Teeth Mother Naked at Last" was the first poem written following Bly's intensive reading of Jung, which had begun in 1969. Jung's association of the unconscious with femininity and the conscious mind with masculinity struck a responsive chord in Bly, who promptly caricatured it in his writings. As Bly explains it in the essay "I Came Out of the Mother Naked" in *Sleepers Joining Hands* (1973), masculine awareness—which Bly identified with rules and morality—defeated the feminine consciousness—identified with nature, compassion, intuition, and poetry—in a struggle for control of the planet. *Sleepers Joining Hands* was an attempt, in Bly's words, to "right [the] spiritual balance" on earth. But for Bly righting the balance naturally meant giving the mother consciousness the upper hand. Bly condemns everything associated (in his own mind, anyway) with the masculine impulse, from literary criticism to the desire to "go out and conquer Africa," and is full of praise for everything associated with the feminine outlook. What Bly really liked about Jung's theories, or what he saw in them, anyway, was their simplicity. The world was neatly divided into two camps: the good and the bad. One is to be disposed of and one is to be saved. All special circumstances, contingencies, and complexities are conveniently ignored.

Of course, the masculine attribute most roundly condemned by Bly during his Jungian phase was poetic form. In an interview published in *Craft* magazine in 1972, Bly went to considerable lengths to indicate that his poetry is written without the assistance of what he refers to as "the stiff part of the mind." After the interviewer gets Bly to admit grudgingly that the poems of *The Light Around the Body* are composed in "high" or poetic language, the interviewer—clearly relishing the idea that he'll go on record as the only person ever to have forced Robert Bly to admit that his poetry is crafted—proudly declares: "That's a matter of craft." But Bly retorts: ". . . what guides this craft is an instinctive sense for when a sentence is alive and when it's not. . . ." When it comes to his "technique" or to what gives birth to a poem, Bly is even more evasive. He simply does not say anything.

Not surprisingly, Bly tried to revise literary history along these same anti-formal lines. All "great poems," he said, "like the *Odyssey*, take[s] [their] form . . . without mind intervention." Bly sought to revolutionize the art of translating poetry in a similar fashion. Knowing the language well wasn't the most important factor in translating poetry, Bly insisted, since "[w]hat you are essentially doing is slipping for a moment into the mood of the other poet . . . into an emotion which you may possibly have experienced at some time." In truth, Bly's ideas about translation merely allowed the translator, as James Dickey put it, to take "as many liberties as [he] wants to take with the original, it being understood that this enables [him] somehow to approach the 'spirit' of the poem [he] is translating." The emergence of public readings of poetry during this time was also given encouragement in Bly's ideas. When you read poetry, Bly explained, the mind intervenes. When you hear poetry, on the other hand, there is less chance of the mind analyzing the work and thereby suppressing a deep subjective interaction with the poem. Criticism of poetry also underwent a drastic change, thanks in part to Bly's theories. Fewer and fewer writers on poetry analyzed what they read. Instead poetry was admired for—to borrow a phrase of Howard Nelson's—its "flowing, rushing, knotting, whirling" energy. An entire way of writing about poetry was quickly becoming obsolete, and it was Bly who had played a major role in drafting the blueprint of its destruction.

Bly provided the generation of poets coming of age in the Seventies with plenty of examples of anti-poetic poetry to accompany his anti-critical rhetoric. The following excerpt, for example, from Bly's "Six Winter Privacy Poems"—which opens the book *Sleepers Joining Hands*—reminded budding poets how easy it was to stand by whatever banality they had first put down on paper:

> My shack has two rooms; I use one.
> The lamplight falls on my chair and table
> and I fly into one of my poems—
> I can't tell you where—
> as if I appeared where I am now,
> in a wet field, snow falling. . . .
>
>   *   *   *
> There is solitude like black mud!
> Sitting in this darkness singing,
> I can't tell if this joy

> is from the body, or the soul, or a third
> place!

Bly wasn't through yet. After all, he was still using the stanza and line—
"antiquated" poetic units of measure. The prose poems of *The Morning Glory*
(1975) and *This Body is Made of Camphor and Gopherwood* (1977) sought, in Bly's
words, to "calm the language down" even more, thereby making it a truer
reflection of the timeless flow of the inner body. "[I]t was as if I had descended
into my body at last," says Bly in the *Selected Poems*, "and that immersion is the
subject of the poems. The joy [of the poetry] lies in its being unfocused":

> The cucumbers are thirsty, their big leaves turn away from the wind. I water
> them after supper; the hose curled near the rhubarb. The wind sound blows
> through the head. . . . What is comforted words help, the sunken islands
> speak to us. . . .
>   In this world animal or vegetable? Others love us, the cabbages love the
> earth, the earth is fond of the heavens—A new age comes close through the dark,
> threatens much, so much is passing away. . . .

Even some of the critics who had previously supported Bly rebelled against
This Body is Made of Camphor and Gopherwood. One of them, Philip Dacey, in a
piece entitled "This Book is Made of Turkey Soup and Star Music," cited by
Nelson, wrote:

> Although Bly, a classic literary demagogue, rails against artifice in
> poetry . . . many of the prose poems in this book are more artificial—pieces
> clearly contrived in a language one is not likely to hear outside the poem—than
> virtually any of, say, Frost's poems in blank verse. Frost and countless others
> achieve the natural or a semblance of it through the artificial; Bly wishes to
> bypass the latter and ends up smack in the middle of it.

Apparently Bly was sensitive to the charges. His next book, *This Tree Will Be
Here for a Thousand Years* (1979)—a group of surrealist country poems much in
the vein of those in *Silence in the Snowy Fields*—was an obvious effort to
conciliate the critics and readers who had grown impatient with his work. But
these poems, written at intervals during the previous sixteen years, are more
literary and less spontaneous than their predecessors. The book was promptly
attacked by Eliot Weinberger—never a supporter of Bly's—who began his
review, which appeared in *The Nation* on November 17, 1979, with the
sentence, "Robert Bly is a windbag, a sentimentalist, a slob in the language."

Bly attempted to start off the decade of the Eighties on a new foot. *The Man in
the Black Coat Turns* (1981) was heralded as the poet's long overdue reconcili-
ation with the masculine consciousness, a "return to the father," as Bly put it.
"To be able to respect your father is such a beautiful thing!" Bly declared in an

interview at the time. Although the surface details of the poems in this book seem to be vaguely "about" masculinity, little else has changed. Indeed, the same undiluted anti-rationalism and anti-formalism that governed the earlier poetry governs almost everything here. This is from "What the Fox Agreed to Do":

> And the shells, the mollusc shells, grow large.
> Smoke twists up through water,
> the moon rockets up from the sea floor.
>
> The fox agrees to leap into the ocean.
> The human being feels a splash around him.
> Hebrews straddle the slippery dolphins.

And this is from the prose poem entitled "Eleven O'Clock at Night" (none of these prose poems were included in the *Selected Poems*):

> I lie alone in my bed; cooking and stories are over at last, and some peace comes. And what did I do today? I wrote down some thoughts on sacrifice that other people had, but couldn't relate them to my own life. I brought my daughter to the bus—on the way to Minneapolis for a haircut—and I waited twenty minutes with her in the somnolent hotel lobby. I wanted the mail to bring some praise for my ego to eat, and was disappointed. I added up my bank balance, and found only $65, when I need over a thousand to pay the bills for this month alone. So this is how my life is passing before the grave?

The critics in Bly's thrall—there were still many of them—responded to this book, as they almost always had, by relinquishing their critical powers: "I risk, of course," said one, "by trying to be too rational (male-conscious), damaging [Bly's] subtle fabrics."

Howard Nelson, in his recent book on Bly, does not view the poetry in *The Man in the Black Coat Turns* as another episode of solipsistic surrealism. He finds it not only full of meaning—an attempt, in his words, to "recover the past"—but full of allusions to the New Testament as well. But then Nelson discovers allusions, "sexual metaphors," "symbols," and coherent imagery everywhere in the Bly *oeuvre*. "The consciousness in the *Snowy Fields*," Nelson avers, "is in fact quite complicated." Nelson's ability to misconstrue Bly's poetry—not to mention his ignoring the poet's numerous statements of intention—is remarkable. Bly's defiantly illogical imagery is said by Nelson to be a "smooth arc of association"—a phrase more easily applied to the poetry of the despised Eliot than to that of Bly. Astonishingly, Nelson asserts that Bly

prizes spontaneity but also believes in revision. For him, the free flow of the mind in and out of itself is neither avant-garde nor necessarily very interesting.

This is not the blatant contradiction of Bly's aesthetic it appears to be, or so Nelson claims. For the "intelligence" Nelson finds running rampant in Bly's poetry is not the mind's intelligence, but the "body's wisdom," the consciousness of nature. "The rational intelligence," explains Nelson, "is not the only intelligence."

John Unterecker, who has contributed a foreword to Nelson's book, resorts to a similar strategy in his discussion of Bly's musical effects. Bly's "high" poetic language, Unterecker says, is "probably largely uncalculated," "perhaps casual in composition," "half-conscious," and written "without a great deal of premeditation." Yet a few sentences later Unterecker acknowledges that Bly "trusts to an ear that he's trained by careful listening. . . ." Now *trained* is very much the opposite of *casual, half-conscious* and *uncalculated.* But Unterecker, like Nelson, wishes to honor Bly's free-associational method while simultaneously claiming some quality of mind for the poetry. Clearly, it is no easy task.

In truth, though, Unterecker and Nelson are only responding to a tack recently taken by Bly himself. In a 1981 essay called "Form that is Neither In nor Out"—which begins, "I have been thinking lately that we have not been very faithful servants of art"—Bly declares:

> . . . I have often thought of form as a prison . . . a kind of dungeon in which heart material gets imprisoned. Suppose I were wrong on that. If so, we need to find a way to speak of form so that its wild or intense quality becomes clear. The distinction between form as prison and form as wildness may correspond to a distinction between kinds of form, in particular, the mechanical and the organic. . . . I maintain then that the more form a poem has—I mean living form—the closer it comes to the wild animal.

This view is reiterated in an essay in the *Selected Poems* entitled "The Prose Poem as an Evolving Form," in which Bly speaks of how "form in art relies on form in nature for its model." But whether it is Nelson's "organic" form, Unterecker's "half-conscious" form, or Bly's "wild" and "living" form, it all bespeaks a willed effort to conflate two irreconcilable attitudes toward poetry. For Bly and his critics, it is not enough for poetry to appeal to a primitive level of consciousness. It must be "composed" by that consciousness too.

Intelligence and form have been praised by Bly in other recent essays and interviews too. "All artists love art," he says in one, "but we miss sometimes in Whitman reminders of what a triumph the intensely worked poem can be." "Before solitude can give any nourishment to the poet, evidently a certain level of literary culture has to be reached." "Writing poetry means a lot of study." "Obsession with image can become a psychic habit as much as obsession with persona."[3]

Robert Bly's recent change of heart is interesting as a part of the cultural history of our time—and anyway, he has every right to change his mind. But his well-publicized shift does nothing to rescue the poems, the majority of which suffer from the two worst poetic excesses of the Sixties: politics and solipsism. This is unfortunate, because Bly has displayed from the start an enormous gift for language, and these excesses have worked against his strongest talent. To this reader, only a handful of the pastoral poems in *Silence in the Snowy Fields*, an equally small number of the "thought" poems from the early Eighties, and the previously suppressed formalist work of the late Forties do not betray this gift. Here is a section of another early poem—entitled "Schoolcraft's Diary Written on The Missouri: 1830"—which we are now seeing for the first time:

> Now night grows old above this riverboat.
> Before I end, I shall include account
> Of incident tonight that moved my wonder.
> At dusk we tied the ship to trees on shore;
> No mortal boat in these night shoals can live.
> At first I heard a cry: then shufflings, steps.
> The muffled sounds on deckoak overhead
> Drew me on deck. The air was chill, and there
> I sensed, because these senses here are sharp
> And must be, something living and unknown.

Far from being evidence of "interior starvation," as Bly claimed they were, these youthful lines hint at what Bly's poetic achievement might have been had he not chosen to abandon formalism for the gratifications of a half-baked surrealism. What we have instead is poetry disfigured by politics and the supposed pleasures he derives from being "wrapped in my joyful flesh."

Notes

1. *Selected Poems*, by Robert Bly: Harper & Row, 1986.

2. *Of Solitude and Silence: Writings on Robert Bly*, edited by Richard Jones and Kate Daniels, Beacon Press, 1981: *Robert Bly: When Sleepers Awake*, edited by Joyce Peseroff, University of Michigan Press, 1984; *Talking All Morning*, a volume of interviews and papers, the University of Michigan Press, 1980; and *Robert Bly: An Introduction to the Poetry*, by Howard Nelson, Columbia University Press, 1984.

3. As John Haines writes in an essay in *Of Solitude and Silence*, by the late Sixties and Seventies "a second and third hand pastoral sureality manifested itself and all kinds of people began writing poems crowded with stone and earth images and forced imagery of darkness. Small, tousled animals were creeping out of all kinds of castles in the oaks and maples, and from little houses in the grass. Moose were sighted in the suburbs of Los Angeles, as I recall, and wolves were baited on the rooftops in San Francisco."

Minnesota Transcendentalist

JOYCE PESEROFF

Mr. Bly has never believed that poetry makes nothing happen. For almost 30 years he has been a busy and energetic advocate for certain spiritual, political and literary values; a publisher, translator and shaman. A man who praises privacy and solitude, he writes poems that rush toward and embrace the world, both the outer world, acutely observed in its glory and decay, and the inner world, to him the source of the soul's ecstasy and grief. Reconciling these two worlds has always been his mission as he writes poems meant, in words he quotes from the French prose poet Francis Ponge, to "nourish the spirit of man by giving him the cosmos to suckle." In "Selected Poems," his new collection, he has shaped from both worlds his record of the body's journey and the soul's quest. This is not just an anthology of Mr. Bly's best work; its 11 new essays and its particular method of organization require a fresh look at the poet's achievement.

The book is arranged in nine sections, each introduced by a short essay. Two longer essays, "Whitman's Line as a Public Form" and "The Prose Poem as an Evolving Form," conclude the book. Although he begins with early poems previously uncollected and ends with excerpts from his most recent volume, Mr. Bly avoids strict chronology. Rather, each section is designed to illustrate a step in the evolution of his poetics.

*　　　*　　　*

The third section, for example, includes poems from "Silence in the Snowy Fields" (1962), written in a rhapsodic mode, as well as others written in the same mode ("adapted from Waley's translations of Chinese poems, Frank O'Connor's translations of Celtic poems, and my own translations of Machado, but a certain gaiety carries them along. The line breaks usually come where the thought ends, and bring a moment of silence") but published only 17 years later in "This Tree Will Be Here for a Thousand Years." Part Five—prose poems from "The Morning Glory" (1975) and some from "The Man in the Black Coat Turns" (1981)—precedes (heavily revised) selections from "Sleepers Joining Hands" (1973) in Part Six. This arrangement allows the poet to

Reprinted from the *New York Times Book Review*, 25 May 1986, 2. Copyright 1986 by The New York Times Company. Reprinted by permission.

contrast prose poems, like "The Starfish" and "A Bouquet of Ten Roses," that "carry us to the new place on their minute detail, on what they give us to see," with those written "to turn away from seeing. . . . While I was still writing the *Morning Glory* poems, I felt a longing to compose a radical or root poem that would speak to what has its back turned to me."

> I sent my brother away.
> I saw him turn and leave. It was a schoolyard.
> I gave him to the dark people passing.
> He learned to sleep alone on the high buttes.

That is from a poem originally titled "The Shadow Goes Away," the long poem in "Sleepers Joining Hands" that immediately follows the poet's 20-page essay, "I Came Out of the Mother Naked." I regret alterations here to this poem and to other long poems. Mr. Bly omits his homage to the Great Mother, preferring to shift emphasis from the female *anima* to male images "suggesting Joseph's betrayal of his brother."

The volume becomes a quest to find a voice to fit the poet and a prosody to fit the poem. After abandoning the iambic "lute of three loudnesses" described in Part One ("I loved the music so much I could have written such lines for the rest of my life, but something in them didn't fit me") and, I surmise, Harvard University, the poet moved to New York. He sank, through solitude, "past . . . stones, past Eros, past family affections." From this period of estrangement came poems of both despair and healing that Mr. Bly would publish 14 years later in "The Light Around the Body." It is only after this period that the poet, who had married and returned to his native Minnesota, composed the poems published in his first book.

*   *   *

One of the pleasures of reading "Selected Poems" is to discover themes, language and imagery that will recur, transformed, throughout the poet's body of work like DNA passed from the acorn to the oak. The poems in Part One may not sound much like Robert Bly, but titles like "Dawn in Threshing Time" and "*from* Four Seasons in the American Woods" indicate subjects the poet would write about again and again. "Where We Must Look for Help" presages the "deep image" poems of psychic connections, mythic comparisons and unexpected junctures:

*   *   *

More surprising is "Schoolcraft's Diary Written on the Missouri: 1830," a three-page dramatic monologue poem including a good deal of narrative. The speaker observes the conflict between "busy whites" with "steel traps hanging, swung from saddle thongs" and the Sioux, "as still as Hudson's blankets winding them." He joins a party of men armed to confront a mysterious white apparition stalking the camp.

*   *   *

As well as demonstrating the poet's early and abiding interest in American history, this long poem marks the beginning of his lifelong reliance on narrative.

Throughout his later work he would adapt narrative techniques to the lyric, just as he would appropriate the rhythms of sentences to replace a prosody based on counting syllables.

*   *   *

Powerful, succinct, poignant, such stories make up another sort of history. The personal connects us to the world's master plot. In fact, Mr. Bly has been able to write successful poems about public events because, for him, the political is personal. His response to the Vietnam War was rooted in grief, not grievance, and he never excluded himself from the darker manifestations of our national consciousness.

*   *   *

But Mr. Bly is a public poet even in poems without overt political content. Although in Part Four he introduces "The Teeth Mother Naked at Last" with a description of the long, cadenced line inspired by the Bible, Christopher Smart, William Blake and Walt Whitman—a line "that embodies power in a direct way . . . that throws or catapults itself into the outer world"—even his most intimate and meditative poems, with their frequent use of the pronoun "we," are designed to instruct and exhort. These poems function like stained-glass windows in a cathedral; their images direct us to wisdom and salvation. Mr. Bly's impulse to teach (some would say preach) unites him to Emerson on his platform, Bronson Alcott in his lyceum and Thoreau (whose nature writings Mr. Bly likens to prose poems) awake in Concord jail. He is, in a sense, the most recent in a line of great American transcendentalist writers.

"Selected Poems" begins with images of "this smoking body plough[ing] toward death" and ends with a series of love poems, including the sexy "At the Time of Peony Blossoming."

*   *   *

It is a mellow ending to a good journey, one that is not over yet.

Robert Bly [Review of *Selected Poems*]

Askold Melnyczuk

My first thought on opening Robert Bly's *Selected Poems* was how much this volume could not contain. Like Ezra Pound half a century earlier, Bly has centered himself in poetry and proceeded to radiate his energies out to nearly all corners of the world of letters. He has been influential as an editor, translater, theorist, and publicist for his gifted contemporaries. Where Pound schooled us in Greek, Latin, and Chinese classics, Bly has tutored us in Spanish (Machado, Neruda, Vallejo), Swedish (Ekelöf, Tranströmer), Norwegian (Hamsun), German (Rilke, Trakl), and even Hindu (Kabir). His public persona has been that of a guru, a bard of the people's court, a hyper-vitaminized skald, a WASP shaman (some would insist on abbreviating that word), a kind of straight Allen Ginsberg. Bly also resembles Pound is his talent for vexing the soberer doctors of letters, who tend to tsk and hiss, *de haut en bas*, at the work of mere masters of spirit.

The *Selected*, like all Bly productions, is an idiosyncratic affair. It is divided into ten parts. Nine of these contain excerpts (often much revised) from both published and unpublished material. A final chapter, "Afterthoughts," offers two brief essays on prosody. Bly introduces the poetry sections with semi-autobiographical prefaces that are variously illuminating and irritating. He is capable of awesome banality: "All poems are journeys. They go from somewhere to somewhere else." His need to personalize the rhetoric of poetic convention produces some quaint locutions: he describes the "English melodic line" as "the lute of three loudnesses." But he also surfaces in the pages as a dues-paying guildsman tirelessly testing rhythm and pitch, carefully building the craft that will carry his voice. Like most of the poets born in the twenties, he began by writing in conventional meters. But "something in it did not fit" him; he continued to cast about until he discovered the loose and placid (though not flaccid) line that is his signature. The swivel and pivot of syllables and consonants in Bly's verse are quiet and regular as the plains and fields of his native Midwest.

Until recently, Bly's poetry has been Janus-faced, revealing alternately a public and a private aspect. Bly is aware of this dualism. He calls the work focusing on the inner life "poems of affinity," while those touching on social and

Reprinted from *Partisan Review* 55, no. 1 (1988): 167-71. Reprinted by permission of the author. Copyright © 1988 by Partisan Review, Inc.

political experience he labels "poems of judgement." In solitude, away from society, Bly suggests, we commune freely with nature and spirit and all that makes us feel large and whole. In community, however, we compromise and are compromised, we are driven by greed, motivated by fear, and live at the mercy of the *tamas gunas*. This book charts the poet's movement toward integrity and wholeness.

The earliest poems here reflect the poet's apprentice status. Tender sentiments are tritely expressed in a diction strightlaced with Wordsworthisms: "For me this season is most sweet," vows the young swain of autumn. The following line, however, redeems that confession by its engaging rhythm and evocative image: "And winter will be stamping of the feet." Had Bly developed along the lines he traced out for himself, he would have become a conventional taxidermist of nature: "The honey gatherers, coming and going, drive/Their endless circles to the hive." A notable exception is the longer "Schoolcraft's Diary Written on the Missouri: 1830" which, though a little fuzzy in details, convincingly fuses narrative, symbolism, and period diction to convey something of the awe and mystery that must have enveloped the forays of the American pioneers. Toward the poem's end, the speaker, having just seen a wounded white bear, declares: "I felt as I had once when through a door,/At ten or twelve, I'd seen my mother bathing." His memory of the accidental trespass of a human taboo illuminates the more public and deliberate violation of the American wilderness.

In later books Bly sought a language with which to limn the struggles of the inner man—or, rather, the interior city:

> Inside the veins there are navies setting forth,
> Tiny explosions at the water lines,
> And seagulls weaving in the wind of the salty blood.
> >   "Waking from Sleep"

The mood of the poems is generally ecstatic: "Oh, on an early morning I think I shall live forever." Bly's sense of the numinous probably owes something to his study of the Christian mystics Boehme and Eckhart, both of whom saw the divine as immanent rather than transcendant. Drawn mainly from *The Silence in the Snowy Fields,* and influenced by Waley's Chinese translations and his own versions of Machado, the best of these poems are lapidary and comprehensive:

> V. *Listening to Bach*
> Inside this music there is someone
> Who is not well described by the names
> Of Jesus, or Jehovah, or the Lord of Hosts!
> >   "Six Winter Privacy Poems"

The counterparts to these terse panegyrics are the public poems, many from the Vietnam era. To evoke the psychic dislocations of a nation divided,

Bly deployed a brand of neosurrealism which came to be known as deep imagism. Simplifying grossly, the technique has the poet juxtapose radically disparate images aimed at detonating an emotional explosion in the reader. Here poems that fail lack inevitability. Their images seem arbitrary and cartoonish:

> Filaments of death grow out.
> The sheriff cuts off his black legs
> And nails them to a tree.
>   "War and Silence"

But the blunt rhetorical strategies can also be unnervingly effective:

> Tonight the burn the rice supplies; tomorrow
> They lecture on Thoreau; tonight the move around the trees;
> Tonight they throw firebombs; tomorrow
> They read the Declaration of Independence; tomorrow
>   they are in church.
>   "Johnson's Cabinet Watched by Ants"

The war also inspired what may be Bly's finest single poem, "The Teeth Mother Naked at Last." Structurally reliant on Whitmanesque anaphora, the poem, part catalogue, part document, keens the loss of America's political innocence. A combination of *Mauberley,* a condensed *Cantos,* and *Howl,* it could be read as the bloody right parenthesis to "When Lilacs Last in the Dooryard Bloomed":

> I know that books are tired of us.
> I *know* they are chaining the Bible to chairs.
> Books don't want to remain in the same room with us anymore.
> New Testaments are escaping . . . dressed as women
>   they slip out after dark.

Pasternak once remarked that a book is nothing more than a "cubic piece of burning, smoking conscience." The pyre Bly lit with his war poems continues to smoulder and disturb our night.

Bly's prose poems deserve an essay of their own. While his meditations on the prosody of prose are provocative, the things themselves embody and magnify some of the weaknesses of Bly's less successful verse. They can be obvious, *faux-näif,* packed with posturing and banal observations. Memorable exceptions include "The Hockey Poem" with its Ovidian metamorphoses, and "The Dead Seal" which, as a meditation on death and physical decay, is every bit as good as Richard Eberhardt's much anthologized "The Groundhog."

A "selected poems" may become either a tombstone or a capstone to a career. In Bly's case, however, it appears to be a stepping stone. The poems included here from his last two books, *The Man in the Black Coat Turns* and *Loving a Woman in Two Worlds* are his finest yet. Previously Bly's community seemed comprised of trees, turtles, horses, and the poet's own soul. Now that humans have entered as subjects of the poems, the tensions between public and private, outward and inward, have diminished. Bly writes about trying to come to terms with his father and about learning his own limitations as a father and a lover:

> I know there is someone
> who tries to teach us.
> He has four ways
> to do that . . .
> . . . I usually ignore
> the earlier three,
> and learn by falling.
> "Four Ways of Knowledge"

He speaks, with startling luminosity, about loving a woman simultaneously muse and mortal:

> And we did what we did, made love attentively, then
> dove into the river, and our bodies joined as calmly
> as the swimmer's shoulders glisten at dawn.
> "The Good Silence"

And his meditations on the sources of our otherness are worth attending to:

> We are bees then; our honey is language.
> Now the honey lies stored in caves
> beneath us, and the sound of words
> carries what we do not.
> "Words Rising"

The ebb and flow of the spirit now surges in every line. The separate profiles of Janus have merged and he looks out at us at last full face.

Robert Bly's *Iron John* and the
New "Lawrentian" Man

STEPHEN KUUSISTO

The public acceptance of *Iron John: A Book About Men* warrants an appraisal of Robert Bly's uncommon work as a "lay analyst." No poet in the United States in recent years has commanded so much attention. As a popularizer of archetypal psychology Bly has found a growing audience through public readings and lectures and more recently through a Bill Moyers television program which highlighted the wilderness "gatherings" of men who have engaged with Bly on a ritualized variant of the *talking cure*. Their stories often involve the elaboration of a highly charged "polytheistic" fairy tale in which "archetypes" or ancient symbols stand for a host of anxieties, instincts, and buried feelings. Gods and Goddesses, old "wise men," crones, lost children, and unlikely humans and animals are frequently described in overtones that are both romantic and metaphysical. The more intangible the archetype, the more important it may be, since Jungian psychology, like medieval alchemy, claims these are the materials which configure the "soul." A fully "individuated" man is a healthy reader of the unconscious.

As a "figure" the archetype may be likened to Dante's Virgil. As a building block in the story shared by the analyst and patient it may be analogous to the Rosetta stone. Once decoded it reveals the architecture of the psyche. In his early retreats, Robert Bly concentrated on the archetype of the "Great Mother" as a representation of the connection between the human mind and the seasonal cycles of the planet. Participants emphasized the "mystique" of story telling and singing in which intuition, reception, and empathy were understood as "Great Mother" characteristics.[1] The "Great Mother" retreats fashioned the idea of a healing synthesis for men in which their buried "feminine" traits would be encouraged. Several poems in Bly's *Selected Poems* describe the masculine search for the feminine principle as a struggle necessitated by the "poverty" of a masculine sensibility. In "A Dream of Retarded Children," Bly recounts a dream which is entirely feminine in its empathy and reception:

Reprinted from *Seneca Review* XXI (1991): 77-86. Reprinted by permission the *Seneca Review*.

That afternoon I had been fishing alone,
Strong wind, some water slipping in the back of the boat.
I was far from home.
Later I woke several times hearing geese.
I dreamt I saw retarded children playing, and one came near,
And her teacher, face open, hair light.
For the first time I forgot my distance;
I took her in my arms and held her.

Waking up, I felt how alone I was.
I walked on the dock,
fishing alone in the far north.

The poem reminds me of Blake's "Enitharmon" with its oneiric division of masculine and feminine experience. What's important is that the feminine unconscious has revealed its underworld of feeling. The poet must admit this messenger. In "Song of a Man Who Has Come Through," D. H. Lawrence wrote:

Oh, for the wonder that bubbles into my soul,
I would be a good fountain, a good well-head,
Would blur no whisper, spoil no expression.

What is the knocking?
What is the knocking at the door in the night?
It is somebody wants to do us harm.

No, no, it is the three strange angels.
Admit them, admit them.

In all of Bly's work, and in the writing of James Hillman and Marie-Louise Von Franz, two well known Jungians, fairy stories and dreams with their "strange angels" are "admitted" because their archetypes speak for and from the world beyond appearance, whether we choose to call this the unconscious or to give it a gnostic name. The figures in our dreams are celebrated as icons: they are presented as figurative proof that everything in nature is alive and connected. In *Anima Mundi,* a collection of essays on archetypal psychology, Hillman notes that when the archetype of Pan is alive "then nature is too, and it is filled with gods, so that the owl's hoot *is* Athena and the mollusk on the shore *is* Aphrodite. These bits of nature are not merely attributes or belongings. They are the gods in their biological forms."

Bly's incorporation of gods and goddesses underscores his insistence that nature is alive and that the planet is a living force. In "An Evening When the Full Moon Rose as the Sun Set," the poet "sees" these figures that remind us of the living universe:

> The sun goes down in the dusty April night.
> "You know it could be alive!"
> The sun is round, massive, compelling, sober, on fire.
> It moves swiftly through the tree stalks of the Lundin
>   grove as we drive past. . . .
> The legs of a bronze god walking at the edge of the world,
>   unseen by many,
> On his archaic errands, doubled up on his own energy.
> He guides his life by his dreams;
> When we look again he is gone.

The figure of the striding god lends to a natural event an anthropomorphic association which restores men to the center of the cosmological drama. The aim of *Iron John* is to discover charged, heroic archetypes which will enable men to personify their masculine instincts and thereby affirm their place in nature in a mythology that stands alongside that of the "Great Mother." "What gender might the water be?" asks Bly, "Is it masculine or feminine?"

> In our society, the earth and all the water in it is considered to be feminine, and by extension, it belongs to women. In the West, the sky belongs to men, and the earth to women; there is a "sky-father" and an "earth-mother." There's nothing wrong with those phrases, but two other phrases have fallen into oblivion: sky-mother and the earth-father.

Bly argues that when woman say the earth is female, "a man feels he has lost the right to breathe." Accordingly, "the Iron John story, which is pre-Greek, does not polarize earth and sky. Iron John lives in the water, under the water. He also lives wholeheartedly on earth; his wildness and hairiness in fact belong to earth and its animals. Neither earth nor water seems exclusively feminine or masculine."

This is "ur" masculinity. Iron John's hair is his emblem of wildness: he is like Enkidu in the Gilgamesh epic, only he's a more expressive form, an achetypal medium who possesses an organic knowledgeability. In the sequencing of Bly's ideas about masculinity, Iron John appears as an episodic reminder of the power of heroic and life-affirming instincts. Men need Iron John because "fierceness" has gone out of them. Bly asserts that the men he's been seeing in his travels (apparently the same ones who followed the psychological cartography of Jung by exploring their "feminine" interiors) have become "soft." Bly says that "the male in the past twenty years has become more thoughtful, more gentle. But by this process he has not become more free. He's a nice boy who pleases not only his mother but also the young woman he is living with."

The problem as Bly sees it is that men have been learning from a matriarchal mythology at the expense of their masculine gods. Sampson has lost his hair to Delilah. In a poem called "Crazy Carlson's Meadow," Bly describes an overgrown field and equates its decline with the collapse of the "fierce" world of the grandfathers:

Crazy Carlson cleared this meadow alone.
Now three blue
jays live in it.
Crazy Carlson cleared it back to the dark firs.
Feminine poplars have stepped out
in front, now
he is dead,
winding their leaves slowly in the motionless October air,

leaves midway between pale green and yellow,
as if a yellow
scarf were floating
six inches down in the Pacific. Old fir branches
above and below make sober
octopus caves,
inviting as the dark-
lidded eyes of those women on islands who live in bark huts.

A clear sky floats over the firs, pure blue,
too pure and deep.
There is no room
for the dark-lidded boys who longed to be Hercules.

There is no room even for Christ.
He broke off
his journey toward the Father,
and leaned back into the Mother's fearful tree.

He sank through the bark. The energies the Sadducees
refused him
turned into nails,
and the wind of Cana turned back to Vinegar.
Blessings on you, my king, broken
on the poplar tree.
Your shoulders quivered
like an aspen leaf before the storm of Empire.

When you died, your inner horse galloped away
into the wind without
you, and disappeared
into the blue sky. Did you both reach the Father's house?
But the suffering is over now, all consequences finished,
the lake closed
again, as before the leaf fell, all forgiven, the path ended.

Now each young man wanders in the sky alone,
ignoring the absent

> moon, not knowing
> where ground is, longing once more for the learning
> of the fierce male who hung for nine days only
> on the windy tree.
> When he got down,
> darkness was there, inside the folds of darkness words hidden.

There is an explicitly "Lawrentian" architecture in this poem as well as in many passages in *Iron John*. Men have lost their vitality to women because they have forgotten the stories of the patriarchs. Like Lawrence, Bly wishes to restore the masculine principle in the mental absolute of archetypal psychology. Both Bly and Lawrence conceive of the feminine as an opposing principle, an "agon" which must be fought. Consequently, this is a book about archetypal initiation which derives its ideas from a corrective impulse. Only men can initiate men. Bly says, "women can change the embryo to a boy, but only men can change the boy to a man. Initiators say that boys need a second birth, this time a birth from men."

In the absence of this initiation men are without effect. Bly describes "a finely tuned young man, ecologically superior to his father, sympathetic to the whole harmony of the universe, [who] himself has little vitality to offer." In contradistinction Bly says: "The strong or life-giving women who graduated from the sixties, so to speak, or who have inherited an older spirit, played an important part in producing this life-preserving, but not life-giving man." Taken a step further, this enervated man lacks the fervent, compensatory, atavistic mythology that will allow him to defend himself against women while at the same time living out his affirmation of the male principle as a cosmological value. Describing the men he encountered at a retreat in 1980 Bly says:

> The "soft" male was able to say, "I can feel your pain, and I consider your life as important as mine, and I will take care of you and comfort you." But he could not say what he wanted, and stick by it. *Resolve* of that kind was a different matter.
>
> In *The Odyssey*, Hermes instructs Odysseus that when he approaches Circe, who stands for a certain kind of matriarchal energy, he is to lift his sword. In these early sessions it was difficult for many of the younger men to distinguish between showing the sword and hurting someone. One man, a kind of incarnation of certain spiritual attitudes of the sixties, a man who had actually lived in a tree for a year outside Santa Cruz, found himself unable to extend his arm when it held a sword. He had learned so well not to hurt anyone that he couldn't lift the steel, even to catch the light of the sun on it. But showing a sword doesn't necessarily mean fighting. It can also suggest a joyful decisiveness.

"Resolve" and "decisiveness" are presented here as masculine virtues. This is the language of combat, a Lawrentian vehicle. In this passage "decisiveness" depends upon the exclusion of any admission that Circe is a "patriarchal" image: she merely stands for "a certain kind of matriarchal energy." In the emergent Yin and Yang of the male/female battle, Odysseus must raise his sword or risk becoming Oedipus or the Christ figure in Bly's "Crazy Carlson" who fails to find the father and falls back "into the mother's fearful tree." In *Fantasia of the Unconscious* Lawrence concludes that domesticity with women represents a sentimental and destructive self-consciousness. When they lost their primal fierceness men also lost their "masculine" connection to the planet.

The "soft" male, living his life in the sphere of the woman, is deprived of his unbridled gods: he is without volition or purpose. In his intimate relationships he practices a "leprous forbearance," a polite but rueful form of parlor chatter in which he never says what he means. The solution is a return to the wild:

> You've got to know that you're a man, and being a man means you must go on alone, ahead of the woman, to break a way through the old world into the new. And you've got to be alone. And you've got to start off ahead. And if you don't know which direction to take, look round for the man your heart will point out to you. And follow—and never look back. Because if Lot's wife, looking back, was turned to a pillar of salt, these miserable men, forever looking back to their women for guidance, they are miserable pillars of half-rotten tears.

This is the Lawrence who once announced that the introduction of woman as school teachers would have disastrous consequences for America. It's the Lawrence who believed that it's better for a man to be a passionate Vronsky that a milksoppish Tolstoi—who, after all, invented "Tolstoi-ism" and wore "that beastly peasant blouse." It's the Lawrence who lost his father twice a day: once to the mines and then to domestic life.

Looking to women for guidance is for Lawrence the greatest of modern illnesses. Masculinity, once a sacrament between the men and boys, has had its spiritual life broken by the intrusive mother-child relationship. Describing the boy who grows up entirely in the mother's domain Lawrence says, "the poor little devil never knows one moment when he is not encompassed by the beautiful, benevolent, idealistic, Botticelli-pure, and finally obscene love-will of the mother."

Iron John fashions its therapeutic plot in the service of this idea. It's a devotional book which argues that men can experience spiritual growth in a consequential way while living in the feminine domestic circle. In metaphorical terms, men must cross from the mother's house to that of the father. Bly cites examples from ritual cultures which sought to ensure the transformation of boys into men through ceremonies. Out in the wild the boys learn that growing up involves a series of wounds and in many instances they receive a ceremonial wound as a sign that they have crossed over into manhood. Bly asserts that once they've been initiated, young men have been "welcomed" into masculinity in a consequential way. They've learned "moistening" myths which "lead the young male far beyond his personal father and into the moistness of the swampy fathers who stretch back century after century."

In *Healing Fiction* James Hillman argues, as all archetypal psychoanalysts argue, that the best denouement in the battle of stories which constitutes therapy is finding a plot that's good for you. In Hillman's example, Freud gives Dora's story a new ending and thereby cures her. Until this moment the patient is a passive character, then the "revisioning of the story into a more intelligent, more imaginative plot" allows for the heroic comedy of self-development to begin. In *Iron John* an imaginative story for men is substituted for the one that's been generated both by television and the domestic world of women. Each has, according to Bly, devalued the role of the father. The fairy tale of Iron John and its refined interpretation combine to form a reverie in which medieval and Romantic images reverberate. As Bachelard has pointed out, in reverie the reader experiences recurring images, an inversion of logical categories, and proliferating ambivalence, all of which allow for multiple readings of symbolic language. The animated phenomenology of the Jungian imagery in Bly's *Iron John* is built on the resurrection of archetypal kings, swords, wild men, lost boys, as well as queens and fair maidens. A lost boy encounters the "genius" of the woods and learns that he must steal the golden key from under the queen's pillow if he's to escape her rule over his temperament. The key frees Iron John from the cage in which civilization has endeavored to secure him. In turn he becomes the "spirit guide" for the boy who would become a man.

The work of Joseph Campbell comes to mind, as well as the very popular books of Robert Johnson, a Jungian analyst who examines the grail legends to illustrate his ideas about becoming a man. The nostalgia for heroic icons suggests that masculinity is a "tabula rasa" or "vessel" onto which traditional constellations must be painted. Bly's archetypes are drawn from medieval romance and he presents them as autonomous metaphysical entities which inhabit the invisible sphere of each man's psychological life. These figures appear too in many of Bly's recent poems: the man in the black coat, the "invisible" bride who stands behind the physical bride, the "prodigal" son, etc. In *Iron John* the folk image which is utterly traditional and which depends upon popular occultist beliefs is presented as a psychological reality for men:

> There is a king in the imaginative or invisible world. We don't know how he got there. Perhaps human beings, after having loved the political king for centuries, lifted him up into the invisible world, or perhaps it went the other way round. At any rate, there is a King in sacred space. From his mythological world he acts as a magnet and rearranges human molecules. He enters the human psyche like a whirlwind, or a tornado, and houses fly up in the air. Whenever the word *king* or *queen* is spoken, something in the body trembles a little.

This interior king enacts an agreement with men: he will serve as an inner warrior, a guarantor of a strong and decisive emotional life if, in turn, the man learns how to protect his King. Bly notes that "a man whose King is gone doesn't know if he has the right to decide even how to spend the day. When my King is weak, I ask my wife or children what is the right thing to do."

In Bly's analysis, the man who temporizes is likely to fall prey to a woman's pertinacity, he becomes a "conductor" of feminine anger, and his warrior gives way. In a Jungian metallurgical metaphor, the man becomes mere copper:

> The more the man agrees to be copper, the more he becomes neither alive or dead, but a third thing, an amorphous, demasculinized, half-alive psychic conductor. I believe that a woman sometimes finds herself channeling the rage of dozens of dead women who could not speak their rage while alive. Conducting that rage is dangerous.

Bly's failure to probe the etiology of Jungian imagery leads to page after page of Masonic prose. The aim of this work is to create for men a revolutionary sense of selfhood, but reading through the book's geometrical arrangements of archetypes I'm reminded of Lawrence's assertion that "the *apparent* mutual understanding, in companionship between a man and a woman, is always an illusion, and always breaks down in the end." The elaboration of a heroic, figurative spirit-journey for men is consequent to such a view. The assumption that "fierceness" is a crucial attribute of the fully developed male is one that Lawrence would have celebrated, but that I cannot.

Note

1. For a fuller treatment of these ideas see "Walking Where the Plows Have Been Turning: Robert Bly and Female Consciousness" by Victoria Harris in *Of Solitude and Silence: Writings on Robert Bly*, edited by Richard Jones and Kate Daniels. (Boston: Beacon Press, 1981).

ESSAYS

◆

Back to the Snowy Fields

Wayne Dodd

Go back now twenty years later and you will still find it, lying silently in ditches beside the road, drifting noiselessly in with the snow at nightfall, standing dry and bristly in a field of weeds: *The spirit of the American prairie.* For that is what Robert Bly discovered for us in *Silence in the Snowy Fields*: the spirit of the American (prairie) landscape. Nowhere a trace, not one blurring linger, of language or perception from another culture or geography (all influences of Spanish, Chinese, Latin American—and other—poets notwithstanding). Just the American land, breathing into and through Bly. And us. I would even go so far as to say, if pressed, that however much else Bly may have contributed to the ferment of American letters, this has been perhaps his most important contribution—aside from the rich offering of the poems themselves. Once we had experienced *Silence in the Snowy Fields*, the body of America was never again the same to us—never again "merely" there, never again *external* to our own locus of spirit, no longer obedient to even the most carefully translated commands from "English" poetry. Since *Silence*, a developing generation of new young poets has been able to take for granted the subtle and important knowledge of our geographical lives that these poems provide. It has come to be a given, something which, once gained, one can never go back from: like self-consciousness. It has become a fundamental fact of, not just a *way* of knowing, but also a *what*.

But perhaps *consciousness* would be the more useful term, because it is *consciousness* that these poems are concerned with, consciousness of the world of solitude, of darkness, of isolation, of silence. That's what these poems are in touch with—the other world: sleep, the hidden, the unseen: what might be called, *the rest of it.* That's what the silence is filled with, what it frees us for: the other half, the realm of dark knowledge, night. Here the fields and rural buildings open out into that large dimension of (our) being. "We are all asleep in the outward man," Bly quotes Boehme, as an epigraph for the book, then goes on to offer poems which, taken all together, call to us, *Wake up! Wake up!*—in and through the inward man. This is the persistent urge one feels in *Silence in the Snowy Fields*: the urge to spiritual perception. We sense the need to

Reprinted, as revised by the author, from *Robert Bly: When Sleepers Awake*, edited by Joyce Peseroff (Ann Arbor: University of Michigan Press, 1984).

discover the other-dimensionality of being. "There is unknown dust that is near us," the poem "Surprised by Evening" begins. "Waves breaking on shores just over the hill,/Trees full of birds that we have never seen,/Nets drawn down with dark fish."

> The evening arrives; we look up and it is there,
> It has come through the nets of the stars,
> Through the tissues of the grass,
> Walking quietly over the asylums of the waters.

Everything, we sense, is fraught with incommensurably greater meaning. In a substantial number of these poems we have the overwhelming sense that somehow we have suddenly broken through a thin covering into a purely subjective landscape. And yet *it* is the one that seems more real; indeed, in those moments we believe that it is *the* real:

> Now we wake, and rise from bed, and eat breakfast—
> Shouts rise from the harbor of the blood,
> Mist, and masts rising, the knock of wooden tackle in the sunlight.
>
> Now we sing, and do tiny dances on the kitchen floor.
> Our whole body is like a harbor at dawn;
> We know that our master has left us for the day.
> ("Waking from Sleep")

> It is a pleasure, also, to be driving
> Toward Chicago, near dark,
> And see the lights in the barns.
> The bare trees more dignified than ever,
> Like a fierce man on his deathbed,
> And the ditches along the road half full of private snow.
> ("Three Kinds of Pleasures")

And in a poem such as "Return to Solitude" there is the implication that entire histories go on in a kind of subjective isolation, a place of solitude:

> What shall we find when we return?
> Friends changed, houses moved,
> Trees perhaps, with new leaves.

There is an urgency about the moments and events in these poems. Everything is darkly radiant with something which, Bly manages to suggest, we urgently need to know.

The dusk has come, a glow in the west, as if seen through the isinglass on old coal stoves, and the cows stand around the barn door; now the farmer looks up at the paling sky reminding him of death, and in the fields the bones of the corn rustle faintly in the last wind, and the half moon stands in the south.

Now the lights from barn windows can be seen through bare trees.

("Fall")

And at such times as these we don't know whether we fall, or rise, into greater awareness.

But of course the physical details, in Bly, are the essential ingredients, for they are the windows we see through, they are the doors we fall through, the vessels we find ourselves in.

Taking the Hands

Taking the hands of someone you love,
You see they are delicate cages . . .
Tiny birds are singing
In the secluded prairies
And in the deep valleys of the hand.

The poems continually plunge inside: ourselves, the landscape, the face of the American prairie. The spiritual content, we feel, does not exist as some detached or detachable "significance"; it is the content of *this* body (or bodies): *these* places, *these* moments, *these* people. And if one should have a sudden epiphany, a lunge to an unconscious knowing of the gestalt of wholeness in some moment, it will likely be while driving toward the Lac Qui Parle River, through small towns with porches built right on the ground. Or while walking in a corn field. Or among odorous weeds. Authentic language, Bly says elsewhere, arises out of a depth, "coming up from . . . every source." And what Bly offers, in the images and language of these poems, is not an excess of originality, but an ecstasy of appropriateness and recognition.

A successful poem, it seems to me, can profitably be talked of as if it were a living thing, through and in whose body we find beauty, density, grace, *further* life. All bodies are different of course, as all persons, all poems, all experiences. But even the most limited glimpse of a person's physical presence, the merest hint, can bring the whole of it rushing into our consciousness: the line of a neck, the sound of a familiar footstep, the lovely curve where hip rounds into flank—suddenly we know the whole of it: person, poem, place. In *Silence in the Snowy Fields* the *whole* Bly is reaching for is that insistent sense of spiritual reality which the *family* of poems must identify. And we know what the family, individual in their bodies will look like:

The light was dawn. Like a man who has come home
After seeing many dark rivers, and will soon go again,

The dawn stood there with a quiet gaze;
Our eyes met through the top leaves of the young ash.

Dawn has come. The clouds floating in the east have turned white.
The fence posts have stopped being a part of the darkness.
The depth has disappeared from the puddles on the ground.
I look up angrily at the light.

("Getting Up Early")

    Poem after poem in this remarkable book successfully enlarges a bare-bones narrative, exemplum-like in its simplicity, with an incomparably greater sense of existence, a complex presence of life. We come to be aware, as Bly is aware, of the abiding presence of a hidden order, the sacred masked by the ordinary. Poems arrive to suddenly opened vistas:

> We know the road; as the moonlight
> Lifts everything, so in a night like this
> The road goes on ahead, it is all clear.
>
> ("After Working")

or to vague, indefinable threats:

> The barn is full of corn, and moving toward us now,
> Like a hulk blown toward us in a storm at sea;
> All the sailors on deck have been blind for many years.
>
> ("Snowfall in the Afternoon")

For there *is* threat in *Silence.* Water:land, dark:daylight, waking:sleeping—these are the antinomies of our life the poems embody. And within the antinomies lies, often, a susceptibility to the forlornness in *Silence*:

> Something homeless is looking on the long roads—
> A dog lost since midnight, a small duck
> Among the odorous reeds,
> Or a tiny box-elder bug searching for the window pane.
> Even the young sunlight is lost on the window pane,
> Moving at night like a diver among the bare branches silently lying on
>   the floor.

Indeed there are times when it is impossible to tell whether the waking is a source more of gain or of loss. Even the beautiful and brilliant (and oft-quoted) "But, at last, the quiet waters of the night will rise,/And our skin shall see far off, as it does under water"—even this is, finally, ambiguous (I think richly so) in its emotional implication. There is a sense of *duende* about the darkness, "like a paling sky reminding [us] of death." So much happens in these poems at the very moment of shift—from day to night, from sleeping to waking, etc. Events suddenly open up like doors, and a world walks strangely and disturbingly in.

Afternoon Sleep

I

I was descending from the mountains of sleep.
Asleep I had gazed east over a sunny field,
And sat on the running board of an old Model A.
I awoke happy, for I had dreamt of my wife,
And the loneliness hiding in grass and weeds
That lies near a man over thirty, and suddenly enters.

II

When Joe Sjolie grew tired, he sold his farm,
Even his bachelor rocker, and did not come back.
He left his dog behind in the cob shed.
The dog refused to take food from strangers.

III

I drove out to that farm when I awoke;
Alone on a hill, sheltered by trees.
The matted grass lay around the house.
When I climbed the porch, the door was open.
Inside were old abandoned books,
And instructions to Norwegian immigrants.

The movement back and forth between dreaming and waking, between unconscious and conscious is a fundamental one in these poems, as in "Remembering in Oslo the Old Picture of the Magna Carta":

The girl in a house dress, pushing open the window,
Is also the fat king sitting under the oak tree,
And garbage men, thumping their cans, are
Crows still cawing.
And the nobles are offering the sheet to the king.
One thing is also another thing, and the doomed galleons,
Hung with trinkets, hove by the coast, and in the blossoms
Of trees are still sailing on their long voyage from Spain;
I too am still shocking grain, as I did as a boy, dog tired,
And my great-grandfather steps on his ship.

Here is a move not only to unconscious knowing, but almost to a kind of *racial* knowledge, sweeping away differences of both time and space in the identification offered in the last two lines. And as in a poem such as "Getting Up

Early," we experience a form of double existence in ourselves. The poem has a sort of commutative effect, causing us suddenly to experience the potent flow of spiritual energy back and forth between the two poles, conscious and unconscious. Or the movement can lead to the momentary experience of pure timelessness, the extension of a perception into endless duration, as in "A Late Spring Day in My Life":

> A silence hovers over the earth:
> The grass lifts lightly in the heat
> Like the ancient wing of a bird.
> A horse gazes steadily at me.

Needless to say, the duration is achieved through the induction, via the images, of a flow at once into and outside of the speaker, as well as backward and forward in time, so that in the experience itself, inside and outside become one, as do past and present. Indeed, it might be worthwhile to note that a sort of reverie, a dreaming recovery, is frequently an effective instrument in these poems for evoking the unconscious.

> We want to go back, to return to the sea,
> The sea of solitary corridors,
> And halls of wild nights,
> Explosions of grief,
> Diving into the sea of death,
> Like the stars of the wheeling Bear:
> ("Return to Solitude")

Memory (Mnemosyne), it should be remembered, was long ago identified as the mother of poetry. And rightly so. Surely a primary force in the impulse to poetry is the need to rescue the life of the individual spirit from the constant fall into unawareness, to recover, in M. L. Rosenthal's words, "past states of existence, isolated and framed and glowing with their own life as well as with the emotion that has recalled them—something in the preset moment that is shared with the past state." Memory, reverie, the unconscious—they share, in some close, symbiotic way, a common, if at times dark, area of the human mind. Memory is perhaps like a heretofore missing conductor, now suddenly completing the circuit that makes possible the flow further into, and out of, ourselves—and our world. It provides in some way, I would guess, the emotional force field that makes possible a sense of temporal simultaneity and spatial diffusion. If poetry depends absolutely on its idiosyncratic truthfulness to the poet's own sense of reality, it depends equally on a powerful stroke of memory, memory of the living quality of an experience that in part was not a conscious experience. For Bly, in *Silence in the Snowy Fields*, this is memory of experience irradiated by meaning and significance—always in danger of being lost. And the poems continually put us in contact with an urgent sense of the numinous, out of which we wake (or fade) into *mere* existence. The second (or middle) section of *Silence* is entitled "Awakening," but the poems there lead one to an awakening that is more an awakening into, than out of, sleep. Here—in dreams, in reveries, in dark descents, in flights into the unconscious—we wake, paradoxically, into the other dimension of ourselves.

And always we are aware of our bodies—stiff-fingered and clumsy with cold, or alive like a harbor at dawn, or alert to the sound of corn stalks in the wind, to the dark pull of a spot of earth we could feel safe in, to the odor of leaves on the wet earth, to the feel of moonlight on our branches. And then we are, at last, fully inside the land of ourselves. "If I reached my hands down, near the earth," we say,

> I could take handfuls of darkness!
> A darkness was always there, which we never noted.

So after *Silence in the Snowy Fields* we were never quite the same again, either. The darkness in us was never the same again. Nor the snow that covers the bare fields waiting always behind our eyes. Nor the barns we hold ourselves to the remembered earth by. Nor the houses we are adrift in—in Minnesota, Ohio, Michigan, Illinois, and elsewhere all over the great body of the land our breath freezes and warms in. Sometimes, now, a cowbell sounds from so deep within us, or the eyes of a horse gaze so clearly into our consciousness, that we wake suddenly into the present which *Silence in the Snowy Fields* seems always to have been a bright—and dark—part of.

The Live World

Paul A. Lacey

If Robert Bly's magazine, *The Sixties*, has an editorial policy, it is to probe the American psyche, to diagnose its ills and offer means for it to become healthy. Whole issues of the magazine are put together as coordinated assaults on the evils of American culture. In critical articles and by precept and example in the poetry it publishes, and especially in the foreign poets whose works it translates, *The Sixties* opposes the egocentricity, formalism, sensationalism, and subservience to dead traditions which its editors see as characterizing modern American writing. Often the magazine connects these failures of the psyche with the larger evils of American society—our involvement in Vietnam, the ugliness of urban life, our misuse of nature. It is the purest consistency which has led Robert Bly to cancel the subscriptions to his magazine of universities which have taken government defense contracts. The argument is frequently farfetched; Bly acknowledges that refusing his magazine to the university library makes no impact on the huge institutes and centers which are supported by defense contracts, but he sees a connection between the failure of our imagination in art and the failure of our moral imagination in the way we act as a nation. And for Bly, particularly, the making of a poem is a moral act, an opening up to new depths in the self, deeper than the ego, from which not only words and images but acts must arise. "All expression of hidden feelings involves opposition to the existing order."

How these preoccupations articulate throughout Bly's work is richly exemplified in the eighth number of *The Sixties* (Spring 1966). The entire issue, which contains translations of nineteenth century German poetry, Bly's review of Lowell's *For the Union Dead*, and a long review of James Wright's poetry, takes coherent form around Bly's introduction to the translations, "The Dead World and the Live World." In this essay, Bly distinguishes two kinds of writers, those who bring us "news of the human mind" and those who bring us "news of the universe." The first produce poetry locked in the ego, while the poetry of the second "reaches out in waves over everything that is alive."

American literature, he argues, is dominated by those who study the human faculties of feeling, will, and intellect as though the human being

Reprinted from *The Inner War* by Paul A. Lacey, copyright © 1972 Fortress Press. Used by permission of Augsburg Fortress.

existed without reference to the rest of existence. "Writers of this kind regard the 'I' as something independent, isolated, entire in itself, and they throw themselves into studying its turns and impulses." The culture which produces literature which never studies the human in relation to the non-human or even in relation to lives in other countries, he argues, "will bomb foreign populations very easily, since it has no sense of anything real beyond its own ego." And the poets, no matter how critical of or alienated from their culture—and surely the vast majority of the writers Bly is criticizing share with him their opposition to the Vietnam War and the social evils which it has come to represent—who give us only "news of the human mind" can only take refuge in the sensational and extreme. "Poets of the sort," he says, referring specifically to the confessional poets, "will accept calmly the extinction of the passenger pigeon or the blue whale."

That is the dead world, the world of the merely human, which, to remain interesting, must be exaggerated and inflated. It is a world without genuine interiority, for Bly. Poems made from the stuff of that world will necessarily deal with the inflation of the ego, with the kind of excessive self-consciousness which Dostoyevski called a disease, with the suffering of alienation from others. The live world, on the other hand, is aware of an additional energy beyond the human energies of feeling, will, and intellect. This energy within the self Bly follows Georg Groddeck in calling the *Gott-natur*, which he translates as the "holy-nature."

> The *Gott-natur* senses the interdependence of all things alive, and longs to bring them all inside a work of art. The work of these poets is an elaborate expression of the *Gott-natur*. What results is a calmness.[1]

He calls for a poetry which goes deep into the human being, "much deeper than the ego, and at the same time is aware of many other beings," which is aware of human nature as a part of nature, and he cites the poetry of Gary Snyder, and Japanese and Chinese poetry as examples of awareness of *Gott-natur*.

The implications of Bly's essay are wide-reaching. To sketch in just a few of the most obvious, the poet of the universe would know both the inner and the outer world as one; he would therefore be a political rebel in his society even if he would not call himself alienated from it; he could not let his nation bomb foreign populations *or* exterminate the passenger pigeon. In his attack on James Dickey's *Buckdancer's Choice*, he says if the anguish of the poems were real, "We would feel terrible remorse as we read, we would stop what we are doing, we would break the television set with an ax, we would throw ourselves on the ground sobbing."[2]

The poetry of the universe should differ from that of others as much in form as in theme. While it tried to bring the whole live world within a poem, the result should be calmness, not the extravagance or self-generated excitement of a Ginsberg or Kerouac. And indeed sparsity, rather than long catalogues of things, characterizes the poetry Bly admires and writes himself. And though critics speak of "subjectivism" when talking about Bly's poetry, he cites with approval Groddeck's claim that Goethe's short poems are impersonal, as though "not created by a person but by nature." The deeply subjective poem, one which reaches the deepest parts of the self, should somehow become impersonal. Emotions would not be suppressed, but excitement over one's experiences or feelings would be channeled and diffused into this universe of which one was a part. The reading of oneself into the world, so typical of the romantic's attempt to overcome the subject-object dichotomy, would not be inappropriate so much as useless as a poetic strategy.

Further light on the poetic forms which might come from this new consciousness of the inner world comes from the article on the poetry of James Wright which appears in the same number of *The Sixties*. The essay is signed "Crunk," the usual signature for the longer critical pieces in the magazine, but the views and sentiments are consistent enough with Bly's that guessing at authorship seems unnecessary.

The essay, which reviews Wright's work from *The Green Wall* (1957) through *The Branch Will Not Break* (1963), takes on in battle virtually the whole American literary establishment to argue that Wright has freed himself from what Crunk sees as the typical American concern for discursive reasoning, tight metrical form, moral and philosophical truisms in poetry. The world of such a poem is, of course, the dead world Bly speaks of; Crunk makes Kenyon College at the height of the Ransom years his symbol for it. Writing a poem meant climbing out of the world into a walled-in garden with tame animals for decoration. "When people praised order in a poem, as they did much in those days, they were praising the ordered world possible to them only in a poem." Crunk's argument is not with order or form, however, so long as the poem can exploit its form to give us inklings of the terror, ferocity, and wildness which exist in the world. "It is the world which has these things in their full force. The work of art shows their tails escaping under the door, and we know by this that they are in the next room."[3]

When the new critics and the poets they arose to explicate spoke of poetry as existing in and of itself, without reference to the world of experience, they were fighting a rearguard action against science and empiricism. When even so sensitive a reader as I. A. Richards could try to save poetry by justifying it as composed of pseudo-statements for the sake of organizing emotions, and so eminent a practitioner as T. S. Eliot was content to speak of poetry as merely a higher form of amusement, the battle was desperate. Poets and critics retreated behind walls like medieval monks, trying to preserve something from the barbarians. Those who climbed the other way, out of the poem as a world "in little," an independent, self-contained "mode of existence," were also those Bly excoriates in his review of *For the Union Dead*, the *Partisan Review* writers, "the alienated establishment intellectual" concerned with the interaction of politics and art.

To go out where the wildness is means to open oneself to guilt, paranoia, self-hatred; to reach through that wildness, in the self and the world, to the calmness Bly speaks of, calls for new ways of making poetry—new models, new expectations, new ways to employ language. Crunk tells us that, after reading Georg Trakl's poetry in 1952–53, James Wright concluded that his own work was not poetry. "It had not helped anyone else to solitude, and had not helped him toward solitude."

On the basis of these two essays in this remarkable issue of *The Sixties*, it is possible to trace out what Robert Bly expects from poetry, what its materials are, and how it should be written. Crunk attacks the critics of Wright's poetry who want "meanings" and "relationships" established by logic and association, arguing that such discursive writing simply goes over already familiar intellectual and psychological ground. Putting "thought" and "meanings" in poetry means simply being able to handle moral platitudes; establishing "relationships" through association means staying within the bounds of those areas of consciousness already mapped, "areas like the old Canadian wilderness that has now become 'rationalized'." Poetry, for Bly, should bring us "news of the universe," and Crunk reminds us that the poet who gets far enough in himself, back into the unmapped regions of the brain, will bring back "some bad news about himself, some anguish that discursive reasoning had for a long time protected him against." Poetry should bring to consciousness what is hidden, not merely from the ego, but from those depths in which we are aware of kinship with the universe. Somehow anguish, bad news, self-hatred, paranoia—all of them necessary consequences of this penetration to deeper levels of consciousness—must be transformed, through the energy of the image, into goodwill toward the self, calmness, and solitude.

When we turn to the poems in Bly's first book, *Silence in the Snowy Fields* (1962), we see how he exemplifies the principles he enunciates in his criticism. What is chiefly significant about the book is not its themes but the forms in which they are developed. In a prefatory statement on his work, Bly speaks of the connection between poetry and simplicity and points out that the structure of the poems is simple—many of them are made up of three parts, with a time lapse between them, and "If there is any poetry in the poems, it is in the white spaces between the stanzas." Winter landscapes occur frequently; darkness, dryness, blankness characterize many of the scenes the poet reflects upon, and loneliness and death are thematic preoccupations. But none of this strikes us as threat or deprivation. Landscape and theme are somehow affirmative, taken into the realm of silence so that we may reflect on them with a kind of detached enjoyment.

We are rarely surprised by anything in Bly's poems; even the tricks of perception are deliberately kept on the surface, rendered most often through similes so that we are kept aware that one thing is not being forcibly *made into* another by a human mind. The mind plays with resemblances for its own enlightenment, but the things themselves keep their own identity. At the same time, because there is no insistence on something *made* by the poet, and we believe that we see connections only because the poet does, we accept that "One thing is also another."

> The darkness drifts down like snow on picked cornfields
> In Wisconsin: and on these black trees
> Scattered, one by one,
> Through the winter fields—
> We see stiff weeds and brownish stubble,
> And white snow left now only in the wheeltracks of the
> 　　combine.
>
> 　　　　　　　　　　　　　　　　("Three Kinds of Pleasures")

The stanza contains four simple adjectives, one unobtrusive simile, two verbs in the active present tense, neither of them very kinetic in effect, and three other verbals. These provide all the *action*, if that is the right word for it, in the stanza. What we have is description which, except for one simile, uses language almost purely *denotatively* or *presentationally*. But the effect is far greater than cataloguing parts of speech can suggest, for the very impersonality of the scene and its independence of an observer, work on the reader, and "we see" becomes the pivot on which everything turns. We become aware not merely of the starkness of black trees scattered among winter fields, but of the play of black and white implied by the simile and repeated by the image of white snow in the wheeltracks. We are used to snow drifting down on dark fields, as we are used to dark wheeltracks through snow; reverse the images and we become aware of the interpenetration of white and black, light and darkness. It is like looking at the Chinese ideograph for nothingness, *mu*, executed in a thick, black flowing image against a stark white surface; one knows that the image *means* emptiness, nothingness, the incomprehensible. It denotes what cannot be denoted. All our ordinary experience leads us to imagine nothingness as like the blank white paper, but that blankness has been violated by another ordinary way of expressing the concept, the written word. The play of black and white, background and foreground, image and imagination, what the eye sees and what the mind's eye conceives, takes us beyond ordinary experience as we contemplate the ideograph. Such an interpenetration of objects and images, where "one thing is also another" while remaining truly itself, characterizes Bly's most effective poetry.

It is not arbitrary association which leads a reader to think of Zen calligraphy of Chinese ideographs in connection with Bly's poetry. The haiku of Japan and the drinking song of fourth century China provide rich models for what he wants to do. His admiration for the lyric poetry of the six dynasties runs through both his criticism and his poetry. In the poetry it not only appears thematically, in such a poem as "Chrysanthemums," dedicated to Tao Yüan-ming, it exerts a profound influence on the form. Flatness of statement, ellipsis, simple metaphors and similes, juxtaposing of images so that a scene and the emotion it evokes flow together, characterize the style of his models. Through this style they reflect the inwardness which is so important to Bly.

The poet in such poetry is not a *maker* who imposes shape upon existence or creates a verbal world to retreat to, but neither is he a *seer* or visionary, as those terms have been used to speak of symbolist or surrealist poetry. For the *seer*, who twists and falsifies ordinary experience for the sake of extracting its inner meaning, frequently succeeds only in freeing locked-up areas of his own psyche. Dreams, fantasies, verbal play, freudian wit, the worlds of unreality and madness typify theme and method for the *seer*. And Bly has some harsh words to say for such poems, which become "like a tank, unable to maneuver on soft ground."

> How strange to think of giving up all ambition!
> Suddenly I see with such clear eyes
> The white flake of snow
> That has just fallen in the horse's mane!

This poem, "Watering the Horse," can serve as an example of how the oriental simplicity of his poetry reveals the inner world. Like a haiku, it does not lead us through the steps of a meditation, but distills the meditation into its conclusion and confirms it by the clarity of image which follows upon it. The notion of giving up ambition, letting go of this world, takes the poet by surprise. Thought produces a feeling: "how strange." Once again, the pivot of the poem is the simple verb, "I see," and once again it carries us into the life of things. Clear sight follows insight; thought, emotion, sight become a single experience, an enlightenment, anchored in the vivid perception of a white flake of snow in a horse's mane.

To speak at such length of a twenty-eight word poem may seem a sad example of breaking a butterfly on the wheel, but perhaps this butterfly is strong enough to survive. In any case, "Watering the Horse" is a good test case for deciding whether one wants to read any more of Bly, for it shows in miniature his strengths and weaknesses. Not every reader will be persuaded of the depth of excitement signaled by two exclamation points in four lines. The poem's terms are so narrow that even the most willing reader may find that he cannot enter the inner world of the poem without some more detailed confirmation of the experience. Even the longer poems in *Silence in the Snowy Fields* will frustrate or please in exactly the same way, however. Scenes are rendered presentationally, as they make their immediate impact on the senses. Vivid images seem to be deliberately suppressed; the verb "to be" predominates, as though the poet's chief purpose is to affirm the simple existence of what he sees. In "Driving Toward the Lac Qui Parle River," some form of "to be" appears five times in the first six-line stanza, always working as a copula to link each sense impression or experience with the rest. Nothing stands subordinate to anything else, because these are not ideas to be linked into an argument but physical images to convey what the poet means by "I am happy."

> I am driving; it is dusk; Minnesota.
> The stubble field catches the last growth of sun.
> The soybeans are breathing on all sides.
> Old men are sitting before their houses on carseats
> In the small towns. I am happy,
> The moon rising above the turkey sheds.

The language and imagery are deliberately flat, but as we look more closely at the buried metaphor in "The stubble field *catches* the last growth of sun," called to our attention only by the turn of phrase in the second half of the line, details lift up from their context. Dead or inanimate things live; the stubble field catches, the sun grows, the soybeans breathe. The old men sitting before their houses and the soybeans breathing partake of the same quiet vitality. In many of Bly's poems, animate and inanimate objects change places or lend their natures to one another, with the effect of stressing liveliness, not deadness. Thus the rising of the moon, a kind of accompaniment to the poet's happiness, becomes a sign of vitality like the sun's growth.

The poet enters this scene in "the small world of the car" which "Plunges through the deep fields of night." For a moment the reader is aware of the worlds represented in the poem, the larger world of living, breathing things and the closed independent world of the car which passes through it. But the car is also a "solitude covered with iron," an image for a peculiarly contemporary hermit's hut, a place of retreat to solitude. "Inner" and "outer" are unhelpful terms for describing these worlds, however, for they commit us to subject-object, good-bad dichotomies despite our best intentions.

These two worlds do not stand over against each other as opponents in a dualistic universe, for, whatever happens in the poetry of *The Light Around the Body* (1967), his second book, Bly does not intend to speak dualistically. He therefore takes what would be a stock image for the evils of industrialism— Detroit and all its works—puts it in a setting which would be a stock image for the simple life, and reverses their usual connotations. The car plunging into the deep fields of night becomes the inner world of man penetrating into the deepness of nature, and nature in turn plunges into the "solitude covered with iron," for the car is "penetrated by the noise of crickets." This last image achieves much the same effect as a famous haiku by Basho, "The Stillness":

> So still:
> into rocks it pierces—
> the locust-shrill.[4]

Just as in Basho's poem stillness and the high-pitched sound of the locust blend natures, become one, and are then capable of piercing into the hardness of rocks, so the insubstantiality of the crickets' sound penetrates the hardness of iron. The two worlds interpenetrate and become one; "inner" and "outer" cannot distinguish their natures, for each borrows attributes from the other. Nothing has a fixed nature, nothing is good or bad; we perceive the holy-nature's energy running through the man-made world of the car as well as through the silent fields and the noise of crickets.

The final stanza of the poem extends this development. "Water kneeling in the moonlight" and lamplight which "falls on all fours in the grass" effect the same kind of interpenetration. The water comes to life in the natural light, while the man-made light comes to life as it falls on the grass. When the poet reaches the river, where for the first time other people enter the poem, the rising moon which was the signature for his happiness in the opening stanza is now full and at its height, covering the river. The poet reaches his destination, physically and spiritually—a flowing river bathed in moonlight, on which a few people in a boat are talking low. The world of nature and the world of men, of human conversation and natural beauty, are one. All the details of the poem, the reversals of expectations, the exchanges of attributes and images of inter-penetration, work together to substantiate the phrase "I am happy."

Speaking of Georg Trakl's influence on James Wright's poetry, Crunk says, "In Trakl a series of images makes a series of events." The same may be said of the best of Bly's poetry. Often we are aware of the events as a series of correspondences between the outward scene and the buried life within the poet. So in "Hunting Pheasants in a Cornfield," the poet asks, "What is so strange about a tree alone in an open field?" and arrives at his answer by describing the scene and discovering that the mind is like the tree, "It stands apart with small creatures near its roots." In "Night" he perceives the same kind of interplay between surface and depth, the high and the subterranean. The box elders are full of joy "Obeying what is beneath them," the butterfly carries loam on his wings, the toad bits of gravel in his skin, as though they too had sprung from the earth itself. Everything lies asleep, obeying the night and what is beneath them, gaining vitality from their chthonic origin. The correspondences are not always explicit or detailed—indeed they could not be without degenerating into the kind of moralistic platitudes inveighed against in *The Sixties*—but in the best poems the reader feels acted on by this hidden life to which the images point. In "Where We Must Look for Help," for example, Bly substitutes the Babylonian account of the flood for the Genesis story, so that the sign of hope does not come with the dove of peace but the "spider-colored crow." The Noah story is gone; what remains is the dove who found no resting place, the swallows who always return home, and the ugly crow—which in Genesis is the first to leave the ark but in this poem flies on the third day. The poem divests these images of any symbolic quality they might have gotten from the original tale. They operate on us, therefore, not as symbols of peace or flight, but as simple, even despised, fellow-creatures. The image of hope and help is ugly, tough, a scavenger.

> The crow, the crow, the spider-colored crow,
> The crow shall find new mud to walk upon.

Silence in the Snowy Fields organizes its poems around the epigraph from Jacob Boehme, "We are all asleep in the outward man." The book is divided into three parts, "Eleven Poems of Solitude," "Awakening," and "Silence on the Roads." While it would be hard to argue that each poem belongs exactly where it is within this arrangement, the groupings themselves tell us something important about the aim of the whole book. The poems of solitude are, for the most part, quiet meditations anchored in and tested by the stark landscape of late fall and winter in the upper midwest of America. Inner and outer cohere and interpenetrate, and the poet speaks of joy and happiness. Solitude brings one kind of awakening, a cleansed perception of the unity of things.

"Awakening," the second section of the poems, touches more directly upon death, sorrow, division between the two worlds. Thom Gunn, arguing that the differentiating human consciousness has not come into Bly's world yet and that it is "a world of total innocence, without evil, and simply for enjoyment," has not sufficiently considered this section of the book. "Unrest," "Awakening," "Depression," and "A Man Writes to a Part of Himself" speak ominously of the dark world. They also demonstrate the burden it places on Bly's imagination when he must deal with the two worlds in opposition. In "A Man Writes to a Part of Himself," the speaker writes as though to his wife, whom he imagines starving, exposed to the elements, hiding in a cave. He describes himself "On the streets of a distant city, laughing/With many appointments," though returning at night to sleep in a bare hotel room, "a room of poverty." The poem is simple and touching; the separation within the self, conveyed by simple contrasts between cave and bare room, sorrow and artificial gaiety, husband and wife, engages our sympathies. At the same time, we recognize that the poem rests on the stereotype of the traveling salesman or businessman away from home. If we could imagine Willy Loman having enough inner life to write a poem, this would be what we would expect. The final lines of the poem put the question:

> Which of us two then is worse off?
> And how did this separation come about?

But only the extreme simplicity of the poem saves it from the effect of the stereotype. It is too easy to see the businessman as representing the dead world completely cut off from the live world represented by a stereotyped feminine nature.

"Silence on the Roads," the final section of the book, contains poems which seem most clearly to represent the clarity of sight which comes when the outward man finally awakes, when he has experienced both the healing of solitude and the unrest and depression of knowing the world of spiritual darkness.

> We know the road; as the moonlight
> Lifts everything, so in a night like this
> The road goes on ahead, it is all clear.

In Bly's first book, there is little of what Thom Gunn and other critics want when they speak of "thought" in poetry. Indeed, Bly's whole program repudiates any such content as valid for the creations of the new imagination. While it is not accurate to say, as Gunn and others have argued, that the world of these poems is prelapsarian, it is true that there are few human beings in the poetry and "it is only by other human beings and their acts that his view of the world can be tested." With *The Light Around the Body* that issue rises in compelling fashion. If the first book had little "argument"—because showing the inner world required little—the second book takes its shape from the argument that we live in two worlds which do not meet as one. Inwardness can be excessively private, and we may need more evidence to be persuaded of the happiness or joy the poet announces than the cluster of images in the poem provides. In *Silence in the Snowy Fields* we are often willing to suspend rational judgment and take the statements as given. In *The Light Around the Body* Bly wants to persuade us, but the poetry does not testify to the coherence of inner and outer world, it criticizes the turmoil and falseness of the latter from the standpoint of a longing for inwardness. When other people enter this poetry, they are intruders and destroyers.

The influence of Boehme, at least as represented by the epigraphs introducing four out of five sections of the book, has increased. The first section, "The Two Worlds," is introduced by a passage which speaks of our being generated out of both the inward and the outward worlds and needing therefore to speak and be understood in two languages. The passage offers no hope that these two languages can be translated into one another or that they are equally capable of telling the truth. In fact, as the passage puts it, "according to the outward man, we are in this world, and according to the inward man, we are in the inward world. . . ." The quotation from Boehme which introduces the second section, "The Various Arts of Poverty and Cruelty," makes the point more explicitly: we have been locked up and led blindfolded by the wise of this world, who have done so with their *art* and rationality, "so that we have had to see with their eyes." "We have been captured by the spirit of the outward world . . . and now death has us," Bly quotes Boehme in the fourth section, "In Praise of Grief."

"Monistic systems develop in ages of comparative tranquility, dualistic and pluralistic systems in ages of doubt and transition. Boehme was dualistic, his attention was fixed both on the sensual and the super-sensual."[5] Certainly Robert Bly is a powerful witness to the turmoil of this age and demands of poetry that it describe the inward changes which grow out of the profound changes in the outward world in our time.

> There is an imagination which realizes the sudden new change in the life of humanity, of which the Nazi camps, the terror of modern wars, the santification of the viciousness of advertising, the turning of everyone into workers, the profundity of associations, is all a part, and the relationships unexplained. . . . There is an imagination which assembles the three kingdoms within one poem: the dark figures of politics, the world of streetcars, and the ocean world.[6]

In *The Light Around the Body* the two worlds are those of the damned and the saved, the evil and the virtuous. The interpenetration between the two worlds for the enrichment of each, which was an important influence in the earlier poetry, rarely occurs in the second book. In "The Two Worlds," for example, the representatives of the outward world are Romans, executives, merchants, accountants, President Johnson's cabinet. They are not ignorant of the inner world; they are its enemies. The conflict between the two worlds is a death-struggle. The inner world is identified with solitude, sorrow, love, and especially with the mother. In "Romans Angry About the Inner World," the Romans seize Drusia, whose crime is that she has "seen our mother/In the other world," and torture her to death, for "The two Romans had put their trust/In the outer world." Romans, executioners, and executives appear in the poem, as though any term would readily substitute for the other. The other world terrifies them; it is "like a thorn/In the ear of a tiny beast!"

"Smothered by the World," "A Dream of Suffocation," and "Watching Television" speak of the horror of this world, where machines and men become interchangeable and "Accountants hover over the earth like helicopters." The events of this world and the consequences of its history are so inimical to the inner world that, as the poet watches television, the body cells "bay" and "the inner streets fill with a chorus of barks." Finally

> The filaments of the soul slowly separate:
> The spirit breaks, a puff of dust floats up,
> Like a house in Nebraska that suddenly explodes.

The poet does not lead us to observe or enter a scene from the calm center of a unified life; we accompany an angry prophet, savagely parodying and condemning the false religion he sees. "The Busy Man Speaks" illustrates the point. The Busy Man intones a two-part creed, first renouncing the faith he will not follow, then affirming his allegiance to the other. He renounces the mother of solitude, of art, of love, of human and physical nature, of Christ. He will give himself only to the father, the foundation for what might be called the religion of outward man, the worship of business, cheerfulness, righteousness, and the practice of the Protestant virtues.

> From the Chase National Bank
> An arm of flame has come, and I am drawn
> To the desert, to the parched places, to the landscape of zeros;
> And I shall give myself away to the father of righteousness,
> The stones of cheerfulness, the steel of money, the father of
>   rocks.

In his criticism, Bly has been preoccupied with defining the new imagination which will explore the unknown country, the "change in inward life which corresponds to the recent changes in outward life." When he catalogues those changes, however—and the list always includes industrialism, modern advertising, concentration camps, and rarely much that is hopeful—we are forced to conclude that his own earlier poetry does not show us *correspondences* but *compensations* or *alternatives* to the changes in outward life. His midwestern landscapes are made timeless by being made historyless, or the history is innocent because naive and unselfconscious. "Some day I will go back, and inhabit again/The sleepy ground where Harding was born."

History has entered the world of *The Light Around the Body*, and timelessness means only that the sins of the past are eternally present, or, as Bly puts it in the title of one poem, "After the Industrial Revolution, All Things Happen at Once.' The blank landscape of the midwest now becomes a palimpsest on which every generation has written its bloody crimes. And we have a vision, in Aldous Huxley's words, of time apprehended as one damned thing after another. Bly telescopes time to bring the Hessians at Trenton, the Whiskey Boys, Coxey's army together as one army, Henry Cabot Lodge, Henry Ford, Charles Wilson together as a single lying sloganeer. Similarly, "As the Asian War Begins" describes Conestoga wagons filled with murderers crossing the Platte River, in "Hatred of Men With Black Hair" those who praise Tshombe and the Portuguese in Angola are those who skinned Little Crow and overthrew Chief Joseph, and in "At a March Against the Vietnam War" the poet sees the darkness the Puritans brushed as they went out to kill turkeys.

> Underneath all the cement of the Pentagon
> There is a drop of Indian blood preserved in snow:
> Preserved from a trail of blood that once led away
> From the stockade, over the snow, the trail now lost.

This stanza sums up American history; the Pentagon, a symbol for irrational, evil power to people who share Bly's political views, stands like an altar over the sacralizing drop of blood, the saint's relic from which it takes its strength. The religion is the worship of power—of business, righteousness, and stones—"We make war/Like a man anointing himself." In "Hearing Men Shout at Night on Macdougal Street," the poet translates the present noise into the sounds of the first New England slave-ships setting out. Politicians—Andrew Jackson, Theodore Roosevelt, John F. Kennedy, Lyndon Johnson, Dean Rusk—become devil-figures in the poetry, and American history becomes demonolatry. Apocalyptic provides the tone—"The world will soon break up into small colonies of the saved,"—but the apocalypticism does not rest in a promise of deliverance but only in a conviction that we must atone for the evil being done. The American self-hatred Crunk spoke of in James Wright's poetry permeates Bly's work in *The Light Around the Body*. The energy and promise of human evolution become perverted into "The Great Society," where man is unnaturally cultivated to change places with the machinery he created to serve him. Evolution and history seemed to have a direction and goal, but they have been lost or perverted: "Hands developed with terrible labor by apes/Hang from the sleeves of evangelists." In "The Fire of Despair Has Been Our Saviour," Bly reflects on the course of human history since the Ice Age, the tracks leading out of the snowbound valley of that life. Those tracks have been lost, even as the trail of blood from the stockade was lost and only one drop of Indian blood remains enshrined under the Pentagon.

> This autumn, I
> Cannot find the road
> That way: the things that we must grasp,
> The signs, are gone, . . .

The Light Around the Body is a despairing book. The solitude Bly invited in his earlier works has given way to isolation; the natural world which he celebrated and through which he saw a spiritual, inner world, the correspondences instinct with value and significance, have gone, and only a pale compensation for the outer world gleams through. The poetry does not speak of hope but only of an apocalyptic day of wrath in which atonement might occur. Bly keeps faith in an inner world, but it stands in judgment on this life rather than infusing it with moral energy.

> . . . where has the road gone? All
> Trace lost, like a ship sinking,
> Where what is left and what goes down both bring despair.
> Not finding the road, we are slowly pulled down.

Since the publication of *The Light Around the Body* Bly has published two small booklets of poetry, *The Morning Glory* (1969), twelve prose poems, and *The Teeth-Mother Naked at Last* (1970), a seven-part antiwar poem. He has also edited an anthology of political poetry, *Forty Poems Touching on Recent American*

History (1970), to which he has contributed a superb preface called "Leaping Up Into Political Poetry," and has continued to publish new poems and translations in various magazines. The recent poetry has come out of a time of testing, an apparent exile from the peace of the inner world. It shows the marks of a hard transition, but it also evidences new power, particularly in the political poetry. This is especially noteworthy, since it was the political poetry of *The Light Around the Body* which was most severely criticized by the critics. Even a friendly critic, Richard Calhoun, said of the political poetry:

> My objection is not to the content but to the poems as poetry. His lines are too often trite, flat, unimaginative—merely rhetorical. . . . There is very little of the sanction of poetry in these poems, even in the pity, which is self pity, and especially in the anger. The poet here has a truth to speak rather than a nightmare to imagine for his reader.[7]

"Writing Again," published in the *Tennessee Poetry Journal*, testifies to the struggle with his material which Bly has gone through.

> Oval
> faces crowding to the window!
> I turn away,
> disturbed—
>
> When I write of moral things,
> the clouds boil
> blackly!
> By day's end
> a room of restless people,
> lifting and putting down things.
>
> Well that is how I have spent this day.
> And what good will it do me in the grave?

On first reading, the poem seems to commemorate a failure, a return to writing which does not eventuate in the kind of poem the poet wants. Disturbance, the threat of storm, and finally a room full of imagined people who move things out of their places: these are at the farthest remove from the silence and solitude out of which the poet had wanted his earlier poems to grow. And the last two lines remind us of the realization which led James Wright to change his approach to poetry: "It had not helped anyone else to solitude, and had not helped him toward solitude."

Yet, as the poem continues to work on us, the final lines speak not of despair but of calm strength. The whole poem then becomes the account of the poet's opening himself to turbulence, turning away from the cheap grace of isolation from others. He may have spent the day in frustration as a poet, but he has kept faith with the moral issues he faces. We could not believe what he writes about moral issues if the clouds did not boil blackly and the room fill with restless people. Only because he has spent the day well, in moral activity, can he ask his final question, which points beyond this day to an examination of the whole life. The poem is a success, describing a failure. It leads us to the right question—What has my work to do with ultimate things?—and leaves the answer open.

In a prefatory note to *The Morning Glory*, Bly speaks of recognizing how independent of us an animal is. "Its world is complete without us. We feel separated at first; later, joyful." The prose poems themselves do not penetrate into that world which is complete without us, however. They read like rough notes from a poet's journal, sketching in external appearances and making a few tentative essays at comparisons which will turn these alien scenes or objects into something from our world. In "A Small Bird's Nest Made of White Reed Fiber," the similes which connect the object with the poet's experience stress disjunction. The simple instinctual architecture of the bird's nest reminds the poet of cloudy transoms over Victorian doors and the tangled hair of nurses in the Crimea. The comparisons convey a sense of deprivation—deprivation of light, of sleep, of love. The nest, made and forgotten, is compared to "our own lives that we will entirely forget in the grave." It is white, but we will be reborn black.

The independence of this world seems to judge the poet. Addressing a dead wren, he says, "Forgive the hours spent listening to radios, and the words of gratitude I did not say to teachers." Elsewhere he says, "There is something spiritual in the rocks with their backs turned to me." A dry thistle shouts at his sleeping senses, "called in from the back of my head," but it speaks of loss, "some love we forget every day." The bottom plate of a turtle's shell is "like the underside of some alien spaceship." Sea imagery occurs frequently in the prose poems, but its effect is to convince us that we are not amphibians, able to move in two worlds. We are land-bound.

The prose poem is at home in French, where writers have been able to employ rhythmic prose and heightened emotion in description to create something neither traditional poetry nor ordinary description or anecdote. But the prose poem has always been an anomaly in English. Following the French model, it becomes a purple patch; refusing to do so, it tends toward flaccidity. Our deepest acquaintance with the form is likely to be in religious tales or parables. The successful prose poem in English depends on resonances set up in the reader's mind which do not rest primarily on pronounced rhythm or especially elaborate metaphorical structure. It is likely to be anchored either in description of nature or in a narrative. One might cite passages from Faulkner, Thomas Wolfe, and James Agee to exemplify the kind of writing where recollection of the past is evoked through such a vibrant poetic prose. Thoreau in *Walden* and in his journals frequently writes a subtler, less mannered kind of nature description with the resonances the effective prose poem must have.

Bly's prose poems lack both emotional intensity and vigor of language. The special difficulties of the form therefore stand out clearly. The poems stand outside what they describe. We are more aware of the observer than of what he observes, and what we perceive is how important it is to him that what he sees should possess deeper meanings. So he experiments with idiosyncratic, peculiar comparisons whose effect is not to join scene and observer's mind but to stress how thoroughly disjoint they are. The poems are diffuse rather than concentrated. The comparisons lack either the inevitability of shared perception or the surprise of vivid insight. The similes are strained; they convey opinions rather than insights. We become aware of the simile as a rhetorical device rather than as a way of seeing.

If there are two stages to our relation to a world which will never be our friend, separation and joy, these poems come from that first stage, no matter how much the poet wants to speak of joy. Their form describes opacity, a closed and indifferent world where rocks turn their backs on us and we ask forgiveness of dead wrens for the failures of our lives.

Yeats says we make rhetoric out of our quarrel with others but poetry out of our quarrel with ourselves. Too often in *The Light Around the Body* we are aware of rhetoric, a sign of judgment from outside the world of the Romans and executives. In his preface to *Forty Poems* Bly speaks of the need to "leap up" into political poetry, first by diving down deep into one's own psyche, then by springing into the national psyche. The poet must leave his own concerns for a time and live in that other realm. When he returns, he brings strange, alien forms of life, "which he then tries to keep alive with his own psychic body." That means writing out of love rather than hatred, showing a care to be identified with the opponent rather than an anxiety to stand separate from him.

Bly calls for a language which "entangles" the personal and the divine, which draws together political life and personal growth into one fabric. The language must be "fragrant"; it must be redolent with the life people know. Such language in a political poem will not be used to express opinions or recommend an action; it will "entangle" poet and reader in a common life—the life of their society and of the universe. Many of the war poems in *The Light Around the Body* are by these standards unsuccessful. But, by these same standards, *The Teeth-Mother Naked at Last* is a fresh, powerful, and profoundly successful work.

The Teeth-Mother brings the political and personal and cosmic together into one long poem. By turns stately and flat, bitter, sorrowful, satiric, and prophetic, the poem works in a multiplicity of tones. We hear the voices of public officials, interrogators of prisoners and soldiers spliced into the extravagant language of surrealism and the equally extravagant, though different, language of satire. Perhaps the nearest analogue for the poem's shape is the greater irregular ode which the romantics developed for speaking simultaneously of several levels of experience. Coleridge's anguished political ode, "Recantation," most closely compares with Bly's poem.

The poem opens with a description of planes and helicopters taking off on missions in Vietnam, an orderly, even beautiful activity which is immediately set in two contexts, the historical and the natural. "This is Hamilton's triumph," an inevitable result toward which American history has always pointed. It has the inevitability too of a natural catastrophe, an event heralding the change of seasons. "This happens when the leaves begin to drop from the trees too early. . . ." Placing the war in these two time-schemes, the historical and the seasonal, gives us an essentially biblical view of it. As the prophets saw the Assyrians and Babylonians as simultaneously heaping guilt on themselves by their evil actions while inescapably working out the will of God, so Bly sees American might as evil in its expression but essentially a helpless agent of power and energy it cannot comprehend. That power is natural and moral in its effect—the change of seasons, the icing over of lake water which drives life deep to the bottom, if it is to survive. By contrast, "Supersabres/like knots of neurotic energy sweep/around and return." The image conveys the whole contrast. American power is knotted, neurotic, turning on itself. It is energy without a proper end.

But the war is not allegorized away. Artillery shells explode, napalm bursts into flame, children and rooms explode, "800 steel pellets fly through the vegetable walls." An American sergeant is also dying, realizing as he does that "the mansions of the dead are empty, he has an empty place/inside him. . . ."

Part II builds on this biblical foundation by placing affirmations of belief in the trinity and on building democratic institutions in Vietnam in ironic juxtaposition against the screams of a tortured prisoner. The President's rallying cry turns into the whines of jets which "pierce like a long needle."

> As soon as the President finishes his press conference,
>   black wings carry off the words,
> bits of flesh still clinging to them.

Ministers, professors, television, and priests are all liars. Their lies set out "like enormous trains of Conestoga wagons. . . ./And a long desire for death flows out, guiding/the enormous caravans from beneath." Again the imagery reminds us of the two contexts of history and nature.

The dying soldier was born with an emptiness he used half his skin to cover. The leaders desire "to take death inside" for the thrill of feeling something. Later on, Part IV describes a fast-revolving black silo within our own bodies, with motorcycles rearing around on the silo's inside walls. The lies become like those knots of neurotic energy, and the President's press conference a chain of nervous tics symptomatic of deep ill. He lies about when the Appalachian Mountains rose, the population of Chicago, the composition of the amniotic fluid, "And the Attorney General lies about the time the sun sets." Emptiness and lies—the signs of a desire to die which has us in thrall. "Do not be angry at the President. . . ./He is drifting sideways toward the dusty places."

Asserting that our lies mean we want to die calls for some causal explanation. In Part III historical cause-and-effect becomes explicitly moral in its working out: "That's what it's like for a rich country to make a war."

> It's because the aluminum window-shade business is
>   doing so well in the United States that we roll fire
>   over entire villages
> It's because the milk trains coming into New Jersey hit
>   the right switches every day that the best Vietnamese
>   men are cut in two by American bullets that follow
>   each other like freight cars.

The causal connections cannot hold logically, but the associations built up by linking milk trains and bullets following like freight cars, window shades and rolling fire create emotional and psychological connectives which do persuade us. Our economic system becomes another grid through which power follows its own volition. Caught in the grip of our economic system, we are its agents and its beneficiaries alike: "That is what it's like to have a gross national product." We are insulated from suffering by our wishes and therefore do not even imagine we have victims.

Essentially the first half of the poem has been organized as a study of power: first the harnessing of energy symbolized in planes and ships; then the energy of the will which turns that other energy into the power of bombing and strafing; finally a comparison of human and mechanical power with cosmic power. The power to kill is like the power to lie; starting out as an assertion of the will to destroy another, it becomes instead an act of self-destruction. A moral causality operates, even through the absolute and amoral laws of economics. *We want to die because we have everything else* would sum up the argument thus far.

Anger and grief break through these sections, but the handling has been almost impersonal, the tone appropriate to describing implacable and unharnessed forces.

The second half of the poem, four shorter sections, is intensely personal. First person pronouns predominate; the emphasis shifts to how *we* feel. "We all feel like tires being run down roads under heavy cars." The black silo revolves inside our own bodies; the New Testaments are fleeing from us. Our emptiness and helplessness spring from sinful pride. Power intoxicates:

> The Marines think that unless they die the rivers will
>   not move.

> They are dying so that mountain shadows can fall north
>   in the afternoon,
> so that the beetle can move along the ground near the
>   fallen twigs.

Judgment and pity have been delicately balanced in the poem. Our indignation at lies has been tempered by pity for the liars; our anger at the savagery of soldiers has been modified by our sorrow for the triviality of their deaths. But in Part VI the poet tests those sometimes contradictory emotions against the vision of a burning child walking toward us. Judgment, pity, indignation, and sorrows are civilized feelings. Before the savage reality of this napalmed child, however,

> I would suddenly go back to my animal brain;
> I would drop on all fours, screaming,
> My vocal chords would turn blue, yours would too,
> It would be two days before I could play with my own
>   children again.

The poem has ranged widely, but it comes back to a single clear focus in the image of the burning child and in the utterly primitive, and deeply humane, response of the scream. The final section of the poem is generated by that image. Exhaustion, the end of struggle, the yielding up to natural power open Part VII. At first this seems to be escape. "I want to sleep awhile in the rays of the sun slanting/over the snow." It is not escape, however, but an opening up to another power, symbolized by the dust shaken from the daffodil and the particles of Babylonian thought passing through the earthworm. The wind working above the earth dispersing pollen and the earthworm working beneath it, refreshing the soil by working the remains of ancient history into it, serve cosmic time. There are ends toward which the world moves by evolution or catastrophe. We can work with these ends or try to oppose them with our own, but the result will be the same. The poem now gathers up the earlier images of natural force, particularly the image of the ice beginning to show its teeth in ponds. Motion speeds up, rushing toward catastrophe; pigs rush over the cliff, like the Gadarene swine. The waters part and huge spheres come to the surface, not bubbles of decay but images of judgment. The luminous globes contain "hairy and ecstatic rock musicians," symbols of a new society, a counter-culture, everything terrifying about the future to a dead generation. And in the ocean is "the teeth-mother, naked at last." The image of the mother appears frequently in Bly's poetry, but nowhere with more terrifying effect than here. In "The Busy Man Speaks," the speaker repudiates all ties to the mother and gives himself away to the father of rocks and righteousness. The mother—protective, nurturing, identified with nature's benevolence—now shows the other aspect of these qualities: savage in defending her children, inexorable in judgment. Divine power uses the Babylonians and the Americans as its instruments, then discards them. It is the Old Testament vision, expressed in surrealistic images.

The poem's final words call for withdrawal and return, withdrawal to the inner world of nature and return as outcasts

> crouched inside the drop of sweat
> that falls again and again
> from the chin of the Protestant tied in the fire.

Only through separation, even at the risk of encapsulation, and identification with the martyrs, can we escape death by freezing, the judgment of offended nature, the teeth-mother.

The poetry which successfully took us into the inner world, and transformed the outer world in the process, exploited images rooted in landscapes and natural settings. It dealt with the present, as Bly says in his prefatory statement in *Silence in the Snowy Fields.* Now the subject matter has broadened out, and Bly deals with history, politics, human guilt, and society's corruptions. To ask that such themes lead to the kind of placidity and quiet joy which marks the earlier poetry would be to ask that Robert Bly become Pollyanna. We must be grateful when any poet tries to tell the truth about such subjects. He has brought the three kingdoms of politics, the streetcar, and the ocean into one poem, but the result is not what he had anticipated in the earlier poetry. To bring these three together and still make one's goal the kind of imagery which leads us into the inner world where we celebrated the holy-nature, will lead to a retreat into sentimentality or despair. Howard Brinton, writing of the circular process by which Jacob Boehme reconciles the inner and outer beings, says:

> In every completed act of the will the soul goes from earth through hell to highest heaven and back to earth again. This is the dialectic of all organic life. Boehme's universe is dramatic to the core, for everywhere the two wills endeavor to enact their appointed roles. Sometimes they fail and the darkness of evil overshadows them. When they succeed, the light of heaven shines.[8]

What Howard Brinton says of Boehme reads like a gloss on Bly's poetry. In *The Light Around the Body*, the darkness of evil overshadows the holy-nature Bly wishes to discover throughout the universe. The vision becomes a Gnostic one, as it must when devil-figures enter a dualistic system. The American self-hatred becomes projected onto history, politics, other men. Though Bly says we must atone, the means of atonement, the possibility of human redemption have not yet entered the poetry thematically; the inner world is as closed to Dean Rusk, Lyndon Johnson, and the Romans and business executives as the Garden of Eden. But surely the apprehension of the holy-nature working in the universe means one must believe that we are all to be saved, whatever that means, or none. In *The Light Around the Body*, the only savior Bly holds out to us is "The Fire of Despair." His pursuit of the inner world image had taken him deeply into things, but not deeply enough to overcome the distinctions between the two worlds.

The Teeth-Mother has both scope and depth. It breaks free almost totally from the hatred, fear, and demonology which weighted down the war poems of *The Light Around the Body*. It is not free from the excesses of political rhetoric, but Bly has plunged into his own psyche and found it like his nation's. He bears his guilt and can therefore speak in both the traditional prophetic voices—the call to judgment and the more tender call to turn and repent.

Notes

1. Robert Bly, "The Dead World and the Live World," *The Sixties*, no. 8 (Spring 1966): 3.

2. Robert Bly, "The Collapse of James Dickey," *The Sixties*, no. 9 (Spring 1967): 74.

3. Crunk, "The Work of James Wright," *The Sixties*, no. 8 (Spring 1966): 52–78.

4. Harold Henderson, *An Introduction to Haiku* (Garden City, N.Y.: Doubleday Anchor Books, 1958), p. 40.

5. Howard H. Brinton, *The Mystic Will* (New York: Macmillan, 1930), p. 8.

6. Robert Bly, "Five Decades of Modern American Poetry," *The Fifties* 1 (1958): 38–39.

7. Richard Calhoun, "On Robert Bly's Protest Poetry," *Tennessee Poetry Journal* (Winter 1969).

8. Brinton, *The Mystic Will*, p. 23.

Robert Bly Alive in Darkness

ANTHONY LIBBY

Often self-consciously, poetry now reassumes its ancient forms. When at Antioch College in the autumn of 1970 Robert Bly began a reading with an American Indian peyote chant, he seemed merely to be accepting a hip convention almost expected by an audience accustomed to Ginsberg and Snyder. Bly chanted for the usual reason, "to lower the consciousness down, until it gets into the stomach and into the chest and farther on." But no such convention had existed in the early fifties, when Bly began to publish his intimations of physical transcendence, poetry of the mystical body, and the conventional mystical terms that have since become so easily available are still inadequate to describe what happens in his unique poetry. To use a characteristic phrase of Bly's, "something important is hidden in there that we don't understand."

Because of the elusively compelling force of its "deep images," Bly's poetry demands interpretation as much as it seems to resist it. When it does not consist of simple deliberately prosy statement, much of it seems obscure, distant, but at the same time it conveys a sense of meaning immediately perceived though seldom paraphrasable in any but its own terms. It is difficult to explain Bly's surrealist poetry, hard to say why some of his imagery moves us so basically and why some appears comparatively contrived, but undeniably his strongest poetry evokes some sort of truth all the more forceful because it exists beneath or beyond any reasoned response. However, what the stomach feels, the mind wants to know. Perhaps the best way to appreciate Bly's irrational evocations is to attempt to explain them logically. If this seems paradoxical, such paradoxes are implicit in the act of analyzing almost all poetry, not merely surrealist poetry, and in any case Bly himself provides ample precedent. Like many mystical poets he writes with large patterns in mind, and behind his explorations into darkness there stands not only a complex poetic theory but also a highly articulated scheme of the psychological development of civilization. This scheme, also like that of other mystical poets (Blake, for instance), is frequently based on logical antithesis suspended in paradox, and only through an understanding of paradoxes simple and profound can we come to terms with Bly's poetry.

Reprinted from *Iowa Review* 3 (Summer 1972): 78–89. Reprinted by permission of the author.

He begins with the intention of creating a truly free associationalism, radically opposed to what he considers the calculated and artificially logical associationalism of Eliot and Pound. In an essay called "Looking for Dragon Smoke" he argues that the formalist obsessions of modern American poets (from Eliot to Charles Olson) have obscured the true psychic bases of poetry. "Our task is not to invent and encourage jargon about 'open form' and breath patterns, but to continue to open new corridors into the psyche by association." His associative and implicitly irrationalist poetry depends not on form but on imagery, primarily on the conception of the "subjective image" developed by Bly and such friends of his as William Duffy and James Wright. The successful subjective image (or "deep image") strikes us with the force of a newly discovered archetype, minor or major, coming from the depths of the poet's subjectivity with a paradoxically universal force, his private revelation made ours. In Bly's "Depression," for instance, the poet describes his psychic state in images which despite their novelty seem more discovered than made.

> I dreamt that men came toward me, carrying thin wires;
> I felt the wires pass in, like fire; they were old Tibetans;
> Dressed in padded clothes, to keep out cold;
> Then three work gloves, lying fingers to fingers,
> In a circle, came toward me, and I awoke.

Like these, Bly's images are almost invariably marked by a surrealist concreteness; not only are psychological or spiritual states felt in material form, but all substances seem to seek greater density. In various poems in *Silence in Snowy Fields,* air frequently becomes water ("the quiet waters of the night"), darkness "drifts down like snow," snow becomes "jewels," moonlight becomes "The sound of the deaf hearing through the bones of their heads," etc. Even when this metaphorical transposition of substances could be interpreted as moving in the opposite direction, toward a reduction of density ("Waterfalls of stone deep in mountains,/ Or a wing flying alone beneath the earth") still we feel a pervasive sense of heaviness, a downward drift.

This imagery suggests the constant preoccupation of *Silence;* the metaphorical flow into greater concreteness reflects the spiritual movement enacted or wished for in most of the poems, a sinking into things, into the earth, usually into darkness, finally into death. Often, as Richard Howard explains in *Alone with America,* spiritual immersion becomes a literal immersion in water. Howard's intelligent though rhetorically somewhat convoluted introduction to Bly centers on the "latent" waters of "that Minnesota mariner," which Howard connects with "the stream the Greeks called *Lethe.*" As Bly writes in "Return to Solitude,"

> We want to go back, to return to the sea,
> The sea of solitary corridors,

> And halls of wild nights,
> Explosions of grief,
> Diving into the sea of death,
> Like the stars of the wheeling Bear.

But though transcendent death by water suggests ancient mystic patterns, Bly's vision of the death which feeds life is neither exactly traditional nor really transcendental. Another main current of imagery in *Silence* suggests interpenetration of body and world. Animism ("The dawn stood there with a quiet gaze;/ Our eyes met through the top leaves of the young ash") is complemented by a sort of bodily surrealism ("Inside me there is a confusion of swallows"). As the psyche is crowded with arcane corporeal images, so the body contains the objects of the world. In the past, for instance in Thoreau, such body-world parallelism and interpenetration has been used to suggest a higher spiritual reality which penetrates all physical being. More recently, in, say, the poetry of Sylvia Plath, the same pattern of imagery has grown into a vision of all physical substance as grotesquely alien to the perceiving consciousness, the body a dead husk imprisoning a sickened spirit, things endowed with terrifying life. While obviously closer to Thoreau, Bly is essentially similar to neither. His animism stems from a perception of vitality in things which connects with the vitality in the body, but which is neither separable from states of physical being nor basically alien to consciousness. Dying into the darkness at the heart of Bly's poetry is not a transcendence of the body but an immersion in the body in turn immersed in the corporeal flow of things. If this elusive immersion is achieved, the body in its fullness contains and is contained by "the inner world," which is this world, not illuminated but condensed to its deepest indivisible essence.

So behind the traditional mystical paradox—the praise of ordinarily negative states, grief and "the death we love," as avenues to holy joy—there exists in Bly the further paradox that spiritual union with the universe must be sought in physical terms. Perhaps for this reason trees play a constant symbolic role in *Silence,* reaching toward emptiness, but always rooted in the earth. In "Poem in Three Parts":

> The strong leaves of the box-elder tree,
> Plunging in the wind, call us to disappear
> Into the wilds of the universe,
> Where we shall sit at the foot of a plant,
> And live forever, like the dust.

The dust, which appears frequently in Bly's poetry, suggest the most corporeal vision of union with the cosmos, a union spiritually more meaningful than the traditional theological dreams of death if only because of its physical inevitability. Bly compares the two visions in "At the Funeral of Great-Aunt Mary."

> The minister tells us that, being
> The sons and daughters of God,
> We rejoice at death, for we go
> To the mansions prepared
> From the foundations of the world.
> Impossible. No one believes it.

> III
> Out on the bare, pioneer field,
> The frail body must wait till dusk
> To be lowered
> In the hot and sandy earth.

The sense of death as physical union with everything becomes a spiritual or moral force in life because it celebrates a loss of self into the other which is more absolute than the ego-loss presumably implied by the death of transcendence; the traditional mystic soul united with god as often seems swollen as lost in oneness. Also the sense of corporeal dissolution of self is, Bly suggests, always with us. Every sleep is a bodily premonition of death. Much of *Silence* concerns periods of transition between waking and sleep, between light and darkness. During such periods the deep image comes close to the surface because the mind sinks to the depths of the body, the body opens to the world.

> The day shall never end, we think:
> We have hair that seems born for the daylight;
> But, at last, the quiet waters of the night will rise,
> And our skin shall see far off, as it does under water.

Perhaps it no longer seems paradoxical that the state of "approaching sleep" is most fully described in "Awakening."

> We are approaching sleep: the chestnut blossoms in the mind
> Mingle with the thoughts of pain
> . . .
> Bodies give off darkness, and chrysanthemums
> Are dark, and horses, . . .
> As the great wheel turns around, grinding
> The living in water.
> . . . the living awakened at last like the dead.

In his second collection of poems, *The Light Around the Body,* Bly's paradoxes are deepened because much of his poetry spreads into another world. Like various other American mystics, most conspicuously Thoreau, Bly becomes interested in the politics of American imperialism, a subject at least superficially uncongenial to mysticism. All but one of the sections of *Light* begin with quotations from Jacob Boehme, the Protestant mystic who influenced the American transcendentalists (through Emerson, who knew him as "Behemen"). "For according to the outward man, we are in this world and according to the inward man, we are in the inward world . . . Since then we are generated out of both worlds, we speak in two languages, and we must be understood also by two languages." The poems of *Light* concern the conflict between the two worlds, in the poet, and in America. So inevitably these poems bring together the two languages of which Boehme speaks, doubling Bly's paradoxes, sometimes confusingly. *Light* still praises grief and maps the progress of the body toward that death which is fulfillment, but while *Silence* emphasized intimations of ultimate union *Light* focuses on obstacles to the good death, one of which is, paradoxically, another sort of death. "Smothered by the World" describes a purgatory between life and death.

> Once more the heavy body mourns!
> It howls outside the hedges of life,
> Pushed out of the enclosure.
> Now it must meet the death outside the death.
> Living outside the gate is one death,
> Cold faces gather along the wall,
> A bag of bones warms itself in a tree.

This death results from basic spiritual distortion in the world. Bly describes it in the same physical terms he used to connect the body and the world, but here the connection has become grotesque. Human consciousness inhabits objects only to suggest a general despair, as in "Those Being Eaten by America."

> The wild houses go on
> With long hair growing from between their toes
> The feet at night get up
> And run down the long white roads by themselves
>
> The dams reverse themselves and want to go stand alone in the desert

The sterile death that follows this despair is occasionally described in terms of whiteness, often snow, but even the darkness which in *Silence* was always the medium of visions has in *Light* changed, become corrupted. "There is another darkness," Bly writes in "Listening to President Kennedy Lie about the Cuban Invasion." "There is a bitter fatigue, adult and sad."

The other darkness, in poems like "Hatred of Men with Black Hair," is described as inhabiting the same deep realms as the darkness of vision.

> The State Department floats in the heavy jellies near the bottom
> Like exhausted crustaceans, like squids who are confused,
> Sending out beams of black light to the open sea.

Both darknesses exist at the root of the mind, which is the source of politics as well as poetry. As the title of "Hatred" suggests, the destructive darkness results from a refusal to acknowledge that more primitive darkness which is the way to union. The American dream of self-proclaimed innocence, so shot through with unacknowledged blackness, leads to a death which cannot reinforce life, if only because it strikes so unnaturally. This vision is dramatized most fully in Bly's later poem "The Teeth Mother Naked at Last," but it is suggested in "At a March against the Vietnam War," which appears in *Light*. Bly says of "a boat/Covered with machine guns":

> It is black,
> The hand reaches out
> and cannot touch it—
> It is that darkness among pine boughs
> That the Puritans brushed
> As they went out to kill turkeys
>
> At the edge of the jungle clearing
> It explodes
> On the ground
>
> We long to abase ourselves
>
> We have carried around this cup of darkness
> We have longed to pour it over our heads

Always, however individually, the poet reflects his time. Primarily *Silence* contains poetry written in the 1950's, a time of comparative political innocence (or naiveté) for American literature, when literary rebellion against America was usually considered a rather solitary and apolitical experience. *Silence* is a book of solitude, of Bly alone with the world; even its few love poems do not involve a recognizable other. *Light* is a book of the sixties, a predominantly political book, like many other books of poetry published since 1966 (the year Bly organized American Writers Against the Vietnam War). But while Bly's development must obviously be understood in terms of our recent history, he might probably have undergone similar changes in any historical context, for in *Light* he is only dramatizing a tension implicit in the paradoxes of *Silence*.

Traditionally, mysticism has existed in potential or actual conflict with more earthy approaches to morality; the conflict surfaces when the mystic theorizes about evil. Having accepted grief and the dissolution of his body as aspects of a vital flow into "the wilds of the universe," Bly must logically confront experiences of grief and death, perhaps unnecessary grief and premature death, much less palatable to those who suffer them. The mystic always returns to the world of men. The perception of dominant and perhaps inherent evil there can blunt his mystic acceptance, or it can become the basis for more strenuous efforts toward transcendence, a denial of the essential reality of certain aspects of the world in favor of higher realities. Allen Ginsberg, for instance, plays more or less seriously with the latter response when he chants, in "Wichita Vortex Sutra": "I here declare the end of the War/Ancient days' Illusion." But because Bly's mysticism remains untranscendental ("The two worlds are both in this world") neither traditional response is really possible. The social fact of pointless death forces a deeper examination of the idea of death as a spiritual good, but Bly is unwilling to deny either vision.

What he attempts to do instead, besides suggesting how the primitive sense of union has been lost, how death has been corrupted, is to create a vision of process toward a new world in which paradoxes resolve themselves. But the approach of this world is itself paradoxical, a terrible movement toward communal death which, like the individual death of *Silence*, is also the approach of birth. As the tension between inner and outer worlds grows more extreme Bly suggests that the center will not hold; however the approaching apocalypse is also described as evolution. The final section of *Light* is called "A Body Not Yet Born." Like the rest of the book it contains images of despairing death, as in "Hurrying Away from the Earth."

> Some men have pierced the chest with a long needle
> To stop the heart from beating any more;
> . . .
> The time for exhortation is past. I have heard
> The iron chairs scraping in asylums,
> . . .
> Men cry when they hear stories of someone rising from the dead.

If the dark night of the soul has become a universal darkness, it carries implications of universal illumination. In "When the Dumb Speak," Bly describes

> . . . a joyful night in which we lose
> Everything, and drift
> Like a radish
> Rising and falling, and the ocean
> At last throws us into the ocean

One ocean flows from the waters of inner experience described throughout much of *Silence*, but the other spreads through time as well as space. "When the Dumb Speak" ends with "images" which evoke traditional Christian visions of the world ending in apocalypse.

> Images of the body shaken in the grave,
> And the grave filled with seawater;

> Fires in the sea
>
> . . .
>
> The house fallen,
> The gold sticks broken,

But "Evolution from the Fish," as its title indicates, describes what is to come not as a Christian end but as an evolutionary change which parallels earlier changes. Here the loss of "everything," which is a loss of self, becomes a participation in the physical development of life from the beginning. "The grandson of fishes" is described

> . . . moving toward his own life
> Like fur, walking. And when the frost comes, he is
> Fur, mammoth fur, growing longer
>
> . . .
>
> He moves toward the animal, the animal with furry head!

As the poem moves into our time the furry-headed one becomes specific, individual, "this long man with the student girl," but in the end he is embarking on another voyage, in darkness, through sleep.

> Serpents rise from the ocean floor with spiral motions,
> A man goes inside a jewel, and sleeps. Do
> Not hold my hands down! Let me raise them!
> A fire is passing up through the soles of my feet!

An earlier version of "Evolution" appeared in 1962 in a brief anthology of poems by Bly, Duffy, and Wright, *The Lion's Tail and Eyes*. Indicatively, it included one additional last line: "I am curving back into the mammoth pool!" By omitting the backward curve Bly alters the final direction of the poem from the past to the future; now the subject is not repeating cycles of existence but a continuing upward spiral into new states of being.

Bly is at his most difficult, to follow and to accept, when he begins to describe the particular nature of the apocalypse to come, and the evolution it heralds. A premonitory poem in *Light*, "Romans Angry about the Inner World," describes that world as "A jagged stone/Flying toward them out of the darkness" and suggests the final articulation of Bly's evolutionary vision. In the poem "executives" watch Roman executioners torture "a woman/ Who has seen our mother/ In the other world." Specifically the lines refer to the mystical cult of Magna Mater, eventually suppressed by the Romans. But the anachronistic presence of the executives implies a comparison between imperial Rome and neoimperialist America, a comparison that goes beyond ordinary politics. Later Bly will elaborate the theory that the mother-goddesses smothered by one empire are returning to haunt the psyche of the other. In his long introduction to "The Teeth Mother Naked at Last" at the Antioch reading, Bly explained a vision of mythic development largely based on the psychological and historical investigations of Jung's disciple Erich Neumann. Originally, as Bly explains Neumann, the world's great religions were based on worship of the female principle, the Great Mother; the Romans and the Jews fought to substitute male gods for the female goddesses, beginning the long western tradition of primacy of the masculine consciousness. Bly defines sexual consciousness in Jungian terms: masculine consciousness involves logic, efficiency, the advancement of material civilization, repression, and control of the natural world; and feminine consciousness involves intuition, creativity, mystic acceptance of the world. Because only women are biologically creative, it is usually the man who feels the aesthetic urge to create with materials outside his own body. However he is truly inspired only if he makes "the great turn" toward the mother, accepting the guidance of the (always female) Muse, and exploring his own feminine consciousness (Jung's anima). Now, though, not only artists but the whole culture is beginning, psychologically, to turn to the Great Mother. "America looks down in the psyche now," Bly said at Antioch, "and it sees the mothers coming up." "That's what's been happening in America in the last fifteen years, that the father consciousness civilization is dying and the mothers are returning."

As the mythic forms of the mothers suggest, this can be a destructive as well as liberating process. Drawing on various mythologies for examples Bly describes the four great mothers in opposed pairs, constructive and destructive: the mother of fertility (Demeter) balanced by the mother of destruction (Kali), the ecstatic mother (Artemis) balanced by the stone mother (Medusa). In this relation to each other they form a cross, or the four main compass points of a circle, and the teeth mother hovers on the circumference between death and stone mothers. To prove his theory, Bly cites widely various bits of evidence of the return of the different mothers. One manifestation of the destructive mothers in the aesthetic consciousness appears, for instance, in deKooning's paintings; Bly is perhaps thinking of works like "Woman I." In a very different sphere, Bly attributes the American violence of Vietnam, often directed against women and children, to our pathologically masculine soldiers' fear of the female, of the mothers, whom they see only in the form of the death mother or the teeth mother. On the other side, Bly sees in hip and liberated life styles the influence of the ecstatic mother, though he explains that the search for the ecstatic mother can fail in a long fall toward the stone mother—the use of drugs, too, dramatizes this paradox, and Bly the comedian does not hesitate to play on the colloquial sense of "stoned."

To those moved by the visionary qualities of Bly's poetry, this theory may present serious problems. How much of it is really believable, how literally does Bly intend it, how necessary is it as a basis for his poetry? Indicatively, little of the theory actually appears in "The Teeth Mother Naked at Last," though it provides a striking title. Bly's vision of the great evolutionary change is felt more convincingly in his poetry—explorations into "the inward world . . . thoughts we have not yet thought" which involve little detailed reference to the mothers—than in his spoken and very explicit explanations of what he thinks now. Bly the performer is enormously compelling, a constantly disarming mixture of vaudeville comedian and oracle, but in retrospect, beyond the range of his personal vibrations, his archetypal sociology does not fully convince. Perhaps in our time any extreme definition of the opposition between male and female consciousness must seem suspect. More important, though, is the tension between Bly's use of the old Jungian archetypes to describe our future, and the constant suggestions in his poetry that the present movement of human consciousness is something new, now hardly dreamed of. Somehow it seems inadequate to describe "the body not yet born" in terms of ancient myths, however they are blended or transmuted to define the world to come. Better to accept Bly's explanations as metaphor, his poems as reality.

For it is the sense of deeply perceived reality in the poetry that leads us in the first place to consider the prose articulation of the theory, and in fact Bly the poet, as he points out, was using the conflict between "masculine" and "feminine" as a metaphor long before he read Neumann and developed his theory. In *Light,* for instance, "The Busy Man Speaks" defines "the mother" in terms of "art," "sorrow," "the ocean;" and "the father" in terms of "The stones of cheerfulness, the steel of money." Still earlier, in *Silence*, women are often associated with liberating death, as in "With Pale Women in Maryland:" "Like those before, we move to the death we love/ With pale women in Maryland."

To see Bly's poetry as dependent on anyone's theory, on Jung's, Neumann's, or even Bly's own, is not only to deny his belief in the irrational psychic sources of poetry but also to dilute the unique force of his poems. If we turn to Jung for explanations, we can say simply that the origin of Bly's deep images is the collective unconscious, that the conflict between the inner and outer worlds is a conflict between anima and persona, that Bly's water imagery is, given his concerns, predictable. Water, Jung says in "Archetypes of the Collective Unconscious," is "no figure of speech, but a living symbol of the dark psyche," the realm "where I experience the other in myself." Even Bly's paradoxical discovery of vitality in death can be explained in terms of Jung's contention, in "Psychological Aspects of the Mother Archetype," that "Nothing can exist without its opposite; the two were one in the beginning and will be one again in the end. Consciousness can only exist through continual recognition of the unconscious, just as everything that lives must pass through many deaths." But to interpret Bly basically in these terms is to oversimplify his paradoxes without really explaining them, as Jung's archetypes inevitably tend to reduce and oversimplify complex individual states of being. Descending into realms initially explored by Jung and later by Neumann, Bly goes beyond both. His greatest strength is his ability to discover in the darkness images that are not archetypal, at least not in the Jungian sense, because they are only beginning to loom into view.

But even if we remain unconvinced by the details of Bly's theory we cannot deny that it remains a fascinating metaphor for states as yet not analytically describable. More important, the mothers metaphor enables Bly to develop and enrich the paradoxes that float up from his inner darkness. He has constructed a vision of mystic evolution that not only refuses to deny but explains the moral dissolution that forms the primary vision of *Light*. The tension between the ecstatic mother and the stone mother provides a theoretical basis for Bly's double conception of darkness, the inspiring darkness of the inner world held in suspension with the terrifying blackness of the outer. "The Teeth Mother Naked at Last," a map of the psychological politics behind an imperial war, is also a record of the collision between inner and outer worlds.

"Teeth Mother," though marked throughout by Bly's characteristic surrealist imagery, differs basically from his earlier poetry. So far it is his only really extensive poem, and its coherence is more theoretical than imagistic. Frequently its deep images give way to flat, almost prosy statement, often far less striking than the visions of *Light*, but in some ways more moving. Bly adopts different tactics in this poem partly because he is writing a sort of propaganda based on juxtaposition of certain facts, but also because it seems impossible, and probably not desirable, to assimilate the actuality of Vietnam into poetry as Bly has previously written it. The Vietnam poems in *Light* primarily concerned the reverberations of war; "Teeth Mother" is often a simple contemplation of unbearable facts. But it also implies an explanation.

> Helicopters flutter overhead. The death-
> bee is coming. Supersabres
> like knots of neurotic energy sweep
> around and return.
> This is Hamilton's triumph.
> This is the advantage of a centralized bank.

Destructive—"neurotic"—machines dominate the poem; despite his moral revulsion, Bly's ability to immerse himself in things enables him to evoke the alien world of machines and mechanical men as fully as he evokes the inner world. Vietnam represents the desperate end of the "masculine" rage for order, the force that created American prosperity but a force basically corrupted by its denial of the inner world. The warrior mentality, recreating itself in machines, opposes not only nature ("800 steel pellets fly through the vegetable walls") but the dark flow of its own humanity, its movement toward the death which completes life. The desire for death as fulfillment, corrupted, becomes a desire for death as grotesque destruction.

> The ministers lie, the professors lie, the television lies,
>   the priests lie . . .
> These lies mean that the country wants to die.
> . . .
> It is a desire to take death inside,
> to feel it burning inside, pushing out strong hairs,
> like a clothes brush in the intestines

In a series of awkward but often striking juxtapositions, Bly suggests that the American rejection of grief and darkness, made possible by wealth, creates the grief of Vietnam. It is:

> because we have so few tears falling on our own hands
> that the Supersabre turns and screams down toward the earth

In the face of this there appears no adequate response, no praise of the grief that follows the denial of grief, no mystical acceptance. Bly the political moralist presents, ironically undercut, the plea of the contemplative dreamer, who sees the corporeal flow of existence very much in terms that suggest *Silence*.

> Tell me about the particles of Babylonian thought that
>   still pass through the earthworm every day,
> Don't tell me about "the frightening laborers who do
>   not read books"

But the dehumanizing outer darkness prevails:

> if one of those children came near that we have set on fire,
> came toward you like a gray barn, walking,
> you would howl like a wind tunnel in a hurricane
> you would tear at your shirt with blue hands,

No response to this, and yet, paradoxically, Bly suggests a response, or at least a way of understanding it. The horribly catalogued violence against human and vegetable nature can be seen in a more distant sense as a natural aspect of the apocalyptic evolutionary change described in more positive terms in the final pages of *Light*. One voice in "Teeth Mother," looking for solace, suggests of the violence of "the Marine battalion," "This happens when the seasons change/ this happens when the leaves begin to drop from the trees too early." Bly undercuts the suggestion of solace, but the comparison remains. Vietnam, in some sense the death of American dreams, is not an end but a transition, in which the teeth mother necessarily appears as an aspect of the ecstatic mother.

> Now the whole nation starts to whirl
> . . .
> pigs rush toward the cliff,

> the waters underneath part: in one ocean luminous globes
>   float up (in them hairy and ecstatic rock musicians)—
> in the other, the teeth mother, naked at last.

The balance, and the sense of cycles evolving, provide no cure to present agony. Bly knows it is the false transcendence of agony, with its attendant repression, which distorts human consciousness in the first place. But the vision of evolution enables Bly to sustain his paradoxical suspension of despair and mystic hope, his sense of death as life. Perhaps that paradox will always defy resolution, but in his latest poetry Bly continues to offer hope for evolution into a state of consciousness in which despair can be replaced by that grief which attends the natural movement of life, which is not inconsistent with joy. At the end of a recent poem read at Antioch, Bly suggests, through paradox now expressed with a clear simplicity, that the conflict between the father and the mother may be resolved by that consciousness now being born.

> More of the fathers are dying each day,
> It's time for the sons.
> Bits of darkness are gathering around the sons,
> The darkness appears as flakes of light.

Robert Bly's *Sleepers Joining Hands*: Shadow and Self

Michael Atkinson

In *Sleepers Joining Hands*, Robert Bly offers his readers a various weave of the personal and the public, the psychological and the political modes of experience. Each mode illuminates the other, though, as I hope to show, the collection is most fundamentally and formally psychological. The layout of the book is pleasantly indirect: two dozen pages of poems, ranging from haiku-like meditation moments to longer poems of protest. Then there is the essay, a short course in the Great Mother, an analysis of the disturbing but finally nourishing configuration of feminine archetypes in the collective unconscious. And finally we have the oneiric title sequence: four poems and a coda, written at different times and published in different places, but here offered as a single structure, a whole.

The poems on either side of the essay seem to point back and forth to each other. And so naturally we ask: what is the relation of the earlier poems to the later sequence? what is the final shape of the book?

The essay points the way. Like most poets who pause to explain themselves, Bly works obliquely. His essay focuses on the work of Bachofen and Neumann; yet the pattern of the book rests firmly on the thought of a successor to the first and the teacher of the second—Carl Jung. The essay coordinates the variety of anima archetypes which inhabit our subconsciousness: the Good Mother who gives us life, the Death Mother who takes it away; the Ecstatic Mother, muse of joy, and the Stone or Teeth Mother who reduces us to the stupor of psychic annihilation. But the title sequence, which is the key to the book's integrity, focuses on two other Jungian dream archetypes—the shadow and the Self.

The symbols of the earlier poems gain resonance in the schematic context of the later sequence: imagist poems move toward plotted action, oracles toward ritual, archetypes toward myth. Here, I would like to present the scheme of the sequence and show its relation to the shorter poems., delineating the system of archetypes that coherently applies throughout the book, linking Biblical allusions to contemporary consciousness and connecting dream images with myth.

Reprinted from *Iowa Review* 7, no. 4 (Fall 1976): 135–53. Reprinted by permission of the author.

After sketching in the profiles of the Great Mother, Bly warns that we should not examine his "poems for evidence of them, for most of [the] poems were written without benefit of them." And further to guide us, he lifts the penultimate paragraph of his essay from Jung: it virtually diagrams the concern and shape of the "Sleepers" sequence, shifting our attention from "the woman within" to the shadow and the Self.

> It would be far better simply to admit our spiritual poverty. . . . The spirit has come down from its fiery high places . . . but when the spirit becomes heavy, it turns to water. . . . Therefore the way of the soul in search of its lost father . . . leads to the water, to the dark mirror that lies at the bottom. Whoever has decided to move toward the state of spiritual poverty . . . goes the way of the soul that leads to the water. [Bly's ellipses]

In Jung's overall schema, the personality striving for full individuation or integration has four aspects, which are personified in our dreams: (1) the ego (or persona), that person (or role) we consider ourselves to be in normal waking consciousness; (2) the shadow, that figure of the same sex as the ego who embodies negative or positive traits which might have been conscious but which have now been repressed; (3) the anima, the woman within the man, that feminine consciousness with which he has to come to terms—or the animus, the man within the woman, representing the male consciousness with which the woman must reconcile herself; and finally, (4) the Self, that perfect wholeness which the individual can become, when he has reconciled himself with his shadow and anima (or she with her shadow and animus) and become his own potentiality for being.

The first poem of the "Sleepers" sequence hearkens back to the time the ego became split from its shadow by repression, and is appropriately entitled "The Shadow Goes Away." It records the fragmentation of the questor, chronicles his separation from that lost aspect which he must again come to recognize in himself. Until he incorporates his shadow, he is powerless to act effectively. We feel his powerlessness as we gaze with him upon "The woman chained to the shore," Andromeda-like, and hear him express his fear of going into the ocean to fight for her, to liberate her. (In mythic compression, the woman *is* the ocean—la mer, la mère—the womb from which he must be reborn whole.) He fears the sea. Juxtaposed to his feeling of impotence is its cause: his loss of the shadow.

Often—perhaps most frequently in dream and art—the shadow is a figure that embodies the negative aspects of the personality; the negativity provides the reason they are repressed. Thus we have Jekyll's hidden Hyde, Dimmesdale's Chillingworth, Gatsby's Wolfsheim, and the like. But, as Jung notes, we may just as easily deny parts of ourselves that—grown wiser—we would consider good. Because something about them threatens the fragile, narrowly defined persona or ego, they too may be repressed. But ultimately they must be admitted to our consciousness and assimilated, or the results will be disastrous. Ishmael's savage Queequeg, Willy Loman's Charley, Macbeth's Banquo: each contains "values that are needed by consciousness, but that exist in a form that makes it difficult to integrate them into one's life."

The protagonist in Bly's poems has a shadow that is protean but consistent. The dreamer first imagines himself a brother (probably Judah) to Joseph of the many colored coat; he recalls selling his brother-shadow into slavery. Joseph contains the qualities the dreamer so desperately needs to complete his life. In Genesis (Chapters 37–50) Joseph is sent into the moral wilderness of Egypt, banished, repressed from the consciousness of the family (except the mind of the father, the wise old man, the Self who yearns for Joseph's return). Despite (or because of) the banishment, Joseph gains mastery over the alien realm, understands its laws by understanding dreams both positive and negative, and eventually provides his brothers with what they need to sustain their lives, when they at last seek him out.

Bly's shape-shifting protagonist repeatedly dreams of selling his brother, notably to be carried away into the desert or out to sea (archetypal equivalents for the unconscious, which may be a realm of danger and potential death for the fragmented and brittle ego). Joseph is transformed into an American Indian: he is "taken in by travelling Sioux," and he learns to "glide about naked, drinking water from his hands, / to tether horses, follow the faint trail through bent grasses." The questor's shadow—and, the poem suggests, ours—is the natural man, the primitive, at home in the world of nature and the unconscious. The pillagers of the tribal village and the Marines who appear late in the poem are intended to remind us how we have duplicated our oppression of the Indian in the bombing of Vietnam. Equations that seem both familiar and strained in political rhetoric are here given greater coherence and vitality in a psychological connection. In each case we have attempted to destroy (or repress) the people who best exemplified the very qualities we most need to acknowledge and cultivate in ourselves—positive shadows.

"The Shadow Goes Away" gives a larger context for a number of the other poems—poems, already integers themselves, now resonate within the larger pattern. "The Condition of the Working Classes: 1970" is blamed not on those above them, but on those they have trod under— blamed not on the oppression that workers might suffer, but on the repression of their shadows, inwardly and outwardly. Thus, we eat "a bread made of the sound of sunken buffalo bones" and drink "a water turned dark by the shadows of Negroes"; the "Sioux dead sleep all night in the rain troughs on the Treasury Building," and because of this our sons are "lost in the immense forest" of the unintegrated unconscious.

As the repression intensifies, so does the terror of living with it. Denying the shadow drives us into the maw of "The Teeth Mother Naked at Last." Here the horror hits its highest pitch and an unfamiliar list toward stereotype and stridence appears. Maybe it is unavoidable—so many have spoken out against the war for so long that even the most telling analysis has deteriorated into formula and finally come to rest in cliché. Bly's poem cannot shake itself free of stereotypy, even though it has considerable power. The power comes not just from its imagery—

> If one of those children came near that we have set on fire, ...
> If one of those children came toward me with both hands
> in the air, fire rising along both elbows
> I would suddenly go back to my animal brain
> I would drop on all fours, screaming,
> my vocal cords would turn blue, so would yours.
> it would be two days before I could play with my own children again

—but from the analysis of cause and effect that is given in the hard terms of imagery which will not allow the luxuries and niceties of rationalization. These cause-effect concatenations generate both the strengths and weaknesses of the poem. I suspect each reader will find different equations effective. But when they work, they work; when they don't, they grate.

The poem begins with a deft and horrific picture of planes lifting off on bombing missions. The first stated cause for the missions—Hamilton's plan for a centralized bank. This is entirely too easy. And, though he does return to such, fortunately Bly gets beyond the familiar accusations of economic materialism to a perspective that still has the capacity to arrest us. He tells us to save the tears we shed for exploding children.

> Don't cry at that—
> Do you cry at the wind pouring out of Canada?
> Do you cry at the reeds shaken at the edge of the sloughs?

He asks us to hold our tears and, Yeatsian but joyless, to see the terrible destruction as a natural law working itself out. The natural wind that shakes the reeds and brings the snow is not just meteorological—it is the inner wind of the spirit that blows where it lists.

> This happens when the seasons change,
> This happens when the leaves begin to drop from the trees
>   too early
> "Kill them: I don't want to see anything moving."
> This happens when the ice begins to show its teeth in the
>   ponds
> This happens when the heavy layers of lake water press
>   down on the fish's head, and send him deeper, where his
>   tail swirls slowly, and his brain passes him pictures
>   of heavy reeds, of vegetation fallen on vegetation . . .
> Hamilton saw all this in detail:
> "Every banana tree slashed, every cooking utensil smashed,
>   every mattress cut."

The key here is the aquatic imagery, which so pervades the poem (and the book). Allegorically read, the passage limns in a picture of repression—a freezing of the sensitive living waters, the ice pressing down on the fish, denizen of the unconscious, our evolutionary precursor. And the dying, descending fish sees the pictures of previous repressions, impressions from the coal age, compressed, petrified, transformed, ancient, yet still leaving, layer upon layer, the imprint of their repression deep in the lake floor, beneath the now frozen surface.

Though it is pretty clear that Hamilton did *not* see all this in detail, we can see that these are natural psychic laws we are following. This is why we lie to others and to ourselves (section II)—to cover with further layers the skin we have already put on things, and so to mask the mask. And from this, a further equation is posited. "These lies mean the country wants to die"—self denial is self denial is self denial. Killing our shadows betokens hunger for our own death.

The poem's other analyses—economic primarily—look best when seen in light of this larger pattern of repression.

> It is because the aluminum window shade business is doing
>> so well in the United States that we roll fire over
>> whole villages

fortunately cedes to

> It is because we have so few women sobbing in back rooms,
> because we have so few children's heads torn apart by high
>> velocity bullets,
> because we have so few tears falling on our own hands
> that the Super Sabre turns and screams down toward the
>> earth.

And it is from this analysis that the poem's final prayer comes:

> Let us drive cars
> up
> the light beams
> to the stars . . .
>
> And return to earth crouched inside the drop of sweat
> that falls
> from the chin of the Protestant tied in the fire.

If we have become cruel it is because we cannot remember our own suffering: in our righteousness we have forgotten our pain. Our only hope lies in remembering.

"The Marines think that unless they die the rivers will not move." At a conscious level, we believe we are fulfilling a chosen, comprehensible destiny; but at the unconscious level we are following the path to a destiny not nearly so manifest, though much more powerfully certain. We are rushing to the edge of the sea as "pigs rush toward the cliff" driven by our own demons and there below us we see our history and our destiny, balanced:

> the waters underneath part: in one ocean luminous globes
> float up (in them hairy ecstatic men—)
> in the other, the teeth mother, naked at last.

She is naked and terrible. But at least we can see her now, as our forebears perhaps could not. In the terror of Vietnam she has become clear to us, our own creation. As Bly explains in his essay, the Teeth Mother "stands for numbness, paralysis, catatonia, being totally spaced out, the psyche torn to bits, arms and legs thrown all over." For the alternative path—the path that leads down into the ocean where "luminous globes float up (in them hairy ecstatic men)"—we must wait until "Sleepers Joining Hands" outlines a map to recovery. Though the outrage of the poem is certainly justified, it looks better in the context of the book as a whole than it does standing alone. "The Teeth Mother Naked at Last" offers a diagram of despair, a brittle anatomy of agony with only a gesture to indicate the possibility of healing, of wholeness.

Here, then, is a picture of the U.S. at our most culturally destructive, annihilating our own shadows—Indians, Blacks, Vietnamese—with whom we must be reunited if we are to have psychic fullness and dimensionality; if we are to be solid enough to cast shadows. Concern for oppression of our shadows pervades the book, essay and poems. But it is neither a continuing accusation nor an extended *mea culpa* that Bly chants, as "Calling to the Badger" shows. This poem, like all of Bly's work on the shadow, is pervaded by a "sadness that rises from the death of the Indians," and that is a sadness for our own loss. "We are driven to Florida like Geronimo" because our imaginations cannot function fully with such a large psychic space blocked out, repressed. Or, in the imagery of "Pilgrim Fish Heads," the Indian we have displaced "vanishes into water. . . . / The Mattapoiset is in league with rotting wood." Thus the denied shadow softens and rots whatever structures we might consciously build.

This backward look over the shadow poems that begin the book can help define the conditions that apply as the title sequence opens. As in most myths (whether the king be impotent, the land waste, or the virgin guarded by a dragon—all of which conditions more or less obtain as we return to the opening of the "Sleepers" sequence) the call to the quest begins with a perception of a lack, an imbalance. Whereas the earlier, shorter poems mainly expressed despair at the loss, "The Shadow Goes Away" proceeds from recognition to restorative action. Our fugitive imaginations are personified in the protagonist who, too, calls to the badger and otter, animals still in touch with the renewing waters of psychic life, the stream that emerges from beneath the ground.

Bly's seeker goes in search of his shadow, which hides in all dark peoples, Negro, Eskimo, Indian, Asian. He enters the inner and outer desert and sees the Sioux "struggling up the mountain in disordered lines" or opens a drawer, a compartment of the unconscious, and sees "small white horses gallop away toward the back" in retreat. He links the destruction of his shadow with his inability to recognize and unite with his anima, the woman within, his own gentleness and intuition:

> I have been divorced five hundred times,
> six hundred times yesterday alone.

Yet even now he has begun to incorporate the shadow's consciousness and values. He will no longer participate in the repression, for he sees where it leads: "The Marines turn to me. They offer me money. / I turn and leave." With the consciousness of the shadow resuscitated, he sees the disfugration of his land. "The suppressed race returns: [it sees] snakes and transistors filling the beaches." Even the planets are despoiled: "The Sea of Tranquility scattered with dead rocks / and black dust resembling diesel oil." Beneath this polluted moon "pilots in armored cockpits [are] finding their way home through moonlit clouds." The equation between past and present betrayals, between Indian and Asian wars, is now complete, clear to the protagonist as well as the reader. Refusing to continue the old path of inner denial and outward oppression, he turns from the zeal of battle to view the littered land with primitive consciousness and compassion. He has begun to assimilate the consciousness of the shadow, and can now continue his journey of integration.

The second poem of the sequence finds the dreamer momentarily awake, noting but not yet comprehending the femininity of the earth on which he finds himself: "fragments of the mother lie open in all low places." But his task here is "Meeting the Man Who Warns Me," and the substance of the warning is that he may not understand, may not proceed further without realizing from a transcendental viewpoint where he has already been.

Dreaming again, the sleeper experiences everywhere the death of the father:

> I dream that the fathers are dying.
> Jehovah is dying, Jesus' father is dying.
> the hired man is asleep inside the oat straw.
> Samson is lying on the ground with his hollow hair.

Even the father's emissary, the Christlike visitor whose circumcising touch puts the protagonist back into a dream, is seen as inhumanly remote, extraterrestrial. The dreamer experiences absolute separation from the presence of the father because he has seen the father only as external; he has not yet recognized the father-energy as a part of himself, waiting to be actualized.

But now that vision can change, for in the paradoxical logic of myth, once the shadow figure has become visible, the light may be seen.

> My shadow is underneath me,
> floating in the dark, in his small boat bobbing among the
>   reeds.
> A fireball floats in the corner of the Eskimo's house—
> It is a light that comes nearer when called!
> A light the spirits turn their heads for,
> suddenly shining over land and sea!
> I taste the heaviness of the dream,
> the northern lights curve up toward the roof of my mouth.
> The energy is inside us. . . .

This energy, this light, is the light of the Self, that truly integrated individual, that near divinity which each human being has the potential to become.

Jung notes that the Self can be symbolized by many sorts of things: a geometric figure, a radiation of light, a tree, stone, well, or any number of "world navel" configurations. But the most prevalent literary and mythical representations of the Self are the babe and the wise old man. It is appropriate that the Self could be represented by youth and age, since it is that nuclear source of energy within us at birth (or reborn in self-discovery), which, if we integrate our lives, comes to the fullness of its wisdom in our maturity. Quite strikingly, as the protagonist of the poem 'sees the light' and realizes that "The energy is inside us," he immediately encounters a personification of the Self:

> I start toward [the light], and I meet an old man.
> . . . .
> And the old man cries out: "I am here.
> Either talk to me about your life, or turn back."

When the protagonist pauses for breath and begins to account for his experience, the rendering is most startling; for it comes from a greater completeness, and a greater mythic awareness than either reader or dreamer knew he had. He begins by announcing his own shadow-including nature and proceeds to recount a mythical journey which neither we nor he knew he had taken.

> "I am the dark spirit that lives in the dark.
> Each of my children is under a leaf he chose from all
>   the leaves in the universe.
> When I was alone, for three years, alone,
> I passed under the earth through the night-water

> I was for three days inside a warm-blooded fish.
> 'Purity of heart is to will one thing.'
> I saw the road."

And when the Self urges him—"Go on! Go on!"—he continues:

> A whale bore me back home, we flew through the air . . .
> Then I was a boy who had never seen the sea!
> It was like a King coming to his own shores.
> I feel the naked touch of the knife,
> I feel the wound,
> this joy I love is like wounds at sea . . ."

Suddenly he has discovered in his own experience, not only the realization of the shadow (which we had shared with him) but also the shape of a quest—complete with a three-day immersion in the belly of a whale, the traditional typological symbol for a descent into the most terrifying aspects of the unconscious (viz. Jonah, Christian iconography, Pinocchio, *et al.*). Until now, he had, like a child born again, forgotten his links with the sea; he was like a king, stranger to his own shore, suddenly realizing the extent of his right and rule. His realization is as sudden as it is complete, as astounding for the dreamer as for the reader. Having thought all the fathers were dead (i.e., having felt the lack of his own origin) he now discovers the light of illumination within himself, and encounters a fatherly wise old man who corresponds to that light in the outer world, only to realize that he, the dreamer himself, is both father and child, "dark spirit" and "boy." Wounded, that is, born and circumcized into the adult male world, the protagonist stops to reflect.

We, too, might take a moment to stop and reflect—to consider the poem's method of proceeding. In the last few paragraphs I have been concerned to establish and outline the continuity of the poem—a continuity which is so far from obvious as to be truly problematic. The obscurity arises, primarily, from the high degree of compression with which the poem was written. (The sequence, I was told casually, was originally five times its present length.) The epiphanic mode, not so unusual in itself, is further complicated by a reversal of the usual relation between outer event and psychic response; here the changing phenomena are dictated by shifts in psychic states (as in dream) rather than the other way around. In order to manage this material, Bly replaces the conventional narrative structure with an implicit and continuous parallelism to Jung's schema of dream imagery in the individuation process.

Though Jung's way of reading the language of dreams is enormously insightful, it is legitimate to ask whether it is so essential a part of our culture that it may be alluded to as a structural principle, as Joyce, say, uses the *Odyssey*. Following archetypal patterns, of course, produces neither merit nor defect in poems, novels, or situation comedies. But requiring external knowledge of patterns is problematic, especially when what is required is not just a general sense of the quest, but Jung's interpretation of it. For without the Jungian frame, and a fair amount of time to apply it, most readers will find some real problems of coherence; and no matter how telling the individual images or how striking the poem's particular emotional effects, difficulties with coherence will diminish the final effect of the poem. Clearly, various readers will count the cost in differing ways—based largely, I suspect, on the ways they have already decided to handle matters such as Eliot's classical eclecticism, Yeats' esotericism, Roethke's Emersonianism, Kinnell's magic, and the like. But a problem that some feel worth overcoming is a problem nevertheless.

The synoptic recollection of the journey of the protagonist, which appears in the last lines of "Meeting the man Who Warns Me," is expanded in "Night Journey in the Cooking Pot," which is a flashback composed of reflections on the experience and meaning of his immersion, of the dark, still uncomprehended part of his quest. Here, again, a problem of continuity confronts us; but the apparently confused and confusing emotional swings of "Night Journey" can be understood once we see that the poem divides itself into two movements, describing two phases of the mythic journey: the departure into the realm of mystery and also the return to the ordinary world. As the seeker begins to reexperience and rearticulate his journey retrospectively, we hear a familiar pattern: "I was born during the night sea journey." That he "love[s] the whale with his warm organ pipes" is less expected, but perfectly consonant: for Bly, this going-out is an *ecstasis*, a standing-outside-of the ego, an ecstasy; it is the return to the world of ordinary men and affairs that proves the difficult leg of the journey.

The departure into the water is a journey into ego-dissolving solitude, a necessary prelude to finding a path of effective action in the ordinary world: "I float on solitude as on water . . . there is a road" (Bly's ellipsis). The poem's first movement explores his privacy, which for Bly is sister word to privilege, not privation. Here we see the rejuvenating exhilaration of going a little crazy in private, deprived of human contact in the "womanless loneliness." The enthusiasm for isolation expressed in "Night Journey" is reinforced and clarified by several of the book's earlier poems. Because it rejuvenates, solitude itself becomes a welcome state, well-captured "In a Mountain Cabin in Norway" where "No one comes to visit us for a week." The short poems which begin the volume deal frequently with solitude in both its aspects, as a going out and as a coming in to center. Ecstasy as *ecstasis* animates "Six Winter Privacy Poems":

> There is a solitude like black mud!
> Sitting in this darkness singing,
> I can't tell if this joy
> is from the body, or the soul, or a third place."

Conversely—as a gloss on "Night Journey's" oracular exhortation "inward, inward, inward"—the "Shack Poem" muses, "How marvelous to be a thought entirely surrounded by brains!"

Finally, of course, this privacy is the solitude of the womb, for the voyage he recalls in "The Night Journey in the Cooking Pot," is the night sea journey in the womb of la mer, notre mère. The cooking pot of the title, like the oven and hearth as Bly explains in his essay, is the province of the woman and symbol of the womb. In the opening movement of "Night Journey" images of rebirth abound: "I feel . . . / the baby whirling in the womb," and "Nuns with faces smoothed by prayer peer out from holes in the earth." When he sees and realizes the possibilities brought by the visitants from the realm of snow and death ("sleeping in anguish like grain, whole, blind in the old grave"), when he intuits the chants of the shamans "with large shoulders covered with furs, / Holy ones with eyes closed," then he comes to rejoice in all signs pointing toward the death that precedes rebirth:

> Leaves slip down, falling through their own branches.
> The tree becomes naked and joyful.
> Leaves fall in the tomby wood.

And it is out of the experience of the retreat, the death, the hibernation that he sings his song of joy.

> Suddenly I love the dancers, leaping
> in the dark . . .
> I start to sing.

But this song is not an easy one, and he knows it. In the second movement of "Night Journey" he faces the difficulty of returning to the world of ordinary experience. Like Buddha, whose ultimate temptation was simply to stay in the oceanic trance of nirvana, like the silent Lazarus and other such questors, this seeker sees how difficult it will be to communicate the joy of going beyond the ego, the personality, the boundaries of our daily round. But like Whitman in "Crossing Brooklyn Ferry," he urges us to realize that we are not separated from him, but united by a common experience we sometimes forget.

> I am not going farther from you
> I am coming nearer,
> green rain carries me nearer you,
> I weave drunkenly about the page,
> I love you,
> I never knew that I loved you
> Until I was swallowed by the invisible.

Here, in his protagonists' plea for understanding, it would seem that we have Bly's apologia for his own method. By writing in the language of dream and vision, he does not hope to remove himself from our experience, for we are all dreamers, and can eventually intuit the scheme of our dreams. If we do not immediately see our waking and sleeping lives as whole and one, it is because the waters of sleep's deep well give the illusion of discontinuity.

> For we are like the branch bent in the water . . .
> Taken out it is whole, it was always whole. . . .
> [Bly's ellipses]

Though he acknowledges that the poem's oracular words may seem skew and difficult, he assures us that when he emerges from the water (night, mother, chaos, unconscious, dream) his speech will be straight as the branch—a promise, as we have seen, difficult to fulfill. What he hopes for (as he said in an earlier poem) is a day in which "if only the fragments in the unconscious would grow as big as the beams in hunting lodges, . . . / we would find holy books in our beds, / Then the Tao Te Ching would come running across the field!" If only.

But such a conclusion is far too optimistic, or else many would have returned and spoken, and redemption would be daily for all men. Bly realizes that—and in the second movement of "Night Journey," the questor suffers the inexorable difficulty of returning to the realm of ordinary experience while preserving his vision. Used to mental traveling, he finds himself constricted by the physical limitations of waking reality: "I think I am the body / the body rushes in and ties me up." Aware of his new clumsiness, he is "ashamed looking at the fish in the water," for he is a fish out. The new being born inside him—the "child in the old moonlit villages of the brain"—is threatened with execution by that Herod, the waking ego and the social system of which, as ego or persona, he finds himself a part. He discovers himself in a role that his deeper, nascent Self had not intended. Hearkening back to the imagery of the early West which characterized "The Shadow Goes Away," he realizes

> Suddenly I am those who run large railroads at dusk,
> who stand around the fallen beast howling,
> who cannot get free, ...
> This is not the perfect freedom of the saints.

Having become one of the very people he would fight against, he realizes the difficulty of action after vision, the dichotomy between what he knows in the absolute realm and the position he occupies in the relative realm. With a fuller understanding he has arrived at the point at which he began the journey we have shared with him in "The Shadow Goes Away."

The personality is divided against itself: with fuller vision now, he sees how he has become his brother's vendor, betrayer of the shadow:

I fall into my own hands,
    fences break down under horses,
cities starve, whole towns of singing women carrying to the
      burial fields
    the look I saw on my father's face,
I sit down again, I hit my own body,
I shout at myself, I see what I have betrayed.
What I have written is not good enough.
Who does it help?
I am ashamed sitting on the edge of my bed.

He is ashamed looking into the limpid pool of his dreams. The poem has moved fully from the ecstasy of the journey to the restrictions of the return. And those restrictions include the difficulty of making the poem "good enough."

In the fourth poem, Bly spells out the nature of the journey as explicitly as possible:

Here is some prose
    Once there was a man who went to a far country
    to get his inheritance and then returned.

This, of course, is (in the phrase of James Joyce and the system of Joseph Campbell) the "monomyth" in its briefest form: the story of the hero who is called from the ordinary world of experience into the realm of the mysterious, where he battles various foes, conquers or converts them, and gains a boon, his "inheritance," a life-restoring elixir with which he recrosses the threshold and with which, after some readjustment, he transforms the world or his vision of it.

Bly uses his water imagery to suggest an intriguing relation between the realm of mystery and the boon snatched from it. The pool, the lake into which he has gazed, the night sea through which he has traveled in dream vision, all now become "Water Drawn Up Into the Head." The questor now encompasses what once encompassed him. In the same way that, in the Judaic tradition, the redeemed feast on the now delicious flesh of the devouring monsters Behemoth, Leviathan, and Ziz, so the very ocean of the night sea journey becomes the elixir which nourishes the poet, granting him the serenity of the final poem and the joy of the "Extra Chorus" which follows it.

This liquid optimism has already found voice in "Water Under the Earth": "everything we need is buried . . . , it's under the water guarded by women." (And in "The Turtle," "huge turtle eggs / lie inland on the floor of the old sea.") The promise of the water is that consciousness can be bathed in, nourished by and brought to rebirth via the fluid world of the unconscious. If tapped, the subterranean sea can yield the healing balm that unites the diverse aspects of fragmented man within his Self and joins him with all other men.

Progression begins with regression, conscious realization with a descent into the unconscious.

> There is a consciousness hovering under the mind's feet,
> advanced civilizations under the footsole,
> climbing at times upon a shoelace!
> It is a willow that knows of the water under the earth,
> I am a father who dips as he passes over underground rivers,
> who can feel his children through all distance and time!

The mind, like a funerary willow, draws the water from beneath the earth and manifests it in leaves and swaying branches: water drawn up into the head produces that fluid and protean vision of the poems Bly has created, nourishes his vision of himself and all men.

"When alone," when in privacy with the wellspring of the unconscious, "we see that great tomb [the material world] is not God," and "We know of Christ, who raised the dead, and started time. / He is not God, and is not called God." Trying to find God outside ourselves, Bly suggests, is to deny the inner springs, the water drawn up into the head. "Best is to let them lose themselves in a river:" best to immerse yourself in the energy of the unconscious, energy of the Self, and learn from your dreams, visions and intuitions that you yourself are the transcendental; and then to drink from that knowledge continuously.

> So rather than saying Christ is God or he is not,
> it is better to forget all that
> and lose yourself in the curved energy.
> I entered that energy one day . . .

The God he discovers himself to be a part of has no name, because he is beyond the pairs of opposites, good and evil, kine and predator:

> We have no name for you, so we say:
> he makes grass grow upon the mountains,
> and gives food to the dark cattle of the sea,
> he feeds the young ravens that call on him.

There is a nascent realization, a new Self, "another being living inside" the poet: "He is looking out of my eyes. / I hear him / in the wind through the bare trees." It is the wind in the barren trees that alerts him to his own birth, it is the death of the old self that so confidently presages the new. And "that is why I am so glad in fall." The poet beside the bare and naked tree trunk waits for true nakedness to come to him as well. And as Jung observes, the tree is often a symbol for the developing self, bringing forth energy from the invisible underground reservoir of the unconscious to be manifested in the world of light and form.

As Ginsberg ended *Howl* with a joyous footnote—not as a palinode, but to affirm the divinity of the horror he chronicled—so to this strange and often painful oneiric journey, Bly appends "An Extra Joyful Chorus for Those Who Have Read This Far." In several ways the chorus alludes heavily to Whitman. Its closing lines (and indeed the very title of the entire "Sleepers Joining Hands" sequence) bear strong resemblance to the opening of the last section of Whitman's poem "The Sleepers":

> The sleepers are very beautiful as they lie unclothed,
> They flow hand in hand over the whole earth from east
>   to west as they lie unclothed.

And, chiasmatically, lines that Whitman uses to close his poem on a cyclical note

> I will stop only a time with the night. . . . and rise
>   betimes.
> I will duly pass the day O my mother and duly return
>   to you

Bly transforms into a paradoxical opening for his "Joyful Chorus":

> I love the Mother.
> I am an enemy of the Mother.

The allusions are clear. Yet, though both poems record psychological night sea journeys, and though both close with affirmations, the similarities between the poems are not continuous. Bly borrows from Whitman for his own ends, as we shall see.

And so with technique. The "Joyful Chorus," Bly's chant of polymorphous identity which echoes and goes beyond his handling of the protean shadow in "The Shadow Goes Away," also recalls Whitman's chants of universal identity. Here again, there are some important differences to balance the similarities. Whitman's sympathetic identifications are usually directed toward the commonplace and the possible, encouraging the reader to follow along:

> I am the actor and the actress. . . . the voter and
>   the politician. . . .
> . . . .
> A shroud I see—and I am the shroud. . . . I wrap a
>   body and lie in the coffin. . . .

Most typically, in the words of "Song of Myself," "I am the man. . . . I suffered. . . . I was there." Bly, on the other hand, opts to include the fantastical and folkloristic along with the ordinary and credible, which encourages the reader to relate these elements to other symbolic quests or to translate them into his own terms, but not to engage directly in the protagonist's own identification:

> I am the ball of fire the woodman cuts out of the
>   wolf's stomach,
> I am the sun that floats over the Witch's house,
> I am the horse sitting in the chestnut tree singing.

While both poets work within the tradition of the psychic quest, Bly is also *referring* to it, and asking the reader to refer to it, schematically.

Like Whitman, Bly makes use of the transcendent power of the aggregate. The catalogue of beautiful and ordinary and terrible beginnings which dominates the first sixty lines of section 15 of "Song of Myself" yields the aggregate exhilaration of Beginning; in "The Sleepers" the catalogue of actor, nominee, stammerer and criminal in an averaged aggregate of sleeping humanity allows Whitman to say

> The soul is always beautiful
> The universe is duly in order. . . . every thing
>   is in its place. . . .
> . . . .
> The diverse shall be no less diverse, but they shall
>   flow and unite . . . they unite now.

For Bly's protagonist the transcendent aggregate is the experience of the completed quest: its component parts, no matter how painful, finally become redeemed because of their place in the whole. Even "fleeing along the ground like a frightened beast" or being "the last inheritor crying out in deserted houses" become fit matter for a "Joyful Chorus" when the protagonist realizes that he is at every moment "an eternal happiness fighting in the long reeds." Each act contains the imprint of all others, and of the completed sequence. Bly's questor images his life everywhere at once and at all stages simultaneously. Perhaps most summatively he is "the man locked inside the oakwomb, / waiting for lightning, only let out on stormy nights." He is that core of life in the tree of the Self, drawn from subterranean waters and waiting, now that the old foliage has died, to manifest himself in the new spring. He is everyone and "no one at all" simultaneously, for he is prior to personality. Thus, in the womb, aching to deliver himself, he can paradoxically say:

> I love the Mother.
> I am an enemy of the Mother, give me my sword.
> I leap into her mouth full of seaweed.

For he honors the womb of the unconscious and arational which he has reentered as embryo, and he honors the rational and masculine desire to translate that primeval wholeness into the articulate world of forms—water to leaves, sea to sword.

Further, he sees and feels the archetypal nature and universal possibility of his experience—new incarnations and new Bethlehems for all men who attend to their dreams:

> Our faces shine with the darkness reflected from the
> Tigris. . . .
> The panther rejoices in the gathering dark.
> Hands rush toward each other through miles of space.
> All the sleepers in the world join hands.

Tiny Poems

HOWARD NELSON

> While dreaming, perhaps, the hand
> Of the man who broadcasts the stars like grain
> Made the lost music start once more
> Like the note from a huge harp,
> And the frail wave came to our lips
> In the form of one or two words that had some truth.
> —Antonio Machado
> tr. Charles Reynolds[1]

Since Bly is a poet who creates books that are not miscellaneous gatherings but rather strive for unity of one sort or another, I have thought it best to base the organization of this study on the individual major collections as Bly has conceived and published them. This chapter, however, will depart from that scheme. Thus far I have skipped over with only passing mention a type of poem represented in both *Snowy Fields* and *Sleepers Joining Hands:* the tiny poem, the poem of three or four or half a dozen lines. I have not done so out of a feeling that these poems are minor. On the contrary, they seem to me a distinctive and significant facet of Bly's work, and so I want to give them some specific attention. Far from being merely a novelty or diversion, this form lends itself to some of Bly's talents and themes in special ways, and one finds within this category some of his most memorable and magical poems.

Many of the tiny poems appeared first, or so far have appeared only, in limited editions from small presses. A number of those I'll be referring to, for example, are from an exquisite, hand-decorated pamphlet, now out of print, entitled *The Loon*, from the Ox Head Press of Marshall, Minnesota. A small press publisher himself, Bly has always contributed to and drawn from this alternative publishing network on which the life and liveliness of poetry in America so largely depend. The list of books, booklets, and broadsides that Bly has published through small presses in a long one, and the titles he has brought out through his own Sixties/Seventies Press include a number of collections that have significantly influenced and enriched contemporary American poetry. It seems appropriate to mention small presses in connection with small

Reprinted from *Robert Bly: An Introduction to the Poetry* by Howard Nelson (New York: Columbia University Press, 1984), 113–27, 241–42. Reprinted by permission of Columbia University Press.

poems, as both represent life far from the giganticism and commercial standards of mass culture, which increasingly dominate mainstream publishing in the United States along with the rest of the society.

In 1966 Bly edited and published an anthology of tiny poems called *The Sea and the Honeycomb*.[2] The book shows him at his trenchant best as an editor. It has an idea with some freshness to it—that the very short poem corresponds to the swiftness of brief emotions, emotions largely ignored in a poetic tradition in which the sonnet has been the shortest form respected—and an introduction and selection of poems that make the idea vivid and alive. The territory Bly ranges over for the poems is, characteristically, wide; the selection, unconventional and eclectic. Among the poets are Spanish Arabs of the early Middle Ages, the Japanese haiku masters, classic moderns from several countries, and the young American poet Saint Geraud (Bill Knott), something of a genius in the very short poem. Also characteristically, the book has a strong bias, and here once again the bias is against the rational element in poetry, and in favor of the associative and intuitive. It is particularly biased against the epigram. The epigram, ruled by wit, irony, and denotative statement, is not only disallowed from the anthology, but from poetry as well: the epigram, Bly says, is "not a poem but a versified idea. . . . a commentary on a suppressed poem."[3] The problem, to put it another way, is that the epigram tends to create with rational and witty statement a tight seal which prevents the waters of the unconscious from entering; it is, therefore, from Bly's point of view, an antipoetic form. (It's interesting to note that when rationalists complain about the sort of poetry they dislike they sometimes use the word "damp." When Bly says that a poem has moisture in it, he is paying it a compliment.)

In his introduction Bly uses an analogy to make concrete his sense of the influence of discursive rationalism in a poem:

> Many of the manuscripts we have of early Greek lyric poets like Alcaeus come down from copies made by scholars in Alexandrian libraries. Sometimes a scholar, after he had copied a brief, intense poem of Alcaeus, written several hundred years earlier, would add to it a composition of his own in the same meter, embodying his own thoughts upon reading the poem. Oddly enough today the same poet writes both parts. If he is skillful in rhythm and tone, the link is almost unnoticeable. An epigram is actually a piece written entirely by the Alexandrian scholar. . . .
>
> An Alexandrian scholar is lurking inside most American poets: the American poet sitting at his desk writes a fine, intense poem of seven or eight lines, then a hand silently appears from somewhere inside his shirt and hastily adds fifteen more lines, telling us what the emotion means, relating it to philosophy, and adding a few moral comments. The invisible scholar is outraged at the idea of anyone writing a brief poem, because he is hardly able to get his chalky hand out of his cloak before the poem is over![4]

Bly's analogies are persistently among the most provocative, telling, and downright interesting moments in contemporary criticism; and if epigrams frequently live by wit, so, in a different form, do Bly's analogies. A second, and a third, complete the introduction's advocacy of the tiny, nonepigrammatic poem:

> *Paradise Lost* is a good example of the long poem. Milton is always there, holding his hand beneath you. He doesn't want you to fall. When angels appear, he suggests the proper attitude to take toward angels. In short, he tells you what to think. He has a huge hand underneath you. In the brief poem, it is all different: the poet takes the reader to the edge of a cliff, as a mother eagle takes its nestling, and then drops him. Readers with a strong imagination enjoy it, and discover they can fly. The others fall down to the rocks where they are killed instantly.
>
> The poet who succeeds in writing a short poem is like a man who has found his way through a stone wall into a valley miles long, where he lives. He walks back up the valley, and opens a door in the wall for an instant to show you where the entrance is. The more imaginative readers are able to slip through in the twenty or thirty seconds it takes to read his poem. Those who expect the poet to give them ideas see only a vague movement on the side of the mountain. Before they have turned all the way around to face the poem, the door is closed.
>
> Readers of recent poetry are used to staggering along under lines swelled with the rhetoric of philosophy courses, experiences under mind-expanding drugs, new criticism—in short, the world of prose. They find it hard at first to concentrate on a short poem, but eventually they learn to find some value in being dropped.[5]

The flying involved in reading tiny poems is a different matter from the flying I referred to in connection with Bly's wildly associative longer poems, such as "Hair" or "An Extra Joyful Chorus." In both cases flying entails associative powers, but in the longer poems the poet carries the reader along with him on broad wings of flowing images and rhetoric; the challenge is not to lose our hold. In the tiny poems, as Bly's metaphor says, it is the reader who must be able to fly on his own.

How much can be accomplished, after all, in a handful of lines that abandon rhyme, the symmetry of set form, and the cutting edge of reason's wit? To some, such poems will seem, no matter whom they are written by, to be works of minimalism and not much more; they will seem to have given up too much—nearly everything. But keeping the Alexandrian scholar out of the poem entirely and relying only on a moment's sliver of seeing and feeling is a discipline that can lead to a freedom and, paradoxically, a great sense of spaciousness. Here is a brief love poem, "Taking the Hands":

> Taking the hands of someone you love,
> You see they are delicate cages . . .
> Tiny birds are singing
> In the secluded prairies
> And in the deep valleys of the hand.
> *(Silence in the Snowy Fields)*

The word "cages" catches a reality of love, yet the birds in those cages sing within expanses of privacy and intimacy. In its five lines the poem follows a smooth arc of associations, from the hands' resemblance to cages, to birds, to the prairies and valleys where they also sing, and from the prairies and valleys back to the hands whose surfaces and creases they, in turn, resemble. The arc becomes a circle so quickly and effortlessly that we arrive back at our starting point before we had realized that we had left it. The fragment implies a whole whose borders are known only to the imagination, and the smallest poems sometimes contain the widest, freshest spaces.

As we know from haiku and the Imagists, the senses can sometimes be sharpened in the very brief poem. A single sight or sound is focused on, inhabited, as if it were a world. Often such sensory pleasure is central in Bly's tiny poems, as in "Grass":

> The cottonwood leaves
> lie naked on the grass
> still chilled from the night.
> *(The Loon)*

But the objectivity of this poem is not typical. As noted before, objectivity is not high among Bly's poetic values, though he has great ability as sheer describer of the physical world. In the tiny poems as nearly everywhere in his work, subjectivity is invited in, and celebrated along with the world it apprehends. (There will be more to say about description and subjectivity in the following chapter, on *The Morning Glory,* where the blend is often extraordinarily rich.) Somewhere at the other end of the spectrum from "Grass" would be "A Cricket in the Wainscoating":

> That song of his is like a boat with black sails.
> Or a window under a redwood tree, warning
> passersby that the tree is about to fall.
> Or a bell made of black tin in a Mexican village.
> Or the hair in the ear of a hundred-year-old man!
> *(This Tree Will Be Here*
> *for A Thousand Years)*

That "is like" is a slender thread; I think it holds. This is decidedly not the more conventional poetic version of a cricket, chirping on some quiet Wordsworthian hearth, and the poem's appeal lies partly in its impulsiveness and humor. Beyond this, however, the smiles do capture in their unexpected associations qualities of the song and its maker. Black seems the right color, tin the right metal, the hair in the ear of a hundred-year-old man the right hair, for the ragged, homely night-song of a tiny, dark, shiny, hidden creature. The sound has a feeling akin to some artifact produced in a Mexican village—

certainly not in a factory in Pittsburgh or Japan. The widow at the foot of the redwood is like the cricket at the foot of nature; their cries have the same urgency and smallness. In this poem it is precisely in the balance between oddness and rightness that the poetry lies.

If, as Bly said in the introduction to *The Sea and the Honeycomb,* brief poems have a special relationship to brief emotions, we might examine a couple of his tiny poems from the stand-point of the emotion they carry. The most obvious effect of a poem of this length is the suddenness with which it accomplishes itself, and the attentiveness and quickness with which it credits its reader. Reading such a poem can be very much like experiencing an emotional sensation or awareness which arrives abruptly, and can pass again just as abruptly. But the poem remains on the page and can be reexperienced and lingered over, and beyond the effect of suddenness, what one often discovers in a good very brief poem is a subtle richness. The brief emotion may be powerful through its purity—just a single clear ray of joy, a single black grain of grief—but also through its delicate shading. For example, consider "Marietta, Minnesota":

> Wonderful Saturday nights
> with girls wandering about!
> New farm machinery
> standing quietly in the cool grass.
> *(The Loon)*

The youth and aimlessness of the girls, and the strange calm of large, brightly painted machines still and stolid on the grass, make a juxtaposition within which an atmosphere of countless evenings in countless small rural towns is captured. One could write a poem on the same subject in a different mood—it might include some young males leaning against their cars smoking—but here the sexual energy floating in the air is not surly but piquant and joyful. Not much may be happening in those towns, but the poet finds this night beautifully fresh and vivid, like the girls and the silent machines he notices. Yet the poem's mood does have its shadow, which is the knowledge of time implicit in its description of its moment. One can hear in the poem's chord of pleasure a note of sadness. One can hear it even in the word "wonderful"—not that Bly uses it with irony, but simply with the awareness, possibly unconscious just then, that part of what makes brightness moving to us is the fact that it fades. The perfect, unmarked machines will lose their oddly impractical brightness soon enough to time and toil, and something similar will happen to the girls. So there is poignance as well as vitality here; in poems, brief ones perhaps especially, what is not said often accents what is.

Another poem, "Kabekona Lake":

> Lots of men could sleep
> on those fir branches
> swaying near the widow's house!

The first two lines join two images, one realistic, one surreal. Energy flows between them tentatively; the branches and the sleeping men sway together duskily. But when we come to the word "widow," a circuit completes itself, and in an instant we not only understand the association of the first two lines but also feel, in a delicate shock of recognition, a remarkable depth of love, loneliness, and sorrow. The poem's emotion is serious, but Philip Dacey, in reviewing *The Loon,* noted first its "humor, tact, and charm"[6]—and clearly those qualities are present as well. Once again a tiny poem possesses a fine emotional shading, a richness within the space of its fourteen words. (The poem has, incidentally, seventeen syllables, but that is no doubt coincidental. Bly has never been interested in the syllable-count aspect of haiku, but rather in its emotional and imaginative effect. In an interview he remarked: "The Japanese say the haiku is a poem in which there's a tiny explosion inside—and if that's not there—I don't care how many syllables it's got—then it's not a haiku. And that little tiny explosion brings the life to this creature.[7])

Bly ended the essay "I Came Out of the Mother Naked," in *Sleepers Joining Hands,* with the following statement: "I see in my own poems and the poems of so many other poets alive now fundamental attempts to right our own spiritual balance, by encouraging those parts in us that are linked with music, with solitude, water, and trees, the parts that grow when we are far from the centers of ambition."[8] A poem of three or four lines may have a special value in this encouragement; with its quickness, smallness, and sharpness it slips past ambition into the present moment, just as a sudden clear perception can sometimes be an awakening:

WATERING THE HORSE

How strange to think of giving up all ambition!
Suddenly I see with such clear eyes
The white flake of snow
That has just fallen in the horse's mane!
(Silence in the Snowy Fields)

One can feel here again the influence of Chinese poetry which I spoke of in discussing *Snowy Fields*—particularly in the theme often expressed by the old Chinese poets, worn out by official duties, beleaguered by tempestuous times: retirement, turning away from the world of affairs to experience a different life, as in this wonderful poem by the Ming poet Yüan Hung-tao, translated by Jonathan Chaves, "On Receiving My Letter of Termination":

The time has come to devote myself to my hiker's stick;
I must have been a Buddhist monk in a former life!
Sick, I see returning home as a kind of pardon.
A stranger here—being fired is like being promoted.

In my cup, thick wine; I get crazy drunk,
eat my fill, then stagger up the green mountain.
The southern sect, the northern sect, I've tried them all;
this hermit has his own school of Zen philosophy.[9]

A difference, of course, is that Yüan's poem describes a turning in a lifetime; Bly's, a turning of consciousness at a certain moment of a single day. Yet in a fundamental way they represent the same movement: a breakthrough into a state of being that is rich through simplicity and immediacy, a breakthrough into "what is." "Watering the Horse" is not a renunciation of ambition; it only says, "How strange to think. . . ." One does not write twenty books without ambition. Yet we need those moments when it all falls away. Ambition per se is not destructive, but that which never allows us to see the flake in the horse's mane takes the universe out of our lives. It is not irrelevant that an animal is close by when such a moment of awareness takes place—the animals are, apparently, masters of being at home in the senses and the present—or that it is a thing as ephemeral as a snowflake that acts as catalyst.

Bly's tiny poems take quick, often affectionate jabs at the preoccupation and clutter of our lives, as in "August Sun":

Strips of August sun come in through shutters.
Baskets of unanswered letters
lie on chairs.
Some foolish man must live here!

Busyness, one of ambition's lower relatives, is addressed specifically, though inversely, in some of the tiny poems. A number of them celebrate "doing nothing," a kind of anti-discipline which can lead to unusual transformation and satisfactions:

A DOING NOTHING POEM

After walking about all afternoon
barefoot,
I have grown long and transparent. . . .
. . . like a seaslug
who has lived along doing nothing
for eighteen thousand years!
(Jumping Out of Bed)

Not only is the seaslug devoid of ambition, but evolution itself has seemingly left it behind. But the poem takes pleasure in imagining such an extraordinary, primal leisure. I think of Whitman, like Bly a poet of the road, saying in Section 27 of "Song of Myself," "If nothing lay more develop'd the quahaug in its callous shell were enough." As human beings we resist that thought, but it is good to keep it in mind for the sake of perspective. Meanwhile, both Bly and Whitman recognize the place of loafing and regression in inviting the soul.

Many of Bly's tiny poems contain animals, partly for reasons mentioned above. He is both delighted and moved by the intentness of nature, of creatures going their own inscrutable ways:

DUCKS

> Two white ducks waddle past my door
> Moving fast:
> They are needed somewhere!
>
> *(Ducks)*

Paradoxically, the poem expresses this very inscrutability by explaining the ducks' motivation, and in distinctly inappropriate human terms. It gives the wrong reason, and thereby somehow manages to get at the truth.

At other times other moods surround a visitation from the animal world:

ALONE

> The river moves silent under the great trees.
> A fish breaks water,
> and then, a few feet farther down, again.
>
> *(The Loon)*

A man feels more alone—yet sometimes, perhaps, less lonely—for being reminded of the animal other, sharing the stream of time with him in a nearly complete separateness. Or possibly I intrude the man where none is intended. Bly may be focusing on the absolute aloneness of a fish jumping in a silent river, with no observor at all to "see" the scene for us, evoking a solitude so great that the human conception of loneliness seems for a moment small and incongruous, out of place in this universe, this calm eternity.

At the same time that he is aware of the otherness of animals, Bly reaches out across the gap between them and the human. Perfectly poised and deeply penetrating, the following poem seems to me among the best of Bly's tiny poems:

THE LOON

> From far out in the center of the naked lake
> the loon's cry rose . . .
> it was the cry of someone who owned very little.
>
> *(The Loon)*

The words "center" and "naked" stretch out the line, but in their effect they move us toward the recognition, made explicit in the final line, of an essential state of being—the voice of a creature, of the thing itself, life simplified and clarified, coming suddenly across the water. Such a response to the cry of loons may have been one reason why Thoreau was fascinated by them, though in "Brute Neighbors," where he gives literature's best-known account of an encounter between man and loon, he emphasizes rather the unpredictable energy of the bird, appearing and disappearing and laughing in the waters of the pond. In the poem the bird, and the natural world of which it is a part, is again distant from us, "far out"—yet why is it that the cry of the loon gets so directly to the heart? Why does it seem, in fact, to rise in the heart and in the mind at the same instant it rises from the lake? There is no explanation for that, but we can note that Bly shares with Thoreau an exceptional ability to translate into words the language they both hear the natural world speaking to the human soul.

Because they are different from us, animals are associated in our minds with that is hidden from us as we remain sitting in the small room of ordinary human consciousness:

FALL

The spider disappears over the side
of the yellow book, like
a door into a room never used.
                                        (*The Loon*)

The sense of other rooms, of the hidden "other," is a sustaining mystery in Bly's poetry. We have seen it in the landscapes of *Snowy Fields,* in the visionary glimpses at the end of *The Light,* and in the spiritual record of "Sleepers Joining Hands." But here again the tiny poem seems especially well-suited for describing the experience, as for example in this one, in which the presence of that "someone" who moves in the music of Bach is felt:

LISTENING TO BACH

There is someone inside this music
who is not well described by the names
of Jesus, or Jehovah, or the Lord of Hosts!
                        ("Six Winter Privacy Poems,"
                        Sleepers Joining Hands)

At times "the other" makes itself known not through an animal or inspired music, but in an intuitive knowledge of another self besides the "I." One of the finest renderings in poetry of the other who both is and is not oneself comes in this poem by Juan Ramón Jiménez, which Bly has translated, "I Am Not I":

> I am not I.
>   I am this one
> walking beside me whom I do not see,
> whom at times I manage to visit,
> and whom at other times I forget;
> who remains calm and silent while I talk,
> and forgives, gently, when I hate,
> who walks where I am not,
> who will remain standing when I die.[10]

Here is a similar poem by Bly which, in its own way, is just as fine:

> When I woke, new snow had fallen.
> I am alone, yet someone else is with me,
> drinking coffee, looking out at the snow.
>   ("Six Winter Privacy Poems,"
>   *Sleepers Joining Hands*)

"Drinking coffee, looking out at the snow": these details communicate the shadowy presence with utmost calm and suggestiveness; it is *physically* there. Again, as in the Bach poem, "someone." As Jiménez says, we sometimes visit, or are visited by, someone beyond us, *this one;* and sometimes that someone is forgotten. For Bly, the possibility of the visit is the possibility of ecstasy, of vision, of new life. The visitor may be many things. It would be hard to exaggerate the importance of the visitor in his poetry.

    The soul of the tiny poem is its suggestiveness, spareness, and swiftness. It lets go everything but the moment of perception, emotion, and intuition, and by doing so it achieves both clarity and mystery. I have tried to move quickly in this survey of Bly's tiny poems, but writing about them one does feel somewhat like the Alexandrian scholar, with his chalky white hand. Having noted a few of their primary effects and recurrent themes, I would like to end this chapter by taking a liberty, and allowing the reader one, by quoting two more tiny poems—the first of which appeared in *Poetry* magazine,[11] the second from "Six Winter Privacy Poems"—without comment.

THE MOOSE

> The Arctic moose drinks at the tundra's edge,
> swirling the watercress with his mouth.
> How fresh the water is, the coolness of the far North.
> A light wind moves through the deep firs.
>
> My shack has two rooms; I use one.
> The lamplight falls on my chair and table
> and I fly into one of my own poems—
> I can't tell you where—

as if I appeared where I am now,
in a wet field, snow falling.

Notes

1. *The Sixties* (Fall 1960), 4:9. Charles Reynolds contributed a number of poems and translations to *The Fifties/Sixties.* He was identified in the contributors notes as living "in seclusion in the Black Hills of South Dakota." Like Crunk, the magazine's regular critic, Charles Reynolds is Robert Bly.

2. Bly, *The Sea and the Honeycomb.* Beacon Press reissued a number of titles originally published by the Sixties/Seventies Press. In the cases of these books, the page numbers in my citations refer to the Beacon editions, as these are likely to be more accessible to the reader.

3. *Ibid.,* p. ix.

4. *Ibid.,* pp. ix–x.

5. *Ibid.,* pp. x–xi.

6. Dacey, "This Book Is Made of Turkey Soup and Star Music," p. 43.

7. Bly, *Talking All Morning,* p. 190.

8. Bly, *Sleepers Joining Hands,* p. 50.

9. Yüan Hung-tao, *Pilgrim of the Clouds,* Jonathan Chaves, tr. (New York: John Weatherhill, Inc., 1978), p. 31.

10. Bly, ed., *Lorca and Jiménez: Selected Poems,* p. 77.

11. *Poetry* (August 1981), 138:284.

"The Body with the Lamp Lit Inside": Robert Bly's New Poems

Ralph J. Mills, Jr.

Prose poems have been appearing with frequency in the work of American poets for the past few years; there have been special issues of magazines devoted to them, and the poet Michael Benedikt has complied a large international anthology of the prose poem which will soon be published. The reasons for interest and practice in this form are doubtless many, but they must surely include the increasingly cosmopolitan atmosphere of our poetry in the last decade and a half and the open, exploratory mood of most writers. When Karl Shapiro selected his prose poem "The Dirty Word" as his favorite piece for the anthology *Poet's Choice* (1962), he did so, his accompanying remarks indicate, as an act of defiance, an assertion of freedom from the "habit" of metrical writing. Shapiro had written the poem long before; St. John Perse had praised it. But its inclusion in the anthology came at a moment which must have been for him one of aesthetic decision, for two years later he published his extraordinary collection of prose poems, *The Bourgeois Poet*.

Had Shapiro been a French poet, there would be nothing startling or newsworthy about a decision to write in this form: some French poets have employed it exclusively or almost exclusively, others have alternated between it and the various possibilities of free or formal verse. At least from Aloysius Bertrand's *Gaspard de la Nuit* (1842) to the present, it has been an integral part of the French poetic tradition. It has appeared in modern German poetry and has been widely used in Spanish and Latin American writing. In American poetry, however, so far as I know, its manifestations have been relatively scarce and scattered, visible occasionally in Williams, Eliot ("Hysteria"), Patchen, and Shapiro, for example. That was the situation until recent years. Now one finds considerable preoccupation and practice with the form among such poets as John Ashbery, Russell Edson, Michael Benedikt, David Ignatow, James Wright, W.S. Merwin, Donald Hall, Vern Rutsala, to name a few, and to the point here, Robert Bly.

I don't propose to offer in this article any general comments on the form of the prose poem itself, which would require a large scholarly acquaintance with European literature I don't possess. From what I do gather, the form is

Reprinted from *Northeast* 3, no. 2 (Winter 1976–77): 37–47. Reprinted by permission of the author.

elastic and accommodating: it may be lyric or dramatic, descriptive or narrative, fabulistic or anecdotal—or some combination of these, or something else entirely. Clearly, the poet is freed of the usual concerns of poetic construction in favor of the greater latitude permitted by the unit of the paragraph. But it does seem that each poet who takes up the prose poem does so for particular reasons which give the resulting work a singular, distinctive character. So, for instance, Baudelaire says in the dedicatory letter to *Paris Spleen:* "Which one of us, in his moments of ambition, has not dreamed of the miracle of a poetic prose, musical, without rhythm and without rhyme, supple enough and rugged enough to adapt itself to the lyrical impulses of the soul, the undulations of reverie, the jibes of conscience?"[1] And to move up to the present, Russell Edson writes in a recent essay on the prose poem: "To find a prose free of the self-consciousness of poetry; a prose more compact than the storyteller's; a prose removed from the formalities of *literature*. . . ."[2] Such passages indicate for us the highly individual approaches taken to the form, as well as the sense of a certain kind of liberation, of poetic elbow-room, that goes with them.

Robert Bly is not a newcomer to the prose poem. It is not possible to say when he first attempted to write in this fashion without information from the poet himself, but a look at his first book, *Silence in the Snow Fields,* discovers two prose poems, "Sunset at a Lake" and "Fall," while the small volume he shares with James Wright and William Duffy, *The Lion's Tail and Eyes,* published the same year, 1962, contains another, "Sparks." So we can guess that Bly has a fairly long familiarity with this type of poem. Recent years have seen him turn to it more often, perhaps as a different and compelling avenue for his imagination's impulses, which in his anti-war poems and his poems of—can we say—mythic and social intent (as in large portions of *The Light Around the Body* and *Sleepers Joining Hands*) were otherwise engaged. Many readers will recognize that *The Morning Glory*[3] is a new, enlarged version of the original chapbook of that title first issued by Kayak Books in 1969 with twelve poems, then reissued in a second edition with twenty poems by the same publisher. The present collection also includes *Point Reyes Poems,* a chapbook initially published by Mudra in 1974, as well as other prose poems gathered from periodicals. Bly's continuing attraction to the potentialities of the form, beyond, that is, the contents of *The Morning Glory,* is attested to by the Fall 1975 issue of *Field,* where three prose poems from a new sequence are printed.

In the course of his career as a poet and thinker, Bly's writings have demonstrated a growing concentration of energies in the direction of the public life as it can be probed inwardly, from beneath, as it were, through imaginative submersion in the "deep mind" (to borrow a term from Donald Hall's essay on Whitman) and the articulation of what is discovered in a poetry that is more and more oracular, as well as surrealist (in Bly's sense of the "leaping" Spanish or Latin American surrealism of Lorca or Vallejo or Neruda) in cast. His latest essays, on the "Mothers" in *Sleepers Joining Hands* and on "The Three Brains" in *Leaping Poetry,* reveal frontiers of concern in the areas of psychology, religion, and something like mystical apprehension (or the bases of it) which are quite congruent with the more extreme metaphoric constructions of a poem such as "Hair" or the title sequence of poems from *Sleepers Joining Hands* with its complex motifs, far-reaching imagery, and its somewhat hermetic air.

Still, a reader who opens *Sleepers Joining Hands* for the first time and begins with the initial group of "Six Winter Privacy Poems" will not feel he has ventured into foreign territory or lost his way, for these poems ar instantly recognizable as parts of the poetic and imaginative world which Bly started to make his own out of solitude, reflection, and attention both to place and its images and to the mind and its rich, unbidden images that rise up drenched from a sea of allusion in the beautiful pieces of *Silence in the Snowy Fields.* Here are the beginning pair of those half-dozen winter poems to illustrate the resonance I've indicated:

> *I*
> About four, a few flakes.
> I empty the teapot out in the snow,
>   feeling shoots of joy in the new cold.
> By nightfall, wind,
> the curtains on the south sway softly.

> *II*
> My shack has two rooms; I use one.
> The lamplight falls on my chair and table
> and I fly into one of my own poems—
> I can't tell you where—
> as if it appeared where I am now,
> in a wet field, snow falling.

The affinity with Bly's earlier poetry—which is emphatically *not* to be taken for duplication or repetition—can be seen even more clearly with a single example from his first book, chosen at random, "September Night with an Old Horse":

> *I*
> Tonight I rode through the cornfield in the moonlight!
> The dying grass is still, waiting for winter,
> And the dark weeds are waiting, as if under water. . . .

> *II*
> In Arabia, the horses live in the tents,
> Near dark gold, and water, and tombs.

> *III*
> How beautiful to walk out at midnight in the moonlight
> Dreaming of animals.

The prose poems of *The Morning Glory* and the poems gathered in another new collection, *Old Man Rubbing His Eyes,*[4] with handsome drawings by Franz Albert Richter, seem to me to emerge from the same primal ground of Bly's imagination as the "Six Winter Privacy Poems" or *Silence in the Snowy Fields* or *Jumping Out of Bed,* where the inward being and the outer world of landscape, objects, creatures, or whatever, coalesce. The product of this fusion is mutual enrichment in a poetry which combines precision and accuracy of detail with the freedom of dreaming. A passage from Gaston Bachelard's *The Poetics of Reverie* is apt here and, I think, suggestive of the sort of process that occurs in Bly's mind and art:

> When a dreamer of reveries has swept aside all the "preoccupations" which were encumbering his everyday life, when he has detached himself from the worry that comes to him from the worry of others, when he is thus truly the *author of his solitude,* when he can finally contemplate a beautiful aspect of the universe without counting the minutes, that dreamer feels a being opening within him. Suddenly such a dreamer is a *world dreamer.* He opens himself to the world, and the world opens itself to him. One has never seen the world well if he has not dreamed what he was seeing. In a reverie of solitude which increases the solitude of the dreamer, two depths pair off, reverberate in echoes which go from the depths of being of the world to a depth of being of the dreamer. Time is suspended. Time no longer has any yesterday and no longer any tomorrow. Time is engulfed in the double depth of the dreamer and the world.[5]

In a poem, "To Live," from *Old Man Rubbing His Eyes,* Bly assumes an unexpected perspective on the procedures of what he calls "'Living.'" The descriptive details of the poem point to activities and a kind of pursuit which destroys an individual's existence in rapid movements. Nothing of the quality of life is tasted in this deadly hunger for the fallen "crumbs." But in the midst of this brief poem Bly sets for contrast an attitude of "Floating," one which seems remarkably close in spirit to that of the dreamer in Bachelard's statement above (just as the posture of "'Living'" would appear to be a fatal extension of the "preoccupations" the dreamer must abandon above in order to enter fully into his reverie:

> "Living" means eating up particles of death,
>   as a child picks up crumbs from around the table.
> "Floating" means letting the crumbs fall behind you on the path.
> To live is to rush ahead eating up your own death,
>   like an endgate, open, hurrying into night.

The poems of *Old Man Rubbing His Eyes* are "floating" poems in the manner Bly implies here, and the same may be said of those in *The Morning Glory:* they are poems of attention, reflectiveness, being, or perhaps of becoming as a state of being, but devoid of will or the pursuit of ends. The "floating" element in this poetry is a type of absorbed passivity and contemplation before a scene, an object, or something else. It is a solitary occupation which dispenses, as Bachelard says, with practical cares and, as I've noted, with the will, in the ordinary meaning of intention, determination, and desire. The effect of such a mental position is a liberation of the mind to dream of the things on which it has come to focus, as in "A Walk":

> It is a pale tree,
> all alone in January snow.
> Beneath, a cottonwood shoot
> eaten pale by a rabbit. . . .
>
> Looking up I see the farmyards with their groves,
> the pines somber,
> made for winter, they knew it would come. . . .
>
> And the cows inside the barn, caring nothing for all this,
> their noses in the incense hay,
> half drunk, dusk comes as it was promised
> to them by *their* savior.

This poem maintains itself fairly near to the outward setting through which Bly passes, concentrating on specific details that evoke a pervasive atmosphere of winter, a calm, cold landscape, sunk in seasonal torpor, only the cows giving the impression of life. It is on them, and also the pine trees, that Bly's imagination exercises freely, generating something of a prescience of their instinctive or fundamental natures: the trees' strange foreknowledge of winter and, stranger still, the promise of dusk made to the cows by an enigmatic, unnamed "saviour." Here as elsewhere in Bly's work the reader is brought not to answers, not to analysis or paraphrase, but to wonder. Finally, if the poem succeeds as it should, he will arrive at a state of "floating" himself, a participation in the timeless dreaming of the poet's vision. The poems of *Old Man Rubbing His Eyes* also turn about a unity of place. Like most of *Silence in the Snowy Fields,* this book has its poetic roots in the farm life and the Minnesota countryside Bly knows so well. "A Walk" is, however, rather modest in its range of associations, its imaginative thrusts. There are poems in this volume which positively soar, "Insect Heads," for instance:

> These insects, golden
> and Arabic, sailing in the husks of galleons,
> their octagonal heads also
> hold sand paintings of the next life.

And there are some poems included which proceed into another dimension, as easily and swiftly as a person steps through a door. This one is called "A Dream on the Night of First Snow":

I woke from a first-day-of-snow dream.
I met a girl in an attic
  who talked of operas, intensely.
Snow has bent the poplar over nearly to the ground,
new snowfall widens the ploughing.
Outside, maple leaves float on rainwater,
  yellow, matted, luminous.
I saw a salamander . . . and took him up . . .
he was cold, when I put him down again,
  he strode over a log
with such confidence, like a chessmaster,
  the front leg first, then the hind
  leg, he rose up like a tractor climbing
  over a hump in the field.
and disappeared toward winter, a caravan going deeper into mountains,
dogs pulling travois,
feathers fluttering on the lances of the arrogant men.

This kind of departure for apparently new realms through a startling, though frequently unobtrusive, shift or jump of association serves at this point as a means for returning to *The Morning Glory* and Bly's practice of the prose poem. The majority of these poems also begin in description which is detailed, objective or factual in character, with the poet sometimes locating himself either at the periphery or in the midst of the observed particulars. The openings of a few poems will demonstrate what I mean:

> A ranger is lifting fingerling trout from a pickup with his scoop. They are weighing the fingerlings for stocking. The man in black boots pours them out of his scoop into a tub set on a scale. . . .
>
>   ("At a Fish Hatchery in Story, Wyoming")

> The orange stripes on his head shoot forward into the future. The slim head stretches forward, the turtle is pushing with all his might, caught now on the edge of my palm. . . .
>
>   *("A Turtle")*

> I am in a cliff-hollow, surrounded by fossils and furry shells. The sea breathes and breathes under the new moon. Suddenly it rises, hurrying into the long crevices in the rock shelves. . . .
>
>   ("Sitting on Some Rocks in Shaw Cove, California")

Such openings, with their generally reserved tone and their close attention to a precise rendering of externals, corresponds with the first sentence of Bly's short prefatory note to the book: "There is an old occult saying: whoever wants to see the invisible has to penetrate more deeply into the visible." The invisible, then, the covert images and associations tied to the visible, lifts into view through exacting meditation on what engages the poet in the actuality he confronts or comes upon. We are drawn close again to Bachelard's ideas of dreaming on the world, for as I understand it, perhaps intuitively from Bly's poems themselves, a hidden or invisible reality becomes available to the poet through an imagery which derives from a process of interpenetration of self and object(s) leading the mind to discovery. In a number of Bly's prose poems this transition from observed things to the highly-charged metaphorical structures imaginative reflection generates is quite rapid; some pieces move almost directly into it. "A Hollow Tree" reveals such a quick shift:

> I bend over an old hollow cottonwood stump, still standing, waist high, and look inside. Early spring. Its Siamese temple walls are all brown and ancient. The walls have been worked on by the intricate ones. Inside the hollow walls there is privacy and secrecy, dim light. And yet some creature has died here.
> On the temple floor feathers, gray feathers, many of them with a fluted white tip. Many feathers. In the silence many feathers.

In this poem the feeling of factual accuracy lasts for only two sentences, just enough to provide a context for what follows and to lead the reader to the place where vision takes command. Without laboring the obvious or trying to reduce the poem's haunting allusiveness by tedious explanation, one can still point to a pattern of association starting with the suggestive erosion of trunk or bark which reminds Bly of Siamese temples and carries him on to an imaginative exploration of—a dreaming on—the stump, its contents, the feathers, reminiscent of death, perhaps sacrifice, and finally the awareness of silence, cumulative time and more deaths. A rough sense of these links does not, of course, *explain* the poem but may help to chart a discernible movement.

"A Hollow Tree" creates a slow, grave prose music, contemplative in kind, which proceeds step by step in its associative development from the beginning gestures of curiosity and observation—that is, from the poet's coming upon the stump in early spring, leaning down to survey its insides. But other Bly prose poems are more electric and elliptical in their progressions. In "A Windy Day at the Shack" the poet's excited mood seems to result immediately from the severe wind- and water-blown surroundings; his mind is bombarded with lightning flashes of perception and visionary insight. Another poem, "Frost on the Window Panes," similar in its volatility, finds the poet keyed-up, ecstatic, and the poem leaps about weightlessly, as it were, among its revelations:

> It is glittery, excited, like so many things laid down silently in the night, with no one watching. Through the two lower panes the watcher can dimly see the three trunks of the maple, sober as Europe. The frost wavers, it hurries over the world, it is like a body that lies in the coffin, and the next moment has disappeared! In its own skin the mind picks up the radio signals of death,

reminders of the molecules flying all about the universe, the icy disembarking, chill fingertips, tulips at head and foot. I look in the upper panes and see more complicated roads . . . ribbons thrown on the road. . . .

The deep reverence Bly feels for the natural world is everywhere evident in these prose poems, as well as in *Old Man Rubbing His Eyes*. Water, trees, hills, grass, shells, tumbleweed, wind, rain, a bird's nest, tidal pools draw his reflective gaze and stir his imagination toward dream. These are recurrent elements of the world his poems make; each is accorded its dignity, the focus of the poet's sensory attentions and his descriptive powers. Bly says, in "Grass from Two Years," "When I write poems, I need to be near grass that no one else sees"; and again in the same poem, further on: "the branch and the grass lie here deserted, a part of the wild things of the world, noticed only for a moment by a heavy, nervous man who sits near them, and feels he has at this moment more joy than anyone alive." Other creatures too elicit has regard. We discover them in poem after poem: fish, an octopus, a turtle, lobsters in a restaurant window, circus elephants, a blue heron, sea lions, gulls, a salamander, a dying seal, a starfish, a porcupine, steers. Wherever such creatures appear, the lines of relationship are traced; nowhere more beautifully, I think, than in "Looking at a Dead Wren in My Hand," a haunting, memorable achievement:

> Forgive the hours spent listening to radios, and the words of gratitude I did not say to teachers. I love your tiny rice-like legs, that are bars of music played in an empty church, and the feminine tail, where no worms of empire have ever slept, and the intense yellow chest that makes tears come. Your tail feathers open like a picket fence, and your bill is brown, with the sorrow of an old Jew whose daughter has married an athelete. The black spot on your head is your own mourning cap.

Yet a poem equally fine, though quite different in location and detail, is "Sunday Morning in Tomales Bay." Bly combines here vividly observed particulars of setting and creature (fog, heron, sea lions) with sudden associative transitions, all of which gives the poem a rewarding, highly-charged energy. Though the poem is a bit long, I quote the whole of it to convey this impression:

> The blue sky suddenly gone—we are in fog—we drift, lost . . . and there's a machine far away, a derrick . . . it is alive! It is a Great Blue Heron! He turns his head and then walks away . . . like some old Hittite empire, all the brutality forgotten, only the rare vases left, and the elegant necks of the women. . . .
> Where he was, heavy bodies are floating—sea lions! We float in among them. The whiskered heads peer over at us attentively, like angels called to look at a baby. They have risen from their sea-mangers to peer at us. Their Magi come to them every day . . . and they gaze at the godless in their wooden boat . . .

After a while the boat drifts nearer the fogged shore . . . boulders on it piled up . . . sea lions, hundreds of them! Some on their backs playing, then the whole shore starts to roll seaward, barking and flapping . . . And the heron slowly ascends, each wing as long as Holland. . . .

The lions are gone, they are somewhere in the water underneath us. At last one head pops up five feet from the boat, looking neither arrogant nor surprised, but like a billfold found in the water, or a mountain that has been rained on for three weeks . . . And the Great Blue Heron flies away thin as a grassblade in the fog. . . .

We can see from such examples how Bly has discovered in the prose poem a complementary form to the free, variable lines of his other poems. In the prose poem he can elaborate more fully if he wishes, use incident, location, or narrative; he can shift readily back and forth between details of the actual scene before him and the imaginative suggestions or associative leaps emanating from them. This strange, marvelous poetic form possesses great flexibility and almost no restrictions: Bly's only boundaries are the margins of his page. One must consider, I believe, *The Morning Glory* a substantial accomplishment both for Bly, in the canon of his writings, and for the prose poem in America, where it can now be seen coming into its own. In the closing poem of this collection Bly enters a barn assumed to be vacant, only to find it occupied by steers. He speaks of these animals at the conclusion in a manner descriptive of all of his own fine prose poems—in fact, it is applicable to the best of Bly's work in any of his books—pointing up their abundance and life, their deep bond with nature, their strength and resilience, their largeness and freedom of body, their intense yet expansive visionary imagination:

These breathing ones do not demand eternal life, they ask only to eat the crushed corn, and the hay, coarse as rivers, and cross the rivers, and sometimes feel an affection run along the heavy nerves. They have the wonder and bewilderment of the whole, with too much flesh, the body with the lamp lit inside, fluttering on a windy night.

Wonder, yes, it is here; but these poems have no excess of flesh. The light glows within them by which we can sit down to read.

Notes

1. *Paris Spleen,* translated by Louise Varèse. New Directions, 1947, p.x.
2. "Portrait of the Winter as a Fat Man," *Field,* 13 (Fall 1976), p. 22
3. *The Morning Glory: Prose Poems.* Harper and Row, 1975.
4. *Old Man Rubbing His Eyes.* Unicorn Press, 1975.
5. *The Poetics of Reverie,* translated by Daniel Russell. Orion Press, 1963, p. 173.

Domesticating the Sublime:
Bly's Latest Poems

CHARLES MOLESWORTH

For more than fifteen years now, Robert Bly has been an unignorable presence in American poetry. In some ways his career has been marked by one peak after another. The sudden impact of his first book, the protest speech at the National Book Awards dinner in March, 1968, the polemics of the *Sixties* magazine, the "discovery" of South American poetry, the theoretical essays on the deep image: each facet of his engagement with poetry in our time was cut with energy and high seriousness, and often both together. Assuming Bly would ever take time to assemble such a traditional volume, his "Collected Poems" might come to less than one hundred pages. Still, Bly's force has brought pressure and influence to bear on dozens of poets in several different ways. Many people have come to think of Bly's work as one great blur, the trailing comet of that first temperamental blast they associate with his role in the poetry of the "late 'sixties." But there has in fact been an unfolding, even clarifying, pattern to Bly's career, and now that he has published his third book in the last five years, his purposes and talents can be better understood. Bly is still, and probably always will be, an extremist, a poet willing to put his talent not only to the test, but to the task of a demanding vision. For him, poetry can never be a "border of ideas," as it was for Pound's Lady Valentine, nor is it a criticism of life in any safe, humanistic way. Bly's poetry is fundamentally a challenge, and what has been clarified in the last fifteen years is the set of terms in which he issues that challenge.

The publication of *This Body is Made of Camphor and Gopherwood* (1977) signals a decisive change in Bly's poetry. Though continuing to use the prose-poem, as he had in *The Morning Glory* (1975), Bly concentrates his vision more directly on ecstatic moments, and writes what must be described as religious poetry. These moments, or nodes of psychic energy, have only a fleeting origin in the discipline of natural history that had lingered so lovingly over the heterogeneous subject matter in *The Morning Glory*. That earlier collection was dominated by a sense of animal delight and keen observation. Its middle section, "The Point Reyes Poems," struck me as Bly's finest work: a celebration of presence and vision, a peripatetic delight in the evidences of process and system that avoided both the disappointments of self-conscious

Reprinted from *Ohio Review* 19, no. 3 (Fall 1978): 56–66. Reprinted by permission of *The Ohio Review*.

closure and the over-reaching of the glib sublime. But Bly, ever aggressive, was obviously not content to rest there. The publication of *This Body is Made of Camphor and Gopherwood* moves Bly beyond *The Morning Glory,* just as *The Light Around the Body* (1967) moved beyond *Silence in the Snowy Fields* (1962). In both instances, a continuity of idiom and style contrasts with a shift in the central subject matter. To simplify the matter grossly, Bly first went from midwestern pastoralism to anti-war polemic, and now he has gone from natural history to religious vision. However, what looks ostensibly like a change in subject can be read as an intensification in style (taking style in the largest sense, as the intersection of temperament and vocation), since the pastoral can readily turn into polemic, as with Vergil's First Eclogue and Milton's "Lycidas." Likewise, celebrations of natural history are often possible only through a sublimated religious yearning, as is apparent in Lucretius, Erasmus, Darwin, and, in some senses, even in Whitman.

Of course this schematizing of Bly's work ignores much detail and over-lapping. To take the most obvious point, *The Light Around The Body* had both pastoral and political polemic as its subject matter. Also, there are in *Camphor and Gopherwood* moments of sheer pastoral delight, and even domestic relaxation, which are not directly religious. And my scheme ignores *Sleepers Joining Hands* (1973), which is best assimilated as a "transitional" volume (what would any scheme do with its transitionals!), part way between the anti-war polemics of the late '60's and the religious-ecstatic poetry of the '70's. In fact, *Sleepers Joining Hands* gathers together Bly's highest utterances in both the polemical and religious modes, "The Teeth Mother" and the title poem, respectively. But the general shape of Bly's growth exhibits at least the outline I have sketched. And I would argue further that the continuity of idiom, contrasted with the shift in subject matter, makes Bly's development both dramatic and instructive; more-over, such change-with-continuity is in fact a working out of poetic problems that remain importantly central in contemporary poetry.

What is distinctive about *Camphor and Gopherwood* is the persistence and dominance in it of the religious impulse. Or, to put it in broader terms, Bly exemplifies the curious persistence of theological modes of experience and feeling in our present-day, secularized culture. This persistence often poses a scandal for criticism. For many readers, especially those with secularized imaginations, Bly's work strikes a thoroughly false, and what is worse, an utterly outmoded, note. For others, the religious is simply assimilated to that other category, the super-charged "poetic," a post-Arnoldian preserve of the literary, where we safely store away all that is not marketable, all that is not "operative" in today's society. These readers are likely to overpraise Bly, to read him with little critical or historical awareness, and to accept his religious yearnings simply as a sort of Jungian compensation and corrective to techno-cratic thought. It is difficult to know a way other than these two alternatives, the dismissive and the obsequious. The former often degenerates into *ad hominem* attacks, while the latter becomes a twisted form of condescension.

But some middle ground might be claimed. Bly, like some of his contemporaries, can be seen as fighting (a rear-guard action? a border skirmish? or the start of a pitched battle?) against the too-pat assumptions of late modernism. In this view, Bly wants to move beyond irony, past the fourth stage of Vico's historical cycle, past the low-mimetic irony of Frye's system, into some challenging affirmation. If we put Bly's work in this sort of context, we can treat its religious impulses seriously and still see how the poems remain essentially poetry and not sacred texts. In other words, Bly writes in such a way as to reaffirm the value of spontaneity, the emphasis on process and sudden illumination often associated with certain trends in modernism (from surrealism to John Cage). But he also wants out of the autotelic trap of modernism, the sense of poetry as "just another" language game. His poetry registers a desire to move beyond what we can call the problem of the symbolic, the modern notion that since reality is constituted by language, everything is (or can be read as) a text. To borrow terms from linguistic theory, there is no signified, and hence there can only be an excess of signifiers; in which case, each code must do what it can to claim autonomy, or else poetry must surrender any claim to a special linguistic status (hence "found poetry," the lingua franca campiness of the epigones of the New York School, etc.). But one way out of the traps of autotelism and excessive self-consciousness is the insistent affirmation of a "beyond," a realm where value is generated and confirmed. This realm becomes the ground of ultimate concern, a place where irony must fall silent or else change itself into celebration. But how can Bly hope to find a language that will take him beyond the ironic, especially when irony often seems the only language?

One key to Bly's latest volume lies in his fascination with the medium of the prose-poem. Baudelaire described the "miracle of a poetic prose, musical, without rhymes and without rhythm, supple enough and rugged enough to adapt itself to the lyrical impulses of the soul, the undulations of the psyche, the prickings of consciousness." Impulses, undulations, prickings: with this category of gestures, each bordering suggestively on half-liberated, half-choked releases of the unspoken, we begin to sense why Bly has turned to the prose-poem. His needs and vision have led him to the point where spontaneous revelations must be somehow both respected for their contact with the marvelous, and incorporated into an everyday idiom, a language both supple and rugged. Bly, in other words, wants to domesticate the sublime.

> We love this body as we love the day we first met the person who led us away from this world, as we love the gift we gave one morning on impulse, in a fraction of a second, that we can still see every day, as we love the human face, fresh after love-making, more full of joy than a wagonload of hay.

The spontaneous ("fraction of a second") becomes the quotidian ("every day"), as the palpable flesh ("this body") is equated with transcendence ("away from this world"). For such eruptions of the marvellous, and such blessed sinkingsback into the everyday, no strict verse form will suffice. Verse, even intense lyric poetry, has traditionally had a public dimension; it cannot be whispered. It can pretend to be overheard, as with "Prufrock," but it almost always has its eye on the larger audience. (Think of Donne, even Catullus, winking at *us* over the shoulder of his mistress.) But prose-poetry sets up a different writer-reader contract by asking the reader to surrender his or her sense of regular measure. Verse promises a return to some unit of measure which implies, however weakly, a mediation between the cry of a revealing truth and the closure of a presentable argument. By their very irregularity, prose-poems *suggest*; the best of them almost always are masterpieces of insinuation. They are less achieved mediations than a sort of self-erasing indicator of something beyond themselves, hushed pointers to the ineffable.

Many of the prose-poems in *Camphor* include passages that announce themselves as dreams; still others suggest a dream-like structure, as does "Galloping Horses." Even "Walking Swiftly," which begins "When I wake . . . ," has the characteristics of a dream-vision, where impulses, undulations, and prickings are the dominant kind of occurrences. Such concern with the texture and (the ultimate moral) meaning of dreams has been crucial to Bly's poetry from the beginning. Articulating such concern in prose-poems seems natural; besides, Bly has never had an ear that was musical at the level of the poetic line. One sensed from the first that he composed by phrases and clauses, that he wanted more a suggestive cadence than a measured rhythm. So the spontaneous "gesture" of the prose-poem has been suited to the "word" of the dream vision. Falling into holes, leaping through and by images: both types of motion are made possible by the spontaneous, insinuating discursiveness of prose poetry. We can summarize this sort of movement as "motile," defined as having the power to move spontaneously, as certain spores and micro-organisms. (A secondary meaning of motile is drawn from psychology, and describes a person whose mental imagery consists of his own bodily motion. This word thus relates the movement of Bly's sentences to his "body-centered" mysticism.)

For Bly, motility represents more than a stylistic tic. It stands for the particular form of heuristic discovery that alone can do justice to his religious imagination. Central to this imagination is the belief, itself a vital part of the Protestant mystical tradition from which Bly borrows much of his imagery, that conversion is most strong when it is most sudden. In *The Varieties of Religious Experience* (1902), William James discusses this phenomenon of sudden conversion. By using the then new notion of a "a field of consciousness," James analyzes the suddenness of religious conversion as resulting from the change in relative importance between what had been centered in the "field" and what had been only marginal to consciousness. And to illustrate such re-polarized fields, or "'uprushes' into ordinary consciousness of energies originating in the subliminal parts of the mind," James refers to cases of post-hypnotic suggestion. This persistence and eventual irruption into a waking state of energies originally discovered in a sleep-like state is, of course, at the center of Bly's poetic project.

What James then goes on to discuss (in the same Lecture X) is the difficulty of ascertaining the "class-mark distinctive of all true converts." James concludes such identification is difficult, if not impossible. Spontaneous conversion leaves no specific evidence; as such, it is indistinguishable from conversion occurring over a protracted period. Likewise with Bly's poetry. Its religious intensity leaves no mark except its own spontaneous, motile discoveries. Bly's political poems, for example, strike many as unsuccessful because they are based on no apparent understanding of social cohesiveness. For Bly, the only important ingredient in the social order is the ecstatic; the ordinary demands of social mediation and historical necessity go largely unregistered in his poetry. And this raises a problem that many readers face with Bly, both in his political and religious visions: they feel his salvation is less suffered than willed. Since there is little social experience in his poems, little evidence of how his conversion affects his daily intercourse with others, the reader must react with inner, subjective criteria. Bly's is essentially an Utopian vision. Furthermore, the negative element of his vision, his sense of satiric correction, can hardly extend beyond labelling the unawakened as unawakened. On the positive side, he preaches not simply to the converted, but to the transformed. The social does not necessarily obliterate the spontaneous, but it remains a fact that when American poets glorify the spontaneous and inner life, then the programmed and exterior life—and hence inevitably society itself—becomes the undesirable.

Now generally religion (as the root of the word tells us) has a social, communal element: one is "bound" not only to a higher force, but bound with others. (Wittgenstein's argument against a private language would apply equally strongly against a private religion.) But Bly's religious intensity has no immediate social content; it is a religion of one. Throughout *Camphor* Bly addresses a "friend." This "friend" can be viewed as the polar opposite of Baudelaire's "hypocrite lecteur," but like some polar opposites, there are strange resemblances. Bly's friend is an interlocutor, a psychological necessity that permits communication to continue; such interlocutors are necessary when the very status of the lyric voice has been called into question. As Walter Benjamin says of Baudelaire, he conceived of his poems as written for an audience that no longer read lyric poetry. So Bly writes his religious meditations for a public that is no longer ostensibly religious. But a more positive perspective on this "friend" would relate him to the friend addressed by George Herbert in *The Temple*. In this sense the friend is not merely a rhetorical crutch, or a way to domesticate the sublime, but the very divinity made companionable. In other words, the friend is the savior, or us, or the savior-in-us, less a social force than a private, inner healer.

My friend, this body is made of camphor and gopherwood. Where it goes, we follow, even into the Ark. As the light comes in sideways from the west over damp spring buds and winter trash, the body comes out hesitatingly, and we are shaken, we weep, how is it that we feel no one has ever loved us?

The Ark is the vessel of love, both the covenant that demonstrates we will be saved, and the body scented with eros. (Gopherwood is traditionally the wood Noah used to construct the Ark. The camphor tree is aromatic, and its gum has legendary ritual uses. Although the *Song of Songs* clearly uses camphor in an erotic metaphor, it developed a certain reputation as an anaphrodisiac. But whether used erotically or ascetically, its odor is sensuous.)

Such religion feeling exists, however, only in a "sideways" light, in the subliminal or marginal consciousness. (This is perhaps why Bly often uses olfactory imagery.) As soon as the feeling is called into the light it may begin to petrify and die:

> Then what is asked of us? To stop sacrificing one energy for another. They are not different energies anyway, not "male" or "female", but whirls of different speeds as they revolve. We must learn to worship both, and give up the idea of one god . . .

Does Platonism lead inevitably to pantheism? Even without tackling that question, we can see how Bly's trust in a realm beyond matter leads him to "recontain" the material as suffused with divinity. Because faith, the "evidence of things that do not appear," is so strong, it can only be located in *every-thing;* and because every thing is thus (at least potentially) sacred, no institutional-ization of religious feeling is permissible. The temple always leaves something outside, something "pro-fane," but Bly cannot accept this. Before any temple he prefers the upright heart, but the upright heart must be prepared to cast down its glance—and its attachments—to the lowliest things. Like many American poets before him, from Whitman to Roethke, Bly believes that what Stevens called "the malady of the quotidian" must be rescued by and for the poetic consciousness. As Emerson argued, "The poet, by an ulterior intellec-tual perception, . . . puts eyes, and a tongue into every dumb and inanimate object." So a wagonload of hay can be full of joy.

But in this religion without priest or hierarchies, what and how should the poet celebrate? If, as Emerson says, "Small and mean things serve as well as great symbols," isn't the worshipful act indistinguishable from the casual, unthinking acts of everyday consciousness? An answer is offered by Emerson:

> Here is the difference betwixt the poet and the mystic, that the last nails a symbol to one sense, which was a true sense for a moment, but soon becomes old and false. For all symbols are fluxional; all language is vehicular and transitive, and is good, as ferries and horses are, for conveyance, not as farms and houses are, for homestead. Mysticism consists in the mistake of an accidental and individual symbol for an universal one. . . . The history of hierarchies seems to show,

that all religious error consisted in making the symbol too stark and solid, and, at last, nothing but an excess of the organ of language.

The poet then becomes a priest of process; he must constantly throw off his own symbols and perceive "the independence of the thought on the symbol, the stability of the thought, the accidency and fugacity of the symbol," as Emerson goes on to say. And what better instrument for such throwing away than the motility of the prose-poem, that most protean of forms? And what better divinity that the yet-to-be disguised as the cast-off, the fugitive cloaked in the forgotten? Bly says:

> The dream said that The One Who Sees The Whole does not have the senses, but the longing for senses. That longing is terrible, and terrifying—the herd of gazelles running over the savannah—and intense and divine, and I saw it lying over the dark floor . . . in layers there.

It is also possible to see here how Bly escapes the problem of the symbolic. As for a true Emersonian, symbolic language is for him transparent, even fugacious. The opacity of language, which has long provided one basis for the autotelic theories of modern poetry—"a poem should not mean, but be"—is simply willed away. Language, for Bly, always offers a way of encapsulating the longing for the senses, and is therefore a way of going beyond the senses.

All this might be taken as another way of saying Bly is a typical post-Romantic poet, that he faces the same problem the symbolists faced, namely, how to discover an entrancing language without a binding social myth, or how to write a liturgy without a theology. In part, Bly's response has been to join that sector of the modernist movement which sacralizes the unconscious. (His closest *poetic* forerunner may be D. H. Lawrence, especially in the "Preface" to the 1927 volume of his poems.) But the most important aspect of the unconscious is that it is a process. *Camphor* is filled with revealing processes, appearances, the comings-on of a guide or the discoveries of a traveller, a catalogue of Poundian *periploi*. But is also records slower processes as well, like falling snow and rising smoke, pilgrimages of a slow, Protozoic time-frame, "the sweetest pools of slowly circling energies." To anchor his sense of a non-binding religion of process, Bly rewrites the Freudian "return of the repressed" as an activity best registered by the body, not sublimated into the "beautiful" or the therapeutic. (This is, among other things, Bly's way of avoiding the "religion of art," that other tendency in modernism which would aestheticize all experience and thus render religion superfluous.)

> We take our first step in words each day, and instantly fall into a hole in the sounds we make. Overly sane afternoons in a room during our twenties come back to us in the form of a son who is mad, every longing another person had that we failed to see returns to us as a squinting of the eyes when we talk, and no sentimentality, only the ruthless body performing its magic . . .

It is the body, the individual human body that best incorporates both the spontaneous discoveries and the longer, slower processes. If the body becomes "the field of consciousness," then bodily ecstasy becomes a sort of sacred unconscious, that is, a something-beyond which can suddenly become central and in turn redefine all value.

I would offer a formulation at this point. What Bly's religion does is to substitute the body for the soul as the privileged term in the traditional body-soul dichotomy. (The negative term then is not soul, but conscious rationality.) This dichotomy has been traced by Paul Ricoeur, in *The Symbolism of Evil*, back to Orphic religion. It was in Orphism that the "body" was first named, and it was there regarded as "an instrument of reiterated punishment." Having named the body as evil, the next step was inevitable: the soul is not a part of the body, it "is not from here; it comes from elsewhere; it is divine." At this crucial point in Western culture, myth is not yet separated into religion and philosophy, but a lasting assumption is made about experience:

> Other cults taught enthusiasm, the possession of the soul by a god. What seems to be original in Orphism is that it interpreted this sudden alteration, this rapture, as an excursion from the body, as a voyage in the other world, rather than as a visitation or a possession. Ecstasy is now seen as manifesting the true nature of the soul, which daily existence hides.

Ricoeur goes on to argue that Greek philosophy was to take this body-soul dichotomy as the basis of its definition of the soul or essence as that which remains identical, the same as itself. Thus the body is seen as change, as the subject and locus of decay, while the soul is eternal and immutable. But for Bly ecstasy is not an excursion from the body; it is an excursion *with* and *into* the body. Ecstasy manifests the true nature of the body, which is to be the evidence of the divine.

Bly's poetry, in *Camphor* especially, is best understood as an attempt to get back to a pre-Orphic sense of the body. The body is sacred for Bly, because as the subject and locus of change and process, it becomes the perfect universal symbol. The body, in *Camphor,* provides the stability, while it is thought that bears the burden of "accidency and fugacity." Paradoxically, it is the very nature of the body-as-process that provides this stability. This "curiously alive and lonely body" is what loves; it "offers to carry us for nothing"; it "is made of energy compacted and whirling." And in a passage which would read more traditionally if we could reverse the poet and put "soul" where he puts "body," Bly says:

> This body longs for itself far out at sea, it floats in the black heavens, it is a brilliant being, locked in the prison of human dullness . . .

Here we see what is distinctive about Bly's religion, as he had made the body equivalent to the Western-Christian Protestant "soul," an entity of nearly unspeakable longings, that has its true abode in the vast beyond, and that can realize its essence only in the momentary gestures of escape and ecstasy.

> Friend, this body is made of camphor and gopherwood. So for two days I gathered ecstasies from my own body, I rose up and down, surrounded only by bare wood and bare air and some gray cloud, and what was inside me came so close to me, and I lived and died!

Ecstasy now manifests what daily existence hides, the true nature of the body. And the body is both a passage to the bare elements and is itself a congeries of religious and erotic scents; it is its own ark and covenant.

It is difficult to transform—or translate, or convert, or institutionalize: whatever the metaphor, the difficulty remains—the ecstasies of one's body into a shareable, communal vision. I think what Bly's poetry enacts, especially in the strengths and weaknesses of *Camphor,* is the persistent desire of American poets simultaneously to celebrate the body and incorporate the universal energies, thus making them available to all. How to domesticate the sublime? Bly's answer seems to be to divinize the *truly* immediate, that is, the data of consciousness not understood as thought, but as bodily sensation. Bodily presence and process—the purview of natural history, with its emphasis on seeing, on turning the given into a specimen by an act of loving attentiveness to detail and change—thus becomes equated with bodily ecstasy—the evidence of religion, with its proffered hope that the bodies of men and women can become one body, which will manifest, in a Blakean way, the transforming and divine energies of the universe.

From Silence to Subversion: Robert Bly's Political Surrealism

WALTER KALAIDJIAN

Working with long, encyclopedic verse forms, Charles Olson and James Merrill at once depart from James Wright's lyric subjectivity and project Merwin's more discursive lyricism into extraliterary registers. Their dialogic negotiations with popular culture and other fields of writing on the one hand question the "literary" status of the American verse canon and, on the other hand, render social history susceptible to poetry's own linguistic powers of cultural critique. Thus, in Olson's and Merrill's textual practice, the contemporary verse epic functions more as a critical than an affective discourse. Similarly, in pursuit of America's social text, Robert Bly, Adrienne Rich, and Gwendolyn Brooks all exceed in different ways the emotive lyricism of the introspective subject. Each interrogates the bourgeois myth of the sovereign self to expose how the conventionally valorized doctrine of individual creativity actually interrupts and impedes poetry's verbal transactions with history. Each collapses the political and disciplinary boundaries dividing confessional verse from the public world as we know it. Experience itself in their writing is mediated by group praxis, while poetic expression emerges as a distinctively intersubjective, rather than solitary, act of the imagination.

In the 1950s, Robert Bly gained a popular following from his irreverent gibes that lampooned American New Criticism and the modernist agenda it espoused. Like Theodore Roethke, he waged a tireless campaign to promote his own literary fame. By the end of the decade, he regularly published fulminations against the Fugitives in his home-grown journal *The Fifties* (1958). "A Wrong Turning in American Poetry" (1963) summed up his quarrel with both the "generation of 1917"—Eliot, Pound, Moore, and Williams—and the later poets of 1947—Karl Shapiro, Robert Lowell, John Berryman, Randall Jarrell, and Howard Nemerov. In this essay Bly advertised his "subjective image" poetry as a corrective to modernism's "objective" and "scientific" milieu.[1] Collaborating with Wright in the late 1950s, he promoted a distinctively private and pastoral sensibility for American verse. His career's founding

Reprined from *Languages of Liberation: The Social Text in Contemporary American Poetry* by Walter Kalaidjian (New York: Columbia University Press, 1989), 123–41, 228–33. Reprinted by permission of Columbia University Press.

moment turned on a decisive break with America's urban present, dramatized in Bly's retreat from New York City to the family farm in rural Minnesota. His early "subjective" poetry not only takes this pastoral flight as its major theme but, more importantly, inscribes it as an immanent feature of its rhetorical forms and verbal style.

Not surprisingly, Bly's "subjective" polemic appealed to a whole generation of mainstream American critics who leaned toward an emotive poetics in a similar effort to unseat New Criticism.[2] Thus, Charles Altieri in *Enlarging the Temple* welcomed Bly's poetics of "radical presence" that "makes visible latent orders of being where nature and consciousness, existential facts and the metaphor or poetic image share the vital life."[3] But for the Frankfurt School theorists, the lyric desire for a consoling, natural presence before social experience was itself underwritten by deeper historical forces. For his part in "Lyric Poetry and Society," Adorno viewed the lyric's social reticence as a symptom of alienation:

> This demand, however, that of the untouched virgin word, is in itself social in nature. It implies a protest against a social condition which every individual experiences as hostile, distant, cold, and oppressive. . . . The idiosyncrasy of poetic thought, opposing the overpowering force of material things, is a form of reaction against the reification of the world, against the rule of the wares of commerce over people which has been spreading since the beginning of the modern era—which, since the Industrial Revolution, has established itself as the ruling force in life.[4]

In reading lyric poetry as a socially mediated discourse, Adorno was careful to separate his approach from vulgar reductions to the poem's social viewpoint, its representation of social events or interests, or the author's biographical or psychic life. Instead, he called for an *immanent* critique of how verse inscribes the social in its linguistic content and poetic forms. In fact, he said, the more authentically a work embodies history, "the more the poem eschews the relation of self to society as an explicit theme and the more it allows this relation to crystallize involuntarily from within the poem" ("Lyric Poetry and Society," p. 61). In the postwar epoch, Bly's career offers a *prima facie* case for how the text of social history always already inhabits even the most intimate expressions of emotive verse. Thus, Bly's obsessive promotion of "subjective" images, now viewed from the vantage point of Adorno's critique, appears less as a visionary alternative to postwar history and more a symptom of resistance to it. Read in this way, the very mainstays of the deep image's pastoral surrealism, its authentic privacy and its psychic distance from everyday life, bespeak a profound unease with America's social milieu.

THE RHETORIC OF THE DEEP IMAGE

The deep image's repression of history is patent in much of Bly's verse, but particularly so in "Depression," published in Bly's first volume, *Silence in the Snowy Fields* (1962). The poem's political subtext is the dramatic spread of American agribusiness that, in the postwar decades, steadily supplanted the small family farmer with giant corporate growers. During the 1950s, the Eisenhower administration rolled back New Deal incentives to small rural farmers such as the health and social services offered through the Farm Security Administration and Rural Electrification Administration. Moreover, throughout the 1950s the American Farm Bureau Federation, and Soil Bank Program in particular, offered generous subsidies to large landowners. In addition, USDA research funds to major land-grant university research and extension programs fostered the growth of expensive high-tech machinery and new methods of capital-intensive farming. Burgeoning agribusiness also fed the chemical industry, which conceived a wide array of pesticides and herbicides, such as DDT, Malathion, Aldrin, Dieldrin, and Endrin, specifically targeted for the giant monoculture combines of the 1950s. It was not until Rachel Carson's devasting exposé *The Silent Spring* (1962) that Americans began to take the environmental impact of such methods seriously. During the 1950s, however, government and business interests waged a largely unchecked campaign to reify farming. The national mood was best summed up by former Secretary of Agriculture Earl Butz's terse dictum: "adapt or perish."[5]

Signs of Midwest agribusiness frequently mar Bly's pastoral landscapes, but "Depression" more radically inscribes industrial references on the body:

> I felt my heart beat like an engine high in the air,
> Like those scaffolding engines standing only on planks;
> My body hung about me like an old grain elevator,
> Useless, clogged, full of blackened wheat.
> My body was sour, my life dishonest, and I fell asleep.
>
> I dreamt that men came toward me, carrying thin wires;
> I felt the wires pass in, like fire; they were old Tibetans,
> Dressed in padded clothes, to keep out cold;
> Then three work gloves, lying fingers to fingers,
> In a circle, came toward me, and I awoke.
>
> Now I want to go back among the dark roots;
> Now I want to see the day pulling its long wing;
> I want to see nothing more than two feet high;
> I want to go down and rest in the black earth of silence.[6]

Divorced from nature, the poet wears the "dishonest" forms of alienated labor, embodied in stanza one's old grain elevator with its "scaffolding engines." Seeking to escape the "sour" and blighted harvest of agribusiness, Bly regresses back toward the deep psychic exotica of stanza two. But even in this dream world, the Old Tibetans of the mind are menaced and dispelled by "Three work gloves, lying fingers to fingers/In a circle." Bly, of course, desperately wants to escape the grim scene of Midwest agribusiness, and so represses it throughout the whole of the last stanza. Nonetheless, the poem's relation to history is "crystallized involuntarily," in Adorno's words, in what he would describe as an immanent feature of the poem's rhetorical makeup.

In "Depression," Bly's unrelenting assertion of the self compensates for the poem's failure to sustain the lyric myth of a world elsewhere. His anaphoric refrain—"I want to see nothing . . . /I want to go down"—is compulsive and, through its repetitive form, signals regression into what Freud theorizes in *Beyond the Pleasure Principle* as the "death instincts."[7] Significantly, no less than nine of the poem's fourteen lines open with "I" or "my." Wholly repressing America's contemporary scene, Bly can only possess visionary privacy finally in "the black earth of silence." These lines carry lyric autonomy to its logical end. The privacy of the subjective image can only be preserved, at last, through the mind's extinction. As "Depression" shows, the poet's early flight from modern middle-class values is profoundly blocked. Despite its lyric critique of America's commercial scene, the poem registers Bly's continuing investment in the mental habits and linguistic forms of bourgeois individualism.

This verbal shortcoming is something that Bly shares with much of American confessional and other brands of postwar "talk" poetry. The deep image's essentially conservative aesthetic, its transparent and seemingly unmediated verbal style, drains his writing in *Silence* of its discursive power. Like Wright, Bly banks on lyric authenticity. He wants to deploy the immediacy of voice, colloquial diction, subjective viewpoints, "natural" locales, and bucolic themes against American consumer culture of the 1950s. Ideally, his pastoral surrealism should blur the boundary separating psychic and political vision, thus freeing landscapes from the signs of reification. But like Wright's cloistral turn from the American present, Bly's pastoral blunts the incisive social critique otherwise registered in his verse. Frequently, the poet fails to craft rhetorical forms that resist advanced consumer capitalism. As "Depression" illustrates, his early work often stages merely a regressive flight from historical pressures.

Beyond disclosing the emotive plenitude of the deep image, Bly's portraits of the Midwest's sprawling agribusiness in poems such as "Depression," "Unrest," and "Awakening" escalated the political stakes of his writing. But more importantly, through translating Third World surrealists in the 1950s, he came to open his local project onto a broader, global critique of American multinational capitalism. Poems such as Pablo Neruda's "The United Fruit Company," for example, alerted Bly to the social injustice of corporate policies in Latin America. A growing critic of American foreign policy in the early 1950s, Bly fulminated against the policies of the United Fruit Company (now Standard Brands) in Guatemala. United Fruit, of course, was a fierce opponent of local minimum wage legislation and land reform throughout Central America. Responding to the 1953 nationalization of 234,000 acres of United Fruit land, the Eisenhower administration ordered a navel blockade of the Guatemalan coast. Moreover, then Secretary of State John Foster Dulles (a former member of the board of directors of United Fruit) and his brother Allen (CIA head and former president of the company) orchestrated a military coup installing pro-American Colonel Carlos Castillo Armas in 1954. The Armas regime, like those of Fulgenscio Batista in Cuba and Anastasio Somoza in Nicaragua, undermined land reform, voting privileges, and labor movements in an effort to foster a cheap pool of labor for American transnational business interests in the Third World.[8]

Silence shows the awakening to political consciousness that later guides Bly's writing in *The Light Around the Body* (1967) and *Sleepers Joining Hands* (1973). But *Silence*'s aesthetic distance from history drains the book of its political force. In "Poem Against the Rich," for example, he filters Third World imperialism through a mystified surrealism: "The rich man in his red hat/Cannot hear/The weeping in the pueblos of the lily,/Or the dark tears in the shacks of corn" (S, 27). Lines like these idealize poverty as a means to rarefied aesthetic vision. Here the poet evades the social abuses of advanced global capitalism by searching out "The tear inside the stone." Bly's failure to deal with political history in *Silence* became increasingly problematic as he faced the growing national crises of the mid-1960s. Little by little, he recognized that his subjective poetics was simply powerless to speak to the 1960s' political assassinations, urban race riots, and the Vietnam War. Responding to America's turbulent history, Bly fashioned a poetic discourse that moved the deep image into public registers. In his next book, *The Light Around the Body*, the poet renounced *Silence*'s solipsism and jettisoned its plain-spoken lyricism.

CULTURAL POETICS IN THE VIETNAM ERA

In the epigraph to *Silence* Bly featured Jacob Boehme's motto: "We are all asleep in the outward man." But in *The Light,* the poet's pastoral dream gives way to a commodified nightmare from which he struggles to awake. Consequently, Bly's next book underscores the constitutive role language plays in shaping political praxis. No longer pastoral, his surrealism adopts a subversive tone, often flouting the half truths and windy abstractions of bureaucratic propaganda. *The Light*'s opening epigraph, also from Boehme, modifies the struggle of inwardness with outwardness, now as a verbal clash: "For according to the outward man, we are in this world, and according to the inward man, we are in the inward world. . . . Since then we are generated out of both worlds, we speak in two languages, and we must be understood also by two languages" (L, 1). In his critical writings, Bly joins the discourse of outwardness to two ideological impulses: "These two strains—puritan fear of the unconscious and the business drive toward dealing in outer things—meet in our poetry to push out the unconscious" (WT, 40). Capitalism's business drive, in other words, reifies the deep image's lyric privacy within what is a public linguistic register.

In *The Light*'s second section, "The Various Arts of Poverty and Cruelty," Bly recognizes that his early pastoral rhetoric was already underwritten by the material culture it sought to transcend. As a result, he crafts the deep image now into a subversive discourse, one that would undermine what Boehme calls the "art and rationality" of outwardness. In "Come With Me," Bly moves beyond *Silence*'s "snowy field" into the junk-space of American consumer society. There he finds the life of things everywhere driven by the reign of the commodity form: "Come with me into those things that have felt this despair for so long—/Those removed Chevrolet wheels that howl with a terrible loneliness, . . . /Those shredded inner tubes abandoned on the shoulders of thruways,/Black and collapsed bodies, that tried and burst,/And were left behind" (L, 13). Poems such as "Come With Me" lament the leveling of the American scene by planned obsolescence, the profit motive, spreading signs of consumerism, car culture, and the growing traffic between country life and suburban sprawl.

Throughout the 1960s, Bly broadened this critique of reification, thus resisting America's push for new economic frontiers in the Third World and Southeast Asia. Faced with the apocalyptic scene of Vietnam, *Silence*'s pastoral aesthetic appeared increasingly bankrupt. By the late 1960s, Bly was an outspoken critic of the war. Along with David Ray, he organized American Writers Against the Vietnam War in 1966. Orchestrating protest readings, demonstrations, and draft card burnings, he assumed a viable public role in the antiwar movement. Moreover, he used his National Book Award acceptance speech in 1968 to foster draft resistance. *The Light*'s antiwar poetry spear-headed this public commitment by probing the ideological forces shaping American policy in Vietnam. In *The Light*'s third section, "The Vietnam War," Bly's assault on the rhetoric of Third World "pacification" was at once a local political action and a psychic critique of American manifest destiny.

To begin with, Bly's political project retrieves America's long-standing desire to capitalize on virgin frontiers. In "Asian Peace Offers Rejected Without Publication," for example, he links military escalation in Vietnam to a standard icon of westward expansion—the railroad: "something inside us/Like a ghost train in the Rockies/About to be buried in the snow!/Its long hoot/Making the owl in the Douglas fir turn his head" (L, 30). This emblem of industrial machinery recalls Thoreau's classic depiction of the steam engine's predatory advance on the American wild: "The whistle of the locomotive penetrates my woods summer and winter, sounding like the scream of a hawk sailing over some farmer's yard, informing me that many restless city merchants are arriving within the circle of the town."⁹ Following Thoreau, Bly depicts the railroad as shuttling between two worlds of experience. It operates as a line of metaphoric exchange between on the one hand the culture, politics, and economy of "restless city merchants," and on the other hand the wilderness of the American unconscious. Through metaphor, Bly fuses nature and culture into an imaginative spectacle. Like Hawthorne's schizophrenic dream of evil in "Young Goodman Brown," Bly's text elicits the scenic "otherness" of the American psyche. There, he witnesses what is anathema to the heritage of Western humanism:

> Tonight they burn the rice-supplies; tomorrow
> They lecture on Thoreau; tonight they move around the trees,
> Tomorrow they pick the twigs from their clothes;
> Tonight they throw the fire-bombs, tomorrow
> They read the Declaration of Independence; tomorrow they are
>   in church.
>
> (L, 5)

In such moments, the poet blurs the "natural" boundaries variously dividing forest and clearing, the night of the unconscious and the lecture hall's rational daylight, tonight's mayhem and tomorrow's justifying rhetoric. Through these uncanny fusions, he joins America's humanistic posturing to its more willful political praxis in the Third World.

Vietnam, of course, was the nation's first televised war, avidly promoted as a media spectacle by America's culture industry. Throughout the 1960s, the war's daily cruelties were instantly broadcast as a kind of grotesque national theatre. The atrocities appeared even more obscene in light of the weekly Pentagon reports of enemy body counts. Bly wrote "Counting Small-Boned Bodies," he says, "after hearing on radio and television, Pentagon 'counts' of North Vietnamese bodies found."¹⁰ Bly's burlesque performance memorably registers the poet's outraged dissent from state propaganda:

> Let's count the bodies over again.
> If we could only make the bodies smaller,
> The size of skulls,
> We could make a whole plain white with skulls in the moonlight!
>
> If we could only make the bodies smaller,
> Maybe we could get
> A whole year's kill in front of us on a desk!
>
> If we could only make the bodies smaller,
> We could fit
> A body into a finger-ring, for a keepsake forever.
>
> (L, 32)

In "Counting," black humor unmasks American consumer society, particularly its penchant for controlling data. Managerial efficiency, of course, is the hallmark of high technology under advanced capitalism. Bly's point is simply that today's sheer exchange of information is itself driven by the forces of reification. The poem's anaphoric refrain lampoons such communication management in a radically hyperbolic parody. The strategy is to estrange America's postwar "telecommunity" through the grim imagery of Vietnam body counts. The poet plays with the desire to tabulate a "whole year's kill" on a desktop or to view it neatly displayed, say, on your personal computer screen. Rereading Pentagon propaganda, Bly's strange persona offers a fateful "keepsake" that weds the war's dehumanizing scene to America's contemporary information economy.

In the early 1970s, Bly's long meditative poem, "The Teeth Mother Naked at Last" (1970), advanced his deep image dissent from Vietnam. Specifically, in it he deploys Jung's program of archetypal therapy as a political critique. Beyond working through the trauma of Vietnam, Bly more unflinchingly notes a personal investment in the sheer power of America's technologic will:

> Massive engines lift beautifully from the deck.
> Wings appear over the trees, wings with eight hundred rivets.
>
> Engines burning a thousand gallons of gasoline a minute sweep
>   over the huts with dirt floors.
>
> (SJH, 18)

In these lines, Bly joins America's war machinery to a deeper libidinal economy driven by the "Teeth Mother" archetype. Reminiscent of James Dickey's "Firebombing," such images describe the shocking knowledge of the Teeth Mother as ecstasy: as "the thrill that leads the President on to lie" (SJH, 21). The poem lays bare what Bly calls the "desire to take death inside" (SJH, 21). Significantly, in the preface to *Forty Poems Touching on Recent American History* (1970), he reflects on the psychic continuity of America's public and personal spheres: "It's clear that many of the events that create our foreign relations and our domestic relations come from more or less hidden impulses in the American psyche. . . . But if that is so, then the poet's main job is to penetrate that husk around the American psyche, and since that psyche is inside *him* too, the writing of political poetry is like the writing of personal poetry, a sudden drive by the poet inward."[11] Reading public history through the deep image, Bly views the racial upheavals of the late 1960s and Vietnam as symptoms of America's troubled political unconscious.

For many critics "Teeth Mother" is a controversial work whose high moral tone verges on the very propaganda it indicts. James F. Mersmann, for example, points out that some of Bly's assaults on the Johnson administration lapse into prosaic didacticism.[12] The poet's aim, however, is not just to mimic propaganda, but to set it in dialogue with the discourse of the deep image. Faithful to the text of Vietnam, Bly aims to unsettle the reader's unthinking complicity in administration propaganda.[13] "Like the Marxists with their notions of false consciousness," writes Charles Molesworth, "Bly posits a common awareness of mundane reality as something to be altered, and if necessary smashed, if we are to uncover the truth (and truth-revealing) relations that shape the polis and the psyche."[14] As Molesworth suggests, Bly deploys the spectacle of Vietnam so as to destroy official state myths of America's democratic mission in the Third World. More to the point, the poet stages his ideological critique through the linguistic resources of poetic discourse.

Ideologies as "world outlooks," according to Louis Althusser, represent "the imaginary relationship of individuals to their real conditions of existence."[15] Through language, ideologies solicit individuals as "subjects" for the material functioning of religious, corporate, and state institutions. Linguistic representation models the subject's attitudes, values, and self-image so as to mirror ideological "truth," now regarded as a "natural" given of everyday life. But by seizing on language as ideology's functional locus, Bly resists its power. His surrealism interrupts the verbal representations through which ideologies enlist subjects for political praxis. Deploying poetry as a linguistic force, Bly subverts the discursive work of America's oppressive domestic and foreign policies in the 1960s.

"Leaping" is the term Bly gives to surrealism's verbal fusions of conventionally unrelated things, images, and discourses.[16] Resting his verse on the depth psychology of Freud, Jung, and Neumann, Bly regards poetry as "something that penetrates for an instant into the unconscious." His surrealist tenet that "one thing is also another thing" (S, 30) enables his radical leaps of psychic association. But more importantly, Bly follows Spanish surrealism in employing such associative leaps in a political dialogue with the empty administration slogans that obscure a more willful praxis. The psychic resources of the deep image underscore the mendacities of bureaucratic rhetoric:

> "From the political point of view, democratic institutions are being
>   built in Vietnam, wouldn't you agree?"

> A green parrot shudders under the fingernails.
> Blood jumps in the pocket.
> The scream lashes like a tail.

> "Let us not be deterred from our task by the voices of dissent. . . ."

> The whines of the jets
> pierce like a long needle.

> As soon as the President finishes his press conference, black
>   wings carry off the words,
> bits of flesh still clinging to them.
>
> (SJH, 20–21)

The "voices of dissent" could deter administrative policy only if they could be heard. The state, however, enforces its regime through verbal repression. Here Bly gauges the intent of bureaucratic language not in what it says but through its censored discourse. The strategy in "Teeth Mother" is both to mimic American propaganda and to voice what it cannot speak. Describing his political poetics in a 1976 interview, Bly says that "it would be wrong to use only part of our language, because in that way you'd be leaving out half of our world. So you have to try and enter that [bureaucratic] language as well as you can and bring it into the poem."[17] Talking back to administrative silences in the deep idiom of psychic association, Bly baffles and unmasks official state rhetoric. Such a dialogic fusion of the languages of our public and unconscious selves makes for a successful political poetics, one that speaks powerfully beyond the privacy of the lyric self.

MATRIARCHAL MEMORY WITHIN THE PATRIARCHAL TRADITION

During the Vietnam decades Bly's subjective aesthetic opened onto the social text of America's public scene. Offering the deep image as a counterstatement to bureaucratic rhetoric, he dissented from the republic's misadventure in Vietnam. Significantly, his political verse both eludes Wright's failed lyricism and takes Merwin's textuality into extraliterary domains. Less viable, however, are Bly's later attempts to elide history through a feminist poetics based in depth psychology. Working from the tradition of Johan Jacob Bachofen, Carl Jung, and Erich Neumann, Bly's feminist verse is contaminated by patriarchal representations that oppress even as they seek to celebrate feminine experience.

As Adrienne Rich has observed, Bly's nostalgia for a prepatriarchal *her*story actually distorts the historical experience of real women:

> This "feminine principle . . ." remains for such writers elusive and abstract and seems to have, for them, little connection with the rising expectations and consciousness of actual women. In fact, Marcuse and Bly might be likened to the Saint-Simonians and Shelley, who likewise insisted theoretically on the impor- tance of the feminine, yet who betrayed much of the time their unconscious patriarchal parochialism.[18]

Such residual sexism, however consciously resisted, underlies Bly's reflections on matriarchy. At the root of this problem is the poet's reliance on Bachofen's *Mother Right* (1861). Briefly, Bachofen hypothesized three universal stages common to all cultures. The first is an oppressive period marked by male dominance and a lack of clearly defined systems of kinship, agriculture, and civil law. But with the rise of matriarchal rule, powerful women come to enjoy civil and religious authority. Bachofen, of course, identified the Golden Age of women's rule with monogamy, agriculture, the domestic arts, and the mysteries of maternal fertility and natural religion. In the final stage, women's "mother right" leads to what he thought of as the more culturally advanced rule of patriarchy. Lacking anthropological data, Bachofen's theory rests on his readings in Greek and Roman literature. Joan Bamberger, however, points out the historical flaws of Bachofen's myth, claiming that anthropology has found little evidence of any social matriarchies.[19] Similarly, in *The Second Sex* Simone de Beauvoir rejects Bachofen, stating that "society has always been male; political power has always been in the hands of men."[20] Not only does Bachofen's theory lack factual support, but his ideas, feminists charge, merely reflect the Victorian stereotypes of his time. Bachofen, of course, defined matriarchal consciousness as a "strange, aimless striving peculiar to women."[21] Compounding this bias, Bachofen's stress on matriarchy as the necessary step "to the education of mankind and particularly of men" relegated women to the position of nurturing patriarchal civilization.[22] Unhappily, Bly is heir to such dubious assumptions about women's domestic roles.

Not surprisingly, the Victorian sexism marking Bachofen's project also shaped other works of the same period. Henry Sumner Maine's *Ancient Law* (1861) sought the genesis of patriarchal rule in biblical scriptures as well as in Greek and Roman law. John F. McLennan's *Primitive Marriage* (1865) and Edward Westermarck's *The History of Human Marriage* (1891) analyzed the nuclear family in terms of women's historic submission to patriarchal authority. Also working within the Bachofen tradition, Henry Morgan was an important influence on Friedrich Engels' *The Origin of the Family, Private Property, and the State* (1884).[23] Bachofen's Victorian bias also persisted, through the influence of Freud, in Jung's thinking about women's psyche.[24] In "Women in Europe" he wrote: "Women's psychology is founded on the principle of Eros, the great binder and loosener, whereas from ancient times the ruling principle ascribed to man is Logos."[25] Moreover, Erich Neumann, another of Bly's key sources, repeated Jung's subliminal sexism.[26] Predictably, Neumann's *The Origins and History of Consciousness* lumped men's and women's psyches into roughly the same stereotypes Bachofen set forth. Neumann also betrayed, at times, a Jungian bias toward projecting unconscious Eros onto woman, who, he says, is "out of her element in consciousness."[27]

Jung's and Neumann's archetypal readings of myth and folklore, as feminists have shown, often consign women to nature, the unconscious, and passive sexual roles.[28] For her part, de Beauvoir argues that such essentialist images cast the feminine as a deviant Other in relation to patriarchal rule. Pushed to the margins of male civil authority and state power, women, she says, have been associated historically with what is "outside" or "beyond":

nature, the unconscious, and the mysteries of life and death.[29] Unfortunately, this is the very problematic that shapes Bly's feminism. Although lamenting sexual division, he ironically perpetuates it by falling into Bachofen's Victorian representations of women. Bly's thematic critique of patriarchy is blocked by the somewhat sexist stereotypes his writing projects. Like Marcuse, Bly associates patriarchal rule with the aggressive repression of erotic life instincts, what Freud and Jung define as Eros. Both Bly and Marcuse identify this century's increasing political totalitarianism, militarism, resource exploitation, and environmental pollution with the death instincts.[30] As a corrective to patriarchy, Bly features the more life-affirming ideals of matriarchy, derived largely from Bachofen's nurturing "mother right."

Working with Jungian theories of archetypal memory, Bly tries to talk back to patriarchy in the idiom of the deep image. But like Bachofen, Jung, and Neumann, he often projects feminine Eros in merely passive rather than empowering images of otherness. Although *Silence* does not foreground sexual division, it betrays an underlying tension between male and female roles. "A Man Writes to a Part of Himself" typifies Bly's early blindness to the feminine vision he would celebrate:

> What cave are you in, hiding, rained on?
> Like a wife, starving, without care,
> Water dripping from your head, bent
> Over ground corn . . .
>
> You raise your face into the rain
> That drives over the valley—
> Forgive me, your husband,
> On the streets of a distant city, laughing,
> With many appointments,
> Though at night going also
> To a bare room, a room of poverty,
> To sleep among a bare pitcher and basin
> In a room with no heat—
>
> Which of us two then is the worse off?
> And how did this separation come about?
> (S, 36)

As his title suggests, in this domestic drama Bly as "a man" condescends to his anima, viewing her as "part of himself." The poem confirms the anima's essentially passive role. Hiding within the cave's wet enclosures, the poet's feminine other is primitive and endures the poverty of earth, nature, and traditional staples. Her masculine counterpart, however, dwells in the distant city, where he enjoys the public sphere of his many appointments. In Bly's family romance, nightfall leads the husband back to a "room of poverty" that, like its pitcher and basin—objects Bly would associate with the feminine—is comfortless and bare. Although questioned, the poet's anima is mute. However penitent, Bly's male pesona has the last word, while his anima remains a silent "other" on the margins of male identity.

Beyond *Silence, The Light* calls this divorce from the feminine into more urgent crisis. Bly's second volume revises *Silence*'s pastoral lyricism, which appears now as a feminine discourse opposed to patriarchy's public rhetoric. As in his Vietnam poetry, Bly's feminist verse draws on satire, burlesque, and black humor to unmask capitalist patriarchy. This dialogue succeeds insofar as it lampoons the reified icons of American consumer society. But because Bly lodges his feminist critique within Bachofen's myth of mother right, he stereotypes women in "natural" roles that are severed from political history:

> Not to the mother of solitude will I give myself
> Away, not to the mother of love, nor to the mother of conver-
>   sation,
> Nor to the mother of art, nor the mother
> Of tears, nor the mother of the ocean;
> Nor to the mother of sorrow, nor the mother
> Of the downcast face, nor the mother of the suffering of death;
> Not to the mother of the night full of crickets,
> Nor the mother of the open fields, nor the mother of Christ.
>
> But I will give myself to the father of righteousness, the father
> Of cheerfulness, who is also the father of rocks,
> Who is also the father of perfect gestures;
> From the Chase National Bank
> An arm of flame has come, and I am drawn
> To the desert, to the parched places, to the landscape of zeros;
> And I shall give myself away to the father of righteousness,
> The stones of cheerfulness, the steel of money, the father of rocks.
>
>   (L, 4)

In "The Busy Man Speaks," Bly escalates the psychosexual conflict explored in "A Man Writes to a Part of Himself." "The Busy Man" renounces *Silence*'s pastoral life in a language that threatens its subjective aesthetic. As in "Counting," the strange persona's anaphoric hyperbole forcefully ridicules partriarchal values. Yet the poem fails to liberate women from the margins of patriarchy's civic power. Granted, the "father of cheerfulness" and "perfect gestures" is an empty figure as he moves through an abstract "landscape of zeros." But the "mother of sorrow" and the "suffering of death," who dwells in nature's dark oceans and open fields, seems equally shallow. Shaping Bly's mother/father division is Jung's Logos/Eros binarism. Although Bly offers his feminine imagery as a progressive alternative to the busy man's deluded pledge, his repetition of "not" and "nor" tends to oppress the mother in a negative otherness to the more aggressive will of the father—here featured in a misguided but still emphatic role. The poem's tone rather perversely registers Bly's unconscious investment in the very patriarchal stances he consciously lampoons. Whether we can sense here some subliminal trace of what Rich describes as Bly's "patriarchal parochialism" ultimately depends on personal reading habits. But if Bly's satire displaces patriarchal representations, his mystification of Woman as nurturing Earth Mother provides actual women little access to public centers of social and political power.

Such sexual division locks him into the same dilemma time after time. In "The Teeth Mother Naked At Last," for example, he would critique patriarchal domination, but the title tends to saddle women with the poem's psychic burden. The repressed feminine, as Neumann's death mother, returns as the violent Other of male civil order. Bly, of course, tries to empower women's otherness in his well-known essay on matriarchy, "I Came Out of the Mother Naked," published in *Sleepers Joining Hands.* But its "feminine" argument is flawed, investing in the very stereotypes that de Beauvoir locates on the passive margins of patriarchal power.[31] Even more troubling is the failure of Bly's feminism in his title piece, "Sleepers Joining Hands," a long Jungian meditation on matriarchy. Here he employs surrealism as a way of fusing the male and female psyches. But falling back on the father's phallic authority, Bly finds sexual difference unmanageable: "I love the Mother./I am an enemy of the Mother, give me my sword" (SJH, 66). Naively endorsing Bachofen's version of women's "mother right," "Sleepers" lacks revisionary force.[32]

Contrasted with Continental theorists of *écriture féminine*, Bly's relegation of women to hearth and home appears woefully lacking. Feminist authors such as Luce Irigaray, and Hélène Cixous pursue more "re-visionary" retrievals of women's experience. The writing of Irigaray, for example, subverts patriarchy's hierarchic oppositions in a multiple play of sexual difference:

> How can we speak to escape their enclosures, patterns, distinctions and oppositions: virginal/deflowered, pure/impure, innocent/knowing? . . . How can we shake off the chains of these terms, free ourselves from their categories, divest ourselves of their names? . . . It's the total movement of our body. No surface holds: no figures, lines, and points; no ground subsists. But there is no abyss. For us, depth does not mean a chasm. Where the earth has no solid crust, there can be no precipice. Our depth is the density of our body, in touch "all" over. There is no above/below, back/front, right side/wrong side, top/bottom in isolation, separate, out of touch. Our "all" intermingles. Without breaks or gaps.[33]

Although Bly embraces a poetics of the body, he neglects such a "gyn/ecology" of feminine sexuality. Failing to reflect critically on the sources of his depth psychology, Bly disfigures what Irigaray calls the "density" of the feminine body and unconscious. The rhetoric of the deep image succeeds when it moves beyond Wright's private lyricism into a public dialogue with America's bureaucratic discourse. Retrieving altered states of consciousness through archetypal reverie further serves to undermine patriarchal assumptions about women. But when Bly asserts nature, the unconscious, mother right, and the rest as intrinsic to the female psyche, rather than part of the cultural network of signs that the feminine disrupts and mobilizes in revolutionary ways, his writing is self-defeating.[34] Beyond the shortcomings of Bly's matriarchal poetry, Adrienne Rich's cultural feminism pursues a more sophisticated inscription of the feminine psyche, herstory, and community.

Notes

1. Robert Bly, "A Wrong Turning in American Poetry," *Choice* (1963), 3:47. Hereafter cited in the text as WT.

2. See Ronald Moran and George S. Lensing, *Four Poets and the Emotive Imagination* (Baton Rouge: Louisiana State University Press, 1976).

3. Charles Altieri, *Enlarging the Temple* (Lewisberg, Pa: Bucknell University Press, 1979), p. 83. Whether Bly has crafted a rhetoric that can stage the meaning of his "deep" vision is open to interpretation. Since *Enlarging the Temple*, Altieri has gone on to argue the limitations of Bly's "immanent" aesthetic contrasted with the more discursive modes of the younger poets of the 1970s. See Charles Altieri, "The Dominant Poetic Mode of the Late Seventies," chapter 2 of his *Self and Sensibility in Contemporary American Poetry* (New York: Cambridge University Press, 1984), pp. 32–51.

4. Theodor W. Adorno, "Lyric Poetry and Society," Bruce Mayo, tr., *Telos* (1974), 20:58.

5. Earl Butz, quoted in Marty Jezer, *The Dark Ages: Life in the United States from 1945–1960* (Boston: South End Press, 1982), p. 162.

6. Robert Bly, *Silence in the Snowy Fields* (Middletown, Conn.: Wesleyan University Press, 1962), p. 37. Hereafter cited in the text as S. Other volumes of Robert Bly's poetry are cited as follows: *The Light Around the Body* (New York: Harper and Row, 1967), L; *Sleepers Joining Hands* (New York: Harper and Row, 1973), SJH.

7. Whether the phenomenon of repetition compulsion, described by Freud in *Beyond the Pleasure Principle* (1920), represents the ego's attempt to master and discharge unconscious tensions or reveals the force of a more radical death instinct which challenges the dominance of the pleasure principle has been a source of heated debate in post-Freudian theory. For a full discussion of repetition compulsion, death instincts, and the pleasure principle, see Sigmund Freud, *Beyond the Pleasure Principle*, in vol. 18 of *The Standard Edition of the Complete Psychological Works of Sigmund Freud*, James Strachey, ed. and tr. (London: The Hogarth Press, 1968), pp. 38–40, 44–45. 55; J. Laplanche and J. B. Pontalis, *The Language of Psycho-Analysis*, Donald Nicholson-Smith, tr. (New York: Norton, 1973), pp. 78–80, 97–103, 322–25; and Samuel Weber, *The Legend of Freud* (Minneapolis: University of Minnesota Press, 1982), pp. 121–25, 130–35.

8. See Peter Lyon, *Eisenhower: Portrait of the Hero* (New York: Little, Brown, 1974), pp. 591–92.

9. Henry David Thoreau, *Walden*, J. Lyndon Shanley, ed. (Princeton: Princeton University Press, 1971), p. 115.

10. Robert Bly, *Talking All Morning: Collected Interviews and Conversations* (Ann Arbor: University of Michigan Press, 1979), p. 78.

11. Robert Bly, "Leaping Up Into Political Poetry," in Robert Bly, ed., *Forty Poems Touching on Recent American History* (Boston: Beacon Press, 1970), p. 10.

12. James F. Mersmann, *Out of the Vietnam Vortex* (Lawrence, Kans.: University Press of Kansas, 1974), p. 124. Discussing Bly's shift to a political poetics, George S. Lensing and Ronald Moran, in *Four Poets and the Emotive Imagination*, note that "the temperate poem becomes baldly topical" (77).

13. An early model for Bly's thoughts on the struggle between unconscious death instincts and civilization is Freud's *Civilization and Its Discontents* (1930): "The fateful question for the human species seems to me to be whether and to what extent their cultural development will succeed in mastering the disturbance of their communal life by the human instinct of aggression and self-destruction." Sigmund Freud, *Civilization and Its Discontents*, vol. 21 of *The Standard Edition*, p. 145.

14. Charles Molesworth, *The Fierce Embrace: A Study of Contemporary American Poetry* (Columbia: University of Missouri Press, 1979), p. 118.

15. Louis Althusser, *Lenin and Philosophy*, Ben Brewster, tr. (Bristol: Western Printing Services, 1971), p. 153. In his chapter "Ideology and the State" Althusser describes this process as an act of "hailing" which transforms individuals into subjects through a process of "interpellation" (162).

16. See Bly's article "Hopping," *The Seventies* (Spring 1972), 1:72.

17. Robert Bly, quoted in Kevin Power, "Conversation with Robert Bly," *Texas Quarterly* (Autumn 1976), 19:93.

18. Adrienne Rich, *Of Woman Born* (New York: Bantam, 1977), pp. 62–63. Hereafter cited as OWB.

19. Joan Bamberger, "The Myth of Matriarchy: Why Men Rule in Primitive Society," in Michelle Zimbalist Rosaldo and Louise Lamphere, eds., *Woman, Culture, and Society* (Stanford: Stanford University Press, 1974), p. 265.

20. Simone de Beauvoir, *The Second Sex*, H. M. Parshley, tr. (New York: Knopf, 1957), p. 70. Both Bamberger and de Beauvoir rely on Claude Lévi-Strauss' distinction between matrilineal descent and matriarchal rule to show that even in quasi-matriarchal societies, such as the Iroquois, women are still reduced to exchange objects and subjected to the guardianship of the ruling father or brother of the extended kinship group. Sarah B. Pomeroy summarizes their point, stating that "there is absolutely no evidence, even in realms where queens were powerful, that women were the dominant class throughout the society." Sarah B. Pomeroy, "A Classical Scholar's Perspective on Matriarchy," in Bernice A. Carroll, ed., *Liberating Women's History* (Urbana: University of Illinois Press, 1976), p. 219. See also Michelle Zimbalist Rosaldo, "Woman, Culture, and Society: A Theoretical Overview," and Sherry B. Ortner, "Is Female to Male as Nature Is to Culture?," in Rosaldo and Lamphere, eds., *Woman, Culture, and Society*, pp. 17–42 and 67–89. Support for the historical existence of matrifocal societies comes from Helen Diner, *Mothers and Amazons: The First Feminine History of Culture* (Garden City, N. Y.: Anchor/Doubleday, 1973), and Elizabeth Gould Davis, *The First Sex* (New York: Putnam, 1971). Margot Alder, in her review of matriarchal thought, makes the point that apart from the historical controversy over matriarchy, it is "important to stress that, contrary to many assumptions, feminists are viewing the idea of matriarchy as a complex one and that their creative use of matriarchy as *vision* and *ideal* would in no way be compromised if suddenly there were 'definite proof' that few matriarchies ever existed." Margot Adler, "Meanings of Matriarchy," in Charlene Spretnak, ed., *The Politics of Women's Spirituality* (Garden City, N. Y.: Anchor/Doubleday, 1982), p. 130.

21. J. J. Bachofen, *Myth, Religion, and Mother Right*, Ralph Manheim, tr. (Princeton: Princeton University Press, 1967), p. 207.

22. Bachofen, *Myth, Religion, and Mother Right*, p. 144. Anne Dickason emphasizes that Bachofen's conception of the feminine is characterized by a passive, maternal role. She argues that in the first stage women are the victims of male aggression, while in the second "mother right" serves merely as a nurturing phase which is finally superseded by the birth of the third, patriarchal culture. See "The Feminine as a Universal," in Mary Vetterling-Braggin, Frederick

A. Elliston, and Jane English, eds., *Feminism and Philosophy* (Totowa, N.J.: Rowman and Littlefield, 1977), pp. 82–84. Similarly, "like many other Victorians," writes Adrienne Rich, "Bachofen is given to sentimental generalizations about women" (OWB, 73). Of Neumann, Rich writes, "However, like Jung, he is primarily concerned with integrating the feminine into the masculine psyche . . . and his bias is clearly masculine" (OWB, 82–83).

23. Feminist writers such as Shulamith Firestone, Kate Millett, and Juliet Mitchell have criticized Engels' economic model for not addressing women's oppression in terms of biological, sexual, and psychodynamic factors. Radical feminist stances such as Firestone's locate patriarchy's origins in the masculine subjugation of women through their biology. Arguing from a psychoanalytic perspective, Juliet Mitchell theorizes Freud's oedipal situation as a universal unconscious complex underlying patriarchy's oppression of women. See Juliet Mitchell, *Woman's Estate* (New York: Random House, 1971), p. 169. More recently, Zillah R. Eisenstein has attempted to fuse radical and socialist feminist critiques of Engels to show how patriarchy reinforces differences in biological sex with specific ideological and economic forces: "Patriarchy precedes capitalism through the existence of the sexual ordering of society which derives from ideological and political interpretations of biological difference. . . . Today, the sexual division of society is based on real differences that have accrued from years of ideological pressure." Zillah R. Eisenstein, "Developing a Theory of Capitalist Patriarchy and Socialist Feminism," in Zillah R. Eisenstein, ed., *Capitalist Patriarchy and the Case for Socialist Feminism* (New York: Monthly Review Press, 1979), p. 25.

24. Bachofen's myth of the struggle between matriarchal and patriarchal societies not only influenced Engels' economic analysis of the evolution of the family, but was a forerunner to Freud's psychological interpretation of history. Bachofen's identification of femininity with natural, biological determinants tended to define matriarchal psychology in terms of material, irrational, and passive characteristics. Similarly, in the representative terms of *Moses and Monotheism*, Freud's mythic description of the origins of patriarchy echoed the Victorian bias of Bachofen's earlier sexism. In Freud's words: "This turning from the mother to the father points . . . to a victory of intellectuality over sensuality—that is, an advance in civilization, since maternity is proved by the evidence of the senses while paternity is an hypothesis, based on an inference and a premise. Taking sides in this way with a thought-process in preference to a sense perception has proved to be a momentous step." Sigmund Freud, *Moses and Monotheism*, in vol. 23 of *The Standard Edition*, p. 114; quoted in Peggy Kamuf, "Writing Like a Woman," in Sally McConnell-Ginet, Ruth Borker, and Nelly Furman, eds., *Women and Language in Literature and Society* (New York: Praeger, 1980), p. 289.

25. C. G. Jung, "Woman in Europe," in *Civilization in Transition*, vol. 10 of *The Collected Works of C. G. Jung*, Sir Herbert Read, ed., R. F. C. Hull, tr. (New York: Pantheon, 1964), p. 123.

26. Although Neumann rejected the historical inaccuracies of the Bachofen problematic, he nevertheless affirmed the usefulness of Bachofen's scheme as a psychological model: "Hence our repeated references to Bachofen, for although his historical evaluation of mythology may be out of date, his interpretation of the symbols has been largely confirmed by modern depth psychology." Erich Neumann, *The Origins and History of Consciousness*, R. F. C. Hull, tr. (Princeton: Princeton University Press, 1970), pp. 265–66.

27. Neumann. *Origins and History*, p. 125.

28. As Marianne Hirsch points out in her article "Mothers and Daughters," *Signs: Journal of Women in Culture and Society* (Autumn 1981), 7:205, even feminist projects based in Jung and Neumann must recognize that in these methodologies "we find not only a male theorist but a developed androcentric system, which, even if deconstructed and redefined, still remains a determining and limiting point of departure." Moreover, as Karen F. Rowe and Susan Gubar have argued, many of the traditional folk tales and myths that Jung and Neumann work with reflect the masculine bias of patriarchal culture to begin with. See Karen F. Rowe, "Feminism

and Fairy Tales," and Susan Gubar, "Mother, Maiden, and the Marriage of Death: Women Writers and an Ancient Myth," in *Women Studies* (1979), 6(3):237–57; 301–15.

29. De Beauvoir, *The Second Sex*, p. 132.

30. See Herbert Marcuse, *Eros and Civilization: A Philosophical Inquiry into Freud*, 2d ed. (Boston: Beacon Press, 1966).

31. "Mother consciousness," Bly writes, "was in the world first, and embodied itself century after century in its favorite images: the night, the sea, animals with curving horns and cleft hooves, the moon, bundles of grain. Four favorite creatures of the Mother were the turtle, the owl, the dove, and the oyster—all womb-shaped, night, or ancient round sea creatures. Matriarchal thinking is intuitive and moves by associative leaps. Bachofen discovered that it favored the left side (the feeling side) of the body" (SJH, 32).

32. This kind of nostalgia, according to Sally R. Binford, Gayle Rubin, and Joan Bamberger, is not only a historical fantasy but reinforces the status quo of patriarchy's mystification of woman as emotive madonna. "Feminist authors," writes Sally R. Binford, "concerned with demonstrating religions based on the Great Goddess often share the assumption, which is sometimes made explicit, that there are enormous psychological and biological differences between the sexes; women are by nature sensitive, loving, and nurturing, while men are aggressive, brutal and violent. As anthropologist Gayle Rubin points out, this is precisely the assumption of conventional sexists, and it cannot be supported by either biological or social science." Sally R. Binford, "Myths and Matriarchies" in Spretnak, ed., *The Politics of Women's Spirituality*, p. 559. Similarly, "The elevation of woman to deity on the one hand," Bamberger writes, "and the downgrading of her to child or chattel on the other, produce the same result. Such visions will not bring her any closer to attaining male socioeconomic and political status." Joan Bamberger, "The Myth of Matriarchy," p. 280.

33. Luce Irigaray, "When Our Lips Speak Together," Carolyn Burke, tr., *Signs* (1980), 6:75.

34. For readings that argue against my reservations about Bly's feminist representations see Victoria Harris, "Walking Where the Plows Have Been Turning: Robert Bly and Female Consciousness," Richard Jones and Kate Daniels, eds., *Of Solitude and Silence: Writings on Robert Bly* (Boston: Beacon Press, 1981), pp. 153–68; and William Virgil Davis, " 'At the Edges of the Light': A Reading of Robert Bly's *Sleepers Joining Hands*," in the same collection, pp. 250–67.

A Sensible Emptiness: Robert Bly
and the Poetics of Immanence

Lawrence Kramer

The poetry of Robert Bly probably evokes the phrase "deep image" for most readers. Deep images are supposed to tap unconscious sources of energy, and the poetry that uses them is thought to give only a sketchy account of the phenomenal world.[1] Everyday reality is only a surface; it becomes significant insofar as it is disturbed by dark forces that rise up from below. Bly has often endorsed this way of looking at his work, in part perhaps because to do so frees him from the burdens of a poetic tradition. The context for his poetry is not a genre or a movement among poetic generations; it is primary truth, known to intuition and expressible in myth. But Bly's poetry does not always comply with the aesthetics of the deep image. There are many lyrics that seem to celebrate pure immediacy for its own sake:

> It is the morning. The country has slept the whole winter.
> Window seats were covered with fur skins, the yard was full
> Of stiff dogs, and hands that clumsily held heavy books.
>
> Now we wake, and rise from bed, and eat breakfast!—
> Shouts rise from the harbour of the blood,
> Mists, and masts rising, the knock of wooden tackle in the sunlight.
> ("Waking from Sleep")[2]

Lines like these have poetic affiliations that Bly's deep image poetry obscures and even denies. My aim in this essay is to argue that Bly's successful poetry always depends on a poetic rather than on an esoteric context, and that his genuine achievement as a poet has little to do with deep images.

Bly's poetic tradition is a specifically American one, and he shares it with several other poets of his generation, especially Gary Snyder and James Wright. What these poets have in common is a feeling for the numinous value of objects divorced from all transcendental glamor. Their values depend on simple, tangible, elemental things, confronted almost without thought. Un-

Reprinted from *Contemporary Literature* 24, no. 4 (Winter 1983): 449–62. Reprinted by permission of The University of Wisconsin Press.

like the thing-intoxicated early Williams, they are not indiscriminate in their appropriation of reality; they are closer to the spirit of Frost's "The fact is the sweetest dream that labor knows," and even closer to the definition of a poetics of immanence given by Walt Whitman:

> An American literat fills his own place . . .
> As he emits himself, facts are showered over with light,
> The day-light is lit with more volatile light—the deep
>   between the setting and rising sun goes deeper many fold,
> Each precise object, condition, combination, process,
>   exhibits a beauty.[3]

The contemporary poem of immanence is written to be a fragment of a lost, privileged presence; it is not concerned with words but with things.[4] Such a poem is meant to carry the facticity of things over into their representation by using a language in which the qualities of bodies—weight, position, texture, mass—is paramount. The logic of argument or narrative breaks down in favor of cinematic cuts from one item to another; Bly's poetry moves by groping forward metonymically:

> The storm is coming. The small farmhouse in Minnesota
> Is hardly strong enough for the storm.
> Darkness, darkness in grass, darkness in trees.
> Even the water in wells trembles.
> Bodies give off darkness, and chrysanthemums
> Are dark, and horses, who are bearing great loads of hay
> To the deep barns where the dark air is moving from corners.
>   ("Awakening," *S*, p. 26)

In lines like these, where the enveloping authority of a Whitmanian ego is lacking, value does not derive from a harmonization of subject and object but from the unspoken assimilation of both to a third, more primitive category. With the help of a rhetoric that shifts freely between personification and objectification, subjects are reduced and objects heightened so that both appear as prereflective fusions of consciousness and materiality—in other words, as bodies. Unrelated presences—horses, chrysanthemums, the corners of barns, the consciousness of the speaker—are drawn together as bodies in the medium of darkness, which is itself a kind of larger body here, diffused but tangible and animate. The traditional emphasis on "materials," as Whitman called them, is exaggerated to such a degree that physical proximity appears as a form of primary awareness or intentionality. Things fill space as materializations of perception: bodies "give off" darkness instead of being dark, and the trembling of water in wells registers an anxious anticipation that belongs to no one in particular, yet belongs where it is. At the same time, subjectivity loses the indeterminate depth that it characteristially derives from subject-object opposition. Any sense of self is primarily physical; any sense of relationship is primarily spatial.

Bly's first book, *Silence in the Snowy Fields* (1962), is an important example of the poetics of immanence. Even before it was published, Donald Hall had celebrated its intimation of "a subjective life which is *general*, and which corresponds to an old objective life of shared experience and knowledge."[5] Already in *Silence*, however, other strains were apparent in Bly's work, and over the years they have become dominant. Political outrage, fueled by the Vietnam war and expressed most stridently in *The Light Around the Body* (1967), led Bly to attempt a fusion of lyric with prophecy. The ambition to tap a collective unconscious impelled him to an archetypal, irrationalist style that many readers, myself included, find histrionic or merely pedantic—a doctrinaire surrealism or Jungian evangelism.[6] But in 1979, Bly published a small book of striking austerity, *This Tree Will Be Here For A Thousand Years*. Collecting poems written since the publication of *Silence*, the new volume tries to recapture the heightened immediacy and "thingy spirit" of the first.

Tree, in fact, is Bly's explicit attempt to return to his origins, both personal and poetic. In his preface, he announces that the newly collected poems are not meant to form a sequel to *Silence* but to complete it; "the two books," he says, "makes one book" (p. 11). And the new half of that book is openly nostalgic, crowded with images that mark moments of origin and departure: first snows, first frosts, first glimpses, first perceptions of physical or emotional distance. Bly's *Tree*-graft is arguably the best measure of his work to date. The double book not only puts his approach to a poetics of immanence into sharp focus, but also—perhaps unwillingly—admits some of the limitations that constrain him.

Tree/Silence will occupy most of my space here, but before turning to it I want to eliminate its competition. It is as important to reject Bly as a poet of deep images as it is to acknowledge him as a poet of bodies and spaces, so for a little while I will be polemical. Bly's style is motivated by a will to subtraction, an urge to simplify that far outdoes Thoreau's. Bly wants experience reduced to its essential elements; to be a poet of space one must clear out the clutter. Part of this simplification is a restriction of the topics of the poetry to three: landscape, history, and the archetypal unconscious. But only the first of these can really endure a minimalist treatment. Bly's landscapes are bucolic, but their numinous physicality gives them the innocence of the pastoral, and it is as a pastoral poet that he must stand or fall. (American poets of immanence prefer pastoral as a genre; William Stafford and Wendell Berry, as well as Wright and Snyder, come to mind.) Bly's sense of history as a purely destructive force, all war and economic exploitation, is itself a pastoral convention: the complaint of Tityrus under the tree, the deserted village smothered by "Trade's unfeeling train." But the convention is maintained with defiant sentimentality; it dismisses the complexity of social good and evil for a melodrama of victims and victimizers. When Bly turns to visions of "the murdered pine" laid low by "Arabic numerals . . . dressed as bankers and sportsmen" ("The Current Administration," *L,* p. 22), or proclaims that "There are lives the executives / Know nothing of, / A leaping of the body, / The body rolling—and I have felt it—" ("Romans Angry about the Inner World," *L,* p. 9), history is reduced to a gush of antibourgeois rhetoric that confuses— sometimes willfully, as here—prophetic rage with self-congratulation.

With archetypes, something similar happens. Bly takes a pentecostal view of the unconscious; he receives the irrational uncritically as a form of revelation. His commentary on the subject tends to be more enchanted than informed.

> You know Freud considered in the first half of his life Eros energy to be the most powerful energy in the unconscious; we could also call that Demeter energy or Good Mother energy. Then, during the First World War, he saw Europe committing suicide, and it came to him that there is another balancing energy involved, which might be called the Death Wish, or the desire to die.[7]

The poetry rarely falls down this badly, but its trouble with archetypes is similar. As a poet, Bly reduces his irrational imagery to the reflex level by refusing to take it seriously enough. His dreamlike passages and surrealist fantasies are typically ambivalent, a blend of terror and ecstasy, delusion and vision. But the poetry is not ambivalent *about* them. The potentially devastating otherness of the mind is broken down into bundles of merely formal attributes, almost ornaments, while Bly unreservedly endorses the "joyful night in which we lose / Everything" in a primal darkness ("When the Dumb Speak," *L,* p. 62). This is easiest to see in poems like "The Busy Man Speaks" (*L,* p. 4), where the plenitude of archetype is denied to the tribe of the poet's villainous executives. The Busy Man gives himself away to the paternal Chase National Bank with its "landscape of zeros" and rejects the maternal spirit that encompasses both "the night full of crickets" and "the suffering of death," both "the mother of the open fields" and "the mother of Christ." The poem satirizes this choice stridently but fails to confront the terrible rigor of the alternative. It is merely glib to say "I shall give myself away" to fertility and mystery when they embrace the kind of pain, isolation, and passivity that the images of the poem ascribe to them. Even in less tendentious pieces, this failure to suffer what is celebrated undermines the impact of Bly's admittedly striking images:

> The blind horse among the cherry trees—
> And bones, sticking from cool earth.
> The heart leaps
> Almost up to the sky!
> ("Wanting to Experience All Things,"
> *L,* p. 160)

The echo of Wordsworth here is a subtle act of self-aggrandizement: Bly's images celebrate the very collision of life and death, wholeness and maiming, that threatens to depress Wordsworth's leaping heart. Yet Bly's easy confidence in the therapeutic value of elementals seems facile when it is set against the bewildered stubbornness with which, say, the narrator of "Resolution and Independence" struggles through "the fear that kills; / And hope that is unwilling to be fed" just to achieve a workable defense mechanism.

That leaves the landscape, and particularly the landscape of Bly's native Minnesota. The rugged countryside, with its severe winters, seems to heighten the bodiliness of everyone and everything within its borders. Even at its hardest and sparest, it remains a *locus amoenus*, one that displaces the pastoral values of abundance and innocence from "the sweet especial rural scene" into a depth of appreciation for a scene that may be neither special nor sweet. Perceived with archaic, animistic simplicity, Minnesota is an austere Arcadia, a parcel of ground that appears sacred because everything inessential has been subtracted from it.

The decisive poem in this pattern of apotheosis is a famous one from *Silence*, "Driving Toward the Lac Qui Parle River." Here, the Minnesota countryside appears as both an animating presence and an animate one. It fills its place like a large projected body, a *corpus* rather than a *genius loci*. To enter this space is to participate in an ecstasy of locations that spreads from one site to another as if handed or breathed around:

> I am driving; it is dusk; Minnesota.
> The stubble field catches the last growth of sun.
> The soybeans are breathing on all sides.
> Old men are sitting before their houses on car seats
> In the small towns. I am happy,
> The moon rising above the turkey sheds. (*S*, p. 20)

Though the time of the scene indicates transience, the spatial relations point to a permanence of presence. Each depleted object is balanced by a vital one: stubble by breathing soybeans, the old men by the young poet, the car seats by the moving car, the failing sun by the rising moon, the empty houses by the turkey sheds. The happiness of the poet does not come from any particular part of the landscape, nor from a subjective integration of the details into a whole. It is simply a fact of being there, not to be distinguished—as the loose syntax indicates—from the fact of the rising moon stationed above the turkey sheds.

"Driving" establishes the mode that the poems of *Tree* would like to recapture: an awed sense of connectedness, a feeling for a perfect but nonrational, inexplicable order in things, a language of pure description that never merely describes. Bly's aim in *Tree* is to find a severe simplicity by submitting attention to a drastic discipline. He looks into his privileged landscape to single out two or three objects, not necessarily related one, which animate each other or their horizon merely by existing together. The objects all belong to the life of rural work and its seasonal imperatives; they are all somehow innocent; and they are all sanctified by their participation in the primary mystery of natural space: "Sometimes when you put your hand into a hollow tree / you touch the dark places between the stars" ("Women We Never See Again," *T*, p. 41).

The *Tree* poems, like those of *Silence*, vacillate between observation and a sort of descriptive rapture. Their strongest impulse is to leap abruptly from bare perception to mystical vision, usually by finding that the merely physical objects at hand have a creaturely dimension, or even a primitive intentionality:

> In small towns the houses are built right on the ground;
> The lamplight falls on all fours in the grass.
> ("Driving Toward the Lac Qui Parle River," *S*, p. 20)

> The day is awake. The bark calls to the rain still in the cloud.
> "Never forget the lonely taste of the white dew."
> ("July Morning," *T*, p. 50)

The release of vision is often triggered, as it is here, by proximity to the earth, particularly the grass, and by the passivity—tranquil, but always tinged with melancholy—that Bly associates with it. Often, too, the threshold of vision is an actual space where a line is drawn between light and darkness—the hollow of a tree, or a lake with reeds: "In the Ashby reeds it is already night, / though it is still day out on the lake" ("Pulling a Rowboat Up Among Lake Reeds," *T*, p. 45).

Bly's animism is a literal attempt to register what he calls "the consciousness *out there* among plants and animals." "I've come to believe," he writes, "that it is important for everyone that the second consciousness appear somehow in the poem, merged or not. It's time. The 'human' poem can become transparent or porous at the end, so that the city, or objects, or the countryside enters" ("The Two Presences," Preface to *Tree*, pp. 9–10). The self-conscious innocence of these remarks makes them a little disingenuous; nothing is really at stake here but an overly naturalistic solution to the problem of subject-object relations that has confronted poetry in English since the Romantics. Nevertheless, Bly's impulse is distinctive. He does not want to emphasize with objects, subtly mastering them in the process, nor does he want to internalize them. What he seeks instead is an impersonal pose, a detachment from both himself and the objects that will allow him to meet them as equals on—literally—the same ground. Unhappy with the mind's tendency to humanize external reality, he tries to limit his own subjectivity by naturalizing it. Unlike Charles Olson, who resists "the lyrical interference of the individual as ego"[8] by programmatically treating persons as things, Bly treats all significant things as living bodies, dispersed locations of sentience.

In *Silence*, Bly's efforts to incorporate himself with otherness usually take the form of oblique, half-acknowledged personifications, like the image of light on all fours from "Driving." In "Solitude Late at Night in the Woods," birch trees paradoxically take on sentience when the poet seems to deny it to them:

> The body is like a November birch facing the full moon
> And reaching into the cold heavens.
> In these trees there is no ambition, no sodden body, no leaves,
> Nothing but bare trunks climbing like cold fire! (S, p. 45)

At first, the metaphorical identification of the solitary body with a desolate single birch tree suggests that the body has become inanimate, that its subjectivity has frozen. But the rhetorical equation of the lack of ambition and sodden body in winter birches with their lack of leaves reverses the implication. Feelings, like leaves, belong to the trees inherently; the birches' lack of ambition and soddenness is not an absence of mind but a passionate concentration of purpose that the poet's body shares. When the poem speaks of "bare trunks climbing like cold fire," the image can refer equally well to the stark positioning of the winter trees or to the strained intensity of their "second consciousness." Likewise, the poet's body can accept identification with both the inner and the outer trees. Their situations, in every sense of the term, are parallel:

> I must return to the trapped fields,
> To the obedient earth.
> The trees shall be reaching all the winter.

The same personification appears in a more attenuated, more disguised form in another poem from *Silence*, "Hunting Pheasants in a Cornfield":

> What is so strange about a tree alone in an open field?
> It is a willow tree. I walk around and around it.
> The body is strangely torn, and cannot leave it.
> At last I sit down beneath it. (S, p. 14)

Here, the tree's subjective presence manifests itself in the inexplicable pull of fellowship between its body and a man's. The strangeness of the experience comes from the poet's participation in the tree's solitude, a feeling, not an inanimate fact, which he feels compelled to cure for both of them. The two "torn" bodies heal into one when the restlessly moving poet sits under the willow, thereby accepting both the tree's stillness and its domination, and taking up Bly's position of richest consciousness, near the earth. The poem underlines this union later on when it refers to "the chill skin of the branches" and declares that "The mind has shed leaves alone for years." With the closing image, the intimacy with the tree dissolves, but the poet recognizes that his identity is that of a body, not a subject:

> I am happy in this ancient place,
> A spot easily caught sight of above the corn,
> If I were a young animal ready to turn home at dusk.

Of course, only a subject can perform such an act of self-reflection, but the poem will acknowledge no paradox; it simply doesn't care.

When the poems in *Tree* "return" to the consciousness *out there* first found in *Silence*, they do it, stringently, without personification. Bly seems to have rejected the figure as too rhetorical, tainted by lyrical interference. No matter how subtilized, it always retains its link to the eighteenth-century pictorial ode, where abstractions are forced to "posture" and naturalness is covertly denied as a value. To realize the "second consciousness" in *Tree*, Bly depends primarily on a movement of language that effaces the presence of his voice, and thus his presence as a subject, as the texture of the poem modulates from sparseness to richness. In recent years, many American poets have tried to acknowledge the power of otherness by writing in a peculiarly "quiet" language, simplified in syntax, sparing of metaphor, and commemorative in intent.[9] The style is one that minimizes the poet's action; the object, the other, borrows his language and seems to write *through* him. Many of the poems in *Tree* begin in this mode, often to the accompaniment of unemphatic first-person pronouns that both signal the poet's presence and dissolve it into a minimalized, anonymous articulation. Then, as the second consciousness takes hold, the "I" is wholly obscured and the eye takes over. The poet's presence merges into the landscape's, and the language, now writing for both the self and the other, shifts from description to figuration or from transparent to intricate syntax.

Elaborate though it is in the telling, this pattern gives the effect of a heightened simplicity, and it can be remarkably compressed:

> How lightly the legs walk over the snow-whitened fields!
> I wander far off, like a daddy-longlegs blown over the water.
> All day I worked alone, hour after hour.
> It is January, easy walking, the big snows still to come.
> ("After a Day of Work," *T*, p. 48)[10]

Each couplet of this poem encapsulates the basic rhythm of dissolving subjectivity. In the first, the poet wavers on the edge of self-estrangement, half-lost in the movement of "the legs"—legs almost no longer his. He recovers his selfhood only long enough to record how far he wanders off from it into the mood of the snow-whitened fields. The image of the daddy-longlegs both completes his effacement—together with his transformation into pure body, a pair of legs that move lightly—and expresses the feathery inwardness that belongs to the fields. The first line of the second couplet brings the poet back to himself, but only in the past tense, which robs his returning identity of any immediacy it might have had. Finally, the closing line absorbs him back into January, the frail, impersonal condition of "easy walking" that has already shaped his consciousness all day.

Another poem, "Nailing a Dock Together," spontaneously discards the satisfactions of selfhood with a gesture that is half generous and half nostalgic. The poet lets his awareness shift away from the pleasure he takes in working with boards—"How I love / putting my wet foot / on the boards I sawed myself!"—to the charismatic presence of a penned horse whose inner freedom works with boards in another way:

> It is a horse whose neck human
> beings have longed to touch for centuries.
> He stands in a stable of invisible wood. (*T*, p. 62)

Once again, there is a movement from reflective awareness to simple sentience, from mind to body—here, to an image of ideal bodiliness. But the visionary leap in this case rebukes the poet as well as obscuring his presence as a subject. His dock is "a ladder stretching back to land," a literal attachment linking him to the earth. It enables him to approach the horse's consciousness, but it also humbles him: the horse does not need such external props. It dwells in a space of its own making more fully than the human body, beset by a longing that spans centuries, can ever do. The seductive neck is not only untouched, but untouchable.

The rigor of Bly's engagement with the second consciousness in *Tree* diffuses itself in the ascetic, quietly mournful tone of the book, and marks it off in yet another way from *Silence*, that origin it can never quite reach. Many of the earlier poems are founded on a sense of irrepressible joy that surges up in the community of feeling between the human and the natural. In a world subject to personification, the mere physical energy of the self can seem to reflect a universal exuberance. Dazzled by bodily existence, the poet can bask in an illusion of innocence and permanence that seems to be a transparent appreciation of reality:

> Oh, on an early morning I think I shall live for ever!
> I am wrapped in my joyful flesh,
> As the grass is wrapped in its clouds of green.
> ("Poem in Three Parts," *S*, p. 21)

Outside of elegy, the will to personify is more often than not a will to celebrate. With personification stripped away, the consciousness of objects appears in a new light, rooted in the pathos of change and the vulnerability of being still or set in place. Bly remarks in his preface that "the second consciousness has a melancholy tone, the tear inside the stone, what Lucretius calls 'the tears of things,' an energy circling downward, felt often in autumn, or moving slowly around apple trees or stars" ("The Two Presences," *T*, pp. 9–10). The surprising substitution of Lucretius for Virgil makes its own kind of sense: the melancholy of Bly's poems reflects a sense of fatality in natural process, an ominous undertone of "night being ripped away from day." The poetry of *Tree* is constantly envisioning things at a vanishing point. In "Late Moon," the farm of the poet's father appears half moonlit, half dark, in "the west that eats it away" (*T*, p. 57), while Bly himself, about to go in, fades into his own shadow as he sees it reaching for the latch. Many of the poems end in startled isolation as something disappears: a rabbit scooting under a granary joist, snow falling from a window, a column of smoke rising over a distant field. *Silence* is also marked at times by the tear within the stone, but the mark is often erased by poems that close with an image of fullness or continuation: people talking in a boat in "Driving," or the moonlit road of "After Working":

> We know the road; as the moonlight
> Lifts everything, so in a night like this
> The road goes on ahead, it is all clear. (*T*, p. 51)

Tree is consistent in refusing to balance its tilt towards desolation. Most of the poems close in muted sadness, some in despair, none in a pleasure without a shadow. The book as a whole is carefully framed between a falling away and a falling inward. The first poem, "October Frost," ends with ears "reaching far away east in the early darkness" (*T*, p. 64), half lost, half (literally) reoriented. The last poem, "Out Picking Up Corn" (*T*, p. 64), lapses into disorientation with the image of a blanket of fog near a cliff—not a description, but a closing metaphor for the self in danger from its own sense of depth.

Bly responds to this entropic movement by setting a new value on the barrenness it leaves behind. Emptiness, or a few objects lodged in a too-open space, is simply the extreme to which a poetics of subtraction can go. Naturally, such a blankness suggests death. The few scattered objects left to be seen turn into memorials, cenotaphic images, of a lost plenitude: "Clods rose above the snow in the plowing west, / like mountain tops, or the chest of graves" ("Roads," *T*, p. 37). One poem, "A Long Walk Before the Snows Began," so surrounds the poet with remnants and absences—"a few grains of white sleet on the leaves," the tracks of mice and a deer—that he is forced to respond by positing his own death, which appears as the gradual withdrawal of other presences from his body.

> I see my body lying stretched out.
> A woman whose face I cannot see stands near my body.
> A column of smoke rises from Vonderharr's field. (*T*, pp. 33–34).

Yet the emptiness can also appear as a rent in the phenomenal world, a site of sudden epiphany like the hollow in the tree that encloses the space between the stars. Bly's ambivalence is genuine on this point. A blank space can stand as a bleak authenticity, the meager reward for the poet's devotion to otherness, or it can give rise to a third consciousness, beyond and including both the self's and the other's, that consoles the bleakness from which it arises: "There are women we love whom we never see again. / They are chestnuts shining in the rain" ("Women We Never See Again," *T*, p. 41). Another poem, "Driving My Parents Home at Christmas," grasps both facets of emptiness at once and incidentally measures the lostness of all origins. On the drive, over a treacherous road, the parents recollect their lives in tiny fragments—"hauling water . . . eating an orange"—but their old age gives this the air of recalling the dead ("their frailty hesitates on the edge of a mountainside") (*T*, p. 47). Ironically, their safe return home is their entry into emptiness: "When they open the door of their house, they disappear." Yet the abyss of their disappearance turns abruptly into a house without walls, in which their presence is recaptured by a dialectical image: "They sit so close to each other . . . as if pressed together by the snow" (ellipsis Bly's). Here, love and mortality fuse in their antagonism, each both repealing and heightening the other.

Bly calls such sensible emptiness as this "a place to live," and the poem that offers the phrase, "An Empty Place," is the key text in *Tree*. It starts with prose, praising empty places as "white and light-footed": "There is a joy in emptiness. One day I saw an empty corncob on the ground, so beautiful, and where each kernel had been, there was a place to live." The joy here is the sleight of mind that turns the fleeting of things into the freedom of light-footedness, transience in time into movement in space; the beauty is the trick of sight that turns vacancy into plenitude, one empty corncob into a landscape of places to live. The poem shifts to verse for a gloss on these sentences, covertly giving them a quasi-scriptural status as a text for explication. The poet's eyes again turn to the ground and find a scattering of debris there. Some of it he reanimates, using figuration to connect the broken to the whole; some of it he leaves as a sign that all breakage is irreparable:

The eyes are drawn to the dusty ground in fall—
small pieces of crushed oyster shell,
like doors into the earth made of mother-of-pearl;
slivers of glass,
a white chicken's feather that still seems excited by the warm blood. (*T*, p. 51)

As a last fragment, the poem brings back the corncob, expanding "room after room in its endless palace." Unfortunately, this leads to a weak ending, a wishful rather than integral identification of the corncob "palace" with Christ's house of many mansions. But the poem's scanty particulars retain the warmth and luminosity that Bly's ascetic attention has given them: miniscule body-fragments, but still warm.

"An Empty Place" is not the only poem in *Tree* marred by tendentiousness. A few others play tired archetypal tricks. Most of the book, though, carries the austere conviction of a backward look that forgives what it cannot recover, and it achieves a somber intensity not present in Bly's work since the darker poems of *Silence*, which it surpasses in harshness and resonance. Taken together, in their essential *dis*continuity, the two books represent Bly and the style of immanence at their strongest. The power of this poetry is limited, but real, even if its "cosmic" proportions are sometimes more fuzzy than suggestive. When Bly's lyrics are ascetic about the memory of immanence, when they are stringent about the placement of bodies on the margins of an emptiness, the emptiness becomes a persuasive sign for the original presences that it displaces. The nostalgia of the text for lost immediacies becomes seductive because the language of the text appears as the impression—a scratch, a scuff, a bruise— left behind by what is not there.

Notes

1. See the opening argument in Jonathan Holden, "The Abstract Image: The Return of Abstract Statement in Contemporary American Poetry," *New England Review*, 3, No. 3 (Spring 1981), 435–49.

2. From *Silence in the Snowy Fields* (Middletown, Conn.: Wesleyan Univ. Press, 1962), p. 13. Further references to this volume will be abbreviated in the text as S. Other texts by Bly referred to in this essay are *The Light Around the Body* (New York: Harper and Row, 1967), indicated in the text as L, and *This Tree Will Be Here For A Thousand Years* (New York: Harper and Row, 1979), indicated as T.

3. Passage deleted from *Leaves of Grass* (1856), reprinted in *Leaves of Grass*, ed. Sculley Bradley and Harold W. Blodgett (New York: Norton, 1973), p. 629.

4. On immanentist poetics, see Charles Altieri: "From Symbolist Thought to Immanence: The Ground of Postmodern American Poetics," *Boundary* 2, 1, No. 3 (Spring 1973), 605–41.

5. Introduction to *Contemporary American Poetry*, ed. Donald Hall (Baltimore: Penguin Books, 1962), 23–24.

6. See Holden, pp. 436–39.

7. Robert Bly, *Talking All Morning* (Ann Arbor: Univ. of Michigan Press, 1980), pp. 224–25.

8. *Selected Writings of Charles Olson*, Robert Creeley, ed. (New York: New Directions, 1966), p. 24.

9. See my "In Quiet Language," *Parnassus*, 6, No. 2 (Spring/Summer 1978), 101–17.

10. "After a Day of Work" from *This Tree Will Be Here For A Thousand Years* by Robert Bly. Copyright ©1979 by Robert Bly. Reprinted by permission of Harper and Row, Publishers, Inc.

Nature, Human Nature, and *Gott-Natur*: Robert Bly in the Seventies

RICHARD P. SUGG

The Morning Glory (1975), *This Body Is Made of Camphor and Gopherwood* (1979), *This Tree Will Be Here for a Thousand Years* (1979), and *News of the Universe: Poems of Twofold Consciousness* (1980) represent a coherent grouping of poems, prose poems, and criticism on a common theme, the presence of consciousness in nature. Compared to the political poetry of *Light* and the Jungian poems of *Sleepers*, the work of this period is characterized, as explained in *News*, by the attraction of the poet's imagination to "*Gott-natur*, which means 'divine instinctuality' from one point of view, but also 'non-human nature.'" Bly argues that the poet attracted to this "*Gott-natur* senses the interdependence of all things alive, and longs to bring them all inside a work of art" (*N*, 281). Bly's poetry of this period always expresses his effort to transcend the single consciousness of the rational, human-centered world by discovering and honoring this second, divinely instinctual consciousness in nonhuman nature, this *Gott-natur*. Bly's psyche during this period is engaged in exploring, in learning to see and to live in, a rediscovered universe of what he calls in *News* "twofold consciousness."

The overarching pattern of these four books follows Bly's increasing commitment to two important beliefs. The first is that the world exhibits a consciousness which is different from that which rationalism associates with, and traditionally limits to, human intellect. The second is that he as a poet is writing about man's rediscovery of this other consciousness, and therefore must devise a form suitable for the poetic expression of twofold consciousness. In *News*, whose critical essays present Bly's most thoughtful and extensive statements on these two tenets, he even proclaims the poetry of twofold consciousness as part of a vast but currently neglected literary tradition which, he argues, deserves to be rediscovered. Tracing Bly's development through these three books of poetry, with help from his essays in *News*, will serve to explain the full significance of this period for the poet's career.

The Morning Glory[1] introduces the prose poem, as uncommon hybrid of prose and poetry[2] that Bly was to help make quite popular during the late seventies. Bly declared in *News* that the prose poem was "the final stage of the unpretentious style," especially suitable for allowing the poet's mind to "sink into the mud of earth . . . where the non-human object can live" (*N*, 131–32). In the epigraph to the book, Bly declares his purpose for the switch from poetry to prose poetry. He admires the joy that gradually comes from learning that nature is "independent" of us, "that it has a physical life and a moral life and a spiritual life that is complete without us." Poetry, however free its form, always implies a shaping control of the subject by the poet. But the prose poem form is designed to preserve the independence of the object from the observer, and also to allow for the expression of unpatterned, spontaneous discoveries. In such poetry, as Bly explained in *News*, "the unconscious passes into the object and returns," a union of spirit and perceiving psyche occurs, and the human "unconscious provides material it would not give off if asked directly" (*N*, 213). Thus Bly's prose poem is meant to be a seemingly formless form, designed to express the aleatory, serendipitous quality of the illuminations that the natural world occasionally presents to the psychically attentive observer.

Bly emphasized that the prose form was inseparable from his theme of honoring twofold consciousness. In an interview he defined its purpose as a way of breaking out of the "mind-hell" (*T*, 116) characteristic of the contemporary world, a psychic state in which the "organizing mind" controls human perception by habituating people to see the world only in terms of generalities and abstractions, in terms of types rather than the individual, single object. Bly considers the organizing mind's habit of automatically converting individual objects to plurals very dangerous, for it "can control poetry entirely" (*T*, 118) if left unchecked. For Bly, then, "the prose poem is an exercise in moving against 'plural consciousness'" (*T*, 118). It is a form intended to balance modern man's intellectually overdeveloped mind by exposing it to the freshness of the body and the unconscious. Bly's psychospiritual goal, then, determines the poem form. In *News*, for instance, he calls these "seeing" poems attempts to heal the "wound" of "city culture" by focusing on one object in nature so intently that the psyche can grant "the whole world its being" (*N*, 250–51).

In *The Morning Glory* Bly presents a range of efforts and experiments with the new prose poem form. Each piece is in prose, of course, but there are a variety of prose poems that test the suitability for the new format of familiar elements of Bly's poetic repertoire. Rapid association, characteristically found in clusters in Bly's leaping poetry, seem too frenetic a motion, and too obviously human-centered, for a prose poem form intent on expressing the consciousness of nature. The concluding sentence of "Looking at a Dry Tumbleweed Brought in from the Snow" proves this. Narratives are sometimes successful, with the plot motion making up for the lack of line and stanza motion, as in "The Hockey Poem," or "Watching Andrei Voznesensky Read in Vancouver." But a narrative parable, "In the Courtyard of the Isleta

Mission," fails because it is too self-consciously didactic. A third effort to match old habits with the new form is represented by "Walking on the Sussex Coast," a good poem which is like a *Silence* poem rendered in prose poem form, especially in the steady tone Bly maintains throughout. Catching the proper tone and voice is sometimes a problem for Bly in these early prose poems; he has said that he did not feel the distinctive "pitches"[3] of his speaking voice enter the prose poem until the work of *This Body*. The most successful starts on the prose poem form in part 1 of *The Morning Glory* are "At a Fish Hatchery in Story, Wyoming," "My Three-Year-Old Daughter Brings Me a Gift," and "Standing Under a Cherry Tree at Night." All three of these evince a sharp focus on specific facts of natural objects, with an imaginative development arising organically from nature observed.

In the middle part of *The Morning Glory* are "The Point Reyes Poems," a group published earlier (1974) as a separate book. These are fine poems; as a group they present a consistency of tone, subject, and speaker lacking in the poems of part 1. This may be simply because Bly has found the sea, whose rhythms and formidability provide a measure for the poet's leaping tendencies. Two of the ten poems attempt to mingle the world of politics with that of nature; "Finding a Salamander on Inverness Ridge" invokes the Vietnam War, and "The Dead Seal at McClure's Beach" speaks of the pollution of the California oil spills. Only the first is in any sense a political poem, and there the comparison between nature and politics does not work, partly because the prose poem form does not support the dialectical tension so crucial to Bly's earlier political poetry.

Part 2's introductory poem, "November Day at McClure's," one of the prose poems which Bly saw fit to include in *News*, makes a striking distinction between the emotions of the human world and nature's instinctuality:

> Alone on the jagged rock at the south end of McClure's beach. The sky low. The sea grows more and more private, as afternoon goes on, the sky comes down closer, the unobserved water rushes out to the horizon, horses galloping in a mountain valley at night. The waves smash up the rock, I find flags of seaweed high on the worn top, forty feet up, thrown up overnight, separated water still pooled there, like the black ducks that fly desolate, forlorn, and joyful over the seething swells, who never "feel pity for themselves," and "do not lie awake weeping for their sins." In their blood cells the vultures coast with furry necks extended, watching over the desert for signs of life to end. It is not our life we need to weep for. Inside us there is some secret. We are following a narrow ledge around a mountain, we are sailing on skeletal eerie craft over the buoyant ocean.

There is an important, early statement of a theme that becomes increasingly important for Bly in the work following *The Morning Glory*, especially in *This Tree* and *Black Coat*. Bly describes the "black ducks that fly desolate, forlorn, and joyful over the seething swells" as magnificent instances of nature's purposeful, instinctual labor. They are aloof from human interpretation, from the pathetic fallacy that Bly here caricatures in quotations imputing human "pity" and human "sin" to the birds. For Bly, like Jung, the pathetic fallacy is a mistake man makes not only about nature but also about himself. Man is not unlike nature, and "inside us there is some secret" which our reason does not see, similar in kind to the divine instinctuality that directs the birds to fly and the ocean to swell. Thus Bly's nature is both similar to and different from human nature, but especially different from mankind's wishes about nature. As in this poem, so in *Black Coat*'s elegy "Mourning Pablo Neruda" Bly refutes the pathetic fallacy so prevalent in an anthropomorphic world, declaring poignantly that dead people whom the living have loved must honor nature's laws "and not come back, / even when we ask them." As a consolation in an elegy, this belief captures the same paradoxical quality of the black ducks flying "desolate, forlorn, and joyful" on nature's rounds. This fine poem makes a powerful statement of the philosophy that moved Bly to write in the prose poem form.

An interesting feature of "The Point Reyes Poems" is Bly's increasing ease with his speaking "I." Several of the poems have a flavor of the diary, with a personal narrator telling anecdotes about, or just making reference to, his intimate life. In one of the best poems, "Walking Among Limantour Dunes," Bly begins, "Thinking of a child soon to be born, I hunch down among the friendly sand grains." From this personal beginning, Bly moves to a meditation on the sympathetic correspondences of nature. Similarly, "Climbing up Mount Vision with My Little Boy" begins as a personal anecdote ("How much I love to feel his small leafy hand curl around my fingers"), though it soon metamorphoses into a pastoral allegory about father trying to help son climb up Mount Vision. But in these poems, as well as the final "The Large Starfish," Bly seems more and more confident in his identity as the speaking "I" of a prose poem, an observant, curious, more open and less emotional personality than the "I" of *Sleepers*. If Bly had to wait until *This Body* to find a convincingly personal voice, then he seems to have first begun to identify his speaker in "The Point Reyes Poems."

The final section of *The Morning Glory* presents several interesting types of prose poems. "Visiting Thomas Hart Benton and His Wife in Kansas City" is successful at evoking the scenes and even the brush strokes of Benton's paintings, and Bly infuses his impressions of Benton with psychological readings of the midwest settlers' psyche. Two poems on grass, "Walking in the Hardanger Vidda" and "Grass From Two Years," especially the latter, are skillful interweavings of the poet's "I" and the natural world. And "A Caterpillar on the Desk," in a less emotional vein, does the same thing. "August Rain" endows the "I" of the earlier family anecdotes with a patriarchal aura, and looks forward to the poems of *The Man in the Black Coat Turns*.

The two concluding poems, "Christmas Eve Service at Midnight at St. Michael's" and "Opening the Door of a Barn I Thought Was Empty on New

Year's Eve," are explicitly religious in theme and image, beautiful expressions of the conjunction of the natural world and the divine instinctuality of *Gott-natur*. The last poem, especially, captures this theme in its description of cows in a barn, with their inherited wisdom from "the instinct reservoir." These creatures possess a limited consciousness, but one different in degree rather than kind from that of humans. Using his metaphor of consciousness as light, Bly characterizes cow consciousness as "too much flesh, the body with the lamp inside, fluttering on a windy night." But rather than expressing a superiority of man to nature, this image unites both man and nature in a continuum of consciousness. Although the cows are "bodies with no St. Theresas," no ecstasy, no "light around the body," still Bly recognizes man's kinship with these beasts and the nature they represent. In important ways, this poem complements the one preceding it, with the priest's sermon "that Christ intended to leave his body behind . . . it is confusing . . . we take our bodies with us when we go." The spiritual theme of these concluding poems of *The Morning Glory* looks forward to the pervasive spirituality of the next book, *This Body*.

THIS BODY IS MADE OF CAMPHOR AND GOPHERWOOD

This Body[4] draws upon imagery that is less directly physical and more metaphysical, even spiritual, than *The Morning Glory*. It is the product of an essentially "religious impulse,"[5] which in its expression occasionally seems bardic and false,[6] but that just as often can be stunningly simple and fine. The book continues the earlier line of development, with perhaps less spontaneous discovery but more sustained, overt praise of the consciousness in nature, the *Gott-natur*. The book's title underscores the sacramental relationship Bly sees between the natural and the spiritual worlds. "Camphor and Gopherwood" are two woods God told Noah in a dream-vision to use to build the Ark. This boat of salvation is the Old Testament symbol of the special relationship between a divinity who most often manifests himself in natural objects rather than face-to-face and a humanity whose faith enables it to interpret such sacramental epiphanies. For Bly, the body is modern man's ark, a physical creation that is inseparable from the spirit it houses and protects, as he images it in the early poem "The Left Hand." The human body, through the divine instinctuality that characterizes its consciousness, is man's link to the *Gott-natur* infusing the entire universe.

As the title suggests, this is Bly's book of the holiness of the body. As the book progresses, the body becomes a metonymy for the divine instinctuality that animates not only all of nature but also the spirit of man and the art he creates. In the first poem, "Walking Swiftly," this energy begins as "heat inside the human body," then is transformed in stages into mankind's highest achievement, powering "the artist [who] walks swiftly to his studio, and carves oceanic waves into the dragon's mane." In "Snowed In" Bly again equates the energy in nature with that in art, proclaiming they "are both the same flow, that starts out close to the soil" but grows and manifests itself in different ways: it "is at home when one or two are present, . . . and in the burnt bone that sketched the elk by smokey light" in the ancient caves of Lascaux.

If the body's energy can transform itself into art, it can also establish links in various ways between man and nature, a basis of correspondence between the two. Several poems treat this theme of correspondence from different angles. "Looking from Inside My Body" compares the conscious and unconscious regions of human personality to sun and moon, and the body to "earth . . . earth things, earthly joined." At night the sun-consciousness "will drop underneath the earth, and travel sizzling along the underneath-ocean-darkness path," the inward road of psychic exploration, which is Bly's major poetic symbol. In this extended correspondence, the significant thing is that the body does not break the circuit the way the rationalists always say it must; in fact, the body consciousness, what Bly in *News* terms "night intelligence" (*N*, 1) provides the most important part of the road to self-knowledge which man must travel.

In "Falling Into Holes in Our Sentences" the body is presented both as a corrective to the spirit, protecting it, but also as a continually changing manifestation of the psyche. It is a "ruthless body performing its magic, transforming each of our confrontations into energy." This body continually creates correspondence between psychic and somatic phenomena. It continually teaches man of the inescapable relationship between body and soul, even by compensating such persona behavior as lecturing "about the confusion of others" by sending a subconscious impulse to accidentally drive the car "off the road."

Another bodily basis of correspondence between man and nature is their shared evolutionary history. In "Coming in For Supper" Bly presents a very specific instance of an ancient ritual, having supper with the family. He locates the power of the occasion in its long psychic history, in "those long dusks—they were a thousand years long then—that fell over the valley from the cave mouth (where we sit)." The poet emphasizes how so much of human evolutionary history was based on learning (slowly) from nature, as in his lament for "the last man killed by flu who knew how to weave a pot of river clay the way the wasps do . . . Now he is dead and only the wasps know in the long river-mud grief." Similarly, in "Snowed In" Bly emphasizes the continuum linking nature to man, based on their shared evolutionary heritage, of the divine instinctuality of *Gott-natur*. A man and a woman are snowed in, but "in the snow storm millions of years come close behind us, nothing is lost, nothing rejected, our bodies are equal to the snow in energy," and ready to affirm themselves again.

"The Origin of the Praise of God" deals most fully with the religious aspect of the body and its *Gott-natur* energy. This poem is placed at the center of the book, and accompanied, as each poem is, by a drawing of a snail that presents a frontal view of the creature's cornucopian trumpet, as if to announce and amplify the importance of the poem. Further, this poem is the only one of the book Bly included in his anthology *News of the Universe*, which is a measure of its significance to his theory of consciousness as well as a testament to its worth as poetry. In this poem Bly brings together the major themes of *This Body*. The presence of a consciousness, a wisdom, in nature, one which man would do well to honor and learn from, is a pervasive theme, emphasized again and again simply by an imagery that consistently represents human energy at the cellular level as indistinguishable from the energy of all living things. At the poem's beginning Bly declares this equivalence, "this body is made of bone and excited protozoa . . . and it is with my body that I love the fields." At the poem's conclusion he repeats this correspondence, and emphasizes as well the divine instinctuality of both nature's and man's fundamental, cellular energies, affirming that "from the dance of the cells praise sentences rise to the throat of the man."

The holiness of the body, and the psychospiritual nature of the human imperative to pursue the inward road of self-exploration, are two major themes of Bly's work, and both are expressed more forcefully in this poem than in any other in the book. Bly's answer to the question implied by the poem's title is that the origin of the praise of God lies in the inescapable impulse of life's most ancient and enduring energies operating at the cellular level. This impulse is nature's evolutionary imperative to increase and multiply, to create new life. Behind the human emotions of two lovers lies the force of millions of years of evolutionary history, urging man at the instinctual level to once again re-create himself. When two people approach each other, then beneath ego consciousness and even beneath the stimulation felt through the five senses, an exchange takes place:

> So the space between two people diminishes, it grows less and less, no one to weep, they merge at last. The sound that pours from the fingertips awakens clouds of cells far inside the body, and beings unknown to us start out in a pilgrimage to their Saviour, to their holy place. Their holy place is a small black stone, that they remember from Protozoic times, when it was rolled away from a door . . . and it was after that they found their friends, who helped them to digest the hard grains of this world. . . . The cloud of cells awakens, intensifies, swarms . . . the cells dance inside beams of sunlight so thin we cannot see them. . . . To them each ray is a vast palace, with thousands of rooms. From the dance of the cells praise sentences rise to the throat of the man praying and singing alone in his room. He lets his arms climb above his head, and says, "Now do you still say you cannot choose the Road?"

As the poem progresses, the poet resorts to overtly religious imagery to express the strength and significance of this *Gott-natur* impulse that moves man. Bly draws on the imagery of the Resurrection of Jesus, perhaps the most potent belief in Christian tradition, to express the urge humans feel to honor the *Gott-natur* by procreating. In Bly's image, the myth of resurrection is powerful precisely because it symbolically reenacts the archetypal event of procreation, whose memory man has carried in the collective unconscious "from Protozoic times." Thus Bly images the journey of the sperm toward the womb as a "pilgrimage" to "the holy place." And a successful impregnation is described as a stone "rolled away from a door," an image taken directly from the biblical account of Christ's Resurrection, where the angel rolled away the stone blocking the sepulcher of Christ.

The poem concludes by describing how this archetypal, *Gott-natur* urge leads to the imperative to "choose the Road," the inward path of psychospiritual exploration. Not only the religious imagery of the last half of the poem, but also the situations at the poem's end of "the man praying and singing," affirming with his whole body, "from the dance of the cells," to the "praise sentences" of his voice, the archetypal "Road," underscores Bly's belief in the essentially religious nature of a body "made of camphor and gopherwood."

THIS TREE WILL BE HERE FOR A THOUSAND YEARS

This book of forty-four poems consists of two parts. The first twenty poems were originally published in 1975 as *Old Man Rubbing His Eyes*,[7] and the remainder were added in 1979. Yet in the introductory essay, "The Two Presences," Bly says that *This Tree* includes all the poems written in the style of his first book, *Silence*, since its publication in 1962, and that affinities of style and subject make his latest book seem like a continuation of the first. Bly's desire to compare his latest work to his first, nearly twenty years older, tells less about the two books than it does about an impulse in the poet that the reader senses in the poetry of *This Tree*, the impulse of a survivor to affirm continuity and order in a world which in human terms is breaking apart. The book's title emphasizes survival and endurance, imaging a pine tree that can grow in terrain where a leafy tree would die, a pine tree that can find its place and stay "for a thousand years." Further, Bly's pine tree symbolizes the mood of a poet growing older, not only strong and long-lived but also "somber, / made for winter, they knew it would come" (*Tr*, 36).

In this book Bly emphasizes a new aspect of the *Gott-natur*, not merely its divine instinctuality but also its profound, even sorrowful fidelity to nature's eternal laws. The poet is neither the curious observer of *The Morning Glory* nor the passionate believer of *This Body*. Rather he is a human who has been through what in "Women We Never See Again" Bly calls the "human war." Consequently, he seeks to infuse in the poetry a psychic weight gained from his newly heightened sense of human frailty. In his essay "The Image as a Form of Intelligence" Bly identified this quality of "psychic weight" as one of the six sources of power in poetry, as significant as imagery or sound or story. He declares that this quality is directly connected to the poet's life and experience, "to grief, turning your face to your own life, absorbing the failures your parents and your own country have suffered."[8] In *This Body* the new tone, and a deeper resonance, comes from Bly's balancing this psychic weight with a deepened appreciation of nonhuman nature's consciousness of eternity, by focusing on what he once referred to as "the old non-human or non-ego energies the ancients imagined so well" (*N*, 80). Much of Bly's effort in *This Tree* is skillfully directed to merging the psychic weight of his own life and the eternal laws of the *Gott-natur,* for the purpose of affirming a relationship between the individual and the eternal that might endure beyond his lifetime. As he says in his essay in the image as intelligence, "when a poet creates a true image, he is gaining knowledge; he is bringing up into consciousness a connection that has been forgotten, perhaps for centuries."[9] Later, in *Black Coat*, Bly puts more emphasis on the dialectical relationship between the psychic weight of personal experience and the general laws of nature, to show that man must live life between the two, that this is what it means to be human in a *Gott-natur* world. Nevertheless, the poems in *This Tree* and even *Black Coat* are intended not only to evince the melancholy tone of psychic weight gained from the poet's personal experience, but also to affirm Bly's metaphysics concerning the interdependence between the individual and the natural laws that sustain him. Bly is writing about much more here than merely the difficulty of his personal life.

Bly's belief that man and nature can "share a consciousness" (*Tr*, 9) is the subject of his introductory essay to *This Tree*. He contrasts human consciousness, "insecure, anxious, massive, earthbound, persistent, cunning, hopeful," and nature's nonhuman consciousness, which not only lacks these qualities but also continually frustrates man's desire to impose human emotions on it, to subordinate its true presence to human wishes about its presence. Bly does see in organic nature a thanatos instinct, an awareness of death, "a melancholy tone, the tear inside the stone, what Lucretius calls 'the tears of things,' an energy circling downward, felt often in autumn" (*Tr*, 9–10). Indeed, this melancholy tone humming through the nature of things is the dominant one in part 1 of *This Tree.* As Bly explains in *News*, "each time a human being's desire-energy leaves his body, and goes out into the hills or forest, the desire-energy whispers to the ear as it leaves: 'You know, one day you will die.'" Bly calls this whisper evidence that the two consciousness "have spoken to each other," and argues that it is good for humans to hear nature's whisper of death, for "it helps the human to come down, to be on the ground" (*N*, 281) and to locate human consciousness in relationship to nature's consciousness.

A further aspect of the *Gott-natur* emphasized in *This Tree* is its primitive, "non-human instinctuality" (*N*, 281), the energy that drives the universe. A powerful expression of this occurs in the introductory poem of part 2 of the book: "Sometimes when you put your hand into a hollow tree / you touch the dark places between the stars." This is a Lawrentian image of the discovery of the palpable presence of the nothingness and the magnitude of infinity and eternity, measured against which all human calculations and ego-emotions pale. Bly once paraphrased Lawrence as saying that "when you look up, in most centuries, you do not see the black sky with the stars," but a humanized version, a painted unbrella, because "humanity prefers that, it is less scary." But "a strong artist will tear holes in the umbrella so you can see the stars again." Bly added, "I like Lawrence's image—it explains a lot to me" (*T*, 255–56). *This Tree* is Bly's conscious attempt to tear holes in the umbrella. Another expression of this sentiment comes from Wallace Stevens's "The Snow Man," selected by Bly for *News*. Stevens declares that man "must have a mind of winter," must look at the world and behold "Nothing that is not there and the nothing that is." *This Tree* provides examples of both.

Part 1 develops two associated themes, death and the breakdown of family relationships. The movement of part 1 is from fall to winter, with a final, coda poem about the psyche of winter existing even in the midst of summer, which underscores Bly's winter as a psychic state, a season of the soul. The theme of death is present from beginning to end. "Writing Again" is a dismissal of the moralistic poetry of Bly's Vietnam period as unsuitable to his present imagination, a passionate exercise that does not answer the question of the poem's conclusion, "what good will it do me in the grave?" Death and eternity are to be the measures of life's acts. Similarly, "Fall Poem" dismisses the ecstatic religious moods of *This Body* as insufficient to his present need. Bly defines the season as one of promise forever unfulfilled: "Something is about to happen! / Christ will return! / But each fall it goes by without happening." In "Dawn in Threshing Time" the rebirth of the day is not enough to lighten the burden of death the poet feels, which he admits he has felt every morning "after thirty," the realization that "he is not strong enough to die." The image of the cradle as well as the rhythm of the last line recall Whitman's famous poem about a similar discovery, "Out of the Cradle Endlessly Rocking." "To Live" repeats the paradox, that the more a man lives, the closer he gets to death, for "To live is to rush ahead eating up your own death." "Listening to a Cricket in the Wainscoting" is a better poem, finding four surreal image equivalents for the cricket's chirp, all of which invoke blackness and death.

"A Long Walk Before the Snows Began" uses Bly's ubiquitous image of snow to suggest the threat of death. In this poem Bly's walk takes him to the recognition that "It must be that I will die one day!" This leads to a vision of himself as dead, in which "I see my body lying stretched out. / A woman whose face I cannot see stands near my body." There is nothing in the poem that suggests resurrection or hope of any sort. Similarly, in "Roads" Bly creates a four-line-elegy, dedicated "In memoriam" to someone unnamed, which only hints at a possible consolation in the image of "the plowing west" that reminds the grieving poet of natural resurrections, of "mountain tops, or the chest of graves." The mood of the poet after the elegy is one of extreme vulnerability. In "Passing An Orchard By Train," the concluding poem of part 1, the season is summer, but the mood is dead-of-winter. The poet declares that "We cannot bear disaster" as nature seems to; as humans, "One slight bruise and we die!" The poet is repelled from nature, back to his fellowman, for comfort; even a stranger on the train, because he is human-kind, is better than this melancholy isolation, which Bly had so often praised in the past as solitude. If Bly is the "old man rubbing his eyes" of the original title, then his tears signify a need for community, for human forgiveness, as the book's first part concludes.

The second theme, the breakdown of family relationships, is entwined with the theme of death. Bly's avowed intention to write a poetry that mingles hints of the poet's personal life amid more impersonal, cosmic themes, in order to evoke the shared consciousness, the interrelationship, between the two worlds, is evident in several poems. "Sitting in Fall Grass" opens with the poet hearing the voices of the cosmos, of wind, ocean, and sun; but in the final stanza the poet is attuned to different voices, speaking of separation and differences, saying "I am not like you . . . / I must live so." In "Thinking of 'Seclusion' " Bly imagines living without family responsibilities. He awakens on a day when there is no work to be done, when even his self-imposed task of writing "looks small beside the growing trees." He fantasizes, jokingly, about what a permanent "seclusion" might mean, no worries about the children, leaving the money problems to the wife, living "your whole life like a drunkard's dream!" The poem presents an unresolved tension between the two worlds, the human and the cosmic; but there is also a sense of shared consciousness, in which the human world seems akin to, even interdependent with, the natural world. Both worlds are part of a farm that to Bly "looks doubly good."

"Digging Worms" expresses more directly Bly's association of the themes of death and the breakdown of the family. The poet is "digging worms behind the chickenhouse," an act of penance as well as self-examination. In stanza 2 he reflects on the relationship between parents and children, a paradoxical one of mutual support and burden. Like tightwire walkers carrying each other, staggering, "along a wire our children balance us / on their shoulders, we balance their graves / on ours." In stanza 3 Bly images the unraveling of family relationships, not only between parents and children but also between husband and wife, in "we unwind / from some kind of cocoon made by lovers . . . until / with one lurch we grow still and look down at our shoes." The poem concludes with a dream of insignificant acts of carelessness adding up until they pull down a "castle," the poet's home.

Part 2 of the book is different in tone from part 1, because it presents not only poems contrasting the different consciousness of nature and man, but also poems expressing their shared consciousness, in which Bly finds a source of consolation. The first poem, "Women We Never See Again," sets the tone by imaging time's infinity and space's immensity as "the dark spaces between the stars." Nature's immensity is both impervious and inviting to human consciousness, a "fortress made of ecstatic blue stone," an edifice bespeaking a second consciousness to which inhabitants of the human world may aspire, by which they may measure their human actions. In "Amazed By an Accumulation of Snow" Bly writes of another manifestation of nature's consciousness of the immensity of the universe. This is a "call" poem, described in *News* as a poem about an instance when "one form of consciousness [calls] to another" (*N*, 35). The last stanza cites several forms of the call, ending with "The horse's hoof kicks up a seashell, and the farmer / finds an Indian stone with a hole all the way through." In similar fashion, Bly draws correspondences in "Pulling a Rowboat Up Among Lake Reeds" between the two presences by associating the darkness of nature and of the human world, including birth and religious sacrifice.

An important way in which Bly emphasizes the difference between the two presences in part 2 is by intentionally demystifying nature, by rendering it impervious to man's tendency to project human emotions upon it. Bly critiques the anthropomorphism of the pathetic fallacy in a series of poems in which he presents nature as not responding to or bearing messages for the ego-centered human, but instead constantly affirming what Bly described in *News* as "news of the universe" (*N*, 281). In "July Morning" Bly begins with a blithe description of nature communing with itself, personified, talking to man—in short, a perfect expression of the pathetic fallacy. A morning dove even "coos" to his audience "a cathedral, / then the two arms of the cross!" But Bly undercuts this falsely romantic view of nature on a July morning by looking beyond the moment, by invoking the laws of time that govern organic nature: the same evocative magic which creates the "rabbit/hopping along the garden" also creates the rabbit's death. Laconically, like Emily Dickenson, Bly ends the poem thus: "After that we will be alone in the deep blue reaches of the river" of time, without the rabbit or a blind faith in July mornings.

In the following poem, "An Empty Place," Bly achieves a similar Dickensonian irony by contrasting the joyful attitude toward nature in the introductory, prose poem stanza with the concluding stanza of poetry. The initial situation of a speaker affirming "a joy in emptiness" because each space offers "a place to live" ultimately gives way to a tone of uncertainty and perhaps even bitterness. The speaker wonders at "a white chicken's feather that still seems excited by the warm blood" now gone forever, and he looks upon an empty corncob, lacking all its kernels, as a "place of many mansions, / which Christ has gone to prepare for us." There is little succor in such a line, uttered by the same poet who wrote in "Fall Poem" of the failure of Christ to fulfill his promise to return. Instead, this poem, like "Prayer Service in an English Church," is precisely about the failure of nature to support human hopes in the orthodox religious terms in which they are so often cast.

Nature's denial of conventional religious interpretations of it forces the poet to break with his socially inculcated habits of looking at it, especially strong in one who was raised as a "Lutheran Boy-god in Minnesota,"[10] and to see nature in a new way. "Fishing on a Lake at Night" represents a turning point in part 2, where the poet is able to accept without despair the elements

and consciousness of nature as independent of conventional religious interpretation. Further, this poem expresses Bly's description in *News* of consciousness
in nature as being "not exactly consciousness, nor psyche, nor intelligence, nor
sentience," but mainly characterized by elemental "energy" (*N*, 286–87). This
energy of nature's consciousness need not be exuberant, like the flying around
associated with the ecstatic body. Light, grass, and snow are elemental energies
in Bly's poetry.

The poem begins by subverting the conventional religious image of God
as man's guiding light. Here the light is an element of nature that "simply
comes," carrying no messages from the supernatural, "bearing no gifts, / as if
the camels had arrived without the Wise Men." But it offers another kind of
solace, for it "is steady, holding us to our old mountain home," to the ancient
sense of human sharing in the *Gott-natur* of the universe. The moon, too,
"arrives without a fuss," but without promises. It is similarly demystified of
supernatural portent; for its light "goes between the boards around the
pulp-cutter's house— / the same fence we pass through by opening the gate."

Part 2 of *This Tree*, unlike part 1, moves through despair to hope. The
concluding twelve poems emphasize the magnitude of nature and the necessity
that human consciousness learn to locate itself within this larger context. In
"Night of the First Snow" the poet envisions man as an assertive "dark vertical
shape to the earth." In the final two stanzas he can distinguish the two
presences, identifying the human and individual aspect of nature's eternal,
repetitive laws. "Solitude of the Two Day Snowstorm" similarly locates the
"frail impulses" of the human, including the family, within the context of
nature's immense forces, symbolized by the snowstorm. But a black crow's
head, not only nature's handiwork but also a totem of human consciousness,
looking "intense, swift, decided," asserts itself against the all-blanketing
snow.

But the melancholy tone remains an important counterpoint during the
final poems of part 2. In "Frost in the Ground" it is the poet's recognition that
"what I have / to say I have not said." In "Late Moon" it is the dying light over
his father's farm, "in the west that eats it away." A similar theme of nature's
laws of time and death occurs in "Black Pony Eating Grass," where the poet
marvels that "In a few years we will die, / yet the grass continues to lift itself
into the horse's teeth." Nature continues living in spite of the inevitability of
death—both man and the stars are "stubborn" in their urge to live. This
paradox is imaged in "Nailing a Dock Together," where "the horse stands
penned, but is also free. / It is a horse whose neck human / beings have longed
to touch for centuries," ever since man's rationalism created a gap between man
and nature. The horse symbolizes the *Gott-natur*, the divine instinctuality of
nature's persistent energy, which can prove an effective antidote to excessive
human melancholy about dying.

This Tree concludes with two poems emphasizing the magnitude of
nature as well as the possibility of humans sharing consciousness with nature.

"An Evening When the Full Moon Rose as the Sun Set" celebrates a visual balance of the two natural forces that govern the world, moon, and sun, which symbolize for Bly nature's nonrational consciousness and man's rational consciousness. The event for Bly, and the poem for the reader, exemplify perfectly a moment and a poetry, as praised in *News*, when "the ancient union of the day intelligence of the human being and the night intelligence of nature become audible, palpable again" (*N*, 4). The poem is a vision of a world under the spell of *Gott-natur*, living "the life of faithfulness," a term underscoring the psychoreligious satisfaction derived from fidelity to nature's archaic forces.

The final poem of *This Tree*, "Out Picking Up Corn," is about the poet's learning to find food in pastures "eaten clean by horse teeth," learning to get nourishment from sources "respectable people do not want to take in." This latter statement could almost serve as a summary of Bly's literary career. But Bly is not desolate, but hopeful. As he did at the conclusion of "Sleepers Joining Hands," here Bly turns to an admixture of religious language and parable to express his new state of mind. He declares, "Surely we do not eat only with our mouths, / or drink only by lifting our hands!" He presents in quotations a Zen-like utterance of a disciple, "My master had gone picking ferns on the mountain." The final image of "walking in fog near the cliff" expresses the poet's sense of himself as older, closer to death, lacking a clear vision of what lies at the end of his road, yet nourished and heartened by the very atmosphere in which he walks. Water has always been a symbol used by Bly to suggest nourishment of the conscious life by the unconscious, as in his elegy for Pablo Neruda. Here the damp fog quenches the poet's thirst through osmosis, as the *Gott-natur* nourishes the human consciousness, just as Bly described in the book's introductory essay on the beneficial interdependence of the two presences.

News of the Universe:
Poems of Twofold Consciousness

In 1980 Robert Bly published *News*, an extensive poetry anthology accompanied by critical essays that are often directly applicable to Bly's own poetry of this period. In *News* Bly argued for nothing less than a new version of Western literary and intellectual history. His poetry selections were chosen to illustrate a tradition that champions the possibility of humanity's achieving "twofold consciousness," which Bly defines as awareness of unity not only within the human psyche, between conscious and unconscious aspects, but also between "the human psyche and nature" (*N*, 5). The fundamental message this literary tradition of twofold consciousness communicates to its audience is "news of the universe," and this news is that man can gain a sense of the possibility of inner, psychic unity by learning to see an external unity in nature.

News begins by briefly tracing the tradition's subjugation by eighteenth-century rationalism, and continues with a fuller treatment of the counterattack led by Blake in England and the continental romantics Goethe, Hölderlin, and Novalis. The largest portion of the anthology deals with the tradition's struggle in the early twentieth century to prevail against the neoclassicism of the Pound-Eliot tradition, as well as with the literature of twofold consciousness's emergence since 1945 as the dominant tradition. Bly defines the major tradition of modernism as the "lineage of double consciousness, or 'full consciousness'" (N, 84). Bly's book even infers the tradition's future from the poetry of other cultures, such as the Eskimo, which seem to have arrived at a unity of consciousness before Western civilization.

Throughout this chapter the essays and even the poetry of News have shed light on Bly's own efforts to write poetry that brings news of the universe and of a rediscovered nature. But his anthology speaks also to concerns that span his entire career. News raises such perennial subjects as Bly's anti-academic stance (imagine this history as opposed to that commonly assigned textbook, the Norton anthology). Also, this literary history argues for Bly's anti-rational epistemology, praising a kind of poetry devoted to exploring beyond the rationalist conception of consciousness, seeking news of the universe rather than "news of the human mind" (N, 281). Finally, the book is a virtual catalog of Bly's acknowledged influences: the European romantics Goethe, Novalis, Blake, and Rilke; non-Western poets such as Kabir, Basho, and some Amerind artists; and, of course, the Spanish surrealists Lorca, Jiménez, and Neruda. Bly himself has translated[11] most of these poems. Many of these writers were either unappreciated or unknown to most American academics and poets twenty-five years ago; this anthology is a reminder that it is Bly who is mainly responsible for their general acceptance today. News, then, is indispensable as Bly's own textbook on himself, not only on his efforts to rediscover nature during this period, but also on many of the major themes and sources that inform his entire career.

Notes

1. *The Morning Glory* (New York, 1975) incorporates *The Morning Glory: Another Thing That Will Never Be My Friend* (San Francisco: Kayak Press, 1969–70) and *Point Reyes Poems* (Half Moon Bay, Calif.: Mudra Press, 1974).

2. William V. Davis, "'In a Low Voice'" *Midwest Quarterly* 25, no. 2 (1984):149–52, discusses the history and poetic validity of the prose poem form.

3. "Recognizing the Image as a Form of Intelligence" *Field* 24 (Spring 1981):18.

4. *This Body is Made of Camphor and Gopherwood* (New York, 1979).

5. Molesworth, *The Fierce Embrace,* 130.

6. See Philip Dacey, "This Book Is Made of Turkey Soup and Star Music," *Parnassus,* Fall–Winter 1978, 34–45.

7. *Old Man Rubbing His Eyes* is reprinted in *This Tree Will Be Here for a Thousand Years* (New York, 1979); hereafter cited in the text as *Tr.*

8. "Recognizing the Image," 18.

9. Ibid., 21.

10. Bly's "Being a Lutheran Boy-god in Minnesota" is an informing presence behind the family poems of this period, especially in its description of Bly's socioreligious role in a Lutheran, Norwegian-American culture that repressed all doctrinal conflict with what Bly found to be a "maddening cheerfulness" (*Growing Up in Minnesota*, ed. Anderson, 211).

11. Bly has translated the work of more than twenty poets, and has written an excellent book on the process and its challenges: *The Eight Stages of Translation* (Boston, 1983).

The Man in the Black Coat Turns and Loving a Woman in Two Worlds

WILLIAM V. DAVIS

The Man in the Black Coat Turns (1981),[1] Bly's tenth book of poems, took him more than ten years to write. Bly's symbolic turn toward home, the self-referential elegy many writers come to, *Black Coat* describes the end of the journey *Silence in the Snowy Fields* began almost twenty years before. But *Black Coat* is more than a simple return to Bly's personal and poetic origins. Bly constantly circles back to beginnings and, with every return, he discovers another beginning. Just so, *Black Coat* is not an end but another new beginning.

Black Coat shares much of its tone and mood, some of its themes, and many of its sources with *Silence*.[2] It also adds the crucial new development of a more personal voice to Bly's canon. The poems in *Black Coat,* together with its companion volume, *Loving a Woman in Two Worlds* (1985), are Bly's most personal and private poems. As such, they tell a good deal about him now, and about where he has been and where he is going.

Black Coat is divided into three sections, the first and third poems in lines, the second, like *Morning Glory* and *This Body,* poems in prose. The prose poems in the central section, which appear almost as carry overs from the earlier books of prose poems, really represent a transitional form. Knowing that he would be dealing with "heavy thought-poems" in *Black Coat,* Bly asks, "What sort of form is proper" for these poems? "Free verse in brief lines doesn't seem right" because it "suggests doubt and hesitation, whereas these thoughts are obsessive, massive, even brutal. And the prose poem form doesn't seem right, because prose poems flow as rivers flow, following gravity around a rock." And since "these thoughts are more like the rocks themselves" they need a new form, "a form that would please the old sober and spontaneous ancestor males." Therefore, Bly "tried to knit the stanzas together in sound, and . . . set [himself] a task of creating stanzas that each have the same number of beats."[3] Although several of the prose poems in this book, "The Dried Sturgeon" (21–22, *Selected* 108), "A Bouquet of Ten Roses" (23–24, *Selected* 107), and "Finding an Old Ant Mansion" (27–30, *Selected* 110–112), in

Reprinted from *Understanding Robert Bly* (Columbia: University of South Carolina Press, 1988), 133–63. Reprinted by permission.

particular, are important poems, only the lined poems in the first and third sections of the book, those "rocks" that create the strongest resistance, and whose "language begins to take on the darkness and engendered quality of matter,"[4] will be considered here.

In one of the prose poems, "Eleven O'Clock at Night," Bly says, "Many times in poems I have escaped—from myself. . . . Now more and more I long for what I cannot escape from" (18). That inescapable essence which the poems in *Black Coat* confront, and the object poems in prose in the earlier books avoid, is a depth of personal existence and experience.

In *Black Coat* Bly opens the door of the self to expose deeper levels of reality. "Snowbanks North of the House" (3–4, *Selected* 148), the first poem in *Black Coat,* is an important transitional poem. Like "great sweeps of snow . . . thoughts that go so far," it goes back to the beginning, to *Silence.* This poem represents one stage of the recovery of the shadow which Bly speaks of in *A Little Book on the Human Shadow*[5] and it also introduces the dominant theme of *Black Coat,* the father-son relationship.

In "Snowbanks . . ." the initial focus is on the father ("The father grieves for his son and will not leave the room where the coffin stands" 3), but later the focus shifts to the son as Bly explores both sides of the father-son dichotomy. The ending of the poem provides the title for the book. The references to "the man in the black coat," the father, and the snow parallel Bly's memory of "My father wearing a large black coat . . . holding a baby up over the snow . . . my brother or myself" in his essay, "Being a Lutheran Boy-God in Minnesota." Bly remembers that "always around [his father] there was a high exhilaration, pursued by grief and depression," that "he had a gift for deep feeling. Other men bobbed like corks around his silence." And he comes to respect his father ("such a beautiful thing!") as a "solitary man" who "is the stone pin that connects this world to the next."[6]

In the second poem, "For My Son Noah, Ten Years Old" (5–6, *Selected* 152), the transition from Bly the speaker as son to Bly the speaker as father has already occurred. Bly says, "The end of the poem suggests that spontaneity reappears in our relationship with our sons when we live in the grief of the return."[7]

The "grief of the return" in terms of the father-son relationship is the theme of the next poem. "The Prodigal Son" (7, *Selected* 147). This theme, as already indicated, runs throughout Bly's work. The poem begins, "The Prodigal Son is kneeling in the husks." Here, even at the outset of the poem, the son is already away from his father, already fallen on hard times, already among the swine ("The swine go on feeding in the sunlight"). The story of the prodigal son is an old story, as is indicated by the references of Tyre and Sidon, cities important in New Testament times, but cities ancient even then, both having been conquered by Alexander the Great, and older even than that (Sidon was one of the most ancient Phoenician cities, founded in the third millenium B.C.). In short, the story is as ancient as the generations of men ("father beyond father beyond father") and as new as the poet's relationship to his own father, who, he says, "is seventy-five years old."

Although this poem is clearly important for Bly's theme, it remains somewhat confusing and enigmatic. The references to the Biblical parable in Luke 15:11–32, to Alexander, the allusion to the Irish folk tale mentioned by Yeats in his *Autobiography*, all deal with fathers and sons and the conflict between them, but the poem stops short of taking a stand on the relationship or making a specific personal statement. The original final line, "What we cannot solve is expressed by the swine,"[8] is indicative of Bly's inability to state his theme clearly; he "cannot solve" it. The revised last line, "Under the water there's a door the pigs have gone through" (7), links the end with the beginning of the poem, and has obvious Jungian associations, but does little to define the dilemma or exorcise the "demons" that possess father-son relationships.[9]

The theme of the father-son relationship, so important in *Black Coat*, is rather new in Bly's thinking although it is a natural outgrowth of the age we live in as well as Bly's interest in myth, fairy tales, Jungian psychology, and his own personal background as a "boy god." Bly has discussed in depth what might be seen as the background to the poems in *Black Coat* on several occasions. Here is a summary of his views: "Historically, the male has changed considerably in the past thirty years." The 1950s male "was vulnerable to collective opinion" and "lacked feminine space . . . lacked compassion, in a way that led directly to the unbalanced pursuit of the Vietnam war. . . . Then, during the '60s, another sort of male appeared." The war "made men question what an adult male really is. And the women's movement encouraged men" until "some men began to see their own feminine side and pay attention to it." Still, the "grief and anguish in the younger males was astounding" and "part of the grief was remoteness from their fathers." Now, "it's possible that men are once more approaching [the] deep male" in the psyche, "the *deep* masculine." "When a boy talks with the hairy man, he is . . . getting into a conversation . . . about something wet, dark, and low—what James Hillman would call 'soul.' And I think that today's males are just about ready to take that step" and be initiated "into the moistness of the swampy fathers who stretch back century after century. . . . After a man has done some work in recovering his wet and muddy feminine side, often he still doesn't feel complete. A few years ago I began to feel diminished by my lack of embodiment of the fruitful male, or the 'moist male.' I found myself missing contact with the male—or should I say my father?. . . . It takes a while for man to overcome" his mother. "The absorption with the mother may last ten, fifteen, twenty years, and then rather naturally, a man turns toward his father."[10] This statement rather clearly summarizes Bly's poetic activity from his beginnings up to the moment of *Black Coat* and through it.

This focus on the father as the first "transformer" of his son's energies is, ideally, followed by exposure of a "wise old man," who "assumes the role of a shaman" and teaches the boy "artistic curiosity and intellectual discipline, values of spirit and soul, the beginnings of a rich inner life." This stage should be followed by an "intensive study of mythology." As Keith Thompson says, "Bly became interested in these themes when his own sons began to grow up, and when, after years of emotional distance, he began to get close to his own father."[11] Bly reports that "the American man is often 40 or 45 before the . . . events of initiation have taken place completely enough to be felt as events." The final stage in the process is "a deepening of feeling toward the religious life."[12]

The first section of *Black Coat,* following the initial poems on the literal father-son relationship, concludes with an elegy on Neruda. Bly wrote "Mourning Pablo Neruda" (11–13, revised in *Selected* 149–151) "in [Neruda's] skinny pitch-enlivened form . . . to honor" the "old reckless dead" man, "and to honor another, William Carlos Williams, I put rocks into the same poem by means of an abrupt line break" (*Selected* 144). Williams, and especially Neruda, are crucial "father-figures" for Bly.[13] and, as he says in the poem, "the dead remain inside / us" (12).

The third section of *Black Coat* opens with "The Grief of Men" (33–34), and important poem for the theme of the entire book. The poem begins with a "Buddhist" who "ordered his boy to bring him, New Year's / morning, a message . . . / he himself had written." The "message," delivered on the first morning of the New Year reads:

> "Busyness has caught you, you have slowed
>   and stopped.
> If you start toward me, I
> will surely come
> to meet you."

The man weeps. Then the poem moves out into nature. The poet hears a "coot" call his Keatsian "darkening call," a "dog's doubt," and sees a silent porcupine, and "fresh waters" that "wash past the tidal sands, / into the delta . . . and are gone." The poem ends with a very personal reference to Bly's Aunt Bertha who died in childbirth and of her husband who "will not lie quiet" but "throws himself against the wall." The uncle is comforted and cared for by men:

> Men come to hold him down.
> My father is there,
> sits by the bed long night after night.

Here, in the figure of the poet's father being there, and caring for another man, Bly makes the first overt reference to the importance and significance of men for other men in this book. The "grief of men" has been traced to a specific personal context, and this poem is a moving introduction to the dominant theme of this section of the book—indeed, to the book as a whole.

"Words Rising" (42–44, revised in *Selected* 169–170), is the prelude to a hymnlike crescendo, the most beautiful musical conclusion in all of Bly's canon, to which the end of *Black Coat* builds. (Bly places "Words Rising" last in the section of poems from *Black Coat* in his *Selected* poems.)

"Words Rising" begins: "I open my journal, write a few / sounds with green ink, and suddenly / fierceness enters me." Then, "the music comes." This fierce music, the way words make and remake the world ("Watery syllables come welling up. . . . / The old earth fragrance remains / in the word 'and.' We experience / 'the' in its lonely suffering. . . . / When a man or woman feeds a few words / with private grief, the shames we knew / before we could invent the wheel / then words grow. . . . / We see a crowd with dusty / palms turned up inside each / verb" [*Selected* 169–170) is the subject of this poem. In the final stanza the words do almost "rise" to a kind of prayer for the world.

> Blessings then on the man who labors
> in his tiny room, writing stanzas on the lamb;
> blessings on the woman who picks the brown
> seeds of solitude in afternoon light
> out of the black seeds of loneliness.
> And blessings on the dictionary maker, huddled among
> his bearded words, and on the setter of songs
> who sleeps at night inside his violin case.
>
> (*Selected* 170)[14]

"A Meditation on Philosophy" (46–47, revised in *Selected* 162–163) looks backward to literal and poetic ancestors and forward to poetic progeny yet to come. It begins with an evocation of Yeats's "The Wild Swans of Coole" and "A Prayer for My Daughter" as Marjorie Perloff has pointed out[15] and the Chinaman "exchanging poems" in stanza four may refer to Yeats's Chinamen in "Lapis Lazuli."[16]

The "restless gloom in my mind" is prelude to the philosophic "meditation" of the rest of the poem. The last two stanzas look forward to the "father" poems still to come in this book and back both to the feminine in *Sleepers* and elsewhere and forward to *Loving a Woman in Two Worlds.* The "thunderstorms longing to come / into the world through the minds of women" and the dream of the father as "an enormous turtle" suggest the "momentary hope that the side of feminine consciousness . . . call[ed] the Ecstatic Mother will return. . . . The turtle is one of the Mother's favorite creatures; the father's metamorphosis thus spells out the return of matriarchy" even though "the text never quite connects the case of Bly's father . . . to the thesis that the Mother consciousness . . . is destroying masculinity."[17] Still, the fact that the father as turtle is "enormous," that his eyes are "open" and that he is "lying on the basement floor" suggests that the grounding for the power and the basis of the final vision will be with the father.[18] In "Four Ways of Knowledge" (51–54, revised in *Selected* 164–167) Bly talks of the "Wild Man" who "turns men to turtles" (53).

As Bly says regarding meditation, "The West misunderstands 'meditation' or sitting because it assumes that the purpose of meditation is to achieve unity. On the contrary, the major value of sitting . . . is to let the sitter experience the real chaos of the brain."[19]

The "meditation" of "A Meditation on Philosophy" serves as a kind of introduction to the next poem, "My Father's Wedding" (48–50, revised in *Selected* 153–155), a poem important to the theme of the book. The most explicit poem, before *Black Coat,* to suggest the quest that is the theme of this book is entitled, appropriately enough, "Finding the Father" (see Chapter Three). In "Finding the Father" the poet begins the search for the father, who "lonely in his whole body" is "waiting for you" (*This Body* 19).

> Today, lonely for my father, I saw
> a log, or branch,
> long, bent, ragged, bark gone.
> I felt lonely for my father when I saw it.

The second through fifth stanzas are an enigmatic and awkward "meditation" on the "invisible limp" which "some men live with." This invisible flaw will become visible no matter how hidden: "If a man, cautious, / hides his limp, / Somebody has to limp it! Things / do it; the surroundings limp." Bly says of himself, "I learned to walk swiftly, easily, / no trace of a limp." And, punning on his "leaping" poetry, "I even leaped a little." But then asks, "Guess where my defect is?" Bly's legacy from his father, from the generations of fathers, the "limp" passed down to him, is what he will shortly characterize as "noble loneliness."

After this rather awkward "meditation," the poet moves to a powerful account of his father's wedding:

> On my father's wedding day,
> no one was there
> to hold him. Noble loneliness
> held him. Since he never asked for pity
> his friends thought he
> was whole. Walking alone he could carry it.
>
> He came in limping. It was a simple
> wedding, three
> or four people. The man in black,
> lifting the book, called for order.
> And the invisible bride
> stepped forward, before his own bride.
>
> He married the invisible bride, not his own.
> In her left

breast she carried the three drops
that wound and kill. He already had
his bark-like skin then,
made rough especially to repel the sympathy

he longed for, didn't need, and wouldn't accept.
So the Bible's
words are read. The man in black
speaks the sentence. When the service
is over, I hold him
in my arms for the first time and the last.

After that he was alone
and I was alone.
Few friends came; he invited few.
His two-story house he turned
into a forest,
where both he and I are the hunters.

(*Selected* 154–155)

This poem, dated 1924, is immediately interesting because its speaker will not be born until 1926. Clearly, the account, which seems to be a literal account of the wedding, has thrown over it the trappings of myth and depth psychology. The "invisible bride" who carries the "three drops / that wound and kill" in her breast, the bride the father marries instead of his own literal bride, is a spectral figure drawn in dream and related to myth. It is fairly clear that Bly has drawn heavily on the fairy tale "Faithful John" for some of the details in this poem.[20] Like the poem, "Faithful John" tells the story of a literal and surrogate father-son relationship, of a marriage in which the bride carries three drops of blood in her breast, and of Faithful John who is turned to stone (as opposed to the "bark-like skin" of the father in the poem—although the log at the beginning of the poem, "ragged, bark gone," is similar to stone in appearance).

Marie-Louise von Franz says that the "Faithful John" fairy tale "mirrors masculine psychology." In an extended commentary on the tale she discusses the "archetypal" theme of this story in which a bride, "contaminated with unconscious impulses which want to become conscious and, because they are not, . . . get at the man's emotional side and influence his moods . . . so [that] he has to cross the bridge of his emotions to find out what the demonic powers are," discovers that "generally they are mainly religious ideas."[21]

Faithful John "is the representative of the transcendent function" and "like Khidr," the "first angel of the throne of Allah" in the 18th Sura of the Koran, "is a representative of the divine principle of the unconscious."[22] In both the theological and the psychological senses of the term, "religious ideas" are predominant at the end of Bly's poem and they are made even more conspicuous in the revision in *Selected.* The "Bible's / words are read" ("So / the words are read" in the *Black Coat* version) and "The man in black / speaks the sentence." On the one hand, this is simply a reference to the "sentence" of a wedding ceremony ("I now pronounce you . . ."); on the other hand, it suggests some sort of punishment, a "sentence" to a life of loneliness, without friendship, which is passed down from generation to generation while the world becomes a kind of forest where men seek for something they never find.

The final three poems in *Black Coat* form a thematic triptych. "Fifty Males Sitting Together" (55–57, revised in *Selected* 145–146)[23] seems to begin where "My Father's Wedding" left off and it anticipates the final poem in the book, "Kneeling Down to Look into a Culvert." In "Fifty Males Sitting Together," "After a long walk in the woods" the poet "turn[s] home, drawn to water." Then the poet finds a "coffinlike shadow," "a massive / masculine shadow," of "fifty males sitting together / . . . lifting something indistinct / up into the resonating night," softening "half" the small lake. The sunlight on "the water still free of shadow, / . . . glows with the high / pink of wounds" (*Selected* 145). Clearly, there is something of rites of initiation here. As Bly says elsewhere, "We can . . . imagine initiation as that moment when the older males together welcome the younger male into the male world."[24]

Then the scene rather abruptly shifts to "the son who lives / protected by the mother," who:

> loses courage,
> goes outdoors to feed with wild
> things, lives among dens
> and huts, eats distance and silence;
> he grows long wings, enters the spiral, ascends.
>
> How far he is from working men when he is done!
> From all men! The males singing
> chant far out
> on the water grounded in downward shadow.
> He cannot go there because
> he has not grieved
> as humans grieve. If someone's
> head was cut
> off, whose was it?
> The father's? Or the mother's Or his?
> The dark comes down slowly, the way
> snow falls, or herds pass a cave mouth.
> I look up at the other shore; it is night.
>
> (*Selected* 146)

This "dark night" here at the end of the poem is one of the main threads which run throughout all of Bly's work. In the third of the "Six Winter Privacy

Poems" "the darkness appears as flakes of light" (*Sleepers* 3); but the image goes back to Bly's beginnings in *Silence* where he speaks of "a darkness [that] was always there, which we never noticed" (*Silence* 60). And the "thin man with no coat" riding "the horse of darkness . . . fast to the east" (*Silence* 52) is the first prefiguration of the man who dons a black coat and dies fighting at the end of this book.

"Crazy Carlson's Meadow" (58–60, revised in *Selected* 160–161) is one of the most complex poems Bly has written. It brings together a cluster of images which, in the aggregate, define much of what he is about in *Black Coat* and in his work as a whole. The poem begins simply enough, with the story of "Crazy Carlson," who "cleared his meadow alone / . . . back to the dark firs" which "make sober / . . . deathlike" caves, "inviting as the dark- / lidded eyes of . . . women . . . who live in bark huts (*Selected* 160). But in these caves:

> There is no room
> for the dark-lidded boys who longed to be Hercules.
> There is no room even for Christ.
> He broke off
> his journey toward the Father,
> and leaned back into the Mother's fearful tree.
>
> (*Selected* 160)

Even Christ's first miracle, the turning of the water into wine at the wedding in Cana (see John 2:1–11), is "refused" ("the wine of Cana turned back to vinegar") and Christ's life "broken / on the poplar tree," like a leaf fallen, has no efficacious effect or abiding significance: "your inner horse . . . galloped away / into the wind without / you, and disappeared / into the blue sky. Your horse never reached your father's house" (59) and thus "all consequences" are "finished."

> Now each young man wanders in the sky alone,
> ignoring the absent
> moon, not knowning
> where ground is, longing once more for the learning
> of the fierce male who hung for nine days only
> on the windy tree.
> Beneath his feet
> there is darkness; inside the folds of darkness words
>   hidden.

The "fierce male" referred to here is Odin, the "All-father," the Norse god who agreed to self-sacrifice on the World Tree, Yggdrasill, in order to acquire the wisdom of the runes. In the *Hávamál* (the Words of the High One) of the *Elder Edda,* a 13th century collection of Norse and Icelandic poems, Odin records his own crucifixion: "I know that I hung / on the windswept tree/

for nine full nights / . . . myself to myself / . . . I grasped the "runes' / . . . Then I began to be fruitful / and to be fertile, / to grow and to prosper; / one word sought / another word from me / one deed sought / another deed from me."[25] Odin's success in achieving the runes, the magical written words that make him an even more powerful god and a poet (Odin is also the god of poetry) able to perform magic with words heretofore hidden in darkness would obviously appeal to a poet who has categorized himself as a boy-god and who wishes, with "fierceness," like this "fierce male" god Odin, to let "words rise."[26]

The final poem of *Black Coat*, "Kneeling Down to Look into a Culvert" (61–62, retitled "Kneeling Down to Peer into a Culvert" in *Selected* 168) is a fitting conclusion to the many themes of the book, what one critic has called "a successful poem in the rather rare genre of the archetypal memory, original because it shows the perspective of the parent who will be replaced."[27] It is the "simple," straightforward poem of a family man, a father, thinking through his life, past, present and future. It begins:

> I kneel down to peer into a culvert.
> The other end seems far away.
> One cone of light floats in the shadowed water.
> This is how our children will look when we are dead.

Here, mentioned again, are a series of things that run throughout the book, throughout the whole of Bly's work: the "kneeling," the "light" floating, the "shadowed water," the "children," the "blue sky" of the next stanza. Indeed, the opening line of the second stanza, "I kneel near floating shadowy water," containing four of his most definitive value words, may be the most succinct, quintessential line in all of Bly.

The poet, having "fathered so many children," wonders, "Are they all born?" One cannot help but read this metaphorically as well as literally, the poet wondering about his poetic "progeny," as he "returns" to the "lake newly made," symbol of the unconscious, and becomes a "water-serpent, throwing water drops / off my head, . . . gray loops trail[ing] behind me" (like "long tails of dragon smoke"?), until "one morning," like the Odin all-father figure the poet has become, when "a feathery head pokes from the water / I fight—it's time—it's right—and am torn to pieces fighting" (62).

As Boehme said, "all beings move onward until the end finds the beginning" and "the beginning . . . swallows the end" and thus "beginning and end turn back into unity."[28]

Thus, here at the end of *Black Coat,* in a ritual that symbolizes a sacrificial death as prelude to a new birth, the poet, like the man in the black coat, fulfills all the implications of the final word of the book's title, and *turns.*

＊   ＊   ＊

Loving a Woman in Two Worlds[29] is Bly's most recent book of poetry, the prelude to his *Selected Poems. Loving* is divided into three sections, the first and last containing twelve poems each, the central section twenty-six. Almost half of the poems are eight lines long or less, and eleven of them are only four lines each. Most of the poems are love poems in one way or another. Several of them are explicit sexual poems and many of the others are symbolically sexual. For Bly this is a book of joy, celebrating the love between man and a woman (three of the poems begin, "A man and a woman . . .") and a man and his family and the family of man. Thus, thematically, the poems court sentimentality, and some succumb to it.

In his introduction to the section of poems from *Loving* in *Selected,* Bly tries to define the fine line that keeps love poems from going "out of tune." "If the poem," he says, "veers too far toward actual events, the eternal feeling is lost in the static of our inadequacies; if we confine the poem only to what we feel, the other person disappears" (*Selected* 172). These are thematic considerations. It is the poetic considerations not mentioned by Bly which often cause the poems in *Loving* to go "out of tune."

Perhaps the most obvious theme poem in the book is "A Third Body" (19, retitled "A Man and a Woman Sit Near Each Other" in *Selected* 181) which appears near the end of the first section.

> A man and a woman sit near each other, and
>   they do not long
> at this moment to be older, or younger, nor born
> in any other nation, or time, or place.
> They are content to be where they are, talking or
>   not-talking.
> Their breaths together feed someone whom we
>   do not know.
> The man sees the way his fingers move;
> he sees her hands close around a book she hands
>   to him.
> They obey a third body that they share in
>   common.
> They have made a promise to love that body.
> Age may come, parting may come, death will
>   come.
> A man and a woman sit near each other;
> as they breathe they feed someone we do not
>   know,
> someone we know of, whom we have never
>   seen.

The "third body" that the man and woman "share in common" and "have made a promise to love," the unseen presence that unites them and unites them with all other men and women, is what Bly is trying to describe in many of the poems in *Loving*. Sometimes it is sex and sometimes it is spirit; usually it is the two mixed together, but always the spiritual predominates. In many ways this "third body" is similar to the "body not yet born" in *Light*. The metaphor runs throughout *Loving* and concludes in the final poem in the book, "In the Month of May" (77–78, *Selected* 192), in the lines:

> I love you with what in me is unfinished.
>
> I love you with what in me is still
> changing, . . .
> . . . what has not found its body (77).

Loving begins with "Fifty Males Sitting Together" (3–5), the revision of a poem brought over from *Black Coat* (55–57). This poem, then, ties *Black Coat* and *Loving* together and illustrates Bly's obsession with continuity and his penchant for revision. Still, if *Loving* begins with a man being initiated both to his own manhood and maleness, it immediately puts him to the test of that initiation in the world of men and, especially, in the world of women.

In rough sequence, the poems in *Loving* follow the course of a relationship. In "The Indigo Bunting" (6–7, *Selected* 175–176), the second poem in the book, the relationship is still distant, casual ("I do not know what will happen. / I have no claim on you" 6) although there is an emotional reaching out on the poet's part:

> I love you where you go
> through the night, not swerving,
> clear as the indigo
> bunting in her flight,
> passing over two
> thousand miles of ocean.

This meeting, and the relationship that results, will be made explicit in the little poem, "The Whole Moisty Night" where the image of the lit lamp from "The Indigo Bunting" is picked up again and the word "wife" implies the consummation of the relationship: "The body meets its wife far out at sea. / Its lamp remains lit the whole moisty night" (10).[30]

The second section of the book begins with "The Roots" (25), a Ramage, a form Bly invented. A Ramage is a poem of eighty-five syllables, distributed among eight lines, in which several sounds are repeated often enough to create an overall tonal structure. "The Roots," a poem about the knowledge of grief and limits, is almost an epistemology of loss. In many ways "The Roots" is a companion poem to "The Grief of Men" in *Black Coat*. Here "the grief of men" is "the love of woman" and this grief, although it "finds roots" in the earth, is limitless. "There are no limits of grief. The loving man / simmers his porcupine stew. Among the tim- / ber growing on earth grief finds roots" (25).[31] What frightens us, as the next poem, "What Frightenes Us" (26), says, is that once "we" descend into "some inner, or innermost cave" there is "no beginning or end"—the "grief" of the human condition stretches out limitlessly in all directions.

The basic thematic focus of *Loving* take Bly in several directions. It leads him to weak or overtly sentimental poems ("The Conditions" 54, and "Seeing You Carry Plants In" 27); to explicit sexual poems ("Ferns" 38, "The Horse of Desire" 65–66, *Selected* 189–190); to moving love poems ("Come with Me" 29 and "In the Month of May" 77–78, *Selected* 192); to poems with the trappings of myth ("Night Frogs" 32–33, "Conversation" 63 and "The Good Silence" 73–74, *Selected* 185–186); and to poems which end in false epiphanies ("At Midocean" 30, *Selected* 179, and "The Artist at Fifty" 52).

Structurally, the book contains examples of most of the forms Bly has worked in throughout his career. There are, as already noted, numerous short, often pithy, poems as well as poems written in "the long Whitman line" ("'Out of the Rolling Ocean, the Crowd . . .'" 8–9, *Selected* 178 and "Returning Poem" 42–43); poems in short staccato lines ("Two People at Dawn" 14–15, "Love Poem in Twos and Threes" 41 and "A Man and a Woman and a Blackbird" 55–57); poems with literary or artistic associations ("A Man and a Woman and a Blackbird" and "Listening to the Köln Concert" 67–68, *Selected* 191); and poems in the prototypical tripartite manner of many of Bly's earliest poems ("In Rainy September" 17–18, *Selected* 174 and "Alone a Few Hours" 46–47); even poems that may not quite be poems ("What We Provide" 50).[32]

In short, Bly seems to be trying for a tour de force here in *Loving,* pulling out all the thematic and structural stops. Even if it is understandable that Bly might well have wanted to try for such a tour de force as prelude to his *Selected Poems,* this mechanical decision may be the main reason this book is not more successful.

Nevertheless, several poems in *Loving* need to be looked at specifically. A particularly candid poem is "Night Frogs" (32–33) where, after stating, "How much I am drawn toward my parents! I walk back / and forth, looking toward the old landing," he says:

> What is it in my father I keep not noticing?
> I cannot remember years of my childhood.
> Some parts of me I cannot find now.
>
> I intended that; I threw some parts of me away
> at ten; others at twenty; a lot at twenty-eight.
> I wanted to thin myself out as a wire is thinned.
> Is there enough left of me now to be honest?

Even though the poem begins in a myth-like setting, "I wake and find myself in the woods, far from the castle," Bly seems to be speaking nakedly both about his life and his work in the lines quoted above.

"Alone a Few Hours" (46–47) is a lovely lyric reminiscent of much of Bly's early work but incorporating his more recent interest in myth, fairy stories and Chinese folklore. As Bly describes it, the poem has had a long history. He says, "This one began about ten years ago as a prose poem and I liked it as a prose poem and finally I worked and worked and worked and . . . put it into stanzas like this in which you count the beats, so many beats a line and every stanza has to have the same number. . . . It's a form of craftsmanship; it's more like making a chest of drawers."[33] Although the stanzas differ in the number of "beats" (either literal stresses or syllables) both in the published version and in the version on the tape (which is quite different) Bly's point is well-taken and his comments reveal several important concerns of his recent career: his constant, continuing obsession with revision (which, of course, has been with him since the beginning) and his increased attention to "craft," a term which, early on, he refused to use or even to talk about.

"Alone a Few Hours" is filled with Bly's most typical catchwords ("today," "alone," "darkened," "naked," "father," "light," "snow," "barn," "rain," "window," "shadows," "lake," "writing table," "love," "field mouse," "stone," "misty") but in this poem he brings them together gently, mellif-lously, to create the quintessential Bly lyric.

> Today I was alone a few hours, and slowly
> windows darkened, leaving me alone, naked,
> with no father or uncle,
> born in no country . . . I was a streak of light
> through the sky,
> a trail in the snow behind the field mouse,
> a thing that has
> simple desires, and one
> or two needs, like a barn darkened by rain.
>
> Something enters from the open window.
> I sense it, and turn slightly
> to the left. Then I notice
> shadows are dear to me, shadows in the weeds
> near the lake,
> and under the writing table where I sit
> writing this.
> "The hermit is not here;
> he is up on the mountain picking ferns."
>
> That's what the hermit's boy told the visitor
> looking for him. Then I realize that I do love,
> at last, that the simple
> joy of the field mouse has come to me.
> I am no longer

> a stone pile visited from below
> by the old ones.
> "It's misty up there . . .
> I don't know where he is . . . I don't think you
>   can find him."

"In the Month of May" (77–78, *Selected* 192), the final poem in *Loving,* is a fitting conclusion to the book. It is a love poem in which the speaker begins by seeing and saying, "how well all things / lean on each other," how well the earth, the seasons, the insects, the fish, the animals all work together. This causes him to "understand / I love you with what in me is unfinished // . . . with what in me is still / changing . . . / what has not found its body." This is "the miraculous" which is "caught on this earth," even though it continues to contain trappings of the otherworld, and even though it is "not yet born." Here Bly explicitly refers to his early poem, "Looking into a Face" (*Light* 53), and evokes the notion so important in all of his work—that of rising to a "body not yet born," which exists "like a light around the body" giving off an aura that makes man more than what he seems to be. The reference to Gabriel (the "man of God" in Hebrew), the archangel who helps Daniel to understand his vision and who tells him that "at the time of the end" there "*shall be* the vision" (Daniel 8:15–17), who foretells the birth of John the Baptist (Luke 1:11–20) and announces the conception of Jesus to Mary (Luke1:26–38), seems to suggest the possibility of an announcement or a vision here at the end of this book. The vision, if it is one, is secular, earthbound, earthy and specific, a reference to the "holy bodies" of "lovers" who are seeking "places / . . . to spend the night."

Thus, *Loving,* and Bly's work to date, fittingly ends with a poem that celebrates that which "is still changing," that which is "unfinished."

Notes

1. Robert Bly, *The Man in the Black Coat Turns* (New York: Dial Press, 1981). Hereafter, references to this book will be included in the text.

2. For parallels between *Black Coat* and *Silence* see William V. Davis's, "'Still the Place Where Creation Does Some Work on Itself': Robert Bly's Most Recent Work," in Joyce Peseroff, ed. *Robert Bly: When Sleepers Awake* (Ann Arbor: University of Michigan Press, 1984) 238–241.

3. Bly, *Selected* 143–144. These seemingly rigid requirements are often difficult to distinguish in many of the poems.

4. Bly, *Selected* 144. In referring to these poems as "rocks" Bly surely must be thinking of Stevens's late dominant poem, *his* final turn toward home, "The Rock," "the habitation of the whole," "the starting point . . . and the end," "the gate / to the enclosure." (See *The Collected Poems of Wallace Stevens* [New York: Random House, 1954] 528.) And one cannot but remember, in this same context, the little poem, "Late Moon" in *This Tree* (57) whose "rocks . . . hum at early dawn." "Late Moon," with its "light over my father's farm" and the poet's "shadow" which "reach[es] for the latch" of his father's door, seems to anticipate, in several significant ways (as already suggested above) the poems in *Black Coat.*

5. Bly, *Book on the Human Shadow* 31–32.

6. Robert Bly, "Being a Lutheran Boy-God in Minnesota," in *Growing Up in Minnesota: Ten Writers Remember Their Childhoods,* ed. Chester Anderson (Minneapolis: University of Minnesota Press, 1976) 205, 217. This essay is a particularly important essay for much of Bly's recent work.

7. Bly, *Book on the Human Shadow* 33.

8. See *The New Republic* 31 Jan. 1981: 28.

9. In this final line Bly alludes to the story in Matthew 8:28–32 in which Jesus casts devils into a herd of swine who then run headlong into the sea as if the water were a door. Bly associates this Biblical story with the Persephone myth, also alluded to in "A Bouquet of Ten Roses" (24). In one account of this myth Persephone is accompanied into Hades by a herd of pigs. Bly refers to the "astonishing detail" of the pigs in the Persephone story and says, "There is a great power in that, and it is somehow related to the pigs Christ drove over the cliff." (See Bly, "Recognizing the Image as a Form of Intelligence," *Field:* 26.)

10. Keith Thompson, "What Men Really Want: Interview with Robert Bly," *New Age* 7 (May, 1982): 31, 33–36, 50–51. One new source for Bly's thinking, mentioned here, is James Hillman, the Jungian analyst whose work, especially in books like *The Myth of Analysis: Three Essays in Archetypal Psychology* (1972), *Re-Visioning Psychology* (1975), and *The Dream and the Underworld* (1979), has had a definitive influence on Bly's recent thinking.

11. Keith Thompson, "Robert Bly on Fathers and Sons," *Esquire* 101 (Apr. 1984): 238.

12. Robert Bly, "Men's initiation rites," *Utne Reader* (Apr./May, 1986): 45, 48–49.

13. Bly visited Williams in 1959. In "Sea Water Pouring Back over Stones" in *Morning Glory,* in a passage using a similar metaphor to the one he uses here, Bly refers to "the gentleness of William Carlos Williams after his strokes" (50). In 1964 Bly met Neruda in Paris and, of course, some of his most important translations are of Neruda.

14. The first words of this stanza are misprinted "Blessing them" in the *Black Coat* text. The "man . . . writing stanzas on the lamb" must be Blake and the "woman, who picks the brown seeds of solitude in afternoon light" is according to Bly, a reference to Emily Dickinson (see Nelson, *Robert Bly: An Introduction* 229), to whom he has already referred in an earlier poem in this book (see "Visiting Emily Dickinson's Grave with Robert Francis" 25–26), while the "dictionary maker" may well be a reference to J. A. H. Murray, editor of the Oxford English Dictionary, conspicuous for his long beard among the "bearded words" of the Oxford English Dictionary.

15. Marjorie Perloff, "Soft Touch," *Parnassus,* 10:1 (Spring/Summer, 1982): 223.

16. Just as Yeats's "Lapis Lazuli" was "inspired" by a carved stone of the Chinese sculptor sent to Yeats as a present, so Bly's poem seems to have been similarly "inspired" by the painting of *The Six Philosophers* from the "Tang" (T'ang) dynasty. Yeats spoke of his poem as an "heroic cry in the midst of despair," (see *Letters on Poetry from W. B. Yeats to Dorothy Wellesley* [New York: Oxford University Press, 1940] 8) a sentiment Bly might well share about his poem.

17. Perloff, "Soft Touch" 224.

18. The reference to the turtle, the creature "most often and most explicitly connected with luminous revelation," (see Libby, "Dreaming of Animals," *Plainsong:* 51) in Bly's poems, harkens back to "The Turtle" in *Sleepers* (5):

> How shiny the turtle is, coming out
> of the water, climbing the rock, as if
> the body inside shone through!
> As if swift turtle wings swept out of darkness,
> crossed some barriers,
> and found new eyes.

19. Bly, *Leaping Poetry* 63.

20. See *The Complete Grimm's Fairy Tales* (New York: Pantheon Books, 1944) 43–51.

21. Marie-Louise von Franz, *The Feminine in Fairy Tales* (New York: Spring Publications, 1976) 3.

22. Marie-Louise von Franz, *Shadow and Evil in Fairy Tales* (Irving, Texas: Spring Publications, 1980) 69, 72–73. Bly has spoken of the "you" in poetry as: "a primitive initiatory force, female in tone," and as "the inner guide, a Khadir or 'Faithful John,'" as well as "the collective 'God'" (see Robert Bly, *Selected Poems of Rainer Maria Rilke* [New York: Harper & Row, 1981] 8).

23. The *Selected* version of "Fifty Males Sitting Together" differs from the version in *Loving a Woman in Two Worlds*. It introduces the poems in that book.

24. Bly, "What Men Really Want" 36.

25. E. O. G. Turville-Petre, *Myth and Religion of the North: The Religion of Ancient Scandinavia* (London: Weidenfeld and Nicolson, 1964) 42. Campbell associates this "Cosmic Tree" from "immemorial antiquity" (Yggdrasill) with Buddha's Bo Tree (the Tree of Enlightenment) and Christ's "Holy Rood (the Tree of Redemption)" (see Campbell, *Hero With a Thousand Faces* 235, n. 31; 33, n. 37; *passim*).

26. It is worth noting here that Bly published his magazine *The Fifties, The Sixties* and *The Seventies* from "Odin House" and that he used as colophon for the magazine an image of Odin in armour, on horseback, his two ravens, which symbolize thought and memory, accompanying him.

27. Donald Wesling, "The Wisdom Writer," *The Nation* 31 Oct. 1981: 447.

28. See Boehme, *Psychologia Vera, Sämmtliche Werke,* vol. 6, ed. K. W. Schiebler (Leipzig: J. A. Barth, 1846) 18–19.

29. Robert Bly, *Loving a Woman in Two Worlds* (New York: Dial Press, 1985). Hereafter, references to this book will be included in the text.

30. "The Whole Moisty Night" is the title poem of a pamphlet of seven love poems Bly published in 1983. In a tape containing eighteen poems from *Loving,* recorded February 25, 1984, entitled "Loving a Woman in Two Worlds," Bly says about "The Whole Moisty Night," "This is one of the first [four line] ones that I did. It came out completely whole. And it gave me hope and I went and did the rest of them."

31. "Porcupine stew" picks up the reference to a porcupine in "The Grief of Men." Among Bly's many animals, the porcupine is an obvious masculine symbol. But Bly may also be thinking here of Galway Kinnell's poem "The Porcupine" where we read, "In character / he resembles us in seven ways" (see Galway Kinnell, *Body Rags* [Boston: Houghton Mifflin, 1967] 56).

32. On the "Loving" tape Bly says about "What We Provide," "Is it quite a poem? I'm not sure."

33. Bly, "Loving" tape.

Captain Bly

Ted Solotaroff

Recently in these pages Gore Vidal remarked that instead of politics Americans have elections. One sees what he means, but it's not quite on the money, because elections matter mostly to the politicians, their PAC groups and their dwindling party loyalists. For the rest of America, elections are a peculiar form of TV entertainment in which the commercial has become the program. The affiliations and ideologies people care about are elsewhere, in what Theodore Roszak fifteen years ago termed "situational groups," the politics of the personal. "In less than a generation's time," he wrote, "every conceivable form of situational belonging has been brought out of the closet and has forced its grievances and its right to exist upon the public consciousness." He was writing about the mitosis of the counterculture, but his observation was no less prescient about its opposition—the pro-lifers, creationists, apocalyptics, neo-conservatives, school vigilantes, et al. There are also the expressive therapeutic groups: The most influential ideology of change in America today is probably that of A.A., not only because it works so dramatically but because it provides a model of psychological and spiritual community, which is what the ethnic, racial, gender, sexual and other situational groups are partly about. The most interesting recent example is the men's movement, a complex phenomenon that appears to derive from A.A., feminism, New Age religion and therapy, environmentalism and the culture and charisma of Robert Bly.

That a poet is the spokesman of a broadly based movement as well as at the top of the charts has, of course, struck many readers but not, I imagine, many poets. They are used to Bly the group leader, publicist, ideologist, translator, mythologist, guru and scold, he having played these roles in the American poetry of the second half of the century, much as Ezra Pound did in that of the first half. Poets are also used to Bly the showman, his hit performance on Bill Moyers's program, which sent the men's movement into media orbit, having been preceded by hundreds of his sold-out poetry readings and seminar star turns.

Like most literary careers that last, Bly's has been formed from the ongoing play of oppositions, but his have been particularly intense: Lutheran

Reprinted from *The Nation* 253, no. 7 (9 September 1991): 270–74. Reprinted by permission of *The Nation* and the author.

and pagan, rural and international, reclusive and engaged, austere and grandiose. These contending traits and inclinations have generated Bly's high
energy and also created a certain rhythm to his career that makes his present
celebrity and function almost predictable. Also they are compacted into a
strongly lived life that personalizes the mythopoetic structure and far-out
counsel of *Iron John* (Addison-Wesley) and gives the book, for all of its
discursiveness and highhandedness, an overall staying power and a kind of
charmed ability to hit paydirt about every third page.

Iron John is less about male identity than it is about what Jungians, following
John Keats, call "soul-making." Much of Bly's soul has been forged and refined
by his relationship with the Wild Man, his favorite name for the tutelary figure
in the fairy tale that he unpacks and unpacks, embroiders and embroiders to
tell the reader how boys psychically become men and men remain psychically
boys.

    Bly grew up, as he says, a "Lutheran Boy-god" in Minnesota, being his
mother's favorite, and in good Freudian fashion, drawing from that a heightened sense of entitlement as well as a tendency to see the world through her
eyes and feel it with her heart, which means he didn't see or feel very much on
his own. In Bly's terms his soul or psyche had a lot of conducting "copper" in
it, which would come in handy as an editor, critic and translator, and not much
of the "iron" of autonomy that he would later have to extract on his own from
the mines of the archetypal warrior king in himself. In short, he grew up "soft,"
like the males of today to whom *Iron John* is mainly addressed. Bly's brother
appears to have been his father's son, the one who took up the family
occupation of farming, the hairy Esau of his tent-dwelling Jacob. His father
was strong, kindly, intensely moral, and alcoholic, creating a particularly
poignant remoteness that broods over *Iron John*, as it does in some of Bly's later
poetry: "the man in the black coat" who appears only to turn away again and
whose haunting absence, along with his mother's haunting presence, has
created Bly's lifelong project and process of fathering one's soul, which is his
particular contribution to the men's movement.

    For the rest, Bly was a well-raised product of Madison, Minnesota, a small
plains community with a Norwegian cultural accent. He was properly clean
and godly, cheerful and repressed, "asleep in the Law," as he puts it in his major
autobiographical poem, "Sleepers Joining Hands." A Lutheran Boy-god who
remains in this state is likely to become a minister, his grandiosity put into the
service of interpreting doctrines and counseling the flock. Bly has, of course,
taken the opposite road, "from the Law to the Legends," as he puts it in *Iron
John*, but the deal he apparently made with his psyche is that the nascent
preacher has gone with him and adapted to his various stages and purposes.

    Bly doesn't talk about his Harvard experience in *Iron John*—he seldom
has in a career otherwise rich in self-revelation—but it was a determinate stage
in which this wounded Boy-god and naïve "ascender" was both endowed and

banished, a literary version of the prince of his fairy tale. Here he is as an editor of the *Harvard Advocate,* reviewing a collection of British poetry edited by Kenneth Rexroth. One sentence tells the tale:

> Perhaps it is unfortunate that Rexroth should have been let loose on the Romantics; there is, I think, a difference between the desire to express personal emotion by increased direct reference to the world of nature, and the desire to overthrow all external discipline of morals of government.

This is, of course, the T.S. Eliot act that many young writers in the postwar era used to put themselves on the cutting edge of modernism. In Bly's case, it suggests that he was turning over in his sleep from the Lutheran law to the Anglican one. The literary air at the time was thick with conservative authority and decorum. It has an archbishop, Eliot; a set of bishops, the New Critics; a martyr, Pound; and lots of acolytes, who were becoming half paralyzed by the dogma that poetry was a hieratic vocation, that the imagination lived, worked and had its being with The Tradition. As Eliot had laid it down, it was mostly Dante and the metaphysical poets, the high Anglicans like himself. The dogma came equipped with Eliot's emphasis on the impersonal, objective image and with a set of literary heresies and fallacies that were meant to nip any revival of Romanticism in the bud.

To subscribe to this ethos typically led a young writer to graduate school or to the pits. Bly chose the latter, having become "overcommitted to what he was not," as Erik Erikson would say, and badly needing to find his way to his own "inner tradition." He ended up in New York, where he spent the next three years being mostly blocked, depressed and poor: the state of "ashes," descent, and grief" that forms a major early stage in his mythic prince's initiation. According to Bly, life reserves this "katabasis" particularly for the grandiose ascender, putting him in touch with the dark, wounded side he had tried to ignore and evade and ministering to the naïveté, passivity and numbness that comes with the apron strings of his entitlement. The road, in short, that leads "from the mother's house to the father's house."

The one poem that Bly published from this period, "Where We Must Look for Help," is based on three types of birds that were sent forth from Noah's ark into the flooded world: the glamorous peaceful dove and the graceful swallows find no land, only the crow does:

> The crow, the crow, the spider-colored
> crow,
> The crow shall find new mud to walk
> upon.

As Bly was to tell Deborah Baker, who has written an excellent biographical essay about him, "It was the first time . . . I ran into the idea of the dark side of the personality being the fruitful one." After a year at the Iowa Writers' Workshop, Bly went to live on a farm his father had bought for him, and a year later, while visiting relatives in Norway, he discovered his new mud lying adjacent to his inner tradition.

In primitive societies, as Bly tells us in *Iron John*, the male initiation is viewed as a second birth, with the elders acting as a "male mother." Bly's were first Georg Trakl, a German, and Gunnar Ekelöf, a Swede. From them he began to grasp the subjective, intuitive, "wild" side of modernism as opposed to the objective, rationalist, "domesticated" one. In their work as in that of the French and Hispanic surrealists—Char, Michaux, Jiménez, Vallejo and Lorca, among others—Bly sensed the missing water, the unconscious, for lack of which he believed Anglo-American poetry was suffering vastation. Increasingly dry, ironical, exhausted, remote, it was itself The Wasteland, while the European poets were still fecund, passionate and present. Returning to the family farm, Bly started a magazine, *The Fifties*, to say so as aggressively as possible and to provide translations of the European and Latin American surrealists in three or four languages, as well as to give welcome to his contemporaries who showed signs of new life and put down those who were dead on their feet. Flying a woodcut of Woden as his logo, Bly almost single-handedly led the charge against the reign of the "Old Fathers" in the middle, joined by the New York School on his right and the West Coast Beats on his left. Neither wing was anywhere near as relentless, reductive and brutal as Bly. He was out to deauthorize as well as replace the Eliot-Pound-Tate tradition, stamping on it well into the next generation—Lowell, Berryman, Delmore Schwartz, Jarrell, Karl Shapiro, whomever. In *Iron John* he chides himself for contributing to the decline of "Zeus energy," attributing it to the demons in his father-wound: a false note from someone who has repeatedly insisted that literature advances by generational strife and deplored the absence of adversarial criticism among poets.

Be that as it may, in the late fifties Bly entered his warrior phase, developing the strategy and service to a cause that in *Iron John* distinguish the warrior from the soldier. Though his magazine was known mainly for its demolition jobs, it also blazed, paved and landscaped a new road. Bly wrote many essays that developed his concept of "leaping" and "wild poetry," both in concept and prosody. In "Looking for Dragon Smoke," Bly hooked together a countertradition to the Christian-rational-industrial one that provided a kind of culture of the Wild Man. It begins with *Gilgamesh,* in which the "psychic forces" of an early civilized society created the hairy, primitive Enkidu as the adversary and eventual companion of the golden Gilgamesh (the first harbinger of *Iron John*). After *Beowulf* (Bly's Nordic touchstone) the "dragon smoke" of inspired association with primal memories is not much in evidence until Blake arrives to give the lie to the Enlightenment, as do the associative freedom and "pagan and heretical elements" in his German contemporaries Novalis,

Goethe and Hölderlin. With Freud and Jung the unconscious is back in business again, and the romantic/symbolist/surrealist wing of modernism provides Bly with a whole range of leaping, dragon smoke poets from Scandinavia south to Spain and across to Latin America to translate, publish and emulate.

Compared with Trakl's images ("On Golgotha God's eyes opened") or Lorca's ("Black horses and dark people are riding over the deep roads of the guitar"), Bly's own early leaps as a poet did not take him very far inward. About a horse wandering in the moonlight, he wrote: "I feel a joy, as if I had thought/Of a pirate ship ploughing through dark flowers." The poems of his first collection, *Silence in the Snowy Fields,* are noticeably restrained, wishing to be admired for the integrity of their mood, mostly a meditative one: a young pastoral poet getting his act together rather than appearing with snakes in his hair or as a messenger from the deeps.

Then, in the mid-sixties, Bly got caught up in the antiwar movement. He became a leading mobilizer of the literary community and provided one of the great moments in the theater of demonstrations when he gave his National Book Award check for his second collection, *The Light Around the Body,* to a draft resister while on the stage at Lincoln Center. Auden said of Yeats, "Mad Ireland hurt you into poetry"; the Vietnam War hurt Bly into writing the kind of poetry he had been calling for and that in places matched Neruda's in its creeping balefulness. Evoking the fallout of evil that has settled in Minnesota, he ends:

> Therefore we will have to
> Go far away
> To atone
> For the suffering of the stringy-chested
> And the short rice-fed ones, quivering
> In the helicopter like wild animals,
> Shot in the chest, taken back to be
>   questioned.

In the course of writing these poems and of editing a collection of antiwar poetry, Bly developed his concept of the intuitive association to reconnect literature with politics, two realms that most criticism and most experience of their "bloody crossroads," in Lionel Trilling's phrase, counseled to keep apart. Bly's position was an early version of the statement, long before it became cant, that the personal was political. As he put it, "A modern man's spiritual life and his growth are increasingly sensitive to the tone and content of a regime." Since much of our foreign and domestic policy comes from more or less hidden impulses in the American psyche, and because that psyche is in the poet too, "the writing of political poetry is like the writing of personal poetry, a sudden drive by the poet inward."

Along with strengthening his own poetry, Bly's involvement turned him into a performer of it. His high-visibility poetry readings developed into a counter-cultural event, the Lutheran Boy-god and warrior now reappearing as the bard. I first caught his act in the early seventies, when he entered a symposium on literary editing dressed in a serape and tapping a Tibetan drum, as though he were a cross between Neruda and Chögyam Trungpa, the meditation guru Bly studied with. After his poetry reading, complete with primitive masks, the other Bly, the literary caretaker, appeared on the panel of editors—sharp, shrewd and no less dominating.

He supported himself by his public appearances; otherwise he remained on his farm, tending to his chores as an editor, publisher, critic and poet and using his solitude to nourish "the parts that grow when we are far from the centers of ambition." Through the writings of Jung, Joseph Campbell, James Hillman and other psychic/cultural explorers he developed his encyclopedic command of the great heuristic myths, legends and folklore that understand us, concentrating on those that involve the female side. He gave lectures on Freud and Jung, as well as on Grimms' Fairy Tales, in the church basement in Madison, his trial by fire in making the esoteric vivid and meaningful to the public. He turned from America's shadow to his own, producing eleven collections of poems, most of them inward, associative, naked—Bly fully joining the tradition he had been staking out. He put out only one issue of *The Seventies*, a noticeably temperate one. The warrior was giving way to the gardener and lover, two roles that Bly lived through and that noticeably "moistened" his poetry in the eighties. They also provided two more stages in the process of male initiation that he took into his work with the men's movement. So did certain personal experiences of shame, guilt and loss, along with the aging process through which the holds that a father and son put on each other can turn into a yearning embrace. So, too, did his awareness that the young men in the literary and New Age circles he visited and who visited him on his farm had been weakened by the feminism of the era, and that male consciousness was in short and despairing supply. It was time, as Bly would say, to do something for the hive again.

Iron John, then, grows not only out of Bly's experience during the past decade in the men's movement but out of the central meanings of his life. If he has bought into the confusion and anxiety of many younger men today, caught between the new sensitivity and the old machismo, he has done so with the capital he has earned from his own growth as a man, a poet, a thinker and a husbandman of the culture. The souled fierceness that he prescribes for staking out and protecting the borders of male identity has provided much of the motive energy for his career as a literary radical. By the same token, his devotion to asserting and cultivating the primalness and primacy of the imagination in a highly domesticated and institutionalized literary culture has led him to view the condition of men in similar terms and to apply the learning he has acquired in the archeology and anthropology of the imagination to remedy it. This authority is finally what makes *Iron John* a serious, ground-breaking book.

The startling public appeal of Bly's therapeutic sermon is not hard to fathom. Based on Jungian psychology, it takes a much more positive measure of human potential for change than does the Freudian model, whose Great Father and Great Mother are pretty strictly one's own and give not much quarter to altering their influence: a foot of freedom here, a pound less grief there. Bly's pagan goodspell is that the gods are still around and within each of us, able to be mobilized or deactivated, as the case may be. Like Rilke's torso of Apollo, they search us out where it aches and command us to treat it and thereby change our lives.

Also, *Iron John* has a lot of specific insight and lore to teach men and employs a very effective method. It takes an old story and gives it a new spin, thereby enlisting the child in us who is still most open to learning and the adult who is keen to escape from his own banality. Along with combining therapy for men, or at the very least clarity, with a course in the world mythology and ethnography of male initiation, *Iron John* is also a spiritual poetry reading in which the words of Blake and Kabir, Rumi and Yeats and many others join Bly's own poems as a kind of accompaniment to the text.

The prominence of poetry in the men's movement is perhaps its most surprising feature; none of the other situational groups seem to be particularly disposed to it, and most poets would tend to agree with Auden that poetry "makes nothing happen." Perhaps it's only an aspect of Bly's influence, but I see it as part of the same reviving interest in the imagination signified by the increasing popularity of poetry readings.

Some people say that the men's movement will have to move into national politics, as the women's movement has done, if it is to survive its trendiness and become socially significant. I'm not so sure. As the bonanza of the Reagan era recedes and the midlife crisis of its favored generation draws on, there are a lot of men in America who have mainly their imaginations to fall back upon. As a social analysis of male distress, *Iron John* is pretty thin stuff; but that's not why it is being read. It's not the *Growing Up Absurd* of the nineties but rather a deeply based counsel of self-empowerment and change. Like the men's movement itself, it offers the sixties generation another crack at the imagination of alternatives they grew up on, right where they most inwardly live and hurt and quest. This is the imagination that they turned in to become Baby Boomers; if it can be let loose in America by this broad, influential and growing situational group, there's no telling what can happen.

OVERVIEWS AND CONCLUSIONS

◆

Which Way to the Future?

Robert Rehder

There is no better witness to the state of contemporary poetry than John Ashbery, and the circumstances of his comments to *Le Monde* in June 1986 are as significant as his remarks themselves. The reporter encountered him in the Palais de Justice at Aix-en-Provence. The occasion was the Fête du livre 1986 on the theme of "Ecritures transatlantiques." James Baldwin was there, Grace Paley, Jayne Anne Philips, Kenneth Koch—and John Ashbery. The reporter noted that while the American authors spoke freely and at length about their work to the French participants, between themselves they exchanged only the minimum number of words. Asked about the state of American poetry, Ashbery replied "dans un français parfait" (in perfect French) that he did not read any contemporary American poets:

> Je lis les poètes anglais du dix-neuvième siècle, l'oeuvre de Maurice Scève: je suis en train de lire les romans de Marivaux. . . . Je crois qu'il y a aujourd'hui des milliers de poètes américains qui ne se lisent pas les uns les autres. (I read the English poets of the nineteenth century, the work of Maurice Scève: I am in the process of reading the novels of Marivaux. . . . I believe that today there are thousands of American poets who do not read each other.) (*Le Monde*, 6 June 1986, 26)

This is a classic self-defense. Ashbery, like any artist faced with someone who wants him to explain himself in terms other than his art, is acting to protect the secret self that is the source of his originality, as if any violation of this fundamental privacy might endanger his creative powers. By his comments he removes himself from the American scene, his native ground, and creates a space around himself, keeping everyone, everything, especially other people's poems, at a distance. His remarks immediately set him apart from his contemporaries. Not only does he not read any of them, he does not read any American authors, old or new. Whitman disappears along with Stevens, and so do *all* contemporary authors, American, British, or French. He reads the English poets of the nineteenth century. He does not specify which. This is an immense, uninscribed, inscrutable block of marble. Although Ashbery is being deliberately old-fashioned and conservative, as befits a truly radical and

This essay was written specifically for this volume and is published here for the first time.

experimental poet, this is nonetheless an important statement in that it demonstrates that Wordsworth's and Coleridge's and Browning's and Hardy's concerns are still with us and that our most radical innovations are grounded in their practice. (This is a point we will return to in talking about Bly.)

The French poets from Baudelaire to Valéry, Eliot declared in 1930, "are now as much in our bones as Shakespeare or Donne."[1] Ashbery who lived for ten years (1955–1965) in Paris, who as all his work shows is well-versed in this poetry, and who speaks "un français parfait," escapes like Houdini from the implications of Eliot's statement. He only admits to reading Maurice Scève (?–1564), an older contemporary of Montaigne, whom many French readers have never heard of (proof in itself of his knowledge of French literature) and Marivaux (1688–1763). Scève has a reputation for obscurity and Marivaux for preciosity and frivolity. Gray remarked that his definition of happiness was "to lie on a sofa and read endless novels by Marivaux and Crebillion." Ashbery could not have chosen two more recherché authors to surprise his French audience, and what the little old lady in Dubuque, Iowa, would have made of it (for whom Harold Ross is alleged to have said *The New Yorker* was intended), who can say? In the case of Marivaux, that it is *novels* makes it even more difficult to establish any relation to Ashbery's work. The combination of authors is an extremely eclectic one, and in this Ashbery conforms absolutely to the norm. If one word describes the present American tradition, it is *eclectic*.

"Thousands of American poets who do not read each other" and who in turn are read only by very small groups—this impression of a very large number of very small, diverse, and relatively isolated units can be confirmed by an afternoon's browsing in the Grolier Bookshop in Cambridge, Massachusetts, or Prairie Lights in Iowa City, Iowa (which must be two of the best poetry bookstores in the United States), or by talking to those who teach contemporary American poetry in American universities or to the poets themselves. There are hundreds of books and hundreds of little magazines, many of which have backlogs of accepted poems that will take them one, two, or more years to publish, and this is without taking any account of unpublished work. There is no one who keeps up, because there is too much to read, too much of it is uninteresting, and too many of the publications are too local and too ephemeral. In addition, there are very few theories as to what is happening and a general sense of lack of pattern and direction.

As the present is always unfinished, any theory of recent or contemporary events can only be extremely tentative, but my own view is that the second great period of American poetry, which can be dated roughly as from Pound's first book, *A Lume Spento* (1908), to his last canto, CXX (1969), is now over (the other great period is that of Whitman and Dickinson), and that so far it has proved impossible to come to terms with all that was discovered in that period. The absence of a sense of development is because this new consciousness is still being worked through and because this was an unusually rich period. This rhythm would appear to be a fundamental one and explains why episodes of high creativity (for persons and cultures) are usually relatively brief. Moreover American poetry, while it has its own dynamics, has never been a closed system and can only be understood within the larger context of European culture. Most of the allegedly new or radical innovations of the past thirty years or so are merely the repetition of things that have been done in the past, notably by the French poets from Mallarmé to Le Breton. The death dates show us the end of an era: Stevens (1955), Frost and Williams (1963), Eliot (1965), Pound (1972). The books that perhaps best indicate the new developments are Ginsberg's *Howl* (1956), Lowell's *Life Studies* (1959), O'Hara's *Lunch Poems* (1964) and Ashbery's *The Double Dream of Spring* (1969).

Where does Bly fit in? Born in 1926, he is of the same generation as Ginsberg (b. 1926), O'Hara (b. 1926), and Ashbery (b. 1927) and knew O'Hara and Ashbery when they were students together at Harvard. His eclecticism is of a different form than Ashbery's. From his interviews and journalism, he emerges as someone who enjoys nothing more than talking about himself. He not only reads all contemporary poets, but is their friend. He is at the center of things. The elaborate, self-important prefaces to the different sections of the *Selected Poems* (and the two "after thoughts") insist so much on his suffering and growth that it is as if he was aware that the poems themselves do not show very much development, as if the autobiography and his awareness of his techniques could somehow validate them. Bly sees himself as the summa of the whole history of English, and indeed, all poetry. He contains multitudes. He is ready to acknowledge the influence of anyone and everyone including himself: Shakespeare, Milton, Smart, Blake, Whitman, Baudelaire, Rilke, Ponge and Jiménez, "Waley's translations of Chinese poems, Frank O'Connor's translations of Celtic poems, and my own translations of Machado."[2] He hides among the multiplicity of his acknowledgements. The succession of names in the essays and interviews is unending, so that it is extremely difficult to trace his actual development, and, in addition, like Ashbery he likes directing attention away from his home ground. Who should the young American poet read? "Well, I think he might read the Spaniards and the South Americans [*sic*] poets. And, of course, the Chinese. . . . The ancient Chinese poetry still seems to me the greatest poetry ever written."[3]

This eclecticism is old-fashioned and European as well as American. Valéry writing in 1919 identifies this "libre coexistance dans tous les esprits cultivés des idées les plus dissemblables" (free coexistence in all cultivated minds of the most dissimilar ideas) as the characteristic of a *modern* epoch. Without any effort, he says, we find in the works of such a period:

> une influence des ballets russes,—un peu du style sombre de Pascal,—beaucoup d'impressions du type Goncourt,—quelque chose de Nietzsche,—quelque chose de Rimbaud,—certains effets dus à la frequentation des peintres, et parfois le ton des publications scientifiques,—le tout parfumé d'un je ne sais quoi de britannique difficile à doser! . . . (the influence of the Russian ballet,—a

little of Pascal's somber style,—many impressions of the Goncourt type,—
something of Nietzsche,—something of Rimbaud,—certain effects due to
frequenting painters, and often the tone of scientific publications—the whole
perfumed by a certain British something difficult to analyze! . . .)[4]

Diversity and heterogeneity of this kind first makes its appearance in *Leaves of
Grass* (1855). Whitman's forms can be understood as a response to this disorder
and freedom, as a way of both allowing and containing this free coexistence of
ideas.

The form of all, or virtually all, of Bly's poems is that of the moment of
experience. This is why they are lyrics and relatively short. They are for the
most part in the first person, usually singular, sometimes, occasionally, in the
third person singular. Experience, consequently, is seen from the inside such
that there is an explicit or implied world of consciousness and
unconsciousness—and the merging of these two. There is a double pressure in
Bly's work: to try to accommodate more of the unconscious and at the same
time to resist meeting the idea and its consequences head-on. Unusual metaphors enter his poems like dreams.

The poems are in one sense historical, passages from the middle of a
continuing story, but they are fragments of an autobiography that seeks to hide
its true nature and to make it impossible to reconstruct the life. Each moment
is clearly and definitely located in space and time. This is one function of the
small details with which the poems are filled. There is a sense of duration and
of the passage of time. The text holds and is a re-experiencing of the temporary.
The unity of the moment depends upon the emotion, although it is one of the
purposes of the poem to invent this unity which is also a reaffirmation of the
wholeness of the perceiver. When the emotion finishes, the poem concludes.
Even so the beginning and ending are to a certain extent arbitrary, and the text
is concerned with the delimitation of twilight zones: between the perceiver and
the object, between one moment and the next, between what is changing and
what is not.

These are poems in which the action is thinking. What happens is
metaphors. Objects are read as if they were language. There is invariably a
scene, a landscape, a connected set of things. The enumeration of the details of
the scene marks the nuances of the perceiver's changing feelings (including his
fantasies). The emotion is projected upon the landscape and analyzed, but, of
course, the landscape is chosen, created out of and in order to manage the
emotion. These poems are essentially descriptive and are pervaded by the sense
of many other similar moments. This form was the creation of Wordsworth
and Coleridge.[5] It is the form of the vast majority of poems written since, and
it appears that we can no more escape from it than we can escape from
ourselves. Bly's "Driving Toward the Lac Qui Parle River," perhaps his
best-known and most-discussed poem, is a perfect example of the form.

I am driving; it is dusk; Minnesota.
The stubble field catches the last growth of sun.
The soybeans are breathing on all sides.
Old men are sitting before their houses on car seats
In the small towns. I am happy,
The moon rising above the turkey sheds.

(Selected Poems, 45)

The title sustains the poem. The poet is in motion—as he so often is: "riding in a car, in Wisconsin / Or Illinois," "driving / Toward Chicago" ("Three Kinds of Pleasures"); "I start out for a walk . . ." ("After Long Busyness"); "I came in . . ." ("After Working"); and "Along the road to Bellingham" ("Early Spring Between Madison and Bellingham"). Like Donne on Good Friday, Wordsworth near Loch Katrine, and the sun in his own poem, he is headed westward, across west central Minnesota. He is changing and so is the landscape. He is in an intermediate, transitional state: between Willmar and Milan, in the twilight ("it is dusk"). As the title makes clear, the poem is about nearness. He comes closer and closer to the river, finally arriving in the dark at the end of the poem. The darkness ensures the obscurity of his final vision.

The title like the form is in the tradition of Wordsworth: "Lines Composed a Few Miles above Tintern Abbey, on Revisiting the Banks of the Wye during a Tour. July 13, 1798." With Wordsworth also, it is a question of nearness (the poem closes with his vivid awareness of his closeness to his sister) and movement toward. He, too, is in motion. His, too, is a summer poem, although if a field has been recently cut, Bly's is probably set toward the end of the summer. Bly's title like Wordsworth's locates his poem in time and space, and more details are furnished in each stanza. What the poem does not tell us is that Bly is on his native ground. He was born in Madison, Minnesota, southwest of Milan, across the river. Thus, this landscape is charged with a personal significance that is hidden in the poem. The presence of unrevealed private meaning, deliberately withheld, appears characteristic of Bly's work. No reason is given in the poem as to why the poet is making this journey. Like his happiness it is unexplained. There is nothing in the description to indicate any special familiarity with his surroundings. Wordsworth is freer. He makes extremely clear his relationship to the various landscapes of his poem.

What most engages our attention in Bly's poem is the name "Lac Qui Parle." This is a master stroke. The notion of a speaking lake invests the whole world with significance, implying the possibility of communicating with objects and thereby changing the nature of our relation to the landscape. That the name is French suggests that the language of objects might be foreign, other than our own, and is in keeping with the poet's arriving at night and hearing "talking," but presumably unable to make out what is said. The possibility of communication is made more problematic by the fact that this is

Lac Qui Parle *River*, whose relation to the speaking lake is unspecified. The force of the river as a destination is weakened by the improbability of anyone driving over a bridge in a car being able to hear muted voices in a boat below and by this being human communication: that people talk to each other is not news. The conclusion is an anticlimax. The people in the boat do not seem to belong to the landscape and no relation is established between the moonlight on the river and their conversation, so that the poet's apparently not understanding them appears gratuitous. The sense of the otherness of things struggles in the poem with this spurious mysteriousness.

The poem's first line, reiterating that the poet is driving, insists on his being in motion and locates the poem securely in both time ("dusk") and space ("Minnesota"). After the title, the name of the state is a very precise reference that enables us to situate the events on a map. Bly compresses as much information as he can into the opening line. This is matched by the terseness of the close of the first stanza and increases its effectiveness. "I am happy" and "The moon rising above the turkey sheds" are thereby as if packed with compressed meaning. By contrast the language of the rest of the poem is slack, a slackness that emphasizes the randomness of the poet's perceptions and the chaotic, unorganized nature of the landscape.

The description of the landscape in a series of self-contained statements in which the various things named are more or less unrelated except by a similar syntax is pure Whitman:

> The paving man leans on his two-handed rammer, the
> reporter's lead flies swiftly over the note-book, the sign-
> painter is lettering with blue and gold.
> The canal boy trots on the tow-path, the book-keeper counts
> at his desk, the shoe-maker waxes his thread, . . .
> Where the yellow-crown'd heron comes to the edge of the
> marsh at night and feeds upon small crabs,
> Where the splash of swimmers and divers cools the warm
> noon,
> Where the katy-did works her chromatic reed on the walnut
> tree over the well, ...
> ("Song of Myself," 15 and 33)[6]

Comparison with Whitman shows the way in which Bly has flattened his language. Whitman is more vigorous. His language draws attention to itself. He very often employs an unusual word in an unusual place. Working with a carefully limited vocabulary, Bly is soft-spoken, if slightly rhetorical, low-key and studiously unadventurous. "Driving Toward the Lac Qui Parle River" is marked by an avoidance of adjectives, and the ones chosen are deliberately ordinary. Bly bets on his metaphors, on the muted act of naming.

Robert Pinsky observes that "the generic plural of 'old men'" is "unlikely," that is, if I understand him, that it is improbable that several old men were sitting in front of their houses on car seats in the small towns between Willmar and Milan that evening, before it became too dark to see them.[7] The point is well-taken. Bly keeps his distance from all the objects in the poem. Things are played down or generalized for the sake of an overall uniformity of effect. "The stubble field," "soybeans," and "men" are disconnected elements. There is no inner logic here. The words that characterize them, "last growth," "breathing," "old," refer in an unspecific way to human life. By contrast "The moon rising above the turkey sheds" is very much stronger and sharper, precise where the other description is diffuse: the moon is just rising and is still near the horizon. Why "turkey sheds"? Almost certainly because there were turkey sheds along the road, and because chicken houses in the Middle West are of different shapes and Bly has already used *houses* once and will use it again in the final stanza, but, more importantly, I believe, because of their distinctive, long, low shape. Turkey sheds are close to the earth—which is the poem's central concern.

The second stanza emphasizes the poet's separation from the world as he drives in the car and the opposition of inside to outside, which produces repeated images of impenetrable blackness. Nothing is seen in the second stanza, and only the faint sound of the crickets is heard. The car is a world apart, an armored solitude. The *iron* insists on the difference between the inside and the outside and at the same time makes the power of the crickets to *penetrate* this *solitude* the more remarkable. There are some problems. Car bodies are steel, not iron. The chirping of crickets is not very loud and does not carry, and it is extremely improbable that crickets could be heard above the noise of an automobile engine. Moreover, crickets are not very often heard in groups. They are solitary. This may be a simple error on Bly's part. He may have had in mind the locust or catydid. Their cacophonous, rasping sound can easily be heard at night driving with the window open, and they are commonly heard as a chorus.

The argument can be made that *iron* and *crickets* are used *poetically*, without regard to reality. Certainly the poet has that right, but that changes the nature of the poem, and if that is the case here, no indication of this is given in the poem, in fact, all the signs are to the contrary. "The deep fields of the night" is a good example of the pressure of the poetic in this sense in Bly's work. Are these the dark, barely visible fields of the Minnesota farms or is the night here seen as a landscape? Bly wants to have it both ways, but because it is not clear the metaphor loses much of its force and the *deep* seems vague and imprecise. Similarly, "this solitude covered with iron" appears euphemistic. The second stanza is wordy and rhetorical. The of-constructions are heavy— four in six lines and at the end of the line in each case—and made heavier by the repetition of "fields of night" and by the fact that the final three lines restate the first three.

Both the second and third stanzas end with an act of incomplete communication. The choice of *noise* to describe the crickets rather than *voices* or even *sound* emphasizes its meaninglessness, separating them from the Lac Qui Parle, but in suggesting or approximating speech, it constitutes another example of nearness. The "small bridge" marks the possibility of crossing the frontier into the world beyond the river. The poet reaches the river, but he does not cross. He appears to go no farther than the middle of the bridge. If the moon and the crickets give us a sense of something beyond in the first and second stanzas, they have no counterpart in the third stanza:

> Nearly to Milan, suddenly a small bridge,
> And water kneeling in the moonlight.
> In small towns the houses are built right on the ground;
> The lamplight falls on all fours on the grass.
> When I reach the river, the full moon covers it.
> A few people are talking low, in a boat.

Every line in the final stanza expresses the idea of nearness: "Nearly," the water "kneeling," the houses "built right on the ground" (the banality of this line almost sinks the whole poem), the lamplight "on all fours on the grass," the moon covering the river and the boat on it, but with different connotations. William V. Davis suggests that "the water 'kneels' and the lamplight 'falls on all fours', apparently to show obedience as well as acquiescence to powers beyond themselves."[8] Kneeling also suggests prayer, and we "fall on all fours" to look for something that is lost, to play—or from exhaustion. The description of the houses is perhaps meant to imply solidity. Covering suggests protectiveness, and the sexual act. The boat on the water repeats in a different way the idea of the car in the night, suggesting both contact and separation. The image of the full moon covering the river contradicts or reverses that of the "water kneeling in the moonlight." The one has the moon on top, the other, the water.

These disparate metaphors do not really add up except insofar as each affirms contact of some kind with earth and water. They resemble a scattering of shots across a target. The effect is of a certain incongruity. The images of the water "kneeling" and the lamplight "on all fours" are strange in that each enforces a shape on things that are amorphous. That that shape is human adds to their incongruity. These personifications are acts of violence done to the reality of the poem. They surprise and keep the reader guessing, but ultimately do not fit. They are pseudo-signs, figures of the incomprehensible.

Wordsworth at moments like this analyzes. He attempts to explain to himself what is happening to him. So does Whitman, so does Stevens. Here the succession of images is a substitute for analysis. The half-human nature of most of the metaphors shows us that we are between subject and object. Their incongruity is a sign of confusion. The poet presumably does not hear what the people in the boat are saying. There is not a sound from the Lac Qui Parle River. The light "covers," there is no illumination. The concluding stanza looks toward the unknown.

This poem and others like it have been called "deep image" poems.[9] This is a misnomer as the depth has been ironed out of the poem. The narrative is in the present tense. Because it is the story of a journey, we are made aware of the passage of time, but minimally. If the three stanzas are a series, surprisingly little is changed if they are rearranged. The poet does not remember anything and there is no thought of the future. Similarly, the description includes very little sense of space. The objects are in no particular relation to each other, especially in the final stanza, where due to the curious beginning of the third line: "In small towns the houses . . . ," it is unclear as to whether these houses are before Milan or Milan itself or merely an item of general knowledge, fictitious houses that are not part of the landscape. As a result, the source of the lamplight is problematic. Neither is there a central image within or beyond the poem, nor do the various images of the poem tell us anything about the unconscious. On the contrary, the way in which Bly sticks to the visible scene, the repetitions, the abruptness of the close, and what could almost be called a certain anti-intellectualism are all examples of self-limitation. The force of the poem is more from things repressed or suppressed than disclosed. The theory of the "deep image" would have us believe that the minimalism of the poem is understatement rather than a refusal to engage in self-analysis.

Kramer's definition of the poem as an example of "the contemporary poem of immanence" is equally unsatisfactory. Such poems, are in his words, "written to be a fragment of a lost privileged presence."[10] Certainly the poem is fragmentary, as it is in the nature of all experience to be fragmentary. There is a difficulty, however, in identifying anything "lost" in "Driving Toward the Lac Qui Parle River" and with the notion of "privileged presence." The presence of the landscape, of the world outside the car, is insisted upon in many ways, but despite the personifications, the soybeans, moon, crickets, grass, and river are not one but many, and this is not simply *nature* because mixed in are the men, car seats, houses, turkey sheds, bridge, and boat. What can "privileged" mean here? And as far as "presence" is concerned, none of these objects stays with us, except the moon. The poet passes them all by and none of them seem to have any particular effect upon him. They do not refer to anything beyond themselves in any clear or specific way. There are no disclosures, which makes it impossible to accept Kramer's interpretation of the poem as leaping "abruptly from bare perception to mystical vision" (Kramer, 455). Everything is seen in the same way. The language does not alter, and there is no vision of anything except the Minnesota countryside.

The houses, lamplight, moonlight, a few people talking in a boat are not in any sense of the word *mystical*. Wordsworth in "the poem on his own life" describing walking home after a dance makes his state of mind explicit:

> Magnificent
> The morning was, a memorable pomp,
> More glorious than I ever had beheld.
> The sea was laughing at a distance; all

> The solid mountains were as bright as clouds,
> Grain-tinctured, drenched in empyrean light; . . .
> Ah, need I say, dear friend, that to the brim
> My heart was full? I made no vows, but vows
> Were then made for me: bond unknown to me
> Was given, that I should be—else sinning greatly—
> A dedicated spirit. On I walked
> In blessedness, which even yet remains.
> (1805; IV.330–335, 340–345)[11]

So in a very different style does Yeats:

> My fiftieth year had come and gone,
> I sat, a solitary man,
> In a crowded London shop,
> An open book and empty cup
> On the marble table-top.
>
> While on the shop and street I gazed
> My body of a sudden blazed;
> And twenty minutes more or less
> It seemed, so great my happiness,
> That I was blessèd and could bless.[12]

These passages leave us in no doubt about the poets' experiences. Now the tendency is to want Wordsworth's intensity, without the rhetoric of "memorable pomp," "glorious," "beheld," "Grain-tinctured," and "empyrean light," without the specificity of his brim-full heart, the vows, bond and blessedness, and emphatic cause-and-effect structure that separates the passage into two parts—description of landscape followed by description of feeling. After the lessons in simplicity of the older Yeats, Pound, Eliot (in *The Waste Land*), Stein, Hemingway, and Williams, many poets have tried to strip down their poems without noticing that very often there is a radical loss of analytic power. Wordsworth meets his subject head-on, which means that everything he adds enables him to go deeper into the subject. From this point of view, Ashbery's interest in "the English poets of the nineteenth century" is perhaps indicative of what he sees as the way forward. Contemporary poets searching for greater suggestiveness and obliqueness commonly go around their subject, missing any point altogether or saying nothing of interest. Understatement can engage a process of diminishing returns or produce silence where speech is needed.

Yeats is much simpler than Wordsworth. He has reduced his scene to a small number of elements: man, shop, book, cup, and table. The verbs are ordinary. For the most part, there is one adjective per noun. The sentences are short. The syntax is uncomplicated. As a result the short lines and rhymes make for a strong, tight structure. The emotion because it is named with the same precision and matter-of-factness as the book, cup, and table is absolutely clear. The figurative *blazed* presents the unexpected increase in intensity of the poet's feelings as well as suggesting their fluid contours and gradual fading. The secular setting of the London shops and the definition of the happiness is such as to remove any specific religious connotations from *blessèd*. There is nothing supernatural here. The moment of illumination is an event in the history of the *body*. The single noun *happiness* and the repeated *was blessèd* and *could bless* without any further development have the same kind of simplicity as *shop, book, cup,* and *table*, a simplicity that is increased by *more or less* and *seemed*, inherent in the experience and in no way a failure of language. The poet knows that he only partially understands what has happened to him, and it is one of the poem's major purposes to make this clear.

All of this is missing in Bly. The context of his metaphors is confused, their inner connection is unclear. If the "kneeling" has religious connotations, they are not confirmed by "on all fours" or the other metaphors. If they are thought to promise something more, that promise is not kept. There is no foundation in the poem for anything approaching Kramer's "mystical vision." Mysticism is the belief in the possibility of experiences of union with or revelations from supernatural persons. There is neither anything religious nor any trace of the supernatural in "Driving Toward the Lac Qui Parle River." There are hints at revelations from the natural world, but they are as if discarded by the poem. At the end we are left with people talking. Another slightly different poem might build to this as a conclusion; in this case it seems a chance conclusion, or rather as if Bly had decided to go in several directions at once instead of choosing one.

The term *immanent* can certainly be applied to the poem in the sense given by *The Shorter Oxford Dictionary* of "an act which is performed entirely within the mind of the subject, and produces no external effect." The significance, such as it is, of the metaphors is withheld from the text. The experience is performed in large part within Bly's mind and "produces no external effect" in the poem. The other sense of *immanent*, "Indwelling, inherent; actually present or abiding *in*; remaining within," does not apply, because there is nothing in or beyond the landscape. The method of description (the enumeration of discrete items, the incongruity of the images, the absence of grammatical connectives between sentences) produces a curiously two-dimensional scene composed of disparate pieces. The landscape is disunified, and there is no exploration of the notion of touching that informs so many of the images.

The promise of a glimpse into the unconscious is never kept. The revelation is not forthcoming. Perhaps this is because Bly cannot completely accept the idea of the unconscious and substitutes instead various pseudo-psychological and pseudo-scientific notions: Jungian archetypes, first, second and third brains, twofold consciousness, father-consciousness, mother-consciousness, and an eclectic collection of religious views. As he has grown older, his ideas appear to have become crankier (see, for example, the interviews published in *Talking All Morning*, 1980). Very often in the poetry the images are a substitute for analysis. They pretend to be metaphors, but in fact do not refer beyond themselves. They mark an end to the thinking. There is a rhetoric of depth—intimations of intimations, a suggestion of the supernatural, or the evocation of some unspecified mystery—but the perspective is an illusion. The poet gestures self-consciously toward a painted horizon.

"Letter to Her" in *Loving a Woman in Two Worlds* (1985) is another example of this evasion of self-analysis.[13] The poem begins with the poet's confession:

> What I did I did.
> I knew that I loved you
> and told you that.
> Then I lied to you
> often so you would love me,
> hid the truth,
> shammed, lied.

The language is simple and direct. The statements pared down as in the best Hemingway and Williams. The strength of Bly's poetry very often resides in such spare, stripped-down, standard subject-verb-object sentences. The sentence also imposes its form in that the only words capitalized at the start of the line are those that begin a sentence (which is true of most of the poems in this volume), a move toward the prose poem. The appeal of the opening is irresistible. The reader is between the two lovers, overhearing their secrets. The act of confession cannot but engage our attention, and the duplicities of everyday life is a drama in which we all participate. We know this world of white and black lies as we know ourselves. These are home truths.

This realism, however, is not sustained. After the powerful first stanza the poem falls apart in assorted images of the natural world and insistent moralizing. The analysis is not continued. The poem runs out of honesty. The poet in the remaining three stanzas examines neither his motives nor the relationship any further; instead he offers a somewhat inconsequential and obscure set of images as self-justification. Again, as in "Driving Toward the Lac Qui Parle River," Bly's metaphors, contrary to what might be expected, are the sign of his abandonment of his subject. The woman in this poem, as in all the poems of *Loving a Woman in Two Worlds* is an extremely shadowy figure—even more shadowy than the poet himself. She almost never speaks and then only a few words. She has no behavior. Her body is mostly metaphors. She exists as the pretext for the poet's emotions. As in the other poems, the poet in "Letter to Her" seems to be most concerned to communicate with himself. After the first stanza the moment of the letter is lost. Despite the images of nature, the poet turns inward rather than outward.

The second stanza is a complete change from the first:

> Once human beings
> in their way do what they do
> they find peakéd
> castles ahead, they see
> lanterns aloft over
> the seal-like masses
> where they love at night.

The language is more complicated, more artificial. The seven lines are a single sentence. The tone is impersonal. There is a shift from the immediacy of the first person to the generality of "human beings." The lovers are assimilated to the species. The "in their way" is at once redundant and tautological, a comprehensive, all-purpose phrase that explains nothing. It is not clear whether this vision of castles is a reward, a punishment, or an evasion, or merely the inevitable consequence of all human action. The specificity of the situation produced by the poet's lies is lost in this totalizing commentary. The exact nature of the "lanterns" and "the seal-like masses" is unclear.

This is the world of fairy stories, of castles in Spain and princesses in towers, a willed dream world. Nothing indicates this more clearly than the imprecise *peakéd* with its archaic accent mark which sets the tone for the rest of the poem. The final three stanzas are stiff and mannered, and instead of following the phrasing of speech as in the first stanza, the lines are divided so as to disrupt the rhythm of ordinary speech. The break after the *o* of *oppossum* and the two breaks after *sun* in the last stanza (so that the two last words of the second and fourth lines are identical, a mock rhyme) are the most obvious examples.

"Letter to Her" appears, in a number of different ways, to affirm the inevitability and necessity of our behavior and that whatever anyone does is right. The poem concludes with the evocation of elemental forces:

> some-
> thing strong guides the sun
> over the sky
> it carries its spark down
> to the northern forests.

The poet's lies are lost in the darkness of the northern forests. Whether the "spark" is the cause or the effect of the lies, redeems or cancels what he has said, or is completely unrelated to it, the poem does not say. Neither is it clear whether this putative force is natural or supernatural. Bly's need is for elemental forces to remain mysterious. The images of the final three stanzas in "Letter to Her," do not, like those in "Driving Toward the Lac Qui Parle River," establish a particular landscape, but both sets of images finally verge on the unknown and produce a generalized portentousness.

This conclusion causes us to re-examine the first stanza, which in the light of the poem as a whole appears to be less simple than we had originally thought. The *that* at the end of the third line is unnecessary. Apparently it is there to mimic the *that* in the second line (although they are grammatically different) in a way analogous to the repetition of *the sun* in the last stanza. Also, the final two lines could be deleted. This would put greater emphases on her love and on the possibility that she would not love him if he told the truth, opening the poem to more truth. The justification of the threefold repetition of his untruthfulness is that it proves the word *often* and demonstrates the frequency of his lies. As it stands, the emphasis is on the poet's lying and leads—unconsciously—to the dream world, to the sham castle and the rhetorical shamming of the final three stanzas. That lies have consequences in human relations is avoided altogether. In the context of the whole poem, the first stanza seems a pretense of honesty rather than the real thing, as if we are asked to admire the poet for being able to admit that he has lied. There is no apology or mention of forgiveness in the poem. The appeal, as usual in Bly, is to beyond the poem, and beyond nature.

There is no "deep image" in any of these poems. On the contrary, "Driving Toward the Lac Qui Parle River" and "Letter to Her" are composed of a succession of deliberately unconnected images. "Letter to Her" can be said to assert the existence of an indwelling, immanent presence, but this is an invented rather than an experienced presence, a wish of the poet that the poem does not fulfill, and, we might say, cannot, because we cannot accept the poet telling lies about our experience. Every life is lived with some sense, even though this sense changes, of what is real, not an idea but a profound feeling of truth, and there are limits, again variable, to how much any author can trespass upon this fundamental and primeval ground. Disbelief can be suspended for Donne's god or Milton's, but Eliot's religious beliefs appear anachronistic and no one believes in Yeats' system. Similarly, it is impossible to believe in Bly's spirit world, and insofar as Bly in his work behaves as if he believes, he appears self-deluding—as do all the critics who tell us that texts are only about other texts or about language.

The major problem of contemporary poetry and, indeed, all art is to go beyond the work of Freud and his successors. Since Wordsworth the most urgent concern of poetry has been the analysis of consciousness. This has included (beginning with Wordsworth) an idea of the unconscious as necessary to the understanding of the dynamics of consciousness. During this period, poetry has derived its energy from working at the edge of what was known, by using the poem to make new discoveries about human behavior and who we are. The theories of Freud and his successors explain so much and so clearly and so simply, and have brought so much new material to consciousness that the majority of poets have not been able to come to terms with it all—which, of course, is not the same as accepting those theories.

The Interpretation of Dreams was published in 1900, and if one accepts Jung's rule of thumb that it takes about forty years for a new idea to be accepted, then Bly's generation is the first to come of age in a culture permeated by the ideas of psychoanalysis—which is a way of understanding the change in American poetry with Ginsberg, O'Hara, and Ashbery. The major poets of the earlier generation, Stevens, Williams, Pound, Eliot, and Crane all grew up in a different world, although traces of the effect of the new psychology and of shared psychological concerns can be found in their work as well. Freud's comment: *"Naja—die Dichter haben das alles gekannt,"* is a clear statement of the contribution of poetry. At the moment, however, American poets appear to be having difficulty in finding their way forward to their own knowledge, a difficulty both in working through the contribution of Freud and his successors, and of continuing the discoveries of Whitman, Rimbaud, Mallarmé, Crane, and Stevens—to name only the most radical of recent poets. Temporarily at least, the cutting edge has been lost.

Much of Bly's poetry is like a replay of Williams's without the sharpness of Williams's vision and the tension of his language. Going back to Boehme or to the later work of Jung, as Bly does, is a refusal to confront the notion of the unconscious, a denial of reality, like his references to indeterminate forces and spirit horses. Poetically, this homemade religion is Confederate money, so much snake oil, impossible to believe in because we know too much about ourselves—and the earth—and because we are never completely convinced that Bly believes in it. The rhetoric is too apparent. Bly's simplicity is his effort to keep this special pleading under control. The unfinished metaphors, the images that turn in upon themselves, such as the "water kneeling in the moonlight," are a way of avoiding any explicit commitment to any system of meaning and of keeping at bay the fantasy world of "Letter to Her."

Bly works between the two extremes of "Driving Toward the Lac Qui Parle River" and "Letter to Her." The poems such as the former stand or fall on the vividness of the observed details, although this vividness is usually muted, because Bly prefers not to engage in sustained description. The scene is for him more important than any single object, although often it has no unity or wholeness except that of the perceiver, and this is limited by his dislike of making definite statements about his own life. Bly resists history. There is a certain impersonality and timelessness about all his poetry. The speaker is ghostly, almost disembodied. He commonly has no past and virtually no experience except the poem, and very often, as in "Driving Toward the Lac Qui Parle River," the action has no particular meaning and the naming of several items of the scene is expected to suffice instead, almost as if a certain configuration of things might, with luck, become significant.

The other extreme is that of "Letter to Her," in which the poet's mood is projected or translated upon the natural world and undefined or extranatural forces are evoked, as if human problems could be resolved by other than human means, as if meaning was other than man-made, an intervention from without the culture or somehow given. The natural world is invested with the poet's fantasy and the whole has the quality of a dream, but one that cannot be interpreted because the full context is withheld. Again objects from the natural world are presented in place of any analysis, as if they were metaphors. There does not in the work of Bly or in that of any other contemporary American poet appear to be any way around the poem of the moment of experience. This is still the form in which we apprehend the world.

Notes

1. T. S. Eliot, "*Baudelaire and the Symbolists. Five Essays.* By Peter Quennell," *The Criterion* 9 (January 1930): 357.

2. Robert Bly, *Selected Poems* (New York: Harper and Row, 1986), 26; hereafter cited as *Selected Poems*.

3. Robert Bly, *Talking All Morning* (Ann Arbor: University of Michigan Press, 1980), 129.

4. Paul Valéry, *Oeuvres*, ed. Jean Hytier (Paris: Gallimard, 1957), I, 992–93.

5. For Wordsworth's contribution, see my *Wordsworth and the Beginnings of Modern Poetry* (London, Croom Helm and Totowa, N.J.: Barnes and Noble, 1981), esp. 201–223.

6. Walt Whitman, *Complete Poetry and Collected Prose* (New York: Library of America, 1982), 201–202, 222.

7. Robert Pinsky, *The Situation of Poetry* (Princeton: Princeton University Press, 1976), 77.

8. William V. Davis, *Understanding Robert Bly* (Columbia: University of South Carolina Press, 1988), 23; hereafter cited as Davis.

9. For references to this discussion, see Davis; 23–25.

10. Lawrence Kramer, "A Sensible Emptiness: Robert Bly and the Poetics of Immanence," *Contemporary Literature* 24 (1983): 450; hereafter cited as Kramer.

11. William Wordsworth, *The Prelude,* 1799, 1805, 1850, ed. Jonathan Wordsworth, M. H. Abrams, and Stephen Gill (New York: W. W. Norton, 1979), 142.

12. W. B. Yeats, *The Collected Poems* (London: Macmillan, 1956), 246.

13. Robert Bly, *Loving a Woman in Two Worlds* (New York: Harper and Row, 1985), 12–13.

The Startling Journeys of Robert Bly

PETER STITT

In his *Selected Poems* (1986), Robert Bly does something unusual for such collections. Most poets simply include within their selected volume everything that they wish to preserve from earlier books; Bly, in contrast, has pared his corpus down to a slim grouping that seems meant to indicate the major directions he sees his work taking. As though to reinforce this notion, he has also written a series of introductions for the sections of the book, making a kind of reader's guide to his own work. The method is inherently didactic, of course, and as such reflects a prominent characteristic of Bly's career. Indeed, so pronounced is this tendency that the figure of Bly as teacher, preacher, and reformer often seems to dominate that of Bly the poet.[1] In one of the miniature essays in the *Selected Poems,* Bly defines the goal of his poetry: "All poems are journeys. They go from somewhere to somewhere else. The best poems take long journeys. I like poetry best that journeys—while remaining in the human scale—to the other world, which may be a place as easily overlooked as a bee's wing."[2]

Though Bly here locates the goal of his poetic journeys at an intimate level of the natural world, elsewhere (especially in earlier theoretical pronouncements) he locates it within a deep layer of the mind, something akin to Freud's subconscious or Jung's collective unconscious. More recently, Bly has tended to put these two aspects of his idea together, as in this passage from another of these introductions:

> . . . at certain moments, particularly moments alone, we can pass into a deep of the mind, and at that instant we may pass as well into a tree or a hill, as when the dreamer traveling to some far place finds himself not farther from the soul but nearer to it, and wakes with the sweet sensation of friendship from other worlds. Whoever dreams in this way leaves judgment behind, at least temporarily, but we never leave mind. For when we pass into a deep of the mind, we become awake to the intelligence of hills and groves. At thirty-two I felt for the first time in adult life an unattached part of my soul join a tree standing in the center of a field. (26)

As Anthony Libby has pointed out, Bly's search for the other world has religious, even mystical implications—though, of course, it is emphatically

This essay was written specifically for this volume and is published here for the first time.

grounded in the physical and real: "So behind the traditional mystical paradox—the praise of ordinarily negative states, grief and 'the death we love,' as avenues to holy joy—there exits in Bly the further paradox that spiritual union with the universe must be sought in physical terms."[3] Among the many poems that exemplify this line of thinking and way of writing is "Gone, Gone, Gone":

> When the wind-sleeve moves in the morning street,
> I walk there, and brood on brown things,
> On green things,
> On the green waves
> Lifting at sea, the green wives, and the brood of heaven.
>
> I hear a faint sound, a bell inside the waves
> Coming from far off . . . and the sweet clear
> Bell of the joys
> Of silence pierces
> Through the roaring of cars, the hum of tires, the
>   closing of doors.
>
> When I hear that sound, a subtle force, a sheath,
> Motherly, wraps me. Inside that sheath
> I need no
> House or land,
> Caught in sweetness as the trout in the running stream. (23)

This is an ecstatic poem; the poet is in the mystical state, transported away from corporeal reality to where everything hums. The poem's final image—the simile comparing the speaker, surrounded by his god-mother's sheath, and the fish, surrounded by a stream—is one of only a few here that are based upon a familiar sense of logic. The images in the first stanza are more typical in being not logical but impressionistic: the "wind-sleeve," the "brown things," the "green things," the "green wives, and the brood of heaven."

Such images constitute one of the two major stylistic signatures of Robert Bly—his use of metaphors so strange that they have been called surrealistic. In fact, metaphor—because it is the journeying device, the figure of speech that, by comparing one image with another, carries the reader from here to there—is the perfect foundational device for Bly. In poems like "Driving Toward the Lac Qui Parle River," we find ourselves moving from the human world to the natural world to the spiritual world, all through the agency of metaphor. The poem contains soybeans that "are breathing on all sides," water that is "kneeling in the moonlight," and lamplight that is falling "on all fours on the grass."[4]

This traveling-through-metaphor technique is one that Bly has been using throughout his career. It is illustrated in pristine fashion by " "Taking the

Hands,'" a poem not reprinted in the *Selected Poems* but that may be found in *Silence in the Snowy Fields* (1962), Bly's first book:

> Taking the hands of someone you love,
> You see they are delicate cages . . .
> Tiny birds are singing
> In the secluded prairies
> And in the deep valleys of the hand. (42)

In its second line, the poem establishes a metaphor that carries the reader from an ordinary pair of hands to the enchanted kingdom of poetry. The metaphor is as simple as the poem is sentimental, and it illustrates clearly how habitually Bly links disparate objects together, how quickly he moves from one to another.

"A Dream of Suffocation," from Bly's second book, *The Light Around the Body* (1967), is another poem not reprinted in the selected volume. Though possessed of the amusing surface use of images we associate with the typical Bly poem, it also has a serious point to make about western civilization:

> Accountants hover over the earth like helicopters,
> Dropping bits of paper engraved with Hegel's name.
> Badgers carry the papers on their fur
> To their den, where the entire family dies in the night.
>
> A chorus girl stands for hours behind her curtains
> Looking out at the street:
> In a window of a trucking service
> There is a branch painted white.
> A stuffed baby alligator grips that branch tightly
> To keep away from the dry leaves on the floor.
>
> The honeycomb at night has strange dreams:
> Small black trains going around and round
> Old warships drowning in the raindrop. (8)

The kind of thinking exemplified by Hegel and the accountants, in Bly's view, is killing both nature (the badgers and alligator) and art (the chorus girl) and is forcing the imaginative life (represented by the apocalyptic dreams of the honeycomb) to retreat into the world of dreams.

These ideas are presented in something like the method of surrealism— which for Bly has its origins more in Jung's notion of the collective unconscious than in Freud's more self-contained model. Bly's method is essentially free association; the imagination is allowed to discover whatever images it deems appropriate to the poem, no matter the logical, literal demands of consciousness. He describes this process in a prose poem, "Eleven O'Clock at

Night," from *The Man in the Black Coat Turns* (1981): "Many times in poems I have escaped—from myself. I sit for hours and at last see a pinhole in the top of the pumpkin, and I slip out that pinhole, gone! The genie expands and is gone; no one can get him back in the bottle again; he is hovering over a car cemetery somewhere" (18). In the poems, of course, the genie makes his journeys through the agency of metaphor.

The other distinctive characteristic of Bly's style results from the way in which he uses metaphor. Often the surface of his poems will be oddly and almost unintentionally funny in its use of figures, even as the content is quite serious. I think this is what Bly is getting at in another of his introductory comments, where he speaks of "a kind of poem I had never written before. . . . Its shape is circular or spiral. The rhythm of the lines is sometimes weak, . . . but a certain gaiety carries them along" (26). "Pilgrim Fish Heads," for example, tells a fairly grim story in images that are both astonishing and delightful:

> It is a Pilgrim village; heavy rain is falling.
> Fish heads lie smiling at the corners of houses.
> Inside, words like "Samson" hang from the rafters.
> Outdoors, the chickens squawk in woody hovels,
> yet the chickens are walking on Calvinist ground.
> The women move through the dark kitchen; their heavy
> skirts bear them down like drowning men.
> Upstairs, beds are like thunderstorms on the bare floor,
> leaving the covers always moist by the rough woods.
> And the eggs! Strange, white, perfect eggs!
> Eggs that even the rain could not move,
> white, painless, with tails even in nightmares.
> And the Indian, damp, musky, asking for a bed.
> The Mattapoiset is in league with rotting wood;
> he has made a conspiracy with the salamander;
> he has made treaties with the cold heads of fishes.
> In the grave he does not rot but vanishes into water.
> The Indian goes on living in the rain-soaked stumps.
> This is our enemy; this is the outcast;
> the one from whom we must protect our nation,
> the one whose dark hair hides us from the sun. (66)

The first half of the poem is saturated with surprising metaphors—smiling fish heads, hanging words, drowning skirts, thunderstorm beds—images that not only can easily bring a startled smile to the lips of the reader but are startling in the outrageous way they have of presenting reality.[5]

The message of the poem is also revolutionary and unsettling, for it means to undercut the basis on which we Americans have organized our society. In his wonderful book *Studies in Classic American Literature,* D. H. Lawrence criticizes the American spirit for its desire to control the world through white technology, for its hatred of anything dark, for its willingness to destroy everything and anything that does not fit the imposed pattern—nature, the subconscious mind, the American Indian. In the second half of his poem, Bly shows his agreement with Lawrence's thinking. Thus the concluding three lines are ironic, delivered from the perspective of some Ben Franklin, General Custer, or Henry Ford. This poet's commitment is to the dark, the primitive, the nonrational.

Bly has always tended to view the world in terms of dualities, polarities. Throughout his career he has argued, with an almost messianic fervor, that there exists an opposition between what we might call a poetry of the Cartesian mind—logical, empirical, straightforward, businesslike—and a poetry of the subconscious mind. Bly strongly feels that the former type of poetry is characteristic of the American literary tradition, just as Cartesian thought is typical of the American mind; thus his program of searching out and translating the work of poets of the latter type—for example, Neruda, Jiménez, Hernandez, Vallejo, Trakl. It is largely because of Bly's efforts in this direction that we have had a poetry of the "deep image" recently in America. Beyond this literary manifestation of the dualist view, Bly has also seen such oppositions in more general situations. At the time of *Sleepers Joining Hands* (1973), for example, he expressed it in sexual terms. It was the insecurity of American masculinity that made us want to rape Vietnam; the feminine principle counseled sensitivity, respect for life, though it also embodied an intense desire to destroy, violently, rapacious masculinity. These forces fought it out in the poems as on the battlefields.

Elsewhere, Bly has referred to "some recent brain research" to prove that human beings have within them a reptile brain (which makes some of us violent, hostile, regressive), a mammalian brain (which makes others of us warm and loving), and an only rudimentarily developed higher consciousness (which might someday rule and harmonize the other two). Whatever the terms Bly has used at a given time (other versions were based on the work of Jung and Ortega y Gasset), of course, all these theories are different versions of one grand theory, expressed at different times in different terms. With Emerson, Bly shares the desire to be the vatic bard who speaks great truths as though from on high. Consequently, he has always presented each new version of his truth as an entirely new truth—I once was lost, he seems to have said with some frequency, but now am found; was blind but now I see. Such is the nature of the preface—dualistically titled "The Two Presences"—of his book *This Tree Will Be Here for a Thousand Years* (1979). Bly's theory (which here is specifically a theory of poetry) says that, in addition to the human consciousness with which we have always been familiar, there is a "consciousness *out there* among plants and animals." In recounting how this revelation came to him, Bly also defines the dominant mood of this other consciousness: "One day sitting depressed in a cabin on the shore of a small lake, I wrote about the depression:

> Mist: no one on the other shore.
> It may be that these trees
> I see have consciousness,
> and this desire to weep comes from them." (9)

At various times during the years since his first book, *Silence in the Snowy Fields* (1962), Bly has written many poems in which he attempts to bring these two consciousnesses together, in balance and harmony. In *This Tree Will Be Here for a Thousand Years,* those poems are finally gathered within the covers of a book.

Unfortunately, the theory fails completely when used as a guide to what is happening in the poems themselves. The problem is not that Bly expresses no relationship between human consciousness and the consciousness of nature in the poems—he does do this, and with something close to a vengeance. What we end up with, however, are not demonstrations of the separate existence of a nature consciousness but something like lessons to man based on the behavior of nature. For an example of this I am going to quote an unfortunate stanza from the poem "The Fallen Tree":

> After a long walk I come down to the shore.
> A cottonwood tree lies stretched out in the grass.
> This tree knocked down by lightning—
> and a hollow the owls made open now to the rain.
> Disasters are all right, if they teach men and women
> to turn their hollow places up. (60)

This seems to be what Bly means by the consciousness of nature; what I see, however, is a didactic poet making use of nature to his own preacherly ends.

Elsewhere Bly's theory is manifested in his employment of what used to be called the pathetic fallacy (I mean to use the term nonpejoratively), wherein the poet transfers his own emotions outward to nature, as in these lines from "Writing Again": "When I write of moral things, / the clouds boil / blackly!" (18). More commonly, and much more typically for Bly, the relationship is expressed through his second favorite poetic device (after the metaphor), the simile. "Listening to a Cricket in the Wainscoting" is composed entirely of a series of successful similes:

> That sound of his is like a boat with black sails.
> Or a widow under a redwood tree, warning
> passersby that the tree is about to fall.
> Or a bell made of black tin in a Mexican village.
> Or the hair in the ear of a hundred-year-old man! (29)

This Tree Will Be Here for a Thousand Years is an uneven book, most seriously marred by its preface; the reader who tries to understand the poems on the basis of Bly's theory is doomed to inevitable frustration. When the preface is ignored, however, it becomes apparent that there are many good poems here, poems not original in their vision or technique, but well-written and pleasurable for all of that. Among the best is "Moving Books to a New Study":

> First snow yesterday, and now more falling.
> Each blade has its own snow balanced on it.
> One mousetrack in the snow ahead,
> the tailmark wavering in
> between the footprints. Dusk in half an hour.
> Looking up I see my parents' grove.
> Somehow neither the Norwegian culture
> nor the American could keep them warm.
> I walk around the barn the long way
> carrying the heavy green book I love through snow. (46)

We see that the son has solved for himself his parents' problem—the book he carries gives culture enough to keep him warm in the snow; indeed, he seems as much in his element as the mouse whose path parallels his.

Even in Bly's most somber book, *The Man in the Black Coat Turns* (1981), the surfaces of his poems crackle with energy and liveliness and show the same fascinating progression of images we have been looking at. The book contains, for example, this passage of self-rebuke:

> How many failures we hide, talking. When I am too public,
> I am a wind-chime, ringing, to cheer up the black
> Angel Moroni, and feed him
> as he comes dancing, prancing, leaving turkey tracks in the
>   mist. (39)

The ultimate conflict in Bly's work has always been between aloneness and community. He began with solitude, in the magnificently introspective poems of *Silence in the Snowy Fields.* Since then he has been very much a public poet—an antiwar activist, a performer on many campuses, the author of political verse. *The Man in the Black Coat Turns,* in fact, seems to embody the dichotomy inherent in Bly's career; the poems enact a surprising disjunction between their surface desire for community and their dark interiors. The speaker appears to want the sense of closeness derived from family life, but in the pattern of his images he clearly longs for separation and solitude. These lines are typical: "The mother puts down her rolling pin and makes no more bread. / And the wife looks at her husband one night at a party, and loves him no more . . ."; "The father . . . / . . . turns away from his wife, and she sleeps alone" (3). Thus the end seems to join the beginning in this poet's work, just as the most dominant feature of his later work—a baroque use of metaphor—is also the dominant feature of his earliest work.[6]

Notes

1. If Bly's tendency to preach was fostered during his upbringing in the strongly religious environment of rural, western Minnesota, it was most fully developed during his extensive activities as a protester against the Vietnam War; as William Matthews has said, "The war was [*sic*] brought on in Bly another similarity to [D. H.] Lawrence, a tendency to preach" ("Thinking About Robert Bly,") in *Robert Bly: When Sleepers Awake,* ed. Joyce Peseroff [Ann Arbor: University of Michigan Press, 1984], 8; hereafter cited as Peseroff).

2. Robert Bly, *Selected Poems* (New York: Harper & Row, 1986), 88. In his interview with Joseph Shakarchi, Bly commented further on the motif of the journey: "I seem to think naturally in journeys and stages. To me this is ordinary common sense. One notices that fairy stories often lay out stages of growth. It has only been after the Christian victory that European man has forgotten these stages; and that is partly because Christianity deals with instantaneous conversion, as if the work had been done by *another*. But in ancient life, growth was thought of as slow, very slow, involving 'stages' and a 'journey'" (Peseroff, 329). Other critics have also noticed the prominence of the journey motif in Bly's work; Howard Nelson's identification of this matter as an aspect of Bly's use of imagery is similar to mine: "The image as Bly sees it is a thing that contains two worlds; association is movement from one place to another" (*Robert Bly: An Introduction to the Poetry* [New York: Columbia University Press, 1984], 82; hereafter cited as Nelson).

3. "Robert Bly Alive in Darkness," in Peseroff, 40. In an earlier passage, Libby relates Bly's search for the spiritual to the way he uses images: "The successful subjective image (or 'deep image') strikes us with the force of a newly discovered archetype, minor or major, coming from the depths of the poet's subjectivity with a paradoxically universal force" (Peseroff, 38). Howard Nelson sees Bly's use of imagery in essentially the same way: "Bly wants in the image a conjunction of the physical and the unknown, the sensory impression and the inner reverberation" (Nelson, 81).

4. *Selected Poems,* 45. Like many critics, Walter Kalaidjian sees Bly's use of imagery as surrealistic; writing specifically of this poem, Kalaidjian says: "Bly's subtle metaphorical shifts from realistic to surrealistic imagery jar our conventional expectations, yet so unobtrusive is his technique that he manages to 'naturalize' his artificial modifiers. He leads his audience to an impression of psychic plenitude through a virtually transparent verbal performance" ("From Silence to Subversion: Robert Bly's Political Surrealism," *Modern Poetry Studies* 11 [1983]: 291; hereafter cited as Kalaidjian).

5. Bly's startling use of imagery and metaphor is of course the major topic of discussion for critics of his work. The most common terms used for this phenomenon are "deep imagery," "surrealism," or (Bly's own term) "leaping poetry." William V. Davis follows Bly in using the latter term: "Bly's notions of 'leaps' in poetry and of 'leaping poetry' are important both as creative principles and as critical tools. He describes 'a leap from the conscious to the unconscious and back again, a leap from the known part of the mind to the unknown part' as one of the necessities of leaping poems, which give off 'constantly flashing light' as they shift from 'light psyche to dark psyche'" (*Understanding Robert Bly* [Columbia: University of South Carolina Press, 1988], 11). Walter Kalaidjian's discussion of Bly's "surrealism" takes account of the often startling nature of his use of imagery: "Bly's surrealist tenent that 'one thing is also another thing' creates radical leaps of association, allowing the poet to identify, for example, the obscurity of the Congo with the darkness within Minnesota wheat mills. This surrealist strategy provides him with the imaginative means for liberating his vision from the utilitarian constitution of landscape" (Kalaidjian, 292–93).

6. Howard Nelson offers this parenthetical comment on the public and private aspects of

Bly's career: "Those who have attended Bly's readings, which regularly run to two and three spirited hours, or have read his interviews, which are both numerous and extremely lively, will note a certain incongruity between his insistence on solitude and silence on one hand and such outpourings of extraversion on the other. . . . An introvert and an extravert live together in Bly's body. He welcomes them both, although in certain later poems . . . the extravert comes in for criticism" (Nelson, 9–10).

Redefining the American Poet

RICHARD P. SUGG

In his seventh decade, Robert Bly has shown no signs of diminishing creativity or unwillingness to journey in new directions. His *Selected Poems* marked a plateau, but not a conclusion, to his forty-year career as a man of letters. Not only new accomplishments, but also further recognitions and awards, undoubtedly await him. Whatever the future holds, any assessment of the achievement of Robert Bly to date must focus on three major areas.

A career is the work of a lifetime, and Robert Bly is one of the few Americans whose life's work justifies the title of poet. His career exemplifies the best of his generation, not only for its long fidelity to his vocation, but also for its example to, and influence upon, others. In a sense, Bly's career redefined the role of the poet for his generation, providing a comprehensive definition of what that vocation might involve. To cite just a few instances in which Bly's example became the model, one might mention the poet's founding of his own magazine and publishing house, or his turning to political poetry and public demonstration during the social crisis of the Vietnam War, or his thirty-year-long labor of translating and promulgating the work of foreign poets to insular Americans, or his development and popularization of the prose poem, or even his choice of a life-style, living on a remote farm and refusing to work for or submit to the university.

However important Bly's career as a man of letters, including his influence upon others, seems today, it will ultimately prove secondary to his achievement as an American poet. As he once wrote of his father, Bly carried the burden a little bit higher up the mountain; he took classic American themes and reinterpreted them for his time. Bly is squarely within the American romantic tradition of Emerson, Whitman, and Hart Crane in his belief that the poet's lifelong task is the elucidation of the human soul. Further, Bly emulates Thoreau in his belief in the integral relationship between the individual psyche and the body politic, and in his concomitant willingness to engage at the psychospiritual level the political issues of his time. Bly not only knows and follows these American poetic traditions, he also writes about them. In his later work, especially, he takes pains to locate himself within a poetic

Reprinted from *Robert Bly,* by Richard P. Sugg (Boston: Twayne, 1986), 142–43. Copyright 1986 and reprinted with the permission of Twayne Publishers, an imprint of Macmillan Publishing Company, New York.

tradition. He has come to write more and more of this centrality of the family of poets to the continuity of the family of man. In this Bly seeks to renew and reaffirm in his poetry the importance of the traditional interdependence of life and the language arts.

Finally, and most importantly, Robert Bly's achievement must rest upon what new elements his vision and his poetic voice have added to the commonweal. It is good, but not sufficient for poetic immortality, to influence one's contemporaries or reaffirm the tradition. Robert Bly's originality lies in his lifelong journey through his psyche toward the goal of personality development, toward selfhood; his achievement lies in his exploration and re-creation in poetry of an imaginative geography of the human psyche landscape. Bly's inward road has taken him along the process that Jung described as individuation and integration; Bly has been faithfully attentive to the unfolding of the many aspects of his developing personality, as well as to his continuing struggle to integrate them into a complete yet multiplicitous soul. To the enduring poetic subjects of nature, politics, the soul, God, the family, death, and human love Robert Bly has brought a constant source of light: himself. Further, he has consciously sought out more universal symbols for the expression of his own psychic journey, since he believes with Jung that the individual and subjective life is always amplified and illuminated when shown against the backdrop of the universal and archetypal. The ultimate achievement of Robert Bly is that at its best his poetry succeeds in awakening, even inspiring, his audience with a sense of human community and possibility that is both psychological and, in the most fundamental sense, religious. Let this stand as his achievement, that sometimes within the spell of his poetry the ancient, elusive dream of aligning perfectly the conscious and unconscious parts of human nature seems almost true: "For we are like the branch bent in the water . . . / Taken out, it is whole, it was always whole. . . ."

Index

♦

Adorno, Theodor W., 195, 197
Agee, James, 128
Alcaeus, 166
Alcott, Bronson, 91
Alexander the Great, 241–42
Aleixandre, Vicente, 82
Althusser, Louis, 202
Altieri, Charles, 7, 9, 16n45, 195, 208n3
American Writers Against the Vietnam War,
    83, 140, 199
Ancient Law, see Maine, Henry Sumner
Anima Mundi, see Hilman, James
Aragon, Louis, 49
"archetypal memory," 249
archetypes, 74, 144, 148, 150, 164, 201,
    214–15, 223, 230–31, 246, 249
Ark, The, 189–90, 193, 228, 259
Arnold, Matthew, 186
Ashbery, John, 17n67, 27, 76, 267–69, 276,
    281
Atkinson, Michael, 10
Auden, W. H., 8, 49, 261, 263
Autobiography, see Yeats, William Butler
"awakening," 54, 138

Bach, Johann Sebastian, 173
Bachelard, Gaston, 102, 179–80, 182
Bachofen, Johann Jacob, 58, 148, 203, 205–7,
    210n24
Baker, Deborah, 259
Baldwin, James, 267
"Bartleby, the Scrivener," *see* Melville, Her-
    man
Basho, 120–21, 238
Baudelaire, Charles, 177, 187, 189, 268–69
"Beats, The," 260

Benedikt, Michael, 11, 176
Benjamin, Walter, 189
Benn, Gottfried, 21
Benton, Thomas Hart, 227
Beowulf, 260
Berry, Wendell, 214
Berryman, John, 83, 194, 260
Bertrand, Aloysius, 176
Beyond the Pleasure Principle, see Freud, Sigmund
Bible, 91, 94, 121, 130–31, 133, 148, 150,
    154, 189–90, 228, 230–31, 241–42,
    246–48, 254, 255n9, 258–59
Blake, William, 74, 91, 97, 135, 193, 238,
    255n14, 260, 263, 269
Bly, Robert, apocalyptic vision, 39, 126,
    141–42, 199, 285
    autobiographical information, 63, 258,
    270–71
    biographical information, 1, 13–14n2, 21,
    36–37, 76–77, 195, 259–60, 269–71
    as "Boy-god," 63–64, 235, 239n10, 241–
    42, 249, 258, 262
    "call" poems, 235
    as critic, 1, 23, 84, 92, 125, 258, 262
    as editor, 92, 258, 262
    "father" poems, 244
    Fulbright grant, 77
    Garrison Prize for Poetry, 28–29 as "guru,"
    92, 257
    at Harvard, 21, 27–29, 76, 90, 258–59
    and *Harvard Advocate*, 259
    use of "landscape," 107–109
    as "lay analyst," 96
    Lutheran heritage, 62–63, 235, 257–59,
    262

use of meditation, 245

and Minnesota, 70, 73, 180, 195, 216, 258, 271–72

as "mystic," 43, 65, 68, 135, 137–38, 140–41, 145, 188, 190–91, 215, 217, 275, 277, 283–84

mythic approaches to the poetry, 10, 71, 74, 143, 157, 231, 242–43, 246, 252–53, 263

National Book Award, 8, 16n50, 80, 83, 185, 199, 261

as pastoral poet, 214

use of poetry as a linguistic force, 202

the poetry of the "subconscious mind," 287

as political activist, 83

as "preacher," 24, 91, 258, 263, 283, 288, 290n1

as "prophet," 74, 124, 129, 214–15

as publisher, 262

as "religious poet," 185–93, 215, 228–31, 235–37, 247, 277, 283–84

revisions of poems, 242, 251, 253, 256n23

and "Romanticism," 80, 129–30, 191, 259, 261

"seamless" canon of, 16n51

use of "second consciousness," 220–21

use of "Self," 148–50, 155, 159–61, 163

self-imposed isolation in New York City, 77, 90, 195, 259

use of "shadow," 148–50, 152–56, 159, 169, 241, 247, 249, 262, 277

"simplicity," 2

structure of poems and canon, 16n51, 48, 84, 89–90, 148, 156, 240, 251–52

"style," 24–25, 53, 60, 83–84, 91, 117, 119, 186, 195, 242

"subjective polemic," 194–95

and surrealism, 21–22, 54–55, 72, 77–80, 85, 88, 119, 129, 133, 135–36, 145, 177, 187, 195, 197–98, 202, 207, 215, 260–61, 284–85, 290n5

"technique," 53, 63, 83–84, 117, 253

as "therapist," 263

as translator, 1, 43, 77, 84, 92, 173–74, 257–58, 260, 292

use of "twofold consciousness," 224, 237–38, 277

"Utopian vision," 189

use of the "Wild Man" myth, 244, 258, 260

BOOKS

Forty Poems Touching on Recent American History, 126–27, 129, 201

Iron John: A Book About Men, 96–103, 258, 260, 262–63

Jumping Out of Bed, 171, 179

Leaping Poetry: An Idea with Poems and Translations, 178

Light Around the Body, The, 2, 3, 8, 9, 10, 17n54, 23–26, 42–50, 53–56, 60, 66, 73, 77, 80, 82–83, 90, 120, 123–127, 129, 133–34, 138–47, 173, 177, 186, 198–99, 206, 214, 224, 251, 254, 261, 285

Lion's Tail and Eyes, The, 142, 177

Little Book on the Human Shadow, A, 241

Loon, The, 165, 168–70, 172–73

Loving a Woman in Two Worlds, 5–6, 12–13, 15n32, 18n75, 18n78, 68–69, 95, 240, 244, 250–54, 278

Lute of Three Loudnesses, The, 76–77

Man in the Black Coat Turns, The, 4, 6, 15n27, 66–67, 85, 89, 95, 226–27, 232, 240–49, 251, 286, 289

Morning Glory, The, 3, 60–61, 83, 85, 89, 126, 128, 168, 177, 179, 181, 184–86, 224, 226–28, 231, 238, 240

Neruda and Vallejo: Selected Poems, 83

News of the Universe: Poems of Twofold Consciousness, 224–26, 229–30, 232–33, 235–38

Old Man Rubbing His Eyes, 179–80, 183, 231, 238n7

Poems for the Ascension of J. P. Morgan, 77

Point Reyes Poems, 177, 226

Sea and the Honeycomb, The, 166, 169, 175

Selected Poems, 5, 6, 74–77, 82, 85–87, 89–91, 92–96, 250, 269, 271, 283, 285, 292

Selected Poems of Rainer Maria Rilke, 256n22

Silence in the Snowy Fields, 2–3, 8–12, 18n78, 23–25, 30, 35–39m, 40–41, 46–47, 53, 62, 65, 71, 77–80, 82, 85–86, 88–89, 93, 107–13, 117–23, 133, 136–38, 139, 140–41, 144, 165, 167, 170, 173, 177–80, 186, 196–99, 205–6, 214, 216–23, 226, 231, 240–41, 248, 261, 285, 288–89

Sleepers Joining Hands, 2–3, 9–10, 12, 53–56, 57–59, 60, 81, 83–84, 89–90, 148–64, 165, 170, 173–74, 177–78, 186, 198, 201–03, 207, 224, 227, 248, 287

Talking All Morning, 88, 278

Teeth Mother Naked at Last, The, 51–52, 73, 81–82, 126, 129, 134

This Body Is Made of Camphor and Gopherwood, 3–4, 62–64, 85, 185–93, 224, 226–28, 231–32, 240

This Tree Will Be Here for a Thousand Years, 4, 14n23, 65, 71, 85, 89, 168, 214, 216–23, 224, 226, 231–37, 287–89

Twenty Poems of Georg Trakl, 78

Twenty Poems of Pablo Neruda, 83

Twenty Poems of Tomas Tranströmer, 83

ESSAYS

"Being a Lutheran Boy-God in Minnesota," 63–64, 235, 239n–10, 241–42, 249, 258, 262

"Dead World and the Live World, The," 114

"Developing the Underneath," 9

"Form That is Neither In nor Out," 87

"I Came Out of the Mother Naked," 10, 55, 58, 83, 90, 170, 207

"Image as a Form of Intelligence, The," 231–32

"Leaping Up into Political Poetry," 8, 16n52, 127, 129

"Looking for Dragon Smoke," 136, 260

"Mind Playing, The," 18n70

"On Current Poetry in America," 13n1

"Poetry in an Age of Expansion," 18n70

"Prose Poem as an Evolving Form, The," 87, 89

"Recognizing the Image as a Form of Intelligence," 16n48, 232, 255n9

"Two Presences, The," 4, 217, 221, 231, 287–88

"Two Stages of an Artist's Life," 15n42, 18n70

"What the Prose Poem Carries With It," 17–18n70

"Whitman's Line as a Public Form," 89

"Wrong Turning in American Poetry, A," 16n48, 194, 199

INDIVIDUAL POEMS

"After a Day of Work," 219–20

"After Long Busyness," 271

"Afternoon Sleep," 111

"After the Industrial Revolution All Things Happen at Once," 125

"After Working," 36–37, 110, 221, 271

"Alone," 172

"Alone a Few Hours," 252–54

"Amazed by an Accumulation of Snow," 65, 235

"Artist at Fifty, The," 68, 252

"Asian Peace Offers Rejected without Publication," 48, 199

"As the Asian War Begins," 125

"At a Fish Hatchery in Story, Wyoming," 181, 226

"At a March Against the Vietnam War," 125, 140

"At Midocean," 252

"At the Funeral of Great-Aunt Mary," 137–38

"At the Time of Peony Blossoming," 91

"August Rain," 61, 227

"August Sun," 171

"Awakening," 122, 138, 197, 213

"Black Pony Eating Grass," 236

"Bouquet of Ten Roses, A," 90, 240, 255n9

"Busy Man Speaks, The," 124, 132, 144, 206, 215

"Calling to the Badger," 153

"Caterpillar on the Desk, A," 227

"Christmas Eve Service at Midnight at St. Michaels," 61, 227–28

"Chrysanthemums," 119

"Climbing Up Mount Vision with My Little Boy," 227

"Come With Me," 199, 252

"Coming in For Supper," 229

"Condition of the Working Classes: 1970, The," 150

"Conditions, The," 252

"Conversation," 252

"Counting Small-Boned Bodies," 200–201

"Crazy Carlson's Meadow," 67, 98–101, 248–49

"Cricket in the Wainscoting, A," 168

"Current Administration, The," 215

"Dawn in Threshing Time," 90, 233

"Dead Seal, The," 94

"Dead Seal at McClure's Beach, The," 226

"Depression," 122, 136, 196–97

"Digging Worms," 234

"Doing Nothing Poem, A," 171

"Dream of Retarded Children, A," 96

"Dream of Suffocation, A," 124, 285

"Dream of What Is Missing, A," 62

"Dream of the Night of First Snow, A," 180–81

"Dried Sturgeon, The," 240

"Driving My Parents Home at Christmas," 222

"Driving Through Minnesota During the Hanoi Bombings," 81

"Driving to Town Late to Mail a Letter," 30

"Driving Toward the Lac Qui Parle River," 31, 70, 79, 109, 119–21, 216–18, 221, 270–75, 277, 279, 280–81, 284, 290n4

"Ducks," 172

Early Spring Between Madison and Bellingham," 271

"Eleven O'Clock at Night," 86, 241, 285–86

"Empty Place, An," 222–23, 235

"Evening When the Full Moon Rose as the Sun Set, An," 97, 237

"Evolution from the Fish," 142

"Executive's Death, The," 50

"Extra Joyful Chorus For Those Who Have Read This Far, An," 56, 160, 162–63, 167

"Fall" (lined poem), 173

"Fall" (prose poem), 109, 177

"Fallen Tree, The," 288

"Falling into Holes in Our Sentences," 63–64, 229

"Fall Poem," 233, 235

"Ferns," 252

"Fifty Males Sitting Together," 247, 251, 256n23

"Finding an Old Ant Mansion," 66, 240

"Finding a Salamander on Inverness Ridge," 226

"Finding the Father," 245

"Fire of Despair Has Been Our Saviour, The," 126

"Fishing on a Lake at Night," 235–36

"For My Son Noah, Ten Years Old," 241

"Four Seasons in the American Woods," 90

"Four Ways of Knowledge," 64, 95, 244

"Frost in the Ground," 236

"Frost on the Window Panes," 182–83

"Galloping Horses," 62, 188

"Getting Up Early," 110–12

"Going Out to Check the Ewes," 63

"Gone, Gone, Gone," 284

"Good Silence, The," 68, 95, 252

"Grass," 168

"Grass from Two Years, 61, 183, 227

"Grief of Men, The," 243, 251, 256n31

"Hair," 54, 57, 167, 178

"Hatred of Men with Black Hair," 82, 125, 139

"Hawk, The," 68

"Hermit, The," 48

"Hearing Men Shout at Night on Macdougal Street," 126

"Hockey Poem, The," 94, 225

"Hollow Tree, A," 182

"Horse of Desire, The," 252

"Hunting Pheasants in a Cornfield," 40, 121, 218–19

"Hurrying Away from the Earth," 141

"I AM NOT I" (translation of Jiménez), 173–74

"In a Train," 30, 79

"In a Mountain Cabin in Norway," 157

"In Rainy September," 252

"Indigo Bunting, The," 251

"Insect Heads," 180

"In the Courtyard of the Isleta Mission," 225–26

"In the Month of May," 68, 251–52, 254

"Johnson's Cabinet Watched by Ants," 94

"July Morning," 217, 235

"Kabekona Lake," 169–70

"Kneeling Down to Look into a Culvert," 247, 249

"Kneeling Down to Peer into a Culvert," 249

"Large Starfish, The," 227

"Late Moon," 221, 236, 254n4

"Late Spring day in My Life, A," 112

"Left Hand, The," 228

"Letter To Her," 278–81

"Listening to a Cricket in the Wainscoting," 233, 288

"Listening to Bach," 173–74

"Listening to President Kennedy Lie about the Cuban Invasion," 48, 139

"Listening to the Köln Concert," 252

"Looking at a Dead Wren in My Hand," 60, 183

"Loon, The," 172–73

"Long Walk Before the Snows Began, A," 221, 233

"Looking at a Dry Tumbleweed Brought in from the Snow," 225

"Looking from Inside My Body," 229

"Looking into a Face," 254

"Love Poem in Twos and Threes," 252

"Man and a Woman and a Blackbird, A," 252

"Man and a Woman Sit Near Each Other, A," 250–51

"Man Writes to a Part of Himself, A," 18n78, 122, 205–6

"Marietta, Minnesota," 169

"Meditation on Philosophy, A," 244–45

"Meeting the Man Who Warns Me," 154, 157

"Moose, The," 174

"Mourning Pablo Neruda," 227, 243

"Moving Books to a New Study," 289

"My Father's Wedding," 245–47

"My Three-Year-Old Daughter Brings Me a Gift," 226

"Nailing a Dock Together," 220, 236

"Night," 121

"Night Frogs," 252

"Night Journey In the Cooking Pot," 55, 157–59

"Night of the First Snow," 236

"November Day at McClure's," 226–27

"October Frost," 221

"Opening an Oyster," 50

"Opening the Door of a Barn I Thought Was Empty on New Year's Eve," 184, 227–28

"Origin of the Praise of God, The," 229–30

"'Out of the Rolling Ocean, the Crowd . . . ,'" 252

"Out Picking Up Corn," 221, 237

"Passing An Orchard By Train," 233–34

"Pilgrim Fish Heads," 153, 286–87

"Poem Against the Rich," 198

"Poem in Three Parts," 79, 137, 220

"Point Reyes Poems, The," 185, 226–27

"Prayer Service in an English Church," 235

"Prodigal Son, The," 241–42

"Pulling a Rowboat Up Among Lake Reeds," 65, 217, 235

"Remembering in Oslo the Old Picture of the Magna Carta," 111

"Returning Poem," 252

"Return to Solitude," 108, 112, 136–37

"Roads," 221, 233

"Romans Angry About the Inner World," 124, 142, 215

"Roots, The," 68, 251–52

"Sacrifice in the Orchard, A," 67

"Schoolcraft's Diary Written on the Missouri: 1830," 88, 90, 93

"Sea Water Pouring Back over Stones," 255

"Seeing You Carry Plants In," 252

"September Night with an Old Horse," 178

"Shack Poem," 59

"Shadow Goes Away, The," 55, 90, 149–50, 153–54, 159, 162

"Shame," 68

"Silence," 31

"Sitting in Fall Grass," 234

"Sitting on Some Rocks in Shaw Cove, California," 181

"Six Winter Privacy Poems," 53, 84, 93, 157, 173–75, 178–79, 247–48

"Sleepers Joining Hands," 10, 55, 58, 153, 173, 178, 207, 237, 258

"Sleet Storm on the Merritt Parkway," 43

"Small Bird's Nest Made of White Reed Fiber, A," 128

"Smothered by the World," 43, 124, 139

"Snowbanks North of the House," 241

"Snowed In," 229

"Snowfall in the Afternoon," 110

"Solitude Late at Night in the Woods," 218

"Solitude of the Two Day Snowstorm," 236

"Sparks," 177

"Standing Under a Cherry Tree at Night," 226

"Starfish, The," 90

"Suddenly Turning Away," 44

"Sunday Morning in Tomales Bay," 183–84

"Sunset at a Lake," 177

"Surprised by Evening," 108

"Taking the Hands," 109, 167, 284–85

"Teeth Mother Naked at Last, The," 3, 9, 14n13, 16n53, 16–17n54, 54, 57, 81, 83, 91, 94, 129–33, 140, 143–47, 150, 153, 186, 201–3; 207

"Thinking of 'Seclusion'," 234

"Third Body, A," 250–51

"Those Being Eaten by America," 43, 139

"Three Kinds of Pleasures," 35–36, 78, 108, 118, 271

"Turning Away from Lies," 48

"Turtle, A," 181

"Turtle, The," 68, 160, 255n18

"Two People at Dawn," 252

"Two Rivers, The," 68

"To Live," 179, 233

"Unrest," 38–39, 122, 197

"Visiting Emily Dickinson's Grave with Robert Francis," 255n14

"Visiting Thomas Hart Benton and His Wife in Kansas City," 227

"Waking from Sleep," 41, 93, 108, 212
"Walk, A," 180
"Walking Among Limantour Dunes," 227
"Walking in the Hardanger Vidda," 227
"Walking on the Sussex Coast," 226
"Walking Swiftly," 188, 228–29
"Walking Where the Plows Have Been Turning," 11
"Wanting to Experience All Things," 215
"War and Silence," 80, 94
"Watching Andrei Voznesensky Read in Vancouver," 225
"Watching Television," 48, 124
"Watering the Horse," 119, 170–71
"Water Drawn Up Into the Head," 160
"Water Under the Earth," 160
"What Frightened Us," 68, 252
"What the Fox Agreed to Do," 67, 86
"What We Provide," 252, 256n32
"When the Dumb Speak," 50, 141–42, 215
"Where We Must Look for Help," 62, 90, 121–22, 259–60
"Whole Moisty Night, The," 251, 256n30
"Windy Day at the Shack, A," 182
"With Pale Women in Maryland," 144
"Woman We Never See Again," 217, 222, 231, 234–35
"Words Rising," 67, 95, 244
"Writing Again," 127–28, 233, 288
Boehme, Jacob, 6–9, 23–24, 40, 42–44, 50, 63, 93, 107, 122–24, 133, 138–39, 198–99, 249, 281
Bosch, Hieronymous, 72
Brecht, Bertolt, 49
Breton, André, 26, 269
Brinton, Howard, 133
Brooks, Cleanth, 1
Brooks, Gwendolyn, 194
Browning, Robert, 268
Buckdancer's Choice, see Dickey, James, 115

Cartesian thought, 287
Catullus, Gaius Valerius, 188
Celtic translations, 269
Chappell, Fred, 5
Char, René, 21, 260
Chief Joseph, 125
Chinese ideographs, 118, 170, 255n16
Chinese translations, 71, 93, 269
Christian tradition, 156, 230–31, 253
Cixous, Hélène, 207
Coleridge, Samuel Taylor, 130, 268, 270

collective unconscious, 144, 148, 231, 285
Collingwood, R. G., 73
"consciousness in nature," 224, 237
Crane, Hart, 281, 292
Creeley, Robert, 17n67, 25, 35
"Crunk," 116, 117, 121, 126

Dacey, Philip, 3, 85, 170
Dante, 96, 259
Darwin, Charles, 186
Davis, William V., 3, 8, 10, 11–12, 15n43, 211n34, 238n2, 274, 290n5
"dead world," 114–16, 120, 122
de Beauvoir, Simone, 204–5, 207, 209n20
"deep image," 6–8, 15n42, 15n43, 16n45, 16n48, 21, 53, 75, 79, 90, 94, 135–36, 138, 144–45, 185, 195, 196–99, 201–202, 205, 207, 212, 274–75, 280, 287
de Goncourt, Edmond, 269–70
de Hernandez, Miguel, 287
Descartes, René, 287
Dickens, Charles, 235
Dickinson, Emily, 255n14, 268
Dickey, James, 84, 115, 201
Donne, John, 188, 268, 271, 280
Dostoyevski, Fyodor Mikhailovich, 115
dream and dream imagery, 38, 55, 96, 97, 111, 119, 148, 150, 154, 156, 158–59, 179, 188, 215, 228, 270, 280–83, 285
Double Dream of Spring, The, see, Ashbery, John
Duffy, William, 136, 142, 177
Duncan, Robert, 9

Eberhardt, Richard, 94
Eckhart, Meister, 93
Ecstatic Mother, 244
Edson, Russell, 17n67, 176–77
The Eighties, 77
Ekelöf, Gunnar, 21, 92, 260
Elder Edda, 248
Eliot, T. S., 21–22, 28, 30, 43, 74, 79–80, 86, 116, 136, 157, 176, 188, 194, 238, 259–60, 268–69, 276, 280–81
Emerson, Ralph Waldo, 8, 72, 91, 139, 157, 190–91, 287, 292
Engels, Friedrich, 204, 210n23
Enkidu, 260
epiphany, 60, 156, 222, 228, 252
Erikson, Erik, 259

fairy tales (folk tales), 71, 97, 242, 246, 253, 259, 262
"Faithful John," see fairy tales

Fantasia of the Unconscious, *see* Lawrence, D. H.
"father-consciousness," 277
father-son relationship, 241–43, 246, 262
Faulkner, William, 128
"female consciousness," 13, 83, 96–98, 122,
     143–44, 148–49, 190, 203, 207–8, 242,
     262, 277, 287
The Fifties, 2, 22, 35, 77, 175, 194, 260
"Firebombing, The," *see* Dickey, James
Ford, Henry, 125, 287
Franklin, Benjamin, 287
Frazier, Sir James, 71
Fredman, Stephen, 11
Freud, Sigmund, 22, 102, 191, 197, 202,
     204–205, 208n7, 209n13, 215, 258,
     261–63, 280–81, 283, 285
Friberg, Ingegard, 8
Frost, Robert, 85, 213, 269
Frye, Northrop, 187
Fugitives, The, 194

Gaspard de la Nuit, *see*, Bertrand, Aloysius
Gilgamesh, Epic, 98, 260
Ginsberg, Allen, 78, 92, 94, 116, 135, 141,
     162, 269, 281
Gitzen, Julian, 10
Goethe, Johann Wolfgang von, 116, 238, 261
Golden Bough, The, *see* Frazier, Sir James
Goodman, Paul, 263
Gott-natur, 115, 244–38
"Great Mother, The" (or Magna Mater), 10,
     12, 55, 58, 60, 90, 96, 98, 142–43,
     148–49, 178, 215, 263
Groddeck, Georg, 115–16
Grolier Bookshop, 268
Growing Up Absurd, *see*, Goodman, Paul
Gunn, Thom, 122–23

haiku, 168, 170
Haines, John, 23, 88
Hall, Donald, 1, 13n2, 76–78, 176–77, 214
Hamilton, Alexander, 51, 130, 151–52
Hamsum, Knut, 92
Hardy, Thomas, 268
Harris, Victoria Frenkel, 11, 13, 103
Haskill, Dennis, 7
Hávamál, The, 248
Hawthorne, Nathaniel, 200
Hayden, Robert, 39
Healing Fiction, *see*, Hillman, James
Hegel, Georg Friedrich Wilhelm, 47, 285
Hemingway, Ernest, 276, 278
Herbert, George, 189

Heyen, William, 75
Hillman, James, 97, 102, 242, 255n10, 262
History of Human Marriage, The, *see*, Wester-
     marck, Edward
Hölderlin, Friedrich, 238, 261
Homer, 84, 100
Howard, Richard, 8, 136
Howl, *see*, Ginsberg, Allen
Huxley, Aldous, 125
Hyde, Lewis, 14n13

Imagists, The, 168
Ignatow, David, 17n67, 78, 176
Interpretation of Dreams, The, *see*, Freud, Sigmund
"inwardness" or inner and outer world, 8,
     23–25, 36, 41–45, 47–48, 53, 71, 73–
     75, 95, 115, 120–21, 123–25, 133, 137,
     141, 144, 156, 177, 179, 198–99, 218,
     220, 230, 237, 261, 270, 278
Iowa Writers' Workshop, 260
Irigaray, Luce, 207

Jackson, Andrew, 47, 126
Jacob-Esau story, *see*, Bible
James, William, 188
Janssens, G. A. M., 13n2
Jarrell, Randall, 194, 260
Jiménez, Juan Ramón, 37, 43, 77, 173–74,
     238, 260, 269, 287
Johnson, Lyndon, B., 126, 133
Johnson, Robert, 102
Jones, Richard, and Kate Daniels, 88, 103
Joyce, James, 156, 160
Jung, C. G., 6, 9–10, 12–13, 17n62, 22, 58,
     64, 66, 83, 96–98, 102–3, 143–45,
     148–49, 155–57, 161, 186, 201–7, 214,
     224, 227, 242, 258, 261–63, 277, 280–
     81, 283, 285, 287, 293

Kabir, 92, 238, 263
Kali, 143
Kalaidjian, Walter, 8–10, 13, 290n4, 290n5
Kant, Immanuel, 47
Keats, John, 58, 243, 258
Kennedy, John F., 47, 126
Kenyon College, 116
Kerouac, Jack, 116
Khidr (or Khadir), 246, 256n22
Kinnell, Galway, 78, 157, 256n31
Koch, Kenneth, 27, 76, 267
Koran, The, 246
Kramer, Lawrence, 275, 277

Langbaum, Robert, 80
"Lapis Lazuli," see Yeats, William Butler
Lascaux, caves of, 229
Lawrence, D. H., 24, 97, 100–101, 103, 191, 232–33, 286–87
"leaping poetry," 60, 63–64, 67–68, 74, 177, 202, 225, 245, 260, 290n5
Leaves of Grass, see Whitman, Walt
Lensing, George, 13n2
Levertov, Denise, 35
Lévi-Strauss, Claude, 209n20
Libby, Anthony, 10, 12–13, 17n62, 283–84
Life Studies, see Lowell, Robert
"Lines Composed a Few Miles above Tintern Abbey, or Revisiting the Banks of the Wye during a Tour, July 13, 1978," see Wordsworth, William
"live world," 114–15, 120, 122
Lorca, Federico Garcia, 21, 43, 82, 177, 238, 260–61
Lord Weary's Castle, see Lowell, Robert
"Love Song of J. Alfred Prufrock, The," see Eliot, T. S.
Lowell, Robert, 27, 29, 73, 76, 78, 114, 116, 194, 260, 269
Lucretius, 186, 221, 232
Lume Spento, A, see Pound, Ezra
Lunch Poems, see O'Hara, Frank

Machado, Antonio, 43, 82, 89, 92–93, 165, 269
Magna Mater, see Great Mother
Maine, Henry Sumner, 204
male-female consciousness, 6, 10, 12–13, 18n75, 83, 98, 143–44, 147, 190, 203–7, 242, 244
Mallarmé, Stéphane, 269, 281
Marcuse, Herbert, 203, 205
Marivaux, Pierre, 267–68
Martinez, Enrique Gonzales, 43
"masculine consciousness," 83, 85, 96–98, 143–44, 149, 190, 203, 242, 246, 262, 277, 287
"matriarchal (or "mother") consciousness," 12, 58, 203–5, 207–8, 211n31, 277
Mauberley, see Pound, Ezra
McLean, Carolyn, 77
McLennan, John F. 204
MacLeish, Archibald, 28
Melville, Herman, 30, 73
men's movement, 257
Merrill, James, 194
Mersmann, James F., 3, 9, 201–2

Merwin, W. S., 17n67, 43, 49, 176, 194, 203
Michaux, Henri, 21, 260
Mills, Ralph J., Jr., 2, 8, 11, 43
Milton, John, 74, 77, 167, 186, 269, 280
Mitchell, Roger, 6
Moby-Dick, see Melville, Herman
Molesworth, Charles, 3, 4, 8, 11, 202
Monroe, Jonathan, 11
Montaigne, 268
Montale, Eugenio, 37
Moore, Marianne, 194
Moran, Ronald, 13n2
Mother Right, see Bachofen, Johann Jacob
Moyers, Bill, 257

Nadja, see Breton, André
Nelson, Cary, 9
Nelson, Howard, 10, 76, 84–88, 209n2
Nemerov, Howard, 194
Neruda, Pablo, 1, 37, 43, 49, 66, 77, 79, 82, 92, 177, 197, 237–38, 243, 255n13, 261, 262, 287
Neumann, Erich, 12, 17n62, 21, 58, 143–44, 148, 202–5, 207
"new brain," 10
New Critics (or New Criticism), 116, 167, 194–95, 259
New York School, 260
Nietzsche, Friedrich, 269–70
"night intelligence," 229
Noah, 190, 228, 259
Norse mythology, 248, 260
Novalis, 238, 260

Oates, Joyce Carol, 3
O'Connor, Frank, 71, 89, 269
Odin, 248–49, 256n26
Odyssey, see Homer
O'Hara, Frank, 269, 281
Olson, Charles, 74, 136, 194, 217
Origin of the Family, Private Property and The State, The, see Engles, Friedrich
Origins and History of Consciousness, The, see Neumann, Erich Orphism, 192
Ortega y Gasset, José, 287
"Out of the Cradle Endlessly Rocking," see Whitman, Walt
Ovid, 94

Pack, Robert, 77
Paley, Grace, 267
Paradise Lost, see Milton, John
Paris Spleen, see Baudelaire, Charles

Pascal, Blaise, 269–70
Pasternak, Boris, 94
Patchen, Kenneth, 176
"pathetic fallacy," 288
"patriarchal (or "father") consciousness," 58, 205
Pentagon demonstration, 83, 126
Perloff, Marjorie, 4, 244
Perse, St.-John, 176
Peseroff, Joyce, 6, 88
Philips, Jayne Anne, 267
Pinsky, Robert, 272
Plath, Sylvia, 137
Platonism, 190
Plumly, Stanley, 3
Poetics of Reverie, The, see Bachelard, Gaston
poetry and politics (or political poetry), 8–9, 24, 43–44, 47, 49, 60, 80, 82–83, 88, 91, 127, 129, 133, 148, 186, 189, 196–203, 214, 224, 226, 261, 289, 292
Poetry of Experience, The, see Langbaum, Robert
Point Reyes poems, 60
Ponge, Francis, 66, 89, 269
Pound, Ezra, 21–23, 39, 74, 79, 92, 94, 136, 185, 191, 194, 238, 257, 259–60, 268–69, 276, 281
Prairie Lights Bookshop, 268
"Prayer for My Daughter, A," *see* Yeats, William Butler
Prelude, The, see Wordsworth, William
Primitive Marriage, see McLennan, John F.
Prodigal Son story, 241–42
prose poems, 3, 6, 11–12, 17n67, 17–18n70, 60, 62, 66, 90, 94, 128–29, 176–77, 181–85, 187–88, 191, 224–27, 240–41, 253, 292
psychological approaches to poetry, 10, 53, 57–58, 63, 136, 143, 148, 162, 178, 188, 202–3, 227, 229, 233, 242, 246–47, 258, 260–61, 277, 280–81, 283, 293
"Psychological Aspects of the Mother Archetype," *see* Jung, C. G.

"radical presence," 7, 195
Ramage, 251
Ransom, John Crowe, 116
Ray, David, 199
"Recantation," *see* Coleridge, Samuel Taylor
religious approaches to poetry, 10, 24, 62, 107, 178, 185–89, 242–44, 246–47, 277, 293

"Resolution and Independence," *see* Wordsworth, William
Rexroth, Kenneth, 2, 259
Reynolds, Charles (Bly's pseudonym), 165, 175
Reynolds, Michael S., 4–5
Rich, Adrienne, 28–29, 76, 194, 203, 207–8
Richards, I. A., 116
Richter, Franz Albert, 179
Ricoeur, Paul, 192
Rilke, Rainer Maria, 23, 37, 43, 58, 92, 238, 263, 269
Rimbaud, Arthur, 269–70, 281
Roethke, Theodore, 157, 190, 194
Roosevelt, Theodore, 47, 126
Rosenthal, M. L., 112
Rosetta Stone, 96
Roszak, Theodore, 257
Rothenberg, Jerome, 7
Rumi, 263
Rusk, Dean, 73, 126, 133
Rutsala, Vern, 176

Saint Geraud (Bill Knott), 166
Scève, Maurice, 267–68
Schwartz, Delmore, 260
Seal, David, 10
Second Sex, The, see de Beauvoir, Simone
Seventies, The, 58, 77, 165, 262
Sexton, Anne, 39, 42
Shakespeare, William, 268–69
Shapiro, Karl, 176, 194, 260
Shelley, Percy Bysshe, 203
Sidon, 241
Silent Spring, The, see Carson, Rachel
Simpson, Louis, 1, 2, 13n2, 43, 77–78
Sitwell, Edith, 28
Sitwell, Sacheverell, 28
Sixties, The, 2, 23, 35, 43, 77, 114, 116–17, 121, 165, 175, 185
Smart, Christopher, 91, 269
"Snow Man, The," *see* Stevens, Wallace
Snyder, Gary, 115, 135, 212, 214
Solzhenitsyn, Aleksandr, 64
"Song of Myself," *see* Whitman, Walt
Song of Songs, 190
Stafford, William, 13n2, 214
Stein, Gertrude, 74, 276
Stevens, Wallace, 40, 190, 233, 254n4, 267, 269, 274, 281
Stitt, Peter, 6, 15n27
Studies in Classic American Litrature, see Lawrence, D. H.

Sugg, Richard P., 10, 16n52
Symbolism of Evil, The, see Ricoeur, Paul

T'ang dynasty, 255
Tao Te Ching, 159
Tate, Allen, 21, 260
Teeth Mother (or Terrible Mother), 57, 132, 143, 148
Temple, The, see Herbert, George
Thomas, Dylan, 28
Thompson, Keith, 243
Thoreau, Henry David, 3, 46, 60, 71–73, 91, 94, 128, 137–38, 173, 199–200, 214, 292
"Three brains," 55–56, 178, 277, 287
Tolstoy, Leo, 46, 57, 101
Trakl, Georg, 1, 21, 37, 43, 77, 79, 92, 117, 121, 260–61, 287
Transcendentalism, 73, 91, 137, 139, 141, 161
translations of Chinese poems, *see* Waley, Arthur
Tranströmer, Tomas, 92
Trilling, Lionel, 261
Trunga, Chögyam, 262
Tyre, 241

unconscious, the, 38, 53, 57–58, 62–64, 83, 112–13, 117, 150, 152–54, 160–61, 164, 166, 191–92, 199–200, 202, 214–15, 225, 229, 237, 246, 249, 260–61, 270, 275, 277, 280–81, 283, 293
Unterecker, John, 87
"United Fruit Company, The," *see* Neruda, Pablo

Valéry, Paul, 268–69
Vallejo, César, 21, 37, 43, 49–50, 77, 79, 82, 92, 177, 260, 287
Varieties of Religious Experience, The, see James, William
Vico, Giambattista, 187

Vidal, Gore, 257
Vietnam War, 2, 3, 8–9, 16n52, 24, 42–43, 47–48, 51–52, 55, 57, 60, 72–73, 83, 91, 93, 114–15, 130, 143, 145–47, 150, 153, 177, 186, 198–200, 202–3, 206, 214, 226, 233, 242, 261, 287, 289, 292
Virgil, 96, 186, 221
von Franz, Marie-Louise, 97, 246

Waley, Arthur, 71, 89, 93, 269
Warren, Robert Penn, 37
Waste Land, The, see Eliot, T. S.
Weinberger, Eliot, 4, 85
Westcott, Glenway, 41
Wesling, Donald, 4, 75
Westermarck, Edward, 204
Whitman, Walt, 10, 43, 74, 87, 91, 94, 158, 162–63, 171–72, 177, 186, 190, 213, 233, 252, 267–70, 272, 274, 281, 292
Wilbur, Richard, 76
"Wild Swans of Coole, The," *see* Yeats, William Butler
Williams, William Carlos, 17n67, 176, 194, 213, 243, 255n13, 269, 276, 278, 281
Wittgenstein, Ludwig, 189
Wolfe, Thomas, 128
Wordsworth, William, 93, 168, 215–16, 268, 270–71, 274–77, 280
Wright, James, 8, 13n2, 25, 43, 49, 77–78, 83, 114, 116–17, 121, 126–27, 136, 142, 176–77, 194, 197, 203, 212, 214

Yeats, William Butler, 39, 129, 151, 157, 242, 244, 261, 263, 276–77, 280
Yggdrasill, 248, 256n25
"Young Goodman Brown," *see* Hawthorne, Nathaniel
Yüan, Hung-Tao, 170

Zen, 118, 171, 237
"Zeus energy," 260